BARNES & NOBLE
ILLUSTRATED
GUIDE TO
AMERICA'S CIVIL WAR SITES

by
Colonel Marshall Michel III (U.S.A.F. ret.)

Concept, Design, and Maps by
Richard J. Berenson

Meredith Wolf Schizer, Editor

Produced by
Berenson Design & Books, Ltd.
New York

This book is dedicated to the National Park Service, which maintains and preserves America's Civil War battlefields, monuments, and historic sites for future generations.

For information address:
Barnes & Noble
122 Fifth Avenue
New York, NY 10011
212-633-4000

Library of Congress Cataloging-in-Publication Data is available on request.

ISBN 0-7607-3829-7

First Printing

BARNES
& NOBLE
BOOKS
NEW YORK

America's only internal war was fought almost 150 years ago. Whether it is called the War Between the States, the Great Rebellion, or the Civil War, that difficult period in our nation's history continues to intrigue us. Today, thousands of Americans participate in vivid Civil War reenactments, while others devote countless hours to keeping historic sites safe from commercial encroachment. The *Barnes & Noble Illustrated Guide to America's Civil War Sites* is a fascinating guide to the many battlefields, museums, and sites that memorialize the war. By visiting these places, readers will discover—or rediscover—the bravery of the millions of ordinary individuals who fought so strongly for their beliefs.

Not every Civil War site is included, since many merely have signposts denoting battlements and battlefields that are lost beneath urban sprawl. But within these pages, readers will find those sites and collections that are most worth exploring—places where the visitor can come away with some sense of what life was like for a participant in the war, or for a loved one waiting at home.

Included also is information on basic military principles and ordnance of the period, including small arms, edged weapons, field artillery, cavalry, battlefield medicine, fortifications, infantry, photography, and various new technologies of the Civil War—submarines, ironclads, and balloons. A timeline and map set the sites in context, and park maps are included with many entries.

While all of the information was scrupulously researched for accuracy, hours and fees may change. It's a good idea to check the Web sites and phone numbers listed in each entry before you go.

Contents

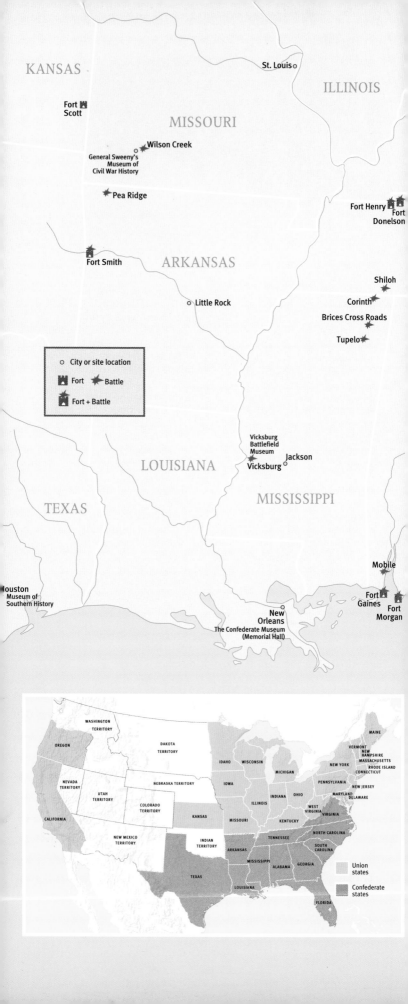

KANSAS

ILLINOIS

St. Louis

Fort
Scott

MISSOURI

Wilson Creek

General Sweeny's
Museum of
Civil War History

Pea Ridge

Fort Henry
Fort
Donelson

ARKANSAS

Fort Smith

Shiloh

Little Rock

Corinth

Brices Cross Roads

Tupelo

City or site location

Fort   Battle

Fort + Battle

Vicksburg
Battlefield
Museum

Jackson

LOUISIANA

Vicksburg

MISSISSIPPI

TEXAS

Mobile

Houston
Museum of
Southern History

Fort
Gaines

Fort
Morgan

New
Orleans
The Confederate Museum
(Memorial Hall)

WASHINGTON
TERRITORY

MAINE

OREGON

DAKOTA
TERRITORY

VERMONT
NEW
HAMPSHIRE
MASSACHUSETTS
RHODE ISLAND
CONNECTICUT

IDAHO

WISCONSIN

NEW YORK

NEVADA
TERRITORY

NEBRASKA TERRITORY

IOWA

MICHIGAN

PENNSYLVANIA

NEW JERSEY

UTAH
TERRITORY

CALIFORNIA

COLORADO
TERRITORY

KANSAS

MISSOURI

INDIANA

OHIO

MARYLAND

DELAWARE

WEST
VIRGINIA VIRGINIA

KENTUCKY

NEW MEXICO
TERRITORY

INDIAN
TERRITORY

ARKANSAS

TENNESSEE

NORTH CAROLINA

SOUTH
CAROLINA

TEXAS

MISSISSIPPI

ALABAMA

GEORGIA

LOUISIANA

Union
states

Confederate
states

FLORIDA

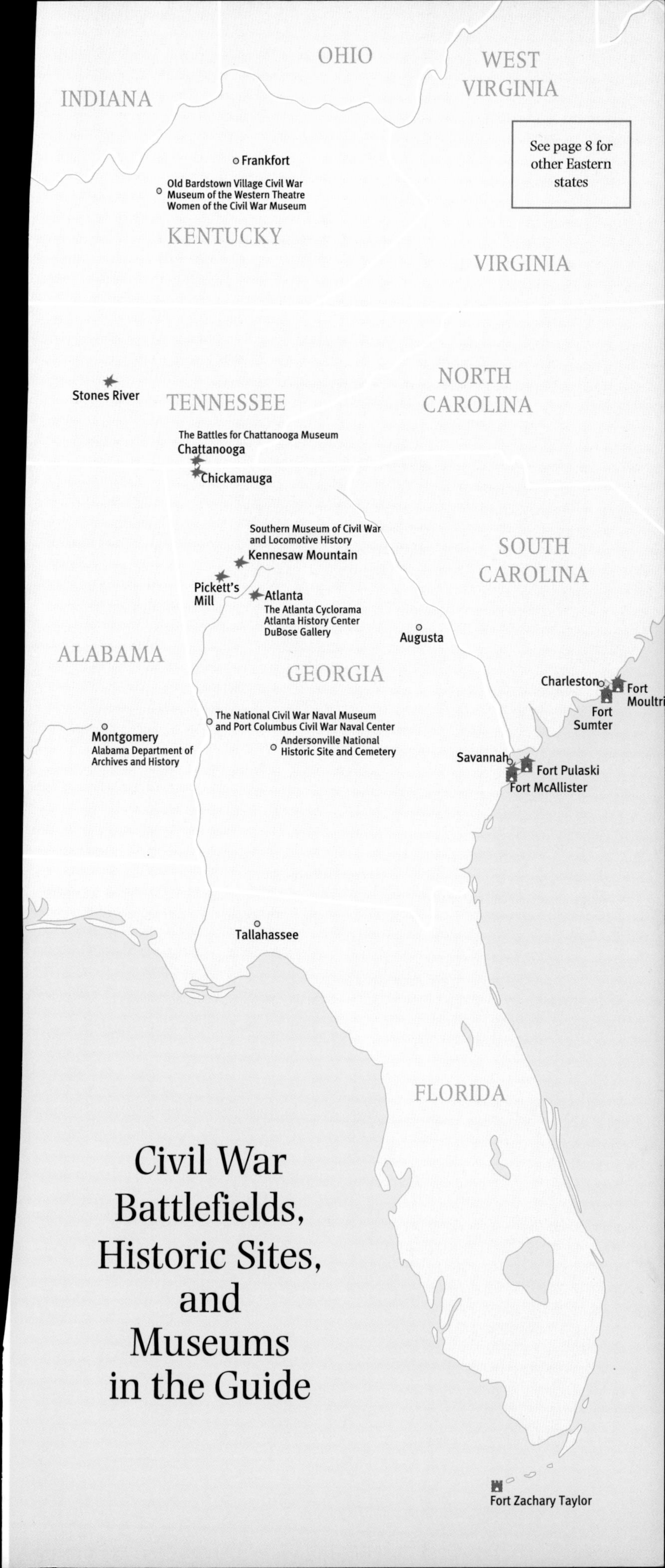

OHIO

WEST VIRGINIA

INDIANA

○ Frankfort

Old Bardstown Village Civil War
Museum of the Western Theatre
Women of the Civil War Museum

KENTUCKY

VIRGINIA

See page 8 for other Eastern states

NORTH CAROLINA

★ Stones River

TENNESSEE

The Battles for Chattanooga Museum
★ Chattanooga
★ Chickamauga

SOUTH CAROLINA

Southern Museum of Civil War
and Locomotive History
★ Kennesaw Mountain

Pickett's ★
Mill

★ Atlanta
The Atlanta Cyclorama
Atlanta History Center
DuBose Gallery

○ Augusta

ALABAMA

GEORGIA

Charleston ○ ▲ Fort
▲ Moultri
Fort
Sumter

The National Civil War Naval Museum
and Port Columbus Civil War Naval Center

○ Montgomery
Alabama Department of
Archives and History

○ Andersonville National
Historic Site and Cemetery

Savannah ○ ▲ Fort Pulaski
▲ Fort McAllister

○ Tallahassee

FLORIDA

Civil War Battlefields, Historic Sites, and Museums in the Guide

▲
Fort Zachary Taylor

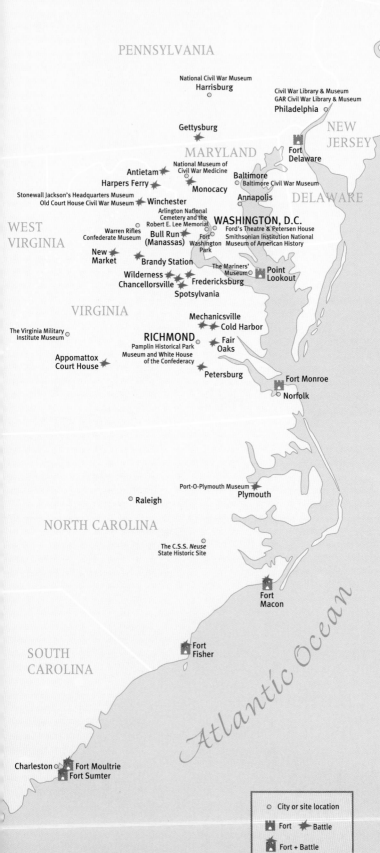

New York State Military Museum
United States Military Academy at West Point and the West Point Museum

NEW YORK

PENNSYLVANIA

National Civil War Museum
Harrisburg

Civil War Library & Museum
GAR Civil War Library & Museum
Philadelphia

Gettysburg

MARYLAND

NEW JERSEY

Fort Delaware

National Museum of Civil War Medicine

Antietam

Baltimore
Baltimore Civil War Museum

Harpers Ferry

Monocacy

Annapolis

DELAWARE

Stonewall Jackson's Headquarters Museum
Old Court House Civil War Museum

Winchester

Arlington National Cemetery and the Robert E. Lee Memorial

WASHINGTON, D.C.

WEST VIRGINIA

Warren Rifles Confederate Museum

Bull Run (Manassas)

Fort Washington Park

Ford's Theatre & Petersen House
Smithsonian Institution National Museum of American History

New Market

Brandy Station

The Mariners' Museum

Point Lookout

Wilderness

Chancellorsville

Fredericksburg

Spotsylvania

VIRGINIA

Mechanicsville

Cold Harbor

The Virginia Military Institute Museum

RICHMOND

Fair Oaks

Pamplin Historical Park Museum and White House of the Confederacy

Appomattox Court House

Petersburg

Fort Monroe

Norfolk

Port-O-Plymouth Museum
Plymouth

Raleigh

NORTH CAROLINA

The C.S.S. Neuse State Historic Site

Fort Macon

SOUTH CAROLINA

Fort Fisher

Atlantic Ocean

Charleston
Fort Moultrie
Fort Sumter

○ City or site location

🏰 Fort   ✦ Battle

🏰 Fort + Battle

Timeline of the War

1859

October 17: Radical abolitionist John Brown seizes the U.S. Armory and Arsenal at Harpers Ferry, Virginia (now West Virginia). The next day, U.S. Marines led by Robert E. Lee storm Brown's hideout and capture him.

December 2: John Brown is hanged for treason and murder.

1860

November 6: Abraham Lincoln is elected 16th President of the United States, with 40 percent of the popular vote.

December 20: South Carolina secedes from the Union.

December 26: Troops at the Federal garrison at Fort Moultrie in Charleston, South Carolina, are withdrawn to Fort Sumter in Charleston Harbor.

1861

January 21: The Union secures Fort Zachary Taylor from secessionists in Florida.

January 29: Kansas is admitted to the Union as a free state.

February 18: Jefferson Davis, former United States Senator and hero of the Mexican War, is inaugurated as President of the Confederate States.

March 4: Abraham Lincoln is inaugurated as President of the United States.

April 12: The Civil War begins when Confederate forces open fire on Fort Sumter in the Charleston, South Carolina, harbor.

April 15: President Abraham Lincoln calls for 75,000 militiamen to serve for three months.

April 19: The Union institutes a blockade against Confederate ports.

Riots begin in Baltimore, Maryland, a Northern city with many Southern sympathizers. On **May 13** martial law is declared.

April 20: Robert E. Lee resigns his commission in the army of the United States. A few days later he accepts command of the Confederate forces of Virginia.

Union forces burn and sink the vessel U.S.S. *Merrimack* in Norfolk, Virginia, before surrendering to Confederate forces. In June the Confederates raise the ship, rebuild it as an ironclad, and rename it the C.S.S. *Virginia.*

April 23: The Union abandons Fort Smith in Arkansas to the Confederates.

May 3: President Lincoln calls for 42,000 volunteers to serve three years each.

July 21: The Union loses the First Battle of Bull Run (Manassas).

July 25: John LaMountain makes the first aerial reconnaissance of the Civil War, ascending by balloon to survey Confederate encampments.

Note: Text in red refers to battles, sites, and sidebars found in this guide.

July 27: President Abraham Lincoln appoints George McClellan as commander of the Department of the Potomac.

August 10: The first major conflict of the Western front, the Battle of Wilson Creek, Missouri, is won by the Confederacy.

August 28–29: One of the first successful invasions of the South results in the surrender of Fort Hatteras, North Carolina.

October 12: The Union navy's first ironclad, the *St. Louis,* is launched on the Mississippi.

November 1: George McClellan is appointed general-in-chief of all Union forces by President Abraham Lincoln.

December 21: The U.S. Congress passes a bill establishing the Medal of Honor. It becomes law July 21, 1862.

1862

January 30: The ironclad U.S.S. *Monitor* is launched.

February 6: Union naval forces capture Fort Henry on the Tennessee River as the North pushes into the South.

February 16: Fort Donelson on the Cumberland River in Tennessee falls to Ulysses S. Grant, whose terms earn him the nickname "Unconditional Surrender" Grant.

March 7–8: The Battle of Pea Ridge preserves Missouri for the Union.

March 8–9: In the Battle of Hampton Roads, Virginia, the Confederate ironclad C.S.S. *Virginia* (*Merrimack*) defeats the Union fleet of wooden ships and the U.S.S. *Monitor* engages the *Virginia* in the first battle of two ironclads. The battle is declared a Union victory.

March 11: President Lincoln relieves George McClellan as general-in-chief, taking command himself. McClellan remains commander of the Army of the Potomac.

March 14: New Bern, North Carolina, is captured by Ambrose Burnside for the Union.

April: The first prisoners arrive at Fort Delaware. By August of 1865, the prison will house 12,500.

April 6–7: At least 24,000 men are killed, wounded, or captured in a two-day battle at Shiloh, Tennessee.

April 10: Union troops overwhelm the defenses of Fort Pulaski in Georgia.

April 12: Federals steal the Confederate train the *General,* but are caught and several are hanged.

April 16: Abraham Lincoln signs an act abolishing slavery in the District of Columbia.

The Confederacy enacts its first military draft.

April 25: Union flag officer David Farragut's brilliant strategies result in the destruction of the Confederate naval fleet at New Orleans and the surrender of the city on April 28.

April 26: The Union's rifled cannons overpower Fort Macon, on the North Carolina coast north of Wilmington, helping prove the point that masonry fortifications have become obsolete.

May 11: The C.S.S. *Virginia* (*Merrimack*) is blown up by her crew to prevent her capture.

June 1: Robert E. Lee assumes command of the Army of Northern Virginia.

June 25–July 1: The Seven Days Battles, near Richmond, result in very heavy losses for both armies but save Richmond for the Confederacy.

July 11: President Lincoln appoints Henry Halleck as general-in-chief.

July 17: Ulysses S. Grant assumes command of the army in the West.

August 28–30: Though outnumbered, Confederate forces defeat Union troops at the Second Battle of Bull Run (Manassas) in Virginia.

September 13–15: Stonewall Jackson and his Confederates reoccupy Harpers Ferry, capturing more than 12,500 Union troops.

September 17: The bloodiest day in U.S. military history comes at Antietam, Maryland, when Robert E. Lee's advancing Confederates are stopped by George McClellan's

Federals. About 25,000 men are killed, wounded, or missing.

September 22: The Preliminary Emancipation Proclamation is issued, causing Britain and France to reconsider recognizing the Confederacy.

October 8: A Union victory at Perryville ends the South's invasion of Kentucky.

November 7: Frustrated by George McClellan's inaction, President Lincoln names Ambrose Burnside to head the Army of the Potomac.

December 12: The ironclad U.S.S. *Cairo* is the first ship sunk by an electrically detonated mine.

December 13: Union forces at Fredericksburg, Virginia, are defeated by Confederates entrenched at Marye's Heights. The Union loses over 10,000 men, the Confederacy over 5000.

December 31: The ironclad U.S.S. *Monitor* is lost at sea off Cape Hatteras.

1863

January 1: President Lincoln issues the Emancipation Proclamation,

The Battle of Galveston (Texas) restores control of the city to the Confederates.

January 2: After three days of fighting, the Battle of Stones River in Tennessee ends in a draw, but the Union sees it as a much-needed victory after the defeat at Fredericksburg.

January 25: President Abraham Lincoln dismisses Ambrose Burnside, replacing him with Joseph Hooker as commander of the Army of the Potomac.

January 27: The Union's *Montauk* attacks Fort McAllister, near Savannah—the first land shelling by an ironclad in naval history.

March 3: The U.S. Congress enacts its first military draft, exempting those who can pay $300 or provide a stand-in.

April 27–May 4: Robert E. Lee defeats a numerically superior Union force at Chancellorsville in Virginia, but almost a fourth of Lee's men are killed, wounded, or missing. Thomas "Stonewall" Jackson is mistakenly shot by his own men. Jackson dies six days later.

June 9: The largest cavalry battle of the war occurs at Brandy Station, Virginia, the first time the Union cavalry proves significantly superior to its Confederate counterpart.

June 28: President Lincoln appoints George Meade commander of the Army of the Potomac.

July 1–3: The South suffers a crippling defeat at Gettysburg, Pennsylvania.

July 4: After holding out for six weeks, Vicksburg, Mississippi surrenders to Ulysses S. Grant's army.

July 9: With the surrender of Port Hudson, in Louisiana, the entire length of the Mississippi River is now under Union control.

July 18: The 54th Massachusetts Infantry Regiment, the first made up entirely of "Negro troops," spearheads the attack on Fort Wagner, South Carolina. More than half the regiment, including its white commander Robert G. Shaw, are killed.

August: The first captured Confederates arrive at Point Lookout, Maryland.

September 1: The Union retakes Fort Smith, in Arkansas.

September 19–20: The Battle of Chickamauga, in Georgia, ends with the Union troops under siege in Chattanooga, Tennessee.

October 16: President Lincoln names Ulysses S. Grant commander of the Military Division of the Mississippi, giving Grant complete authority over all operations in the West.

November 19: At the dedication of the National Cemetery at Gettysburg, President Lincoln delivers a speech known today as the Gettysburg Address.

November 23–25: The siege of Chattanooga ends in a Union victory.

1864

February 17: The Confederate submarine C.S.S. *H. L. Hunley* sinks the U.S.S. *Housatonic* in Charleston harbor, becoming the first submarine to sink a ship in combat. The *Hunley* also sinks.

February 24: The first Union prisoners of war arrive at Camp Sumter, later to be known as Andersonville, the most notorious of the Confederate prisons. Of the more than 45,000 men imprisoned here, nearly 13,000 die.

March 12: Ulysses S. Grant becomes commander of all the armies of the United States, with Henry Halleck as his chief of staff and William T. Sherman as commander in the West.

April 20: Confederate forces are able to capture Plymouth, North Carolina, after sinking defending Union ships.

May 4: The Overland Campaign begins, a massive offensive involving all the Union armies. Major battles include The Wilderness (May 5–6), Spotsylvania (May 8–19), and Cold Harbor (June 3–12). At Cold Harbor, the Union army loses 7000 men in the first hour.

May 11: The Union cavalry wins its first major victory, outside Richmond when Philip Sheridan's forces clash with those of J.E.B. Stuart, resulting in Stuart's death.

May 15: A Confederate force of about 5000 defeats a Union force of close to 10,000 at the Battle of New Market, Virginia.

May 27–28: The first and possibly worst defeat of General William T. Sherman's Atlanta campaign comes at Pickett's Mill in Georgia.

June 10: On his way to destroy Sherman's supply train in Tennessee, Nathan Bedford Forrest's small cavalry force encounters Samuel Sturgis's larger force at Brices Cross Roads in Mississippi and defeats the Union troops in a brilliant tactical maneuver.

June 15: Ulysses S. Grant begins the nine-month siege of Petersburg, Virginia.

June 27–July 1: William T. Sherman's Union army of more than 100,000 battles Joseph Johnston's 50,000 Confederates in a failed frontal assault at Kennesaw Mountain, Georgia. Johnston wins, but then evacuates the area on July 2 as Sherman begins flanking maneuvers anew.

July 9: Union troops lose the Battle of Monocacy in Frederick, Maryland, but buy time to reinforce the defenses of Washington, D.C., thwarting the Confederate attempt to invade the North.

July 14: Union major general A. J. Smith's forces defeat Confederate general Nathan Bedford Forrest at Tupelo, Mississippi.

July 22: William T. Sherman and the Union win the Battle of Atlanta. The city surrenders six weeks later.

August 5: Union rear admiral David Farragut's fleet steams by Forts Morgan and Gaines in Alabama. After two weeks of shelling, the forts surrender.

September 2: Atlanta surrenders to William T. Sherman.

October 21–23: The Union wins the largest battle fought west of the Mississippi, ending organized Confederate military operations in Missouri.

November 8: Abraham Lincoln decisively defeats Democrat George McClellan for the U.S. presidency.

November 16: General William T. Sherman begins a March to the Sea with 62,000 troops.

December 13: After two years of Union attempts to capture Fort McAllister in Georgia from the water, a land assault takes the fort in less than half an hour.

December 15–16: John Bell Hood's Confederate Army of Tennessee is soundly defeated at Nashville by a Union force led by George H. Thomas.

December 21: General William T. Sherman captures Savannah, leaving behind a 300-mile-long and 60-mile-wide path of destruction across Georgia.

1865

January 15: Robert E. Lee's last supply route from Europe is closed when Fort Fisher falls in defense of Wilmington, North Carolina.

January 23–24: The last battle of the ironclads occurs on the James River, when Confederate ships attack General Grant's headquarters at City Point, Virginia.

January 31: The U.S. Congress passes the 13th amendment to the Constitution, abolishing slavery in the United States. After ratification by the states, it takes effect on December 6, 1865.

February 6: Robert E. Lee takes command of all the Confederate armies.

March 2: The Shenandoah Valley campaign comes to an end when General Jubal Early's cavalry is defeated by General Philip Sheridan's forces at Waynesboro.

March 4: "With malice toward none; with charity for all." President Lincoln sets forth his postwar plans in his second inaugural speech.

March 12: To prevent capture, the crew of the C.S.S. *Neuse* destroys the last-produced ironclad before the ship has seen any action.

March 13: The Confederate Congress passes General Order 14, approving the use of Negro troops in the Confederate army.

April 2: The Confederate line is broken at Petersburg, and Lee and his army evacuate the town. Richmond, capital of the Confederacy, is also evacuated.

April 3: Union troops occupy Richmond.

April 9: Robert E. Lee agrees to an unconditional surrender to Ulysses S. Grant at Appomattox Court House in Virginia.

April 14: The U.S. flag is raised over Fort Sumter by Robert Anderson, who surrendered the fort on the same date four years earlier.

President and Mrs. Lincoln attend a play at Ford's Theatre. John Wilkes Booth shoots the President in the head and escapes. The President is carried to a house across the street, where he dies the next morning.

April 15: Vice President Andrew Johnson assumes the presidency.

April 18: Confederate general Joseph Johnston surrenders to General William T. Sherman in North Carolina. The terms are signed on April 26.

April 26: John Wilkes Booth is shot and killed when found hiding in a barn in Virginia.

May 10: The President of the Confederacy, Jefferson Davis, is captured near Irwinville, Georgia.

President Andrew Johnson declares all armed resistance to the government of the United States has ended.

May 23–24: Two days of parades in Washington, D.C., by Union soldiers celebrate their victory.

May 29: President Andrew Johnson grants a general amnesty to those who were involved in "the existing rebellion."

June 23: Stand Watie is the last Confederate general to lay down arms. He is also the only Indian who became a general in the Civil War.

July 7: Four of those who conspired with Booth to assassinate President Abraham Lincoln are executed by hanging.

November 5: The C.S.S. *Shenandoah*, a very successful Confederate commercial raider, is surrendered to British authorities in Liverpool, England—the last Confederate unit to surrender.

November 10: Captain Henry Wirz, the superintendent of Andersonville prison, is hanged—the only Confederate officer to be executed for war crimes.

Fort Gaines

The War of 1812 demonstrated that America needed adequate defenses for its long coastline, and a group of forts called the Third System was begun to meet this need. Fort Gaines, on Dauphin Island in Alabama, was a late Third System masonry fort, designed to keep enemy ships out of western Mobile Bay and repulse an attack from the land. It is a relatively simple fort because its mission was to defend a minor channel into Mobile Bay, while the larger Fort Morgan (*see* Fort Morgan) across the bay guarded the main channel. Fort Gaines was a completely new design, with ten guns on top of five-foot-thick walls of brick and sand and a dry moat that extends 35 feet from the base of the walls. In 1862, the Confederates took over the fort and turned it into a formidable defensive position.

Fort Gaines was attacked from the land side by Union forces on August 3, 1864, just before the Battle of Mobile Bay. The fort played a relatively minor part in the battle because Union admiral David Farragut entered Mobile Bay by the large channel next to Fort Morgan, out of the range of Fort Gaines's guns. Fort Gaines, cut off by both land and sea, surrendered on August 8.

Fort Gaines Historic Site

The northwest bastion of Fort Gaines is preserved in its original condition, and visitors can roam the fort and explore a wide variety of tunnels, living quarters, and various battlements. They can also visit the blacksmith shop, kitchen, and bakery. Civil War cannons are on display along with a battery for two of the three 6-inch disappearing cannons that were installed between 1890 and 1910 as a part of an improvement program. On the land side are the remains of the sloping brick walls covered with earth to absorb cannon shells.

The United States sold Fort Gaines to the City of Mobile in 1926, and the city in turn gave the property to the Alabama Department of Conservation, which deeded it to the Dauphin Island Park and Beach Board. The fort has a museum with a gift shop and an information desk. A ferry runs across Mobile Bay between Fort Gaines and Fort Morgan. The trip takes approximately 30 minutes.

Visitor Information

251-861-6992;
www.dauphinisland.org/fort.htm
Hours: Daily 9 a.m. until 5 p.m.; during daylight savings time, 9 a.m. until 6 p.m.; closed Thanksgiving and December 25.
Admission: Minimal fee for adults and children 7 to 13; free to younger children. Groups should call in advance for two-for-one admission.
Accessibility: Handicapped accessible.
Special Events: Recreation of an 1862 Confederate Christmas at Fort Gaines each December. Annual "Damn the Torpedoes" events in August on the anniversary of the battle. Reenactments are staged October to May.
Getting There: Take I-10 to state highway 193 and go south to Dauphin Island. Turn left at the water tower and go three miles to Fort Gaines, which is on the eastern end of Bienville Boulevard at the tip of Dauphin Island.

The Mobile Bay Ferry runs from Dauphin Island 8 a.m. until 6:30 p.m., and from Fort Morgan, 8:45 a.m. until 7:15 p.m. Schedules vary, so it is advisable to call first. Minimal fee per person. Cars and motor homes can also be accommodated. Discounts are available for round-trip travel. For ferry information, call 251-540-7787.

Fort Morgan and the Battle of Mobile Bay

Fort Morgan was another of the Third System forts built to defend the country's coastline after the War of 1812. Along with the smaller Fort

Gaines across the channel on Dauphin Island, the large brick fort was intended to protect the main entrance to Mobile Bay and the city of Mobile. Begun in 1819 and completed in 1834, Fort Morgan was taken over by Confederate forces when the Civil War began. The two forts protected the city of Mobile from assault by sea, although for most of the war, Union warships patrolled outside Mobile Bay, successfully stopping blockade runners. Then, in the summer of 1864, Union admiral David Farragut planned an attack to break through the Confederate defenses and enter Mobile Bay.

The Defense of Mobile Bay

Confederate admiral Franklin Buchanan, the former captain of the C.S.S. *Virginia (Merrimack)*, commanded Mobile's defenses. Under his command was the powerful new ironclad ram C.S.S. *Tennessee*, but the rest of his sea force consisted of three small, virtually useless wooden gunboats, the *Selma*, the *Morgan*, and the *Gaines*. Part of Mobile's defenses were "torpedoes"—or what today would be called moored mines—laid in the water between Fort Gaines and Fort Morgan. These mines were considered by some (including Farragut) to be "uncivilized," but they were formidable weapons.

Farragut's Plan

Admiral Farragut's plan was simple. He divided his force into two columns, with 14 steam-powered

Farragut's fleet trades fire with Fort Morgan and three enemy gunboats, led by the Tennessee. *At center above, the monitor* Tecumseh *founders after striking a mine. The Rains keg torpedo, inset, was made from small beer kegs and held below the water surface by an anchor.*

wooden warships in one and his four ironclad monitors (the *Tecumseh*, the *Manhattan*, the *Winnebago*, and the *Chickasaw*) in the other. The two columns would proceed down the main channel next to Fort Morgan, out of the range of Fort Gaines's guns. The monitors, which were virtually unsinkable by hits above the waterline, would lead the attack by passing next to Fort Morgan. They would fire grapeshot at the fort to force the Confederate gunners to take cover, while the faster wooden ships would follow in a separate column with Farragut's flagship, the *Hartford*, second in line. The wooden ships would keep the monitors between them and the fort, and each of the first four wooden ships would have a small ship lashed to her side opposite the fort for added firepower and protection.

Once past the fort and inside the harbor, the wooden ships would harass the slower *Tennessee* and wait for the Union monitors to complete their passage and join the attack on the Confederate ironclad. Farragut ordered his commanders to stay in the marked channel to avoid the mines in the bay. As a diversion,

Union forces had landed on Dauphin Island and attacked Fort Gaines from the land side a few days before Farragut attacked.

Farragut's Attack

At six a.m. on August 5, 1864, Farragut's fleet made its move. In Mobile, the cathedral bell sounded the alarm, and other bells in the city joined in. Soon the citizens could see the Union ships entering the bay, helped by the flood tide, while the thunder of cannon fire rolled across the water. From time to time the smoke was so dense that the vessels disappeared, but still the firing continued.

Confederate admiral Buchanan and the *Tennessee*, along with the three gunboats, stood just past Fort Morgan inside the bay, waiting to engage the first Union ships through the channel. The monitor *Tecumseh* led the Union ironclad line past Fort Morgan; but when the *Tecumseh*'s captain saw the *Tennessee*, the Union monitor broke formation and headed straight for the Confederate ironclad. The *Tecumseh* had just turned when a terrific explosion shook the bay and a huge pillar of smoke rose

from the sea. The *Tecumseh* had struck a mine. Its stern rose slowly; and then, with the propeller still spinning, the monitor slipped beneath the waves. Only 21 of the 114 men aboard escaped.

Both sides began to cheer, the Union sailors because they believed the sinking ship was the *Tennessee*, the Confederates because they knew it was the *Tecumseh*. At Fort Morgan, the guns turned on the lead wooden ship, the *Brooklyn*, thinking it was Farragut's flagship. The *Brooklyn*, under heavy fire and fearing there were mines in her path, stopped and then reversed her engines.

"Damn the Torpedoes!"

Farragut, strapped on the rigging high above the *Hartford*'s deck, watched in dismay as the *Brooklyn* stopped in front of him and began to move backward. In a moment, the *Brooklyn* would back into the *Hartford*, throwing the column into chaos directly in front of Fort Morgan's guns. The *Brooklyn* signaled it was backing up because of "torpedoes in the channel." Farragut became immortal with his next command, "Damn the torpedoes! Full speed ahead!"

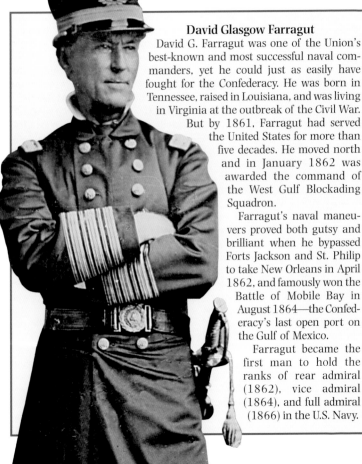

David Glasgow Farragut

David G. Farragut was one of the Union's best-known and most successful naval commanders, yet he could just as easily have fought for the Confederacy. He was born in Tennessee, raised in Louisiana, and was living in Virginia at the outbreak of the Civil War. But by 1861, Farragut had served the United States for more than five decades. He moved north and in January 1862 was awarded the command of the West Gulf Blockading Squadron.

Farragut's naval maneuvers proved both gutsy and brilliant when he bypassed Forts Jackson and St. Philip to take New Orleans in April 1862, and famously won the Battle of Mobile Bay in August 1864—the Confederacy's last open port on the Gulf of Mexico.

Farragut became the first man to hold the ranks of rear admiral (1862), vice admiral (1864), and full admiral (1866) in the U.S. Navy.

Farragut led the rest of the column of ships around the outside of the *Brooklyn* and into the minefield while the *Brooklyn* struggled to get under way again. As they pressed through the minefield, sailors on the wooden Union ships heard the pop of mines' detonators as their ships brushed against them, but the Confederate mines failed to explode, probably because they had been in the water too long.

As the Union ships entered the bay, Admiral Buchanan on the *Tennessee* tried to ram them, but the wooden ships were too agile. While the guns of the *Tennessee* damaged ship after ship, the Union warships slipped away in pursuit of the three small Confederate gunboats. The *Gaines* was run aground, the *Morgan* fled to Mobile, and the *Selma* surrendered.

Soon only the *Tennessee*, remained. Farragut and Buchanan steered their ships toward each other to try to ram, but the two ships skidded off each other. The *Tennessee* raked the *Hartford*'s deck with cannon fire, causing heavy casualties, and fought on. However, the Confederate ironclad was doomed by a design flaw—her steering cables were not properly protected. As the *Tennessee* was hit again and again by concentrated fire, her steering mechanism finally gave out. Soon the ironclad was unable to maneuver. After two hours of pounding, and with serious wounds sustained by Admiral Buchanan, the *Tennessee* struck its colors.

Fort Morgan was one of many Third System forts built for coastal protection before the Civil War. The forts sat low, so their bottom tier of artillery could ricochet cannonballs across the water to hit enemy ships at the waterline.

Fort Morgan Falls

The next day, cut off by land and sea, Fort Gaines surrendered. Fort Morgan was soon cut off from land by the Union army force and was shelled by Farragut's vessels. It held out for over two weeks but finally surrendered on August 23. Even with the forts out of action, Farragut was unable to move his ships in close enough to bombard the city—Mobile Bay was too shallow. Mobile held out until the end of the war. Nevertheless, the victory over Fort Morgan was an important one for the Union. It closed one of the South's essential supply routes—used to receive ammunition and other necessities as well as to ship cotton and produce to Europe.

Fort Morgan Historic Site

The Fort Morgan Museum shows the evolution of American coastal defense fortifications from 1834 through World War II. The museum's collection includes artillery pieces, military uniforms, small arms, and memorabilia from the 19th century through World War II. Archival collections with original photographs, manuscripts, and documents from the period are accessible for research. The Mobile Bay ferry departs from the grounds for trips across the bay to Fort Gaines, on Dauphin Island (*see* Fort Gaines).

Visitor Information
251-540-7125
Hours: Grounds and fort—daily, June through September, 8 a.m. until 7 p.m.; October through February, 8 a.m. until 5 p.m.; March through May, 8 a.m. until 6 p.m. Museum—weekdays, 8 a.m. until 5 p.m.; Saturday and Sunday, 9 a.m. until 5 p.m.
Closed Thanksgiving, December 25, and New Year's Day.
Special Events: Guides and enactors conduct a daily living-history program during the summer at the museum. There are special programs the first weekend in August, including "Living History Encampment." Tuesday evenings during the summer, guides conduct candle-light tours of the fort.
Admission: Minimal fee for adults and children 6 to 12; free to younger children.
Accessibility: Partial accessibility; calling in advance is recommended
Getting There: From I-10, take state highway 59 to Gulf Shores. At Gulf Shores, proceed west 22 miles on state highway 180 to Fort Morgan.

The Mobile Bay Ferry runs from Fort Morgan, 8:45 a.m. until 7:15 p.m. and from Dauphin Island 8 a.m. until 6:30 p.m. Schedules vary, so it is advisable to call first. Minimal fee per person. Cars and motor homes can also be accommodated. Discounts are available for round-trip travel. For ferry information, call 251-540-7787.

The Alabama Department of Archives and History

The Alabama Department of Archives and History in Montgomery, Alabama, contains a very large collection of original and secondary materials on the Civil War. Among the records are Confederate army records, soldiers' personal correspondence and artifacts, and public documents from the period.

Some of the military records of special interest include Alabama Confederate Service Cards, which contain information about individual soldiers from Alabama, including the date and place of enlistment, company and regiment, a list of the engagements the soldier took part in, whether he was killed, captured, or wounded, and the date of parole; Confederate Military Unit history files; original Alabama Confederate muster rolls; Confederate pension files; Civil War and Reconstruction subject files that include narrative accounts of campaigns, and the biographies of general officers; bound volumes of the Loyalty Oaths taken by former Confederate soldiers; hand-drawn Civil War maps of specific campaigns; and the 1907 and 1921 censuses of Confederate soldiers in Alabama.

In addition, the collection includes letters, diaries, and manuscripts from Confederate soldiers and their families and photographs of Confederate officers including Robert E. Lee, P.G.T. Beauregard, John Tyler Morgan, Stonewall Jackson, and J.E.B. Stuart, as well as many others. Public records from the period are also archived here, such as the correspondence and appointments files of Alabama's Civil War governors; Alabama newspapers from the Civil War period; 1867 voter registration lists which record the efforts to extend suffrage to the millions of freedmen across the South; and pamphlets written during and after the war on such subjects as states rights, abolition, secession, specific military campaigns, and Reconstruction.

The archive building contains a Military Gallery devoted to Alabama soldiers and displays the weapons and possessions that they took with them to war. The collection includes a Civil War soldier's knapsack and its contents (including a piece of "hardtack" over 100 years old), Civil War era homespun uniforms dyed butternut brown, a bulky three-pound Ketchum hand grenade, and blue-decorated plates from the famous raider C.S.S. *Alabama.*

A new wing is scheduled to open in 2004.

Visitor Information
334-242-4435;
www.archives.state.al.us
Hours: Monday to Friday and the first Saturday of the month, 8:30 a.m. until 4:30 p.m.; the reference and research room is closed on Mondays; closed on Sundays and all state holidays.
Admission: Free.
Accessibility: The building is handicapped accessible.
Directions: The archives is located at 624 Washington Avenue, just south of the state capitol building in Montgomery.

Fort Smith

Construction of Fort Smith, located on the Arkansas River on the site of an earlier fort by the same name, was completed in 1846. Dogged by funding and labor problems, it had less than half the intended number of buildings, with thinner walls, and several uncompleted cannon platforms.

At the outset of the Civil War, the commander of Fort Smith, Captain Samuel Sturgis, realized that Arkansas would secede and his two companies of cavalry would not be able to defend the post. Sturgis evacuated Fort Smith on April 23, 1861, and the Arkansas state militia quickly occupied it, using it as a Confederate staging area for battles in Missouri and Arkansas.

On July 17, 1863, Union forces won a major victory at Honey Springs in the Indian Territory (present-day Oklahoma), allowing Union troops to retake Fort Smith two months later. They immediately began to build a line of rifle pits, trenches, and artillery emplacements about a mile outside of the fort.

As the war turned against the Confederates, they gave up on large operations and began to focus on small unit actions such as raiding supply trains and harassing Union garrisons in Missouri, northwest Arkansas, and the Indian Territory. They hoped to divert much-needed Union troops west from the main battles. Confederate colonel Stand Watie's Indian forces were a major thorn in the Union's side. Watie—a Cherokee who had moved to the Indian Territory from Georgia in 1837—had joined the Confederate army when the war began, raised a regiment of Cherokees, and was promoted to colonel. His men fought with distinction in a number of battles, notably Pea Ridge. Watie was promoted to brigadier general in May 1864, and celebrated a month later with a remarkable feat, capturing the Union supply steamship *J. R. Williams*.

In late July 1864, Watie began a series of attacks around Fort Smith to try to lure Federal cavalry units out from behind the fortifications. However, the Union cavalry's horses were suffering from heat and lack of forage, so the Federals refused to be drawn any distance from the fort.

Watie finally decided to move on Fort Smith. He launched a surprise attack on July 31 that captured some Union outposts. The Union forces fell back along their line of fortifications, and two companies of the 1st Kansas Colored Infantry, firing from rifle pits, stopped Watie's men. The Confederates brought up a battery of 6-pound howitzers and began to shell the Union fortifications, but the Union countered with four rifled 10-pounder Parrott guns manned by the 2nd Kansas Battery. In a brief, one-sided artillery duel, the Parrotts took a heavy toll on Watie's men, and the Confederates were barely able to withdraw their guns in a frantic retreat. The next day there were sporadic artillery duels, but that night the Confederates departed, ending the threat to Fort Smith.

Watie and his Indian forces continued to harass the Union for the rest of the war. He did not surrender until June 23, 1865, and was the last Confederate general to lay down his arms, as well as having the distinction of being the only Indian to achieve the rank of general in the Civil War.

For the rest of the war, Fort Smith served as a supply post and a refugee camp, but when the war ended Fort Smith's usefulness ended with it. The fort did not age well, and within a few years both of the buildings that housed officers burned down. In the summer of 1871, U.S. Army troops left Fort Smith for the last time.

Fort Smith National Historic Site

The site includes the remains of two frontier forts and the Federal Court for the Western District of Arkansas. One building, which served as the

Stand Watie *was the last Confederate general to lay down his arms.*

barracks, courthouse, and jail, and is now the Visitors Center, is located in the center of the park. The exhibits there focus on Fort Smith's military history from 1817 to 1871.

On the grounds, paved and gravel paths mark the locations of the walls that surrounded Fort Smith, and the floor plans of three historic buildings have also been marked out for the visitor.

The Commissary Storehouse is located at the northwest corner of the Fort Smith site. The interior of the first floor is restored to its 1850s appearance, and audio and visual exhibits explain the history and use of the commissary building from 1838 to the present.

South of the Visitors Center is a reconstruction of the 1886 gallows on the original site used for Federal executions from 1873 to 1896. Nooses are hung on the gallows on the anniversaries of the executions, and on those days park rangers give programs discussing the executions and how they related to the Federal court. The Visitors Center also offers audio and visual exhibits on these executions.

Visitor Information
479-783-3961; www.nps.gov/fosm
Hours: Daily, 9 a.m. until 5 p.m.; closed Thanksgiving, December 25, and New Year's Day.

Admission: Small per-family charge or minimal charge for adults; free for those under 17. National Parks Pass, Golden Eagle, Golden Age, and Golden Access are honored.
Accessibility: Most park facilities are handicapped accessible; a wheelchair is available to borrow.
Special Events: During the summer, the 2nd Kansas Battery–Living History Artillery Crew presents demonstrations of 1812-era and Civil War artillery at the park.
Getting There: From the regional airport: Follow I-540 to the Rogers Avenue exit, and follow Rogers Avenue downtown, almost to the river.

From I-40 west: Take I-540 south to the Rogers Avenue exit and proceed west on Rogers Avenue almost to the river.

From I-40 east: Take exit 64B and go six miles east. Make the first right after crossing the bridge over the Arkansas River to the fort grounds.

From downtown: From Garrison Avenue, turn south at Fourth Street. Turn right onto Garland Avenue. At the end of the next block is the entrance to the main parking lot. Parking is also available on Third Street.

The City of Fort Smith operates a trolley that visits all museums and attractions in the downtown area. The trolley leaves from the city's Visitor Information Center.

The Battle of Pea Ridge

In late December 1861, Union general Samuel Curtis was appointed commander of the Union Army of the Southwest and was told to drive Confederate general Sterling "Old Pap" Price out of Missouri, where he had been fighting Union soldiers for several months. When Curtis moved south and began to press the Confederates, Price decided not to fight and retreated into Arkansas.

There, Price combined his 8000 men of the Missouri State Guard with General Benjamin McCulloch's 8700 Arkansas, Texas, and Louisiana soldiers. However, although Price and McCulloch had won a battle together at Wilson Creek in August, they had sharp disagreements and were barely on speaking terms. The problem was so severe that Confederate President Jefferson Davis created the Military District of the Trans-Mississippi on January 10, 1862, and placed Major General Earl Van Dorn in overall command. It

was to prove a serious mistake.

On February 17, Curtis's Army of the Southwest—four divisions with about 10,000 men and 49 cannons—invaded northwest Arkansas and the Confederacy. As they moved into an area known as Pea Ridge, the Confederates fell back in a disorganized retreat. They burned their own storehouses in Cross Hollows and then moved on to Fayetteville, the major Confederate supply depot in northwestern Arkansas. Thinking they were still being pursued, the Confederates burned more supplies in Fayetteville and vandalized homes and businesses before moving into the Boston Mountains.

Meanwhile, Curtis prudently decided to stop and dig in. His troops were tired, the weather was terrible, and he was at the tail of a long supply line. He set up a solid defensive position facing south in the heights above the Little Sugar Creek Road, east of the town of Bentonville, then sent two divisions to forage for food

Elkhorn Tavern was the scene of bitter fighting on both days of the battle.

ordered a long night march to come around behind the Union forces. He commanded Price and McCulloch each to lead a division along Bentonville Detour, a road that traveled around and north of Curtis's right flank. Price and McCulloch argued against the maneuver because the men and horses were exhausted, but Van Dorn would not be dissuaded.

On March 6, in terrible weather and almost out of food, the Confederate forces began their miserable trek with Price's division and Van Dorn, still riding in his warm ambulance, in the lead. During the night, many Confederates dropped out, and McCulloch's trailing division fell farther and farther behind Price and Van Dorn. By dawn on March 7, McCulloch's force was so far behind that Van Dorn decided to split his forces. He ordered McCulloch's division to turn south early, on the east side of the high ground called Big Mountain and Pea Ridge. The two forces would rejoin around noon at Elkhorn Tavern atop the broad plateau of Pea Ridge. There the Confederates would deploy for battle and advance upon the unsuspecting Federals from the north.

Unfortunately for the Confederates, Curtis had learned that Van Dorn was on the move. He was now faced with the tricky task of moving out of his fortifications and turning his entire army 180 degrees to face north, then meeting an attack by a numerically superior enemy. While he executed this maneuver, he sent out forces commanded by Union colonel Peter J. Osterhaus to attack and delay the Confederates. When they intercepted McCulloch's division, Osterhaus's heavily outnumbered forward elements skirmished briefly with the Confederates but were quickly routed and fell back to join the rest of their division.

Osterhaus asked for reinforcements and began to shell the advancing Confederates. McCulloch, surprised to be engaged, deployed for battle, then rode forward to try to

at Cross Hollows and another two divisions to forage around McKissick's Creek. If Confederates attacked from the south, the Union forces would come together and fight in the positions above the Little Sugar Creek Road.

General Van Dorn was determined to attack Curtis, and rushed to join generals Price and McCulloch. During the trip, Van Dorn's boat capsized while crossing an icy river and when he arrived on March 2, he was exhausted and suffering from chills and fever. Van Dorn heard that Curtis had split his forces, and he decided to surprise the Union forces while they were still separated. When Van Dorn's newly combined "Army of the West" moved out the next morning, it had 16,000 men and 65 guns, a 3-to-2 advantage in manpower and a 4-to-3 advantage in artillery over Curtis's forces. It was the greatest matériel superiority the Confederacy would achieve in the entire war. Included in the force was a brigade of Cherokee Indians commanded by the bearded, eccentric 300-pound General Albert J. Pike.

Van Dorn wanted speed and surprise, so he ordered the soldiers to carry only their weapons, 40 rounds of ammunition, a blanket, and three days' rations. Things began to go wrong almost immediately. After sitting all winter, the Confederate soldiers were out of shape for a rapid march, and it did not help that Van Dorn led the force from a cot in a rapidly moving ambulance. In addition, the Confederates had to march in freezing temperatures through snow and over ice-covered roads. For two days—cold, tired, hungry, and generally miserable—the Confederates marched. On March 6, they arrived close to the Union positions.

But rather than attack the Sugar Creek Road fortifications, Van Dorn

In the Battle of Pea Ridge, *five hundred Federal cavalrymen and artillerymen fire at 8000 attacking Confederates. During the charge, the cavalry regiments became so hopelessly intermixed it took nearly two hours for the Confederates to regain order. This lull gave the Federals the time they needed to regroup and prepare a defense.*

assess the strength of the Union forces. He rode right into a small force from the 36th Illinois, who shot him dead. Brigadier General James M. McIntosh took over the division, but when he rode forward he too was killed by fire, from a different company of the 36th Illinois. Now Colonel Louis Hébert was the ranking officer in McCulloch's division, but Hébert was leading an attack on the flanks and had no idea he was in command.

Curtis sent Colonel Jefferson C. Davis's division to help Osterhaus, but the numerically superior Confederates slowly pushed the Federals back. Then, suddenly, Union forces captured Hébert while he was lost in the smoke of the battle. The now leaderless Confederates fell apart and abandoned the battlefield. About half of the division started the long trek north around Big Mountain toward Elkhorn Tavern to join Price and Van Dorn.

Osterhaus had routed a much larger Confederate force, killed two general officers, and completely spoiled Van Dorn's ambitious plan.

To the east, Van Dorn led Price's division toward Colonel Eugene A. Carr's Union forces, set up on the steep northern slope of Pea Ridge near Elkhorn Tavern. Carr's men had a commanding view of Van Dorn's forces as they moved down Cross Timber Hollow, a deep and narrow valley. When the Confederates began to climb up the steep slope from Cross Timber Hollow to Pea Ridge, Carr's forces opened fire.

Van Dorn was caught by surprise. The low ground in Cross Timber Hollow was filled with smoke, and it was several hours before Van Dorn realized his forces outnumbered the Union forces. Then he ordered a full-scale attack, and the Confederate forces pushed back the Union flanks and reached high ground. As night fell, the Confederates controlled Elkhorn Tavern and Telegraph Road, but their situation was deteriorating rapidly. The remnants of McCulloch's division marched all night to join Van Dorn at Elkhorn Tavern, but they were exhausted, almost starving, and proved to be virtually useless. The rest of the Confederate forces were also tired and weak from hunger and, to make matters worse, were almost out of ammunition. The Union forces, on the other hand, had plenty of food, water, and ammunition. That night, Osterhaus and Davis arrived from the west, and Curtis consolidated his forces and prepared for the next day.

The next morning, Curtis deployed his entire army against the Confederates, one of the few times in the Civil War an entire army was on line. Curtis waited to see if Van Dorn would continue to attack. When nothing happened, at about eight

an extensive effort to return the battlefield to its 1862 appearance. Today the 4300-acre park appears almost exactly as it did during the March 1862 battle, and these days it is one of the best-preserved Civil War battlefields in the nation. In addition to duplicating the natural environment, the National Park Service reconstructed the Elkhorn Tavern on its original site, which was the scene of bitter fighting on both days.

The newly renovated Visitors Center is located just off U.S. route 62 on the park's south side. It contains a museum with both permanent and rotating exhibits, a bookstore, restrooms, and a picnic area. A seven-mile self-guided automobile tour is available from 8 a.m. until 4:30 p.m. There is also an 11-mile equestrian trail and a 10-mile hiking trail. The Elkhorn Tavern is open for tours from Memorial Day until the third week in October.

Visitor Information

479-451-8122; www.nps.gov/peri/
Hours: Daily, 8 a.m. until 5 p.m.; closed Thanksgiving, December 25, and New Year's Day.

Admission: Minimal fee per person or small fee per vehicle. National Parks Pass, Golden Eagle, Golden Age, and Golden Access are honored.

Accessibility: The Visitors Center, tour road, and most tour stops are handicapped accessible. The Elkhorn Tavern and trails are not accessible by wheelchair. Wayside and audiovisual exhibits are not designed for hearing or visually impaired visitors.

Special Events: On the weekend closest to the anniversary of the battle, there are commemorative ceremonies and special programs. Other special remembrance activities are scheduled on Memorial Day and Veterans Day. The park conducts living-history demonstrations, educational presentations, and talks on Saturdays and Sundays throughout the summer.

Getting There: The park is 90 miles northeast of Fort Smith, Arkansas, and 80 miles southwest of Springfield, Missouri.

From Fort Smith: Take I-540 north toward Fayetteville, Arkansas. Take the U.S. 62 exit and follow signs to the park.

From Springfield: Take U.S. 60 to Monett, Missouri, then go south on state Route 37 to Gateway, Arkansas. Follow U.S. 62 west to the park.

a.m. Curtis began an attack of his own. For two hours, Federal cannons shelled the Confederates, creeping forward to fire from ever closer range. The Confederate artillery, virtually out of ammunition, could not respond. Then Curtis ordered an attack and his four divisions, "yelling at the top of their lungs," charged forward.

Van Dorn ordered a withdrawal and then galloped away from the battle while it still raged. The starving, exhausted Confederates, now without a commander, broke and ran. The next day they reassembled and made their way south. During the retreat, many men left ranks to forage for food, some of whom never returned.

At Pea Ridge, the outnumbered and outgunned Union forces celebrated an uncommon early victory over the Confederates. It was to prove a disastrous defeat for the Confederates, since it not only secured the Federal hold on northwestern Arkansas but also assured Union control of Missouri. For the rest of the war, guerrillas would savage the state, but the Union never came close to losing control of it.

Pea Ridge National Military Park

While Union and Confederate veterans groups placed markers on the battlefield after the war, it was not until the late 1950s that the land was purchased for the formal park. In 1962 the Visitors Center opened, and the workers at the park began

Fort Point National Historic Site

Fort Point is the only Third System masonry fort on the West Coast of the United States, and part of its importance is that it shows the beginnings of America as a Pacific power. Fort Point was built on the shores of San Francisco Bay by the U.S. Army Corps of Engineers between 1853 and 1861, and was rushed to completion when the Civil War began. It was a standard Third System fort, pentagon shaped and intended to mount 126 cannons. As the war progressed, it became clear that brick forts had been made obsolete by rifled cannons and that the Confederacy was unlikely to send a fleet to invade San Francisco, but the fort remained in service until 1886.

Fort Point was the base of operations for the construction of the Golden Gate Bridge between 1933 and 1937. It was also one of the few coastal forts to serve a potentially useful purpose in World War II, when searchlights and cannons were mounted there as part of the antisubmarine defenses for the Bay Area.

On the first floor of the fort is a museum that describes the fort's construction. There are also other exhibits on the fort's second and third floors. The museum's permanent photographic exhibition includes "Ready & Forward: Equality for the Buffalo Soldiers," depicting the difficulties faced by African American soldiers. The so-called Buffalo Soldiers were African American troops in the 9th and 10th Cavalry. These regiments were created by Congressional legislation in 1866, and most of the Buffalo Soldiers had served in black units during the Civil War. During the Civil War, on the Union side there were 186,000 black combat troops, 130 infantry regiments, 7 cavalry regiments, and 19 artillery regiments. Black troops fought in 449 major and minor engagements, and 16 black soldiers and four black sailors earned the Congressional Medal of Honor.

Other exhibits include "Women at War," showing the importance of women during the Civil War, and "Constructing the Golden Gate Bridge," with photos of the construction of the bridge, many taken from Fort Point while it was the construction headquarters.

Throughout the day, the fort's museum theater features two videos, *Fort Point, Guardian of the Golden Gate*, a 30-minute video about the history of Fort Point through World War II, and *Building the Golden Gate Bridge*, which provides historical insights into this engineering marvel.

Visitor Information

415-556-1693; www.nps.gov/fopo

Hours: Friday to Sunday, 10 a.m. until 5 p.m.; closed Thanksgiving, December 25, and New Year's Day; the bookstore is open 10 a.m. until 4:30 p.m. Note: Hours are limited because of work on the Golden Gate Bridge. Call for information.

Accessibility: Only the main floor of Fort Point, including the museum, theater, and bookstore, is wheelchair accessible. Portable toilets are available outside of Fort Point, about 140 yards down the main road on the right side.

Admission: Free.

Special Programs: Regular cannon-loading demonstrations show how a Napoleon 12-pounder cannon was loaded and fired. Call for information.

Getting There: From the north: Proceed over the Golden Gate Bridge on U.S. 101 south, staying in the farthest right lane. After passing through the tollgate, take the first available exit to the right, continuing in a circle to the right, and through an underpass. Proceed through the parking lot on the right until reaching the stop sign. Turn left onto Lincoln Boulevard and proceed to Long Avenue, which dead ends at the fort.

From the south: Take U.S. 101 north toward the Golden Gate Bridge, stay in the farthest right lane and take the "Last San Francisco Exit." Proceed through the parking lot on the right until reaching the stop sign. Turn left onto Lincoln Boulevard and proceed to Long Avenue, which dead ends at the fort.

From the southeast: Take 25th Avenue to Lincoln Boulevard. Follow the road for about 1/4 mile and turn left onto Long Avenue until it dead ends at the fort.

By public transportation: San Francisco MUNI buses 28 & 29 stop at the Golden Gate toll plaza area. There is a path that leads down to the fort. For more information about bus routes in the Bay Area call 415-817-1717.

FORTIFICATIONS

Fortifications during the Civil War were made up of masonry or earthen coastal forts, temporary tactical field fortifications like trenches and semipermanent structures, and major field fortifications of thick walls with ditches and other obstacles in front of them.

Waterside Fortifications

The classic Civil War coastal fort was a "Third System" fort, originally built to defend against British or other European naval attacks. Many became famous during the war—Fort Sumter, Fort Pulaski, Fort Macon, and Fort Morgan, to name a few. Their predecessors were built in the late 1700s, the "First System" open earthwork forts such as Fort McHenry in Baltimore. They were fashioned in the European star shape, with a single tier of guns that fired over the walls. In the early 1800s, the "Second System" forts were built, of either masonry-faced earth or all masonry, with the guns firing through openings in the walls.

The British brushed past these forts in the War of 1812, to the chagrin of the United States government. In 1816, President James Monroe launched a program to protect the coast without having to maintain a large navy, by building Third System forts. The Coastal Fortifications Board implemented this massive defense project. They were to be made of masonry with multitiered gun emplace-ments, designed to engage wooden ships with smoothbore cannons. A line of Third System forts was built from Louisiana to Maine, and by the outset of the Civil War, most large seaports and major river mouths were protected by one or more Third System forts.

The pentagon-shaped forts were impressive, usually protected by 50-foot-high, 7-foot-thick walls and covering over two acres of land. Most were designed to mount about 125 guns on three tiers of cannons. The forts sat low, near the waterline, so their lowest tier of artillery could ricochet cannonballs across the water to hit enemy ships.

When the Civil War began, the Confederacy quickly took possession of the Third System forts in their territory, most famously Fort Sumter. However, soon after the war began, they learned that the accuracy and penetrating power of rifled artillery allowed quick destruction of a Third System fort's brick walls. Once Union attackers were able to get rifled cannons within range of the forts, a Third System fort was doomed. For most of the war, these forts were unable to perform their designed purpose.

However, waterside forts were still useful, and during the war both sides began to build new forts at strategic positions. Some were built on the seacoast, but most were built on riverbanks. Most were Confed-erate, and the forts were built to

Fort Monroe's original mission was to protect the entrance to Hampton Roads and the several Virginia ports that had access to its waters. During the Civil War, it was quickly reinforced so that it would not fall to Confederate forces. This 15-inch Rodman Columbiad, "The Lincoln Gun," was part of the fort's significant armament.

Wickerwork cylindrical baskets, called gabions, were set in position and filled with dirt to stabilize earthworks and protect troops from small-arms fire.

FORTIFICATIONS *(continued)*

withstand rifled artillery by incorporating thick earthen walls. Many were formidable, such as Fort Fisher. Others, such as Fort Henry and Fort Donelson, were very poorly constructed and quickly fell. Nevertheless, the new earthen forts obstructed Union water movements and had to be dealt with, most commonly by bypassing them or, if they had to be attacked, by doing so from the land side. A common Union tactic was to shell river forts with ironclads, allowing troop ships to go by and land on unprotected shorelines. From the landing points, the troops would move to their objectives.

Tactical Field Fortifications

At the beginning of the war, much of the land combat was face-to-face, but the rifled musket gave an advantage to entrenched defenders. Units began to throw up tactical field fortifications to strengthen their positions and allow small forces to withstand an attack. They were made with whatever was on hand—stones, earth, and wood—as long as it could be handled easily and rapidly. Their main purpose was to provide cover and protection. Such fortifications could be as simple as holes hacked through house walls or as elaborate as semipermanent fortifications.

These fortifications were not only for defenders—attacking armies tended to fortify their positions so they could stay close to a dug-in enemy with security against unexpected attacks. Even before they began an attack, units often prepared defensive positions to give them a place to fall back to if things went badly.

As an example of how a tactical fortification developed, infantry might be told to dig in quickly. They would first make skirmish pits or rifle trenches—what would today be called foxholes—by piling up earth, rocks, wood, and other materials in front of their position. Once that was done, trenches were dug. The dirt from the trenches was used to cover the materials in front, and soon a wall, called a parapet, was complete. At this point, if there was time, logs were placed on top of the parapet with a gap between the parapet and the logs. The infantry could fire through the gap while the logs protected their heads. Finally, a "skid" was attached, a log jammed between the back of the trench and the log on top of the parapet, so artillery did not knock the logs down into the trench. The trenches were made in a zigzag pattern, called a traverse, so if part of the trench was taken, the conquerors could not fire down the whole trench. Using these techniques, an infantry force could quickly set up a strong defensive position and make attacks very costly.

As Union armies penetrated deeper into the South, they found it vital to protect important points from Confederate cavalry attacks. Blockhouses and stockades were generally used to protect critical points such as railroad bridges, trestles, and river fords, while larger fortifications protected critical supply depots.

Major Field Fortifications

The Union siege of Petersburg would have been recognized in the Middle Ages. Once Ulysses S. Grant realized he could not capture Petersburg quickly, his troops began a siege. They first built siege lines, fortifications to protect their siege guns and soldiers from sharpshooters inside the city. Once this was done, the

Union troops began digging trenches close to the Confederate lines to set up points where they could fire on the Rebels with mortars, small arms, and artillery at close range. Then they began lengthening their trench lines, planning to keep stretching the Confederate lines until they were so thin a breakthrough would be easy.

The basic Confederate fortifications around Petersburg differed very little from those 150 years before, simply because traditional designs and methods worked well. Civil War weapons were more effective—especially rifled artillery, which hit with greater force and accuracy and could penetrate more deeply than smoothbores—but there were no new methods of breaking packed soil. The defenders' response was simple—build thicker walls with more cheap, readily available dirt.

Major field fortifications around Petersburg were different from tactical field fortifications, which were intended to provide protection for the defenders. Major field fortifications were designed both to protect the garrison and as a particular obstacle for an enemy. If the defensive fire did not break up the original assault, the fortifications were designed to stop the attack while more firepower was mobilized.

These fortifications were built with a centuries-old formula, adjusted for new weapons. A major fieldwork had troops on top of a thick earth wall, or parapet. The wall was generally eight feet high, tall enough not only to allow the defenders to fire down on the enemy, but also to prevent direct fire from reaching inside. It also cut off the enemy's view of the interior fortifications. Artillery was either mounted on barbettes high enough to fire over the parapet or in embrasure mountings, openings cut in the wall itself.

A critical part of the major field fortification was a ditch immediately in front of the wall. The ditch had to be at least 12 feet wide at the top and no less than six feet deep. The six-foot-deep ditch, combined with an eight-foot parapet, presented a 14-foot obstacle for an attacking body of troops to scale under fire.

If this was not enough, another important part of a major field fortification was obstacles placed immediately in front of the ditch and in the ditch itself. A common obstacle was an abatis, a tight line of long trees with pointed ends. These obstacles were meant to check the momentum of an attack and delay the troops under heavy fire from the walls above.

In practice, it was found that no matter how intense the fire or how strong the obstacles, a few assaulting troops were almost always able to reach the ditch. There they died.

In the end, Petersburg was captured because Grant had the manpower to keep expanding the Union trenches. He was also able to interrupt the Confederate supply lines, and this combination allowed him to take Petersburg despite its formidable, if classic, major field fortifications.

Bombproof quarters protected Union troops from enemy fire during the siege of Petersburg. Wooden barrels served as chimneys for heating the earthwork barracks.

27

Fort Delaware State Park

In 1847, Congress recognized the need to protect the ports of Wilmington and Philadelphia and authorized the construction of Fort Delaware—the largest Third System coastal defense fort in the country—on Pea Patch Island in the Delaware River. The fort, completed in 1859, is a standard pentagon-shaped fort, with 32-foot-high masonry walls that vary in thickness from 7 to 30 feet and are surrounded by a 30-foot-wide moat. A drawbridge crosses the moat on the southwest side leading to the main entrance, and there were three tiers for guns. Its circular granite stairways are unique to this fort.

As the Civil War developed, it became clear the Confederacy would not mount naval invasions of the Union and, over the protests of the fort's commander, Fort Delaware became a prisoner-of-war camp housing Confederate soldiers, political detainees, foreign blockade-runners, and Union deserters. In April 1862, the first prisoners were sent there—258 Confederates captured at the Battle of Kernstown, Virginia (the only battle "Stonewall" Jackson ever lost). As more prisoners arrived, sheds were built on the parade ground in the center of the fort, and ultimately wooden barracks were constructed outside the fort to accommodate even more prisoners. By April 1863, barracks had been erected to house 10,000 prisoners. Most of the Confederates captured at Gettysburg were imprisoned at Fort Delaware after the battle, and by August 1863 there were 12,500 prisoners on the island.

The accommodations and supplies were inadequate for the cold Delaware winters. Upon arrival, each prisoner was given one set of clothes, including a thin overcoat, and one light blanket. Coal stoves provided heat, but at times there was only one stove for every 200 men. The extreme cold, combined with poor shelter, inadequate rations, unsanitary conditions, and the overall dampness of the island, contributed to a very high death rate among the Confederate soldiers, who were unaccustomed to the cold. Many prisoners also suffered from smallpox, measles, and dysentery.

In mid-1863, a hospital was built on the island, and from then until the end of the war it housed several hundred soldiers each month. Union doctors and inspectors who visited Fort Delaware condemned the conditions there, and after the death of 317 Confederates and 14 political prisoners in September 1863—not even a cold month—one Union officer said "the mortality is to me fearful and it is melancholy proof . . . of the unfitness of this wet island as a depot for large numbers of men." Both the Confederate soldiers and their Union guards identified the dampness of the island as a major cause of the sickness there. (At that time, the island was much lower than it is today and very marshy. More than 2 million cubic yards of soil have been brought in to raise the level of the land and make it drier.)

Even in prison, the prisoners tried to remain civilized. They staged debates and held concerts, and even formed associations to tend the sick. Some set up businesses to get money to buy extra food and supplies, or to use for gambling. Toward the end of the war a handwritten newspaper, the *Prison Times*, appeared, which included advertisements for the various prison businesses.

Many prisoners attempted to escape, not an insignificant task from the island. Escape involved swimming across the Delaware River and avoiding the patrol boats and sharks; but a number tried, and up to several hundred were successful (Confederate and Union numbers vary considerably on this point). There were a large number of Confederate sympathizers in Delaware willing to help those that made it ashore. Interestingly, a number of Confederate soldiers also defected to the Union army.

Among the approximately 3000 political prisoners housed at Fort Delaware were Colonel Burton H. Harrison, private secretary to Jefferson Davis, and Governor E. R. Lubbock of Texas, both captured after the war. Lubbock was not released until 1866, the last prisoner at the fort.

After the war, the fort was used for a variety of purposes before the state of Delaware acquired it from the Federal government in 1947, and then put the island up for sale in 1949. To save the fort, on January 14, 1950, a group of 20 citizens founded the Fort Delaware Society. They launched an extensive lobbying effort, and in 1951 the Delaware legislature declared Fort Delaware a state park.

Today the fort is open for tours and houses a museum and the W. Emerson Wilson Memorial Civil War Library. It offers audiovisual programs, walking tours, a gift shop, and an extensive series of living-history programs. The museum mainly contains artifacts found over the years in and around the fort, left by the people who lived on Pea Patch Island. There are also weapons from the Civil War era, as well as a detailed model of the fort and the outbuildings and barracks as they appeared in 1864, and many restored rooms and other areas in the fort. The library contains over 1000 volumes about Fort Delaware and other Civil War subjects, while the archives contain hundreds of letters, diaries, photos, and other documents pertaining to Civil War–era prisoners and guards. The archives also contain over 56,000 file cards on Confederate and Union soldiers who were on the island.

Outside the museum is the Prison Camp Trail, an easy walk of less than a mile around the prison grounds. The fort has two impressive cannons that are fired regularly—a 32-pounder seacoast artillery cannon, Model 1851, and a larger 8-inch Columbiad on the northwest bastion of the ramparts. The Columbiad is the only one of its kind in the country still being fired.

Visitor Information

302-834-7941;
www.destateparks.com/fdsp/fdsp.htm
Hours: Open weekends and holidays from late April to September, and Wednesdays through Sundays from mid-June to Labor Day; closed Mondays and Tuesdays, except when holidays fall on those days. Call for precise times and ferry sailings.
Admission: Moderate fee for adults and children; admission includes the ferry ride and travel on to Fort Mott State Park in New Jersey. Finn's Point National Cemetery, where 2400 of the Confederate prisoners who died at Fort Delaware are buried, is near Fort Mott.
Accessibility: The ferry, dock area, and ground level of the fort are handicapped accessible.
Special Events: There are numerous special events at the fort, including an annual Garrison Weekend, with 200 reenactors portraying Confederate prisoners, Union soldiers, and civilians. On many weekends, period-clad historic interpreters meet the visitors' tram at the fort and lead regular tours. On some weekends, reenactors portray the members of the 1st Delaware Heavy Artillery, organized at Fort Delaware. This unit was made up of Confederate prisoners who defected to the Union army and guarded their former colleagues. For specific dates and times, contact the park office.
Getting There: Fort Delaware is located on Pea Patch Island, 16 miles south of Wilmington, Delaware, in the Delaware River.

By car: From I-95, take exit 4A to Delaware route 1 south. Follow Route 1 to the highway 72/Delaware City exit. Take highway 72/9 south to Delaware City and take a left turn at the traffic light on Clinton Street. The boat dock is on the right at the end of Clinton Street.

The ferry departs every hour on the hour from the dock adjacent to the park office at Battery Park at the end of Clinton Road. It is a half-mile, 10-minute ferry ride to Pea Patch Island. On the island, a tram takes visitors to the fort.

Ford's Theatre and the Petersen House

On March 4, 1865, Abraham Lincoln was inaugurated for his second term in office. Though the Civil War still raged, it was evident that the Confederacy's days were numbered. Well-known actor John Wilkes Booth—a fanatic Confederate sympathizer—was in the crowd that gathered in front of the Capitol to hear the President's inaugural speech. (There is a photo that purportedly shows Booth near the President at the inauguration.) Lincoln's conciliatory speech included the ringing words, "With malice toward none, with charity for all . . ."

Booth was the guest of his fiancée, Lucy Hale, daughter of the abolitionist former senator John Hale of New Hampshire, soon to be ambassador to Spain. Later Booth said to a friend, "What an excellent chance I had to kill the President, if I had wished, on Inauguration Day!"

The inaugural assemblage would have been stunned to know that Booth had already planned an audacious strike to kidnap Lincoln. Booth and a group of conspirators planned to seize the President, take him to Richmond, and hold him in exchange for Confederate soldiers languishing in Union prison camps.

Booth had learned that Lincoln might soon be visiting a veterans hospital just outside of Washington, and it seemed like an ideal time to seize the President in his carriage. On March 15, Booth met with the conspirators to finalize the plan, but at the last moment he learned that the President's trip had been cancelled. The plan was dropped, and on March 18, the day after he had planned to kidnap Lincoln, Booth calmly performed at Ford's Theatre as Duke Pescara in *The Apostate.*

Less than a month later, on April 9, Robert E. Lee surrendered his army, and the plan to kidnap Lincoln now appeared totally unnecessary. But on April 11, Lincoln spoke from the White House to a crowd gathered outside, and Booth was there again when Lincoln said he was in favor of offering the vote to "very intelligent" African

Americans and those who served the Union as soldiers. Booth was incensed, and told a friend, "That will be the last speech he ever makes . . . this country was formed for the white not for the black man. . . . African slavery is one of [its] greatest blessings." By now Booth had decided not just to kidnap the President, but to assassinate him. He gathered many of those with whom he had previously conspired and offered an even bolder plan— the assassination of Lincoln, Vice President Andrew Johnson, and Secretary of State William H. Seward. Booth hoped the resulting chaos and weakness in the government would reinvigorate the Southern cause.

Booth was the son of the eccentric Junius Booth, one of the most famous actors on the American stage. While not considered as fine an actor as his father, the son was no hack. A fiery-eyed, handsome ladies' man, the young Booth made the equivalent of a quarter of a million dollars when he was at the zenith of his stage career. He had spent several years in Richmond, Virginia, just before the Civil War, and had become attached to the Southern way of life. He even briefly joined a Richmond militia unit, the Richmond Grays, and attended the abolitionist John Brown's hanging. When the war began, Booth respected his mother's wishes and did not join the Confederate army. Instead, he moved north and continued his acting career while performing various small acts of smuggling for the Confederacy.

After a brief hiatus from acting during the spring and summer of 1864, Booth moved back to Washington and stayed at the National Hotel, where he met Lucy Hale after her family moved in there in January of 1865.

Booth, like many transient actors, used the Ford's Theatre address to receive his mail. On the morning of Friday, April 14, Booth met Lucy Hale at

John Wilkes Booth, Lincoln's assassin

On the night of the assassination, *two private boxes had been combined for the presidential party. The Treasury flag, directly behind and above the framed portrait fronting the box, caught Booth's spur as he leapt to the stage.*

the National Hotel, and then went to Ford's to pick up his mail. There he learned the President was planning to attend the evening performance of *Our American Cousin* accompanied by General Ulysses S. Grant. The time was now right for the assassination attempt. Booth knew every line of the play, and he apparently calculated the greatest laughter in the theater would be taking place about ten fifteen p.m. and that only one actor, Harry Hawk (a friend of Booth's), would be on stage. This would be the time to assassinate both the President and the general.

But Grant's wife, Julia Dent Grant, had no desire to be in the company of Mary Lincoln. On several earlier occasions she had been an embarrassed witness to Mary's irrational outbursts. This time Julia made certain to have her husband decline the invitation—probably saving his life as a result.

After learning that the Grants had departed for their home in New Jersey, Booth held a meeting with his coconspirators, telling them he would still assassinate Lincoln at the theater that night. Simultaneously, George Atzerodt was to kill Vice President Andrew Johnson at Johnson's residence at the Kirkwood Hotel; and Lewis Thorton Powell, a semideranged former Confederate soldier, would kill Secretary of State William Seward. David Herold would take Powell to Seward's home and then help him escape from Washington. The group would then meet at the Navy Yard Bridge and escape to Maryland.

Booth went into Ford's Theatre half a dozen times that day without raising any suspicion. At one point he invited several Ford's Theatre employees out for a drink at Taltavul's Star Saloon, next door to the theater. Afterward, he returned to the theater and traveled the route he would use in the assassination. He slipped into the State Box and apparently rehearsed everything except his final leap to the stage. Then he went out the back of the theater and returned to the National Hotel to rest and have dinner.

After dinner, Booth put on calf-length boots, new spurs, black clothes, and a black hat. Into his pocket he put a compass, a loaded single-shot derringer pistol, and a razor-sharp knife with a 7 1/4-inch blade. The pistol—manufactured by Henry Derringer of Philadelphia—was about 6 inches long with a 2 1/2-inch barrel and fired a large .44-caliber bullet. There was also a small box in the butt of the gun for

One of many illustrations published shortly after the assassination. Left, Booth's 44-caliber derringer on display at the museum.

an extra percussion cap.

That night one of Lincoln's guards, policeman John F. Parker, reported to the White House at seven p.m.—three hours late. Parker had become a presidential guard the previous November, but he had a record of bad conduct, including being drunk on duty. When he arrived at the White House, he was told to go to Ford's Theatre and wait for the President's party to arrive. Though Lincoln also had a military force to protect him—the Union Light Guard—one of their officers said later, "It had never been thought necessary for him to be guarded when going out for an evening . . . he preferred not to be accompanied in such fashion, when mingling with the people in such places."

The presidential party—the Lincolns and their guests, Major Henry Rathbone and his fiancée (and stepsister) Clara Harris—arrived at Ford's at about eight thirty p.m. As Lincoln entered, the band struck up "Hail to the Chief." There was cheering and applause as the party moved to the State Box—the only box occupied that night. Entry to the box was through an outer door, then a small vestibule, and finally an inner door.

After the party was seated, Parker took a seat just outside the box. He could only hear the play, so he left his post—perhaps with Lincoln's permission—and found a spot where he could also see the performance. At the intermission, he met two other men who worked for the President—Charles Forbes, Lincoln's footman, and Francis P. Burke, Lincoln's coachman. The three went next door for a drink at Taltavul's. (Whether Parker ever returned to the theater that night is unknown for certain; but when the President was shot, it seems Parker was not at his post.)

Booth arrived at Ford's at about nine thirty p.m., left his horse in the rear alley, and went to Taltavul's and requested a whiskey and water. He then entered Ford's lobby at about seven minutes after ten and mounted the stairs to the door that opened into Lincoln's State Box. Charles Forbes, the President's footman, was seated next to the door, and Booth apparently handed him a card and was allowed to enter. Booth then opened the door and entered the vestibule. Quietly he pushed a piece of wood between the door and the wall, jamming the door shut (he had apparently found the wood supporting an orchestra member's stand on one of his earlier visits and hid it in the box).

At about ten fifteen p.m. he opened the inside door behind where the President was sitting. Lincoln had turned to his left and was looking down into the audience when Booth put his derringer behind Lincoln's head near the left ear and pulled the trigger. The soft lead bullet went through the base of the skull and lodged behind the right eye. Because of the laughter in the theater, not all of the patrons heard the shot. Rathbone jumped up and grabbed for Booth, but the assassin pulled out his knife and slit Rathbone's left arm from elbow to shoulder. Rathbone thought Booth shouted a word that sounded like "Freedom!" and then jumped over the side of the box to the stage floor, about 11 feet below. He apparently caught one of his spurs on the U.S. Treasury Guards flag displayed on the front of the State Box and was thrown off balance. When he hit the floor, he snapped the fibula bone in his left leg just above the ankle. Thrusting both hands in the air and flashing the knife theatrically, Booth crossed the stage in front of more than 1000 spectators. He almost certainly shouted something as he went. Legend has it was "*Sic semper tyrannis*" (Latin for Thus always to tyrants), but not all eyewitnesses agreed on Booth's words or even if there were any.

Mrs. Lincoln screamed. Charles Leale, a 23-year-old army surgeon, was first in the box. He found it covered with Rathbone's blood but there appeared to be none from the President as his wife held him upright. Leale felt no pulse, then lay the President down on the floor. Leale had assumed that both Lincoln and Rathbone had been stabbed; but once the President's upper clothing was removed, he could find no knife wound. It was only then that he located a small wound in the back of the skull.

Additional help arrived, and Leale began to apply artificial respiration. Eventually, Lincoln's breathing resumed feebly. While satisfied that "instant death would not occur," Leale held out little hope of recovery. "His wound is mortal."

Several soldiers from Battery C, Independent Pennsylvania Artillery, took the President in their arms and carried him out of the theater and across the street into a four-story house at 453 (now 516) Tenth Street. A tailor named William Petersen kept a shop in the basement and rented the remaining rooms to lodgers. Lincoln was taken to a small bedroom at the end of the hallway.

Throughout that night, as many as 90 people—including 16 physicians—crowded into the tiny room. Surgeon General Joseph K. Barnes treated the stricken President. Finally, at seven twenty-two in the morning, Barnes, unable to find Lincoln's pulse, stated, "He is gone." Lincoln's pastor, Dr. Phineas Gurley, knelt by the bedside. The rest of the men in the room knelt with him. Gurley prayed aloud, all in attendance said, "Amen." Secretary of War Edwin M. Stanton gave the most fitting eulogy—"Now he belongs to the ages."

The Hunt for the Conspirators

George Atzerodt never left the bar at the Kirkwood Hotel, so Vice President Andrew Johnson was not attacked. Secretary of State Seward was recovering from a broken arm and broken jaw as a result of a carriage accident when Lewis Powell attacked him. Powell stabbed Seward in the throat, but the brace around Seward's broken jaw saved his life. Although he was severely injured, he recovered and eventually returned to his post as Secretary of State.

Booth and fellow conspirator

Presidential Artifacts

During the early morning of April 15, 1865, while Lincoln was still alive, the doctors attending the President used a metal probe to locate the .44-caliber bullet lodged in his brain. It was not removed until the autopsy and it was not considered appropriate to display the bullet until 1956, when it was shown publicly. Now it can be seen, along with fragments of Lincoln's skull, at the National Museum of Health and Medicine in Washington, D.C. The museum, which is a division of the Armed Forces Institute of Pathology (AFIP), is located at Elder and Georgia Avenue, NW, and is open 10 a.m. until 5 p.m. daily. The phone number is 202-782-2200. The Presidential display also includes the "life mask" plaster molds of Lincoln's head and hands.

The rocker in which Lincoln sat was confiscated by the War Department as evidence during the trial of the conspirators. It was kept by Secretary of War Edwin Stanton in his office until 1866. Today it is in the Henry Ford Museum in Dearborn, Michigan.

A **reward poster** *issued by the War Department for Booth, Surratt, and Herold*

David Herold escaped from the city separately, then rendezvoused and headed to the Surratt Tavern in Surrattsville, Maryland. There they acquired supplies and proceeded to the house of Dr. Samuel Mudd, arriving about four a.m. on April 15. Mudd, a coconspirator, treated Booth's broken leg. The next night Booth and Herold arrived at the home of Confederate sympathizer

Samuel Cox, where they stayed for four days.

From April 20 to April 24 the two moved from the home of one Confederate sympathizer to another in Virginia and Maryland. While they were on the move, Booth and Herold met three former Confederate soldiers, and when Herold boasted they were the men who killed President Lincoln, the soldiers took them to the Garrett farm near Bowling Green, Virginia. On April 24, 25 members of the 16th New York Cavalry, under the command of Lieutenant Edward Doherty, found one of the three Confederates and forced him to tell them where Booth was. In the early morning hours of April 26, the column of soldiers entered the Garrett farm and found Booth and Herold asleep in the tobacco shed. Herold quickly surrendered, but Booth refused. At about four a.m., while Doherty was trying to coax Booth into surrendering, the tobacco shed was set afire and Booth, still armed, was shot by Sergeant Boston Corbett. Booth was dragged still alive from the burning shed, shot in the neck and paralyzed from the neck down. His final words were, "Tell my mother I did it for my country . . . useless, useless." In his pocket was a photograph of Lucy Hale.

The other conspirators were soon arrested. Four were hanged, three sentenced to life in prison, and one given six years at hard labor. In 1869, President Andrew Johnson pardoned the surviving conspirators.

The conspirators hanged. *The image of Mary Surratt, Lewis Paine, David Herold, and George Atzerodt was taken by Alexander Gardner, the only authorized photographer.*

Ford's Theatre, left, as it appeared in 1865. Taltavul's Star Saloon, where Booth often stopped for a drink before his performances, is just to the right of the theater.

Ford's Theatre National Historic Site

Ford's Theatre was a large theater and one of the finest in Washington. Converted from a church to a theater in 1861, it seated about 1600 people. John Thomson Ford, the builder of Ford's Theatre, was imprisoned for more than a month after Lincoln's assassination. He was finally acquitted of complicity, but was forced to sell the theater. On June 9, 1893, while 490 clerks of the Record and Pension Division of the War Department were working at their offices in the building, workmen in the basement were removing portions of the building's foundation. The building collapsed and 18 employees were killed immediately. Several more died later, and many more were injured. The National Park Service acquired the theater in 1933, and the entire interior was reconstructed in the 1960s to recreate its historic appearance on the night of the assassination. The building was fully restored in 1968 and since that time has been maintained by the National Park Service as a Lincoln museum. The exterior walls are the only portions remaining of the 19th century theater, but the interior is fully restored and the flag-draped presidential box is in almost original condition.

In 1940 the War Department offered to the Department of the Interior numerous items related to the Lincoln assassination. These items included the derringer that Booth used and the knife with which he stabbed Major Rathbone. Today most of these items are displayed in the museum in the basement of Ford's Theatre. In addition to the gun and the knife, there are the clothes Lincoln wore the night he was killed with the bullet hole colored by his blood, the flag that draped his coffin, the Treasury Guards regimental flag that caught Booth's spur, and a top hat belonging to Lincoln.

Visitor Information

202-426-6924; www.nps.gov/foth
Hours: Theater, museum and the Petersen House (where Lincoln was taken), daily, 9 a.m. until 5 p.m.; closed December 25. The theater is also closed for matinees, rehearsals, and workshops, but the museum and the Petersen House remain open at those times. Call for details.
Admission: Free (although this may change in the near future).
Special Events: Park rangers give daily talks from 9:15 a.m. until 4:15 p.m. on the history of the building and the events surrounding Lincoln's assassination. The Petersen House is included in the tour of the theater.
Accessibility: The orchestra level of the theater is wheelchair accessible. The Petersen House is not handicapped accessible.
Getting There: Ford's Theatre is located in central Washington, D.C., near the intersection of 10th and E Streets in the northwest section of the city. It is a block north of the FBI building on Pennsylvania Avenue. Metro Rail and Metro buses service the area. The closest Metro Rail station is Metro Center at 11th and G Streets.

The Smithsonian Institution's National Museum of American History, Behring Center

The National Museum of American History, Behring Center, includes among its collection thousands of Civil War–related artifacts, photographs, and memorabilia. The Civil War had an impact on every aspect of American life, which is reflected throughout the museum in examinations of communications, agriculture, transportation, politics, and American culture.

History of the Museum

The National Museum of American History (NMAH) is part of the Smithsonian Institution, the largest museum complex in the world. The institution is named for the man who bequeathed it to the American people, James Smithson, who, when he died in 1829, left more than $500,000 to establish an institution whose purpose was the "increase and diffusion of knowledge."

The first Smithsonian building was what came to be known as the Castle, which opened in 1855. Many of the exhibitions displayed in the Castle would eventually be the genesis of the history museum's collection, including engineering, industrial, and scientific items, and inventions transferred from the U.S. Patent Office.

During the Civil War, where the museum now stands was an area known as the White Lot, so called because it was enclosed with a white wooden fence. Often, passersby would see President Lincoln here, accompanied by military officers, trying out a new weapon, such as a breech-loading rifle or a revolver. Just beyond the lot, toward the then half-finished Washington Monument, was grazing land for cows, sheep, goats, and pigs; and beyond that, where the Lincoln Memorial now stands, was swampland. What is now Constitution Avenue was the Washington Canal, a fetid, silted-up waterway used as a dumping ground by butchers at the nearby Center Market; and on the site of the Air and Space Museum was a hospital ministering to the war's casualties.

The current American history museum opened in 1964 as the Museum of History and Technology. In 1980 its name was changed to the National Museum of American History, to better reflect its mission of preserving, collecting, and exhibiting all facets of American history and culture, and in 2000, philanthropist Kenneth E. Behring donated $80 million to the museum, after which the name was changed to the National Museum of American History, Behring Center.

Civil War Items in the Museum

The museum has three floors of exhibitions, plus a lower level with a food court and a museum store. In general, exhibitions on the first floor

In the exhibit "The Telegraph of the Civil War," *a photograph of the U.S. Military Telegraph Construction Corps shows some of the 150-man team setting poles and stringing wire to keep the central telegraph office in contact with the armies in the field. A telegraph battery wagon, inset right, was equipped with an operator's table and attached instruments and a portable battery to supply the electric current.*

The steam engine General Haupt *was named for Brigadier General Hermann Haupt, chief of construction and transportation, U.S. Military Railroads. Haupt, standing at far right, performed miracles in rushing troops forward and evacuating supplies threatened with capture.*

relate to commerce (industry, agriculture, communications, science, shipping); those on the second floor deal with communal life, family, and how people interact; and the third floor exhibitions relate to politics, the military, and popular culture.

The museum will be undergoing renovations for the next several years, and exhibitions may be moved or closed as necessary.

On the first floor, *The Information Age* exhibition includes a section on "The Telegraph of the Civil War," highlighting the ways in which Samuel Morse's relatively new invention was used by commanders on both sides to keep track of distant battles and the movement of supplies. Following the First Battle of Bull Run (First Manassas), Congress established the Military Telegraph Service and authorized the takeover of all telegraph lines needed for the war effort.

Over the course of the war, the Union added 15,000 miles of new telegraph lines, and the Confederacy about one thousand. Both sides developed codes to hamper wiretapping, but these weren't always successful. Confederate commander George "Lightning" Ellsworth once kept Union forces scrambling for hours by tapping their lines and relaying false information in the guise of a Union private crouched under a desk at a headquarters under fire.

"In all history," wrote General William T. Sherman in 1860, "no nation of mere agriculturists ever made successful war against a nation of mechanics." The proof of that statement is evident in the exhibit *Engines of Change, The American Industrial Revolution, 1790–1860,* which focuses on the impact of industrialization in the country

as a whole and brings into sharp perspective the advantage the industrial north had over the largely agrarian south.

While walking through the section dedicated to the development of the American rail system, consider the fact that at the beginning of the war, of the more than 31,000 miles of rail in the U.S., nearly three quarters were in the north and west. Railroads were integral to the transfer of troops and supplies, as demonstrated by the 1860 Map of Transportation Routes that clearly demonstrates the importance of both rails and canals during the war.

Railroad buffs will be especially interested in the John Bull on display. The oldest locomotive in operating condition in the world, it pulled freight and transported passengers between New York and Philadelphia until the last year of the war.

More than 85 percent of the nation's manufacturing industry was located in the north, as well as the majority of the natural resources used in production of items such as steel and iron. A display on the Tredegar Iron Works in Richmond focuses on the use of slaves at the iron works (nearly 200,000 slaves worked in Southern industry), and is a reminder that this

The field jacket of Confederate Colonel John F. Mosby. Mosby's Rangers was a unit of partisans operating in northern Virginia that drained the strength of the invading enemy and became a constant factor in Union campaign strategy.

The Tredegar Iron Works drew waterpower from the James River to operate its machinery. At the close of the war, Confederate troops set fire to the factory to keep it from Union capture, but employees put out the flames as fast as they were set.

was one of the few large plants in the South.

Some 1100 cannons were forged at Tredegar between 1861 and 1865, and it was also the South's major producer of locomotives. Shoemaking shops, a firebrick factory, a sawmill, and a tannery were also included in the works. A reporter for the *Charleston Mercury* in August 1861 described it as "an establishment of which the whole South may be justly proud, and to which we are mainly indebted for the ordnance necessary to prosecute this war with energy and success." Its machinery operated day and night until the final year of the war, when the South's supply of raw materials was exhausted.

Both the North and the South profited from innovations in armaments. Armories, such as those featured here from Springfield, Massachusetts (America's first national armory, built in 1794), and Harpers Ferry, (West) Virginia, were able to mass-produce rifles because of the innovation of interchangeable parts, as demonstrated by a Robbins & Lawrence military rifle.

The 1855 Blanchard lathe displayed here is accompanied by a film showing how this gunstock machine operated. There's also a Colt revolver, patented in 1836 by Samuel Colt as the first repeating pistol with revolving chambers.

In the agriculture exhibition, "The Cotton Kingdom" section highlights the antebellum dependence of northern factories on the cotton harvested in the South. And many in the Confederacy believed that the dependence of Europe's factories—

especially those in Great Britain—on the South's supply of raw cotton would bring aid and recognition to the Southern cause.

Looking at a steam-powered cotton gin, it's hard to fathom how something so small could have had such a huge impact on the South's economy. Eli Whitney took just 10 days to develop the gin, which processed cotton far more efficiently than a team of slaves could.

On the second floor, the *First Ladies: Political Role and Public Image* exhibition (one of the museum's most popular, with its display of inaugural gowns) highlights both Mrs. Abraham Lincoln and Mrs. Ulysses S. Grant during their stays in the White House.

In the section "First Lady as the Nation's Hostess," Mrs. Lincoln's aversion to formal state dinners ("Public receptions are more democratic than stupid state dinners and more in keeping with the institutions of our country.") and Mrs. Grant's extravagant entertaining are examined. There's an interesting feature about Elizabeth Keckley, Mrs. Lincoln's African American dressmaker, who became her confidant and best friend.

"First Ladies in Mourning" includes an impressive presentation on the aftermath of the Lincoln assassination, with items such as a lapel mourning watch owned by Mrs. Lincoln, photographs of the funeral procession (it lasted for weeks and in Chicago featured 36 young women in white surrounding the hearse as it passed under an elaborate arch), and a memorial card showing the spirit of George

Washington embracing the fallen President.

Within These Walls . . . showcases 200 years of American history encompassed in one house—a two-and-a-half-story frame structure built in the 1760s in Ipswich, Massachusetts, dismantled and reassembled in the museum in 1966, eventually to become the centerpiece of an exhibit on five periods in American history as represented by five families who lived in the house.

Josiah and Lucy Caldwell, who lived here from 1822 until 1865, were passionate abolitionists and leaders of the movement in Ipswich, as reflected in the items displayed in their parlor. These include a commemorative plate with a scene from Harriet Beecher Stowe's Uncle Tom's Cabin, a reproduction of an alphabet book for children featuring abolitionist rhymes ("F is the heart-sick Fugitive, The slave who runs away"), and a reproduction of an 1830 newspaper ad announcing a meeting of the Ipswich Female Anti-Slavery Society hosted by Lucy. Visitors can also hear "Get Off the Track," an abolitionist song written in 1844, and read about the movement's efforts to raise money for slaves who escaped to the North.

Communities in a Changing Nation, The Promise of 19th Century America focuses on what the promise of America meant to three communities, one of them the slaves and free blacks in the low country of South Carolina, from Charleston to Waccamaw Neck. (The other two communities are Jewish immigrants in Cincinnati, Ohio, and industrial workers in Bridgeport, Connecticut.)

A map showing the concentration of slaves at the beginning of the war illustrates that in several states, such as South Carolina, slaves constituted more than half the population. The fear that their numerical superiority produced in the white population (intensified after the

Emancipation Proclamation in 1862) is detailed, along with a copy of a list of free blacks in 1861 Charleston, typical of those compiled to enable local governments to restrict their rights and movements.

In a section on the lives of free blacks in Charleston, copies of the minutes of groups such as the Friendly Moralist Society and the Brown Fellowship Society indicate the ways in which free blacks tried to help slaves while also striving to distinguish themselves as free and productive citizens. It was a tight wire to balance upon, especially when there were revolts such as the one led by Denmark Vesey in 1822 that led to harsh penalties visited upon both slave and free blacks.

Recorded personal recollections of former slaves expose in matter-of-fact language the horror of life on a plantation, both for house slaves (many of them children) and those who worked in the fields. The recollections of a female slave demonstrate the fact that, on average, those between the ages of 19 and 44 bore a child every year, so that even as they were working they were often pregnant, recovering from childbirth, or taking care of infants.

The role of blacks in the Civil War is explored, with a section on Susie King Taylor, an African American nurse who cared for Union soldiers in the 33rd U.S. Colored Troops and later wrote a book about her experiences. The 33rd was one of the infantry regiments of the 1st South Carolina Colored Infantry, which fought along the Georgia-Florida coast and participated in the occupation of Jacksonville, Florida. Following their first engagement, their white commanding officer wrote that they had fought "with astonishing coolness and bravery. . . . They behaved gloriously, and

In 1863, the Emancipation Proclamation freed Confederate slaves and authorized the use of "colored troops." This color lithograph underscored the Union's efforts to recruit African Americans to bolster its depleted ranks. By the end of the war, about 186,000 men had enlisted.

COME AND JOIN US BROTHERS.
PUBLISHED BY THE SUPERVISORY COMMITTEE FOR RECRUITING COLORED REGIMENTS
1210 CHESTNUT ST. PHILADELPHIA

deserve all praise."

The American Presidency: A Glorious Burden, on the third floor, explores 200 years of the most honored office in the land, the men who have held that office, and their impact on history. Artifacts such as a broadcloth coat worn by Abraham Lincoln as part of his office suit, an engraving of an 1862 Lincoln cabinet meeting, the original cast of Abraham Lincoln's hands taken by sculptor Leonard Volk in May 1860, two days after Lincoln was nominated for President (his right hand is still swollen from all the hand-shaking), and a Spencer repeating rifle used by Lincoln for target practice are among the hundreds of items on display.

Among the photographs is a particularly poignant one of Lincoln with his son Thomas, known as Tad, who died of tuberculosis six years after his father's assassination, at the age of 18. (Of Lincoln's four sons, only Robert lived to maturity.) Tad was famous for his exploits in the White House, among them buying food from the vendors along Pennsylvania Avenue, many of whom were disabled veterans, then setting up his own stand in the lobby of the White House to sell the food to those waiting to see the President, with the purpose of giving the profits to the Sanitary Commission, the equivalent of the Red Cross.

"The Long and Final Ride: The Funeral of Abraham Lincoln" displays artifacts, photographs, and illustrations from the two-week trek of the eight-coach train that carried the slain President's body home to Illinois. Among these are the drum and flag used at ceremonies in New York City, the top hat Lincoln was wearing the night he was assassinated, and a mourning ring with Lincoln's image as an ivory cameo.

The reverence afforded Lincoln as martyr wasn't enough to forestall his value as an advertising icon. So there is also a poster extolling Lincoln-brand oranges, a box of Lincoln Tea ("the best blood purifier"), and Lincoln Logs, created in 1916 by John Lloyd Wright (son of architect Frank Lloyd Wright) to enable children to build log cabins that supposedly resembled Lincoln's boyhood home.

Also on this floor is General Philip Sheridan's horse Winchester, who died in 1878. He was preserved, mounted, enclosed in a large glass case, and presented to the Smithsonian in 1922. Originally called Rienzi, the horse was renamed Winchester in honor of one of Sheridan's most famous victories. The Mexican saddle on Winchester, valued at the time between two thousand and three thousand dollars, was presented to Sheridan in appreciation for his services along the Texas coast of the Gulf of Mexico after the war.

Nearby is the National Firearms Study Gallery, perhaps its most intriguing display being a collection of more than two dozen miniatures. "Breech-Loading and Repeating Arms of the Civil War" includes an 1865 Miller breech-loading rifle and

Abraham Lincoln *with his son Tad. Tad accompanied the President on his visit to General Grant's camp at City Point and to Petersburg and Richmond at the war's end.*

Sheridan's horse, Rienzi, was renamed Winchester following a pivotal battle between Sheridan and Jubal Early in Virginia's Shenandoah Valley in 1864. While Sheridan slept in the town of Winchester 20 miles away, Early attacked Sheridan's encamped troops. The Union forces were driven from their camps and fell into a chaotic retreat. The rout was halted with the arrival of Sheridan on Rienzi, galloping toward his troops, yelling at them to turn back. The Union forces did carry the day, in celebration of which Rienzi's name was changed.

an 1863 Remington breech-loading carbine. "Civil War: The Confederacy" displays an 1852 Palmetto musket and an 1863 Richmond rifle, while "Civil War: The Union" has an 1861 Requa-Billinghurst battery gun used to defend bridges (a forerunner of the machine gun, it fired 175 rounds per minute) and an 1860 Henry repeating rifle capable of firing 15 rounds before reloading, which is why Confederate soldiers described it as "that damned Yankee rifle they load on Sunday and shoot all week."

Other arms featured include an 1861 Colt rifle musket (the first rifle muskets awarded a Federal contract), an 1860 Savage navy percussion revolver (its peculiar dual triggers—one for rotating the cylinder and cocking the hammer and another for firing—unbalanced the gun and made it difficult to aim), and an 1865 Remington army percussion revolver.

In November 2004, the NMAH will open a new exhibition called *The Price of Freedom*, which will examine major military events in the nation's history. Among the items displayed will be artifacts from the museum's Civil War collection, including the chairs used by Grant and Lee at Appomattox.

Visitor Information

202-357-2700 (voice),
202-357-1729 (TTY);
www.americanhistory.si.edu
Hours: Daily, 10 a.m. until 5:30 p.m.; closed December 25. The Information Center in the Smithsonian Castle is open from 9 a.m. until 5:30 p.m.

Special Events: There are dozens of public events scheduled throughout the year, the largest of which is the Folklife Festival held every June and July. For specific information, consult the museum's Web site.
Admission: Free.
Accessibility: The museum is accessible by wheelchair and stroller, as are its facilities and exhibitions.
Getting There: The museum is located at 14th Street and Constitution Avenue, NW. Parking is extremely limited in this area. There are two-hour parking spots on the Mall, and small parking lots at the Washington Monument and the Jefferson Memorial, also with two-hour parking. Parking is available for longer periods along Ohio Drive between the Lincoln and Jefferson Memorials.

From Virginia: Take I-395 into the city and onto 14th Street. Proceed north on 14th Street to Independence Avenue and the Mall.

From Maryland: Take I-495 (the Beltway) to U.S 50 west. Follow Route 50 into the city, where it becomes New York Avenue, then south on 6th Street, NW, to Constitution Avenue and the Mall.

By subway: Get off at the Smithsonian Station (orange and blue lines), which exits at 12th Street and Jefferson Drive, NW, onto the Mall, two blocks from the museum.

By bus: The 30s bus route has stops at 7th and at 9th Streets on the Mall, and at 15th and Pennsylvania Avenue, from which you turn right if you're traveling east, left if you're traveling west. Walk one block on 15th Street to Constitution Avenue and then left one-half block on Constitution Avenue.

Fort Zachary Taylor Historic State Park

Fort Zachary Taylor, located in Key West, Florida, was the second of two five-sided masonry forts commissioned after the War of 1812—known as Third System forts (*see* Fortifications, page 25)—built to protect the Florida Keys and the Gulf of Mexico. The first, Fort Jefferson, was built on the Dry Tortugas island chain, some 70 miles west of Key West.

Fort Jefferson was begun in the early 1830s and Fort Taylor in 1845, but progress on both forts was slow for a variety of factors, including shortages of material, occasional hurricanes, and general isolation. By the end of 1860, Fort Jefferson was virtually complete, but Fort Taylor—the more important because of its proximity to Key West harbor—was not. However, it did have mounted cannons—Rodmans, Columbiads, and Parrott rifles—and the living quarters were usable.

When Lincoln was elected President, tensions began to mount in secessionist Key West. The commander in charge of the fort's construction, Lieutenant Edward Hunt, began to take precautions in consultation with the commander of the small Union garrison in the town, West Pointer Captain John Brannon. Brannon learned that the Union garrison in Charleston, in a situation similar to his, had withdrawn to Fort Sumter, so when shots were fired on January 9, 1861, at a ship attempting to resupply Fort Sumter, Brannon realized he had to act. Even though he had no orders, on January 21, Brannon quietly marched his troops down to the fort, crossed the moat on the land side, and closed the drawbridge behind him. The fort, though not complete, was quite secure. It had three tiers of casemates with two tower bastions on each flank, and the third level gave a splendid view of the Florida Straits and of the entire island of Key West.

Before the Confederates could react, Union ships began to arrive with supplies and reinforcements, and by early February the fort and town were firmly in Union hands. The harbor became a vital part of the Union blockade as the Key West Naval Station, home to the Eastern Gulf Blockading Squadron. The squadron had approximately 32 ships responsible for keeping Confederate blockade-runners from slipping into ports all along the Florida coast. This was critical for the Union, since Confederate blockade-runners used ports in Bermuda and Cuba as jump-off points for their runs to the Southern ports.

Brannon was promoted to brigadier general almost immediately after the war began, as a reward for his quick thinking. He later commanded an infantry division with distinction, including at Chickamauga, where it suffered 38 percent casualties.

Beginning in 1968, volunteers began to excavate the gun rooms, recovering guns and ammunition from the Civil War. The result of their work is one of the largest collections of heavy Civil War "siege and fort" cannons in the United States, including 14 cannons: two 10-inch (300-pounder) army Parrott rifles, two 10-inch Columbiads (Model 1844), seven 10-inch Rodman guns (Model 1861), one 8-inch siege mortar (Model 1840), and two 8-inch Columbiads (Model 1844).

Today Fort Zachary Taylor Historic State Park covers 87 acres. It was placed on the National Register of Historic Places in 1971 and two years later was designated a National Historic Landmark. The park offers daily tours of the fort at noon and two p.m. Fort Taylor's "sister fort," Fort Jefferson, is located on Garden Key in the Dry Tortugas. Tour boats from Key West visit it regularly on day trips.

Visitor Information

305-292-6713; www.dep.state.fl.us/parks/district5/fortzacharytaylor/index.asp

Hours: Daily, 8 a.m. until sundown.
Admission: Minimal per-car fee.
Accessibility: Handicapped accessible.
Special Events: Key West's pivotal role in the Civil War is commemorated during the city's annual Heritage Festival & Civil War Days held at the park in late February or early March. Reenactors portray Union and Confederate forces, with a Union camp inside the fort and a Confederate encampment set up outside on the park grounds. May is Florida State Parks month, with numerous activities scheduled at Fort Taylor. Call for further information.
Getting There: Fort Zachary Taylor is located at the end of Southard Street on Truman Annex in Key West.

Andersonville National Historic Site and Cemetery

Camp Sumter, to use its official name, was one of the most notorious Civil War prisoner-of-war camps. Open for less than a year and a half, Andersonville, as it was usually called, became a metaphor for the atrocities both Northern and Southern soldiers experienced as prisoners of war. Of the more than 45,000 prisoners who entered the camp, nearly 13,000 died of dysentery, gangrene, diarrhea, scurvy, and other diseases. Although death rates were high in many of the other 150 Civil War prisons on both sides, none were close to that of Andersonville.

Until 1863, the Union and Confederate armies regularly exchanged prisoners of war, so large prisoner-of-war camps were unnecessary. The exchanges ended when the Confederacy refused to exchange African American prisoners and the Union realized the Confederacy was running short of manpower. For both sides, the result was a huge influx of prisoners they were ill equipped to handle, but the situation was much worse in the Confederacy.

Andersonville's Beginnings

In November of 1863, Confederate captains W. Sidney Winder and Boyce Charwick were sent to scout out a site suitable for a prisoner-of-war camp. They found a plot of land in Andersonville, a small village in Sumter County, Georgia, in a pine forest with a stream running through it. The forest would provide timber for the buildings as well as for heating and cooking. The site was close to a railroad and seemingly well out of the reach of the Union forces. There were also a large number of slaves in the area who could be used to build the prison and its support buildings, which was envisioned to hold up to 10,000 prisoners.

Captain Richard B. Winder was sent to Andersonville to construct the prison in late December of 1863. Instead of barracks, an open-air stockade was planned. In January, slaves from local farms began to build a stockade enclosure about 1000 feet long and almost 800 feet wide. The massive walls of the stockade were made of square-cut pine logs standing 15 to 20 feet high and set in a five-foot-deep wall trench. The enclosure was built so the stream, called the Stockade Branch, would run through the middle of the stockade and supply water for the prisoners. There was also a light fence, known appropriately as the deadline, approximately 25 feet inside the stockade wall. It was a "no-go" zone to keep the prisoners away from the wall; anyone crossing this line was supposed to be shot immediately by sentries posted around the stockade wall.

Andersonville's Inmates

When Union forces began to threaten Richmond in early 1864, Confederate officials moved 600 Union prisoners from Richmond to Andersonville. When they arrived on February 24, 1864, one wall of the stockade was still not complete. Artillery was put in front of the stockade opening to prevent escapes

Federal prisoners camp near the stockade and the deadline. Prisoners lived in filth, squalor, and congestion that left only 35 square feet of room to every man. Lookouts watched for escapees from observation posts above.

until the work was finished.

Conditions in the camp deteriorated in April 1864 when more and more prisoners were brought to Andersonville. At the same time, it became more difficult to obtain supplies from the beleaguered Confederacy. Also in April, Confederate brigadier general John H. Winder, in charge of all Union prisoners of war east of the Mississippi, sent Swiss-born Captain Henry Wirz to assume command of the prison. (John Winder was the father of W. Sidney Winder, who selected the prison site, and he was also related to Richard B. Winder, who was in charge of construction.)

By early June, prisoners were arriving at the rate of 400 a day, and the number of prisoners in the stockade had increased to about 26,000. That month the stockade was enlarged to the north by a work crew of 100 whites and 30 African American Union prisoners. On July 1, the northern extension was opened. The prisoners quickly tore down the original north stockade wall, and used the wood for fuel and building materials. Still, inside the stockade there were only a few crude shelters rigged by the prisoners with whatever material they could scavenge. Many prisoners had no shelter of any kind, and they had

Huts of every description were used to shelter inmates from the elements. Most were constructed from strips of cloth or canvas, old blankets, or even a ragged coat.

no clothing except for what they wore when they were captured. Food was short, and the camp had few medical facilities to combat the rampant disease and malnutrition. Captain Wirz requested additional supplies from General Winder and the Confederacy's War Department, but Winder was indifferent; the Confederacy barely had enough for its own troops.

During this time, Andersonville's regular army guards were reassigned to front-line units. This left Wirz with the poorly trained local militia—mostly older men and boys—as prison guards, whose main responsibility was to prevent prisoners from escaping, not to maintain order. Inside the stockade, chaos reigned. Organized gangs of Union prisoners began attacking and stealing from other prisoners. Wirz allowed other Union prisoners to organize their own police force to impose order, and the "officers" hanged several of the most violent attackers.

The guard and hospital facilities outside the prison stockade used the same creek that ran through the stockade for bathing and all manner

"Wuld that I was an artist & had the material to paint this camp & all its horors on the tounge of some eloquent Statesman and had the privleage of expressing my mind to our hon. rulers in Washington, I should gloery to describe this hell on earth where it takes 7 of its ocupiants to make a shadow."
—*From the diary of Sergeant David Kennedy, 9th Ohio Cavalry*

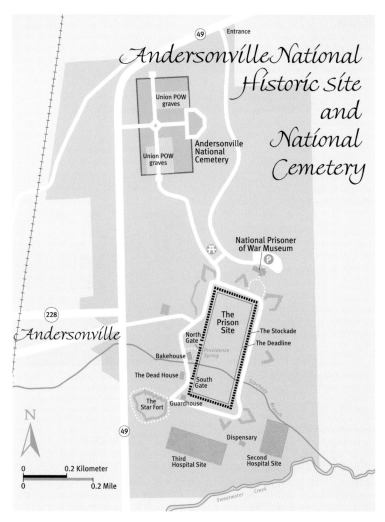

Andersonville National Historic Site and National Cemetery

Union POW graves

Andersonville National Cemetery

Union POW graves

Entrance

National Prisoner of War Museum

Andersonville

The Prison Site

The Stockade

The Deadline

North Gate

Providence Spring

Bakehouse

The Dead House

South Gate

The Star Fort

Guardhouse

Stockade Branch

N

Dispensary

Third Hospital Site

Second Hospital Site

Sweetwater Creek

0   0.2 Kilometer

0   0.2 Mile

of human and animal waste disposal. Since these facilities were upstream of the stockade, the prisoners' water supply was totally polluted, causing extensive disease in an already malnourished population.

By August 1864, the prison population had grown to over 33,000. Then, mercifully, the situation changed. Sherman's troops were on the move in Georgia. Union cavalry was now in striking distance of Andersonville, and most of the prisoners were moved to other camps. By mid-November, only about 1500 prisoners and a few guards remained. The number gradually increased to about 5000, where it remained until the war ended. In May 1865, the Andersonville prison was closed.

Shortly after Andersonville's liberation, wood engravings made from photographs of the prisoners appeared in *Harper's Weekly*. The photographs, coming just after Lincoln's assassination, raised an outcry in the North. Prominent Confederate leaders, including General Robert E. Lee, Secretary of War James Seddon, and several Confederate generals and politicians,

were charged with "conspiring to injure the health and destroy the lives of United States soldiers held as prisoners by the Confederate States." Captain Henry Wirz, the Andersonville commander, was one of those charged. President Andrew Johnson dropped the charges against the Confederate leaders but allowed Wirz, the only remaining member of the Confederate staff at the prison, to be tried. Deservedly or not, Wirz had to answer for all of Andersonville's misery. After two months of testimony, Wirz was found guilty and was hanged on November 10, 1865—the only member of the Confederacy executed for war crimes. Brigadier General John H. Winder, Wirz's superior at Andersonville, had died of a heart attack the previous February, before the war was over. Had he lived, he probably would have been hanged instead of Wirz.

The public outcry over conditions suffered by prisoners at Andersonville helped make this issue one of worldwide concern and eventually led to the drafting of the Geneva Conventions on treatment of prisoners of war.

Andersonville National Cemetery and National Prisoner of War Museum

After the war ended, the plot of ground near the prison where nearly 13,000 Union soldiers were buried was established as Andersonville National Cemetery on July 26, 1865. Only 460 of the graves there are marked "Unknown U.S. Soldier," thanks to a list of the dead kept by Union soldier Dorence Atwater. While a prisoner at Andersonville, Atwater was assigned to keep burial records of all the Union dead. Atwater feared that the Confederates' records might be lost, and he secretly kept a copy himself. After the war, Atwater accompanied Clara Barton and others from the American Red Cross to Andersonville to help identify and mark the graves.

The prison itself reverted to private hands until the Grand Army of the Republic of Georgia acquired the land in 1891. They erected stone monuments on parts of the prison, including the four corners of the inner stockade. Today the U.S. Department of the Interior, National Park Service administers Andersonville National Cemetery as a part of the 495-acre Andersonville National Historic Site. It also serves as a memorial to all American prisoners of war. The initial interments were of those who died in the nearby prisoner-of-war camp, but today the cemetery contains more than 18,000 bodies of veterans and is still open for military burials. A one-hour audio driving tour gives specific information on the historic prison site and the cemetery.

The National Prisoner of War Museum is included in the park. A 27-minute film, *Echoes of Captivity,* is shown every half hour from 9 a.m. until 4:30 p.m. The exhibits in the museum are organized by theme, including "Capture," "Living Conditions," "Those Who Wait," and "Escape and Freedom." The central corridor focuses on Civil War prisons and Andersonville National Cemetery.

The visitor will find a number of archaeological digs around the park and camp. The excavation project began in early 1987 when the National Park Service proposed reconstructing parts of the inner prison stockade at Andersonville so visitors could better visualize the conditions in the stockade. The excavations continue as an attempt to better understand the prison conditions and provide other historical details.

During the 1990 excavations, archaeologists found a tunnel along the southern stockade wall, the only prisoner escape tunnel found so far at Andersonville. That escape failed.

The dead were interred in waiting trenches by fellow prisoners who gladly volunteered to have an oppportunity to get out into the fresh air.

Visitor Information

229-924-0343; www.nps.gov/ande

Hours: Park grounds are open daily, 8 a.m. until 5 p.m.; the National Prisoner of War Museum is open daily 8:30 a.m. until 5 p.m. but closed Thanksgiving Day, December 25, and New Year's Day; the audio driving tour is available from 8:30 a.m. until 4:30 p.m.

Admission: There is no charge to enter the park grounds; there is a minimal fee for the audio driving tour.

Accessibility: Handicapped parking is available. The National Prisoner of War Museum is wheelchair accessible, with a wheelchair available. The historic prison site is not easily accessible to someone with physical limitations.

Getting There: The park is about 55 miles southwest of Macon, Georgia.

From I-75 south: Take exit 135 (state highway 127, Perry/Marshallville exit). Turn right onto route 127. Stay to the left onto state route 224 to Montezuma, Georgia (20 miles) and turn right on state highway 26. Follow Route 26 to state highway 49, turn left on Route 49 and follow it about six miles to the park entrance on your left.

From I-75 north: Take exit 101. Follow U.S. 280 west to Americus, then turn right onto state highway 49 north to Andersonville. The park entrance is on the right.

PRISONERS OF WAR

Prisoners of war were one of the thorniest issues of the Civil War. Initially, the expectation of a short war meant that prisoners would be paroled and exchanged and then, after a period, allowed to return to fight. In December 1861, the U.S. Congress passed a resolution in favor of these types of prisoner exchanges, and in July 1862, Union general John Dix and Confederate general D. H. Hill made a formal parole agreement that President Lincoln accepted. The result was that neither side needed long-term prisoner-of-war camps.

Problems arose when the Union began to use black soldiers. In December 1862, Confederate President Jefferson Davis ordered that white officers commanding black regiments be treated not as prisoners of war but rather as leaders of slave rebellions, which was punishable by death. In May 1863, the Confederate Congress formalized Davis's order and said that any blacks captured would be considered slaves in rebellion and treated according to the laws of the states where they were captured—a sure death sentence. In response, the Union War Department halted the exchange and parole of Confederate officers.

The halt of officers had relatively little effect; but in mid-July, Union Secretary of War Edwin Stanton halted the exchange of enlisted men. This resulted in an explosion in the number of prisoners on both sides, and a scramble to find places to house them. While both sides wanted to return to the original arrangements, the Confederates refused to budge on their treatment of black Union soldiers and their white officers. The issue languished, and both sides' positions hardened.

Union generals acknowledged the suffering the situation caused their prisoners of war, but by the summer of 1864 they suggested that not paroling Confederate prisoners would shorten the war because the Confederates were running short of troops. Ulysses S. Grant wrote in August, "We ought not to make a single exchange nor release a prisoner on any pretext until the war closes. . . . it is hard on our men held in Southern prisons . . . but it is humanity to those . . . who fight our battles. Every [Confederate we release] becomes an active soldier against us immediately." In October 1864, Stanton gave Grant authority to make all decisions on prisoners of war. In early 1865, with the war well in hand, Grant began a slow exchange of prisoners.

In the end, about 215,000 Union soldiers and about 195,000 Confederate soldiers had been prisoners of war. Approximately 30,000 Union prisoners and 26,000 Confederates died in prison camps, or about 9 percent of all deaths in the Civil War.

Prisoners await their rations at Andersonville Prison. Food, gambling, and the hope of escape were the highlights of prison life—everything else was monotonous routine.

The Atlanta Cyclorama

A cyclorama consists of theater seats mounted on a turntable, which rotates so the audience can have a full 360-degree view of a huge circular painting of a story. The Atlanta Cyclorama's painting portrays the Battle of Atlanta, on July 22, 1864. The battle actually took place where the Cyclorama is located today, and this exhibit puts the audience about 50 feet above the battle. As the platform revolves, the visitors have ringside seats of the battle, complete with shouting, hoofbeats, and cannon fire to go with the narration.

The painting captures the vigorous combat that took place that day as Confederate general John Bell Hood's men desperately tried to save the city from William T. Sherman's advancing troops. The vivid scenes capture the ecology of the area—worn-down gullies, red-clay roads, bridges, fences, and a partially completed brick house with combat raging around it. The fine detail of the painting makes it possible to pick out individuals, such as Sherman on a hill far in the distance, watching the battle; Union general John A. "Blackjack" Logan of the Federal Army of Tennessee dashing into combat on his charger; a soldier being taken to an ambulance after being shot in the face; and another soldier offering water to a wounded comrade. A 30-foot-wide diorama of the battle with cannons, railroad ties, and over 130 carefully scaled figures (including Clark Gable in *Gone With The Wind*) make it a decidedly three-dimensional battle scene. The strength of the painting is not merely its historical accuracy but its transcendence—it could be any Civil War battle.

The cyclorama phenomenon seems to have begun in Europe in the 1880s and then spread to the United States. Logan commissioned the Atlanta painting as part of his failed campaign for the vice presidency of the United States in 1884. It was originally titled "Logan's Great Battle," but the depiction of Logan charging fearlessly into battle is historically inaccurate. It took 11 German artists 22 months to complete at a cost of $42,000, and it is the world's largest oil painting,

The **Battle of Atlanta** *depicts a charge led by General "Blackjack" Logan, temporary commander of the Army of the Tennessee after the death of General James McPherson. Other events shown include the intense battle in the vicinity of the Troup-Hurt House, where Confederate general John Bell Hood was unsuccessful in stopping the Federal attack. On September 1, 1864, Sherman's troops captured the city of Atlanta, but not before Hood destroyed the railroad yards.*

standing 42 feet tall, 358 feet in circumference, and weighing 9000 pounds. The cyclorama has been presented since 1893—the longest running show in the country.

The Cyclorama building also houses a number of other exhibits, including weapons, displays, and photographs. There are several touch-screen computers that trace the daily action of the war on all fronts during the Union Army's advance through Georgia. The main exhibit is the steam locomotive *Texas,* which played a leading role in the "Great Locomotive Chase" in April 1862. (Its counterpart, the *General,* sits less than an hour away, at the Southern Museum of Civil War and Locomotive History. *See* that entry, page 79.)

Visitor Information
404-624-1071;
www.webguide.com/cyclorama.html
www.roadsidegeorgia.com/site/
cyclorama.html
Hours: June 1 to Labor Day, 9:30 a.m. until 5:30 p.m. and the rest of the year until 4:30; closed Martin Luther King Day, Thanksgiving, December 25, and New Year's Day. The Cyclorama show begins every half hour and is preceded by a 15-minute video describing the events leading up to the battle.

Admission: Minimal fee for adults and children 6 through 12.

Accessibility: The Cyclorama is fully accessible; tapes are available for the show in a variety of languages.

Getting There: From outside Atlanta, take I-75 to I-20 east to exit 59A (Boulevard). Follow the signs to the Cyclorama, located next to the Atlanta Zoo in Grant Park.

By public transportation: From the West End MARTA station, take the #97 bus to Grant Park.

Atlanta History Center DuBose Gallery

The 9200-square-foot exhibit *Turning Point: The American Civil War,* in the Atlanta History Center, features one of the finest private collections of Civil War objects in the world.

The gallery is divided into six chronologically organized rooms, each with interactive learning stations and various exhibits. The 1400 artifacts displayed in *Turning Point* take the visitor through the Civil War in broad strokes, while also incorporating the stories of the individual soldiers and civilians.

The first room, "The Year of Crisis: 1860," illustrates the extent to which differences over the slavery issue had divided the country for many years, but was brought to a head by the election of Abraham Lincoln in 1860. "A War of Ideals: 1861" shows through firsthand accounts that the vast majority of Civil War soldiers had volunteered to fight because they believed strongly in the ideals espoused in their regions. The displays highlight the variety of brightly colored uniforms and various elaborate military accoutrements the new volunteers thought would be essential in a war. The display also points out that the new soldiers expected the war to be over quickly—"One good battle and those (Yankees/Rebels) will quit!"

The next room, "Ideals Under Fire: 1862," interprets both sides' dawning realization that the war—which had already resulted in well over 200,000 casualties—would be a long, drawn-out conflict. Uniformed mannequins of soldiers from both sides show that they had become experienced veterans and had discarded their extravagant equipment. Now they fought without colorful or elaborate uniforms, huge knives, and the other extras the first volunteers carried. Of interest is a stand where the visitor can heft an almost nine-pound muzzle-loading rifle— the standard infantry arm—as well as a soldier's pack. Along with the combat equipment are amputation kits, a bloodstained Confederate battle flag, religious objects, and more-worldly possessions such as cards, dice, and whiskey bottles.

"A War of Resources, A Test of Will: 1863," in the fourth room, shows the situation as the war settled into a long, bloody struggle. Union industry and manpower were slowly taking over, but the Confederacy was able to develop war industries and slip in weapons and supplies through the Union blockade of Southern ports.

As the war progressed, the burden increased on civilians, especially women. A diorama of a female worker rolling and filling paper-cartridge ammunition by hand in a small-arms factory is poignantly contrasted with a nearby parlor diorama in which another woman in a black mourning dress grieves over the loss of her husband, perhaps by one of these bullets. There are also side-by-side comparisons of Union and Confederate weapons, showing clearly the differences between the two.

The room entitled "Year of Decision: 1864" notes that by August 1864, opposition to the war in the North threatened to stop the fighting. Pro-peace Democrats called for a negotiated peace, and if the Confederate armies could hold Atlanta and Richmond, the South might yet gain a negotiated settlement. Finally, after a summer of miserable campaigns, General

William T. Sherman's army cut the last railroad line into Atlanta. The rapid fall of the city after this move, combined with Admiral David Farragut's securing of Mobile Bay, ensured Lincoln's reelection in November and doomed the Confederacy.

Large displays show the new systems of fortifications that made frontal attacks so costly that year, as well as descriptions of the defense of and attacks on Atlanta. An especially symbolic display is an uprooted railroad track twisted around a pine tree, the trademark "Sherman necktie" emblematic of the Union armies' destruction of Confederate rail lines as they moved through the South.

Other items include the Confederate flag that flew over Atlanta at the time of its capture, a United States flag purported to have been on Farragut's flagship at the Battle of Mobile Bay, the only known surviving Federal six-wheeled supply wagon, the sword of the Union officer who forced the mayor of Atlanta to give up the "keys to the city," and a poll book of the type used by Union soldiers to vote in the 1864 election (they voted overwhelmingly for Lincoln).

The final room, "The Search for

A woman assembles minié cartridges in an ammunition factory.

Meaning: 1865 to 2000," focuses on the end of the war, on Reconstruction, and on the aftermath and its relevance to the United States. It was one of the defining moments in American history, and out of the war came such concrete and far-reaching political changes as the 13th, 14th, and 15th Amendments to the Constitution, as well as the overall change in the role of the Federal government and its relations with the states. A video discusses how the Civil War has been interpreted since it ended.

The room features a variety of artifacts associated with the end of the war, including Confederate general John B. Gordon's dress uniform coat (conceivably worn at the Appomattox surrender), an original copy of General Robert E. Lee's final farewell message to his troops in General Order No. 9, Sherman's general order ending hostilities in North Carolina, and the logbooks of the sea raider C.S.S. *Shenandoah*, the last Confederate unit to surrender, in November 1865. A reproduction of a memorial statue to a Civil War soldier is also on display. A huge number of similar statues sprang up in communities across the country on both sides of the conflict. Once the

The typical Union infantryman, *left, was dressed in a blue government-issue uniform. Confederate soldiers provided much of their own clothing. The official color was gray, but many soldiers wore yellow brown—clothes dyed in butternut or walnut hulls.*

In 1861, thinking the war would last only a few months, volunteer soldiers brought along such unnecessary items as a 55-piece, 25-pound mess set and a traveling six-bottle bar. More-practical items included shaving sets and a portable coffee boiler.

immediacy of the war had passed and memories both faded and intensified, veterans from both sides began to hold reunions, often jointly. The DuBose collection contains a large number of the badges worn by the veterans at these various post-war reunions.

One of the most interesting separate collections in the gallery is the Thomas Swift Dickey Civil War Ordnance Collection, which contains artillery projectiles from both sides. Dickey is known as the "father of Civil War projectile collecting," and this collection shows why. For those who think Civil War cannons fired only cannon balls and some variation of grapeshot, this collection is a real eye opener, with hundreds of shells and "bolts" (solid foot-

ball-shape rounds fired by rifled cannon) in an incredible and bewildering variety of shapes and sizes.

Visitor Information

404-814-4000;
www.atlhist.org/exhibitions/html/turningpoint.htm
Hours: Monday to Saturday, 10 a.m. until 5:30 p.m.; closed Sunday, Martin Luther King Day, Presidents' Day, Memorial Day, Independence Day, Labor Day, Columbus Day, and Veterans Day, noon until 5:30 p.m.; closed Thanksgiving, December 24 and 25, and New Year's Day.
Admission: High fee for adults, mod-

Using a metal detector to comb battlefields, Thomas Swift Dickey accumulated the largest and most comprehensive collection of Civil War artillery projectiles in the United States. Careful research of the battles, including gun emplacement positions, projectile trajectory, battle strategy, and topography, helped him anticipate where artifacts would be found.

The Ketcham Grenades, left, used by Federal troops, had wooden tails to make sure they would land on their nose where the impact fuse was located. The fuse, or plunger, was not inserted until it was about to be thrown.

Two companies *of sharpshooters used the James Target Rifle during the siege of Yorktown in 1862. Equipped with a 4-power telescopic sight, the 14-pound rifle fired a .45-caliber bullet and was accurate up to 500 yards.*

erate fee for children 3–17. General admission includes the Atlanta History Center and gardens, and tours of two historic homes, Swan House and the Tullie Smith Farm.

Accessibility: The Atlanta History Museum is fully accessible to people with disabilities. Video presentations at the History Center are subtitled, and visitor maps are available in English, French, German, Japanese, and Spanish.

Special Events: There are guided tours of the DuBose Collection at 2 p.m. and 3 p.m., Saturday and Sunday. Costumed interpreters give tours on the second and fourth Sunday of each month from 2 p.m. until 4 p.m. There is a large Civil War encampment on the grounds one weekend in July. Call for information.

Getting There: The museum is in the center of Atlanta, Georgia, in the Buckhead neighborhood, 15 minutes from downtown, just off I-75. Take I-75 to the West Paces Ferry Road exit (exit 255). At the end of the ramp, turn left onto Northside Parkway. At the next intersection, turn right onto West Paces Ferry Road. Go approximately 2.7 miles. Turn right onto Andrews Drive. (Do not confuse this road with West Andrews Drive or Andrews Court, which are also off West Paces Ferry.) The Atlanta History Center is on the left.

By public transportation: Take MARTA to the Lenox rail station. Transfer to bus #23 to Peachtree and West Paces Ferry Road. Walk three blocks west on West Paces Ferry Road to the pedestrian entrance in front of the Atlanta History Center. Or take the more infrequent MARTA bus #40, which goes directly past the Atlanta History Center; however, there is no scheduled stop here, and you must inform the driver where you intend to get off. This bus runs only Monday through Friday.

The Battles of Chickamauga and Chattanooga

In the spring of 1863, Lincoln ordered General William S. Rosecrans, the commander of the 60,000-man Army of the Cumberland, to take Chattanooga and the rest of east Tennessee. Chattanooga was a vital railway junction. Its capture by the Union would close one of the South's principal east–west transportation routes, and it would simplify a Union invasion of Georgia. East Tennessee's fertile farmland was important militarily because it supported the Confederate armies, but it was equally important politically. Many of the East Tennesseans were Unionists; some of them had enlisted in the Union Army, while others hid in the mountains and sabotaged the railways. Lincoln badly wanted to free these Union loyalists from the "rebel yoke."

Standing in Rosecrans's way was General Braxton Bragg's 43,000-strong Army of Tennessee. The terrain favored the defense, but Rosecrans outmaneuvered Bragg, driving him back to Chattanooga. With some more clever maneuvering, Rosecrans forced Bragg to abandon the town.

But then Rosecrans made a mistake. He divided his forces into three columns, sending them through three separate valleys in a way that made it impossible for them to reinforce one another. This gave Bragg an opportunity. But try as he might to attack these vulnerable forces, he could not get his subordinates to attack. They did not respect him and repeatedly ignored his orders. Rosecrans soon realized his vulnera-

bility and ordered his generals to reunite.

The Rock of Chickamauga

With reinforcements from east Tennessee, Virginia, and Mississippi, Bragg planned to use his now 66,000 men to outflank Rosecrans by crossing Chickamauga Creek. However, Rosecrans figured out Bragg's plan, and during the night he moved General George H. Thomas's corps northeastward, protecting the route back to Chattanooga. At dawn on September 19, the two armies were facing each other over a stretch of several miles along the banks of the Chickamauga. The fighting began shortly after dawn when Thomas sent an infantry division to reconnoiter the Confederate forces. By midafternoon, major fighting had spread along a jagged line some three miles long. When the battle ended for the day, both sides had suffered heavy losses but had little to show for it. That night, Rosecrans drew the Union forces together into a more compact defensive line. On the Confederate side, Bragg had been further reinforced when General James Longstreet (ironically, Rosecrans's former West Point roommate) arrived from Virginia with two fresh brigades.

The Confederate attack was to begin at sunrise the next morning and move north to south. General D. H. Hill's corps was supposed to attack first, but Hill did not receive the order until seven thirty that morning. Bragg waited impatiently

Confederate reenactors, left, pose next to a Civil War cannon at the site where the Battle of Chickamauga took place.

as Hill, perhaps showing his disdain for Bragg, slowly moved his troops into position. About nine thirty a.m. the attack began, and the extreme left of the Union line fell back initially, but then stiffened. As the attack rolled south, all along the line the Confederates were repelled by Rosecrans's men, solidly dug in behind log breastworks cut and erected the night before. Bragg's planned flanking maneuver turned into a bloody frontal assault.

About eleven a.m., as Longstreet's men were poised to strike the Union right center, they had an amazing stroke of luck. A Union staff officer riding from Thomas's headquarters reported to Rosecrans that one of the Union divisions had fallen out of line and the center of the Union line was exposed. Rosecrans immediately ordered a division out of the line to fill the gap. But the report was wrong—there was no gap. As the Union division followed orders and pulled out of the line, it created a real gap where none had actually existed before. Longstreet's forces struck that precise spot, and in a few minutes the entire Union right flank was split, shattered, and fleeing the field. Rosecrans fled the battlefield, along with generals Thomas Crittenden

and Alexander McDowell McCook. On the extreme right of the Union line, Colonel John T. Wilder's Indiana "Lightning Brigade," armed with Spencer repeating carbines, made a strong stand but finally had to fall back to keep from being completely cut off.

As the battle paused, Thomas, in command of the remaining Union forces by default, formed a new defensive line quickly on Snodgrass Hill (also known as Horseshoe Ridge). Longstreet realized if he could take Thomas's position, the Confederates could destroy the Union army. Longstreet's men vigorously assaulted Thomas's line again and again as the Union troops ran low on ammunition. Confederate success seemed assured until a Union reserve division arrived just in time to stop the Confederates from enveloping Thomas's right flank. Without orders from Rosecrans, these reserves had been moved forward by their commander, General Gordon Granger, who sensed they were needed. Granger's initiative saved the day for the Union.

Longstreet's men tried again to take the hill throughout the day, but were repulsed. At nightfall, Thomas began to withdraw his force to the town of Rossville. One Union general noted that night that "the army is simply a mob . . . [with] neither organization nor discipline."

A battlefield sketch by artist Alfred Waud portrays Confederate troops at Chickamauga advancing to attack the Union line dimly seen through the gunsmoke.

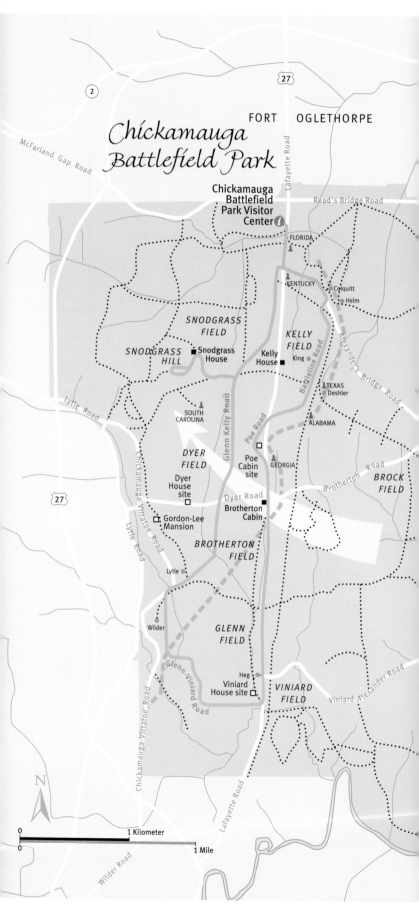

Chickamauga Battlefield Park

FORT OGLETHORPE

Chickamauga Battlefield Park Visitor Center

McFarland Gap Road

Read's Bridge Road

Lafayette Road

FLORIDA

KENTUCKY

Colquitt
Helm

SNODGRASS FIELD

SNODGRASS HILL

Snodgrass House

KELLY FIELD

Kelly House

King

TEXAS
Deshler

SOUTH CAROLINA

Lytle Road

Battleline Road

Alexander's Bridge Road

ALABAMA

DYER FIELD

Poe Road

Poe Cabin site

GEORGIA

Glenn Kelly Road

Brotherton Road

BROCK FIELD

Dyer House site

Dyer Road

Brotherton Cabin

27

Gordon-Lee Mansion

Chickamauga-Vittatoe Road

BROTHERTON FIELD

Lytle

Lytle Road

Wilder

GLENN FIELD

Glenn-Viniard Road

Heg

Viniard House site

VINIARD FIELD

Viniard-Alexander Road

Chickamauga-Vittatoe Road

Lafayette Road

N

0   1 Kilometer
0   1 Mile

Wilder Road

Thomas held the line at Rossville Gap and along Missionary Ridge until the evening of the next day, September 21, which allowed the rest of the Union army to withdraw successfully to Chattanooga, Tennessee. By morning of September 22, all the Union troops were in the town. After the battle, the Union commanders (other than Thomas and Wilder) were severely criticized by the Northern press for leaving the battlefield, and Thomas was given the well-earned nickname The Rock of Chickamauga.

During this bloody battle, the Union suffered a little over 16,000 casualties, the Confederates almost 18,500.

Siege in Chattanooga

Bragg refused to pursue the shattered Union army to Chattanooga, despite the urgings of Longstreet and other Confederate commanders. Instead, Confederate troops took up siege positions around the town on Missionary Ridge, Lookout Mountain, and in the Chattanooga Valley. They controlled river and train traffic to the city. Rosecrans's horses started to starve and his men went on short rations.

Determined to rescue them, Lincoln sent 20,000 troops and more than 3000 horses and mules. This force, including troops under General William T. Sherman, as well as a force under General Joseph Hooker, was the largest troop movement ever by rail.

Meanwhile, command of the two hostile armies had undergone a considerable change since the resounding Confederate victory at Chickamauga. Relations between Bragg and his commanders had deteriorated to the point that Confederate President Jefferson Davis came to Tennessee personally to settle the dispute. Davis felt an allegiance to Bragg, who had helped him during the Mexican War, so Davis sided with Bragg. On the Union side, Granger was given the Fourth Corps; the hero of Chickamauga, Thomas, took command of the Army of the Cumberland, replacing Rosecrans; and General Ulysses S. Grant was given overall command of the newly organized Military Division of Mississippi.

Grant Helps Break the Siege

When Grant arrived in Chattanooga on October 23, he found that Thomas had already drawn up a plan to shorten the supply lines of his besieged and starving army. The night of October 26, 1500 Union troops on pontoons floated down the river from Chattanooga while another force supported them from the shore. Protected by a heavy fog, the Union troops set up a new bridge, and after a brief, sharp fight with Confederate troops, they established the new, short Union supply line, known as the Cracker Line.

The disputes between Bragg and his commanders again became an issue. Bragg either failed to understand what was taking place on the Union side or simply wanted to get the rebellious Longstreet out of his sight; so early in November, Bragg ordered Longstreet and 15,000 men to march against General Ambrose Burnside, who had taken Knoxville. The Confederate Army in front of Chattanooga was now reduced to two corps, General William Hardee on the right and General John Breckinridge on the left of Missionary Ridge. General Carter Stevenson and a small force also occupied Lookout Mountain.

Grant learned that Longstreet was moving toward Burnside, but he felt the best way to aid the Union general was to attack Bragg at Chattanooga, forcing Bragg to recall Longstreet.

Grant ordered Thomas to attack on November 23. With surprising ease, the Union troops drove the Confederates to the base of Missionary Ridge, capturing Orchard Knob, a little more than a mile in front of the ridge. Thomas's forces dug in, set up artillery, and waited for the next phase of the plan.

On November 24, Sherman was supposed to attack Tunnel Hill, but the terrain and well-fortified Confederate defenders prompted him to cancel the attack. Meanwhile, Hooker moved to take Lookout Mountain. The Confederates fell back to a plateau halfway up the slope as the three Union divisions moved up the steep mountain, immersed in a unique but common weather phenomenon on the mountain, a layer of fog that descends toward the valley below but stops about halfway down the peak. The fog moved in and out as the three Union divisions joined and pushed toward a house on the plateau, the home of wealthy Chattanooga industrialist Robert Cravens. The engagement was later romantically called The Battle Above the Clouds. During the night, the Confederate forces withdrew from Lookout Mountain and marched to Missionary Ridge, where they joined their comrades.

On November 25, Grant planned for Sherman and Hooker to attack Missionary Ridge from the wings, while Thomas was to stay put in the Union center. Yet, like most battle plans, Grant's did not survive the

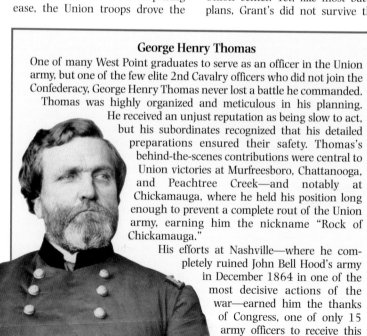

George Henry Thomas

One of many West Point graduates to serve as an officer in the Union army, but one of the few elite 2nd Cavalry officers who did not join the Confederacy, George Henry Thomas never lost a battle he commanded. Thomas was highly organized and meticulous in his planning. He received an unjust reputation as being slow to act, but his subordinates recognized that his detailed preparations ensured their safety. Thomas's behind-the-scenes contributions were central to Union victories at Murfreesboro, Chattanooga, and Peachtree Creek—and notably at Chickamauga, where he held his position long enough to prevent a complete rout of the Union army, earning him the nickname "Rock of Chickamauga."

His efforts at Nashville—where he completely ruined John Bell Hood's army in December 1864 in one of the most decisive actions of the war—earned him the thanks of Congress, one of only 15 army officers to receive this honor for their service during the war.

first engagement. Sherman and Hooker were both rebuffed, so Grant ordered Thomas to attack the Confederate center on Missionary Ridge.

The terrain favored the defense. In front of the Union forces, the ridge rose steeply upward and was strewn with rocks, boulders, and natural ravines. At the foot of the ridge was a line of prepared Confederate defenses, with more halfway up the hill and a seemingly solid line of breastworks at the top. However, Bragg's Confederates at the base of the ridge were disorganized and had conflicting orders. The Union troops advanced and broke through the line, where Grant expected them to halt and reorganize. But after the Union troops took the first positions, they found that staying in place put them under murderous fire from the crest of the ridge; it seemed safest to continue the charge up to the top. When Grant saw the troops continue on toward the summit without orders, he was appalled and reportedly asked Thomas and Granger, "Who ordered those men up the hill?" When he got no answer, he muttered, "Someone will suffer for it, if it turns out badly."

It did not. The Union troops followed the retreating Confederates so closely that the Confederates on the crest hesitated to fire for fear of hitting their own men. Even worse for the defenders, the formidable-looking Confederate fortifications at the top of the ridge were poorly designed and exposed the defenders to a withering crossfire from advancing Union troops. General "Little Phil" Sheridan's troops even came very close to capturing Bragg and a number of other high-ranking Confederate officers; they had to flee, and Sheridan took a large number of guns and prisoners. Hooker, meanwhile, had finally gotten into position and was rolling up the Confederate's left.

Many Confederate units panicked, but some rallied on a ridge about 500 yards to the rear, while the units on the right wing continued to hold Sherman, preventing a rout. Grant ordered Thomas and Sherman to pursue Bragg, but the Confederates set up defenses at Taylor's Ridge and sent the Union soldiers reeling back with heavy casualties. Grant stopped the pursuit at that point.

In the end, the battle cost the Union about 5800 casualties and the Confederates about 6700, but it was a complete Union offensive victory against an enemy that had every advantage of terrain. The rail center of Chattanooga was now in Union hands, as well as Knoxville and the fertile east Tennessee area with its Union sympathizers.

Appropriately, the battle had an impact on the commanders. Bragg asked to be relieved from his command and went to Richmond to become military advisor to President Davis. A few months later, in March 1864, President Lincoln promoted Grant to command of all Union armies in the field, with specific instructions to lead the attack against General Robert E. Lee in Virginia.

Chickamauga & Chattanooga National Military Park

The Chickamauga & Chattanooga National Military Park (known to many as Chick/Chatt) was formed by a resolution of Congress in 1890 to commemorate "some of the most remarkable maneuvers and brilliant fighting in the war of the rebellion." When it was completed in 1895, Chickamauga & Chattanooga became the United States's first national military park. Today, the park has approximately 700 monuments, 250 cannons, and 650 markers, scattered over 8000 acres in Georgia and Tennessee. The park consists of several separate areas: Chickamauga Battlefield, Point Park, and Lookout Mountain Battlefield; a series of "reservations" (small parks) along Missionary Ridge, and the Orchard Knob Reservation. There are two visitors centers, one at the Chickamauga battlefield and one at the top of Lookout Mountain.

The Chickamauga Battlefield Park Headquarters and Visitors Center is at the north entrance to Chickamauga Battlefield on U.S. 27. Every half hour the Center shows a 26-minute multimedia presentation that explains the Battle of Chickamauga and its significance in the Civil War. Library facilities are also available. Exhibits describe the cause of the war, the Battle of Chickamauga, and the history of the park, along with a fiber-optic map detailing the course of the battle and an artillery display with various field artillery cannons used during the war. Visitors can also see the Claud E. and Zenada O. Fuller Collection of American Military Arms, considered one of the premier collections of

U.S. military shoulder arms.

A seven-mile, self-guided automobile tour narrated by a rental tape begins at the Visitors Center and can be easily followed along the road. The low, square monuments around the park mark the sites of various army and corps headquarters, while other monuments and metal tablets—red for Confederate and blue for Union—show the location of various units during the battle. Large triangular stacks of cannonballs on the battlefield mark the places where eight brigade commanders died, including Lincoln's brother-in-law, Benjamin H. Helm. There are over 1400 markers and monuments to other units located across the park—the most on any U.S. battlefield.

Notable points on the battlefield tour include: The **Brotherton Cabin,** behind which is a wooded area where Longstreet's forces broke through the gap in the Union lines and started the rout. The cabin was built later but it is the same design and construction as cabins at the time of the battle. The **Wilder Monument,** honoring Wilder and his Spencer-carbine-wielding troops who tried unsuccessfully to hold back Longstreet's attack. The top of the 85-foot-high monument offers an excellent view of the battlefield. **Snodgrass Hill,** the knob where Thomas rallied fleeing troops from the center of the shattered Union line and held the Confederates long enough to allow the Union forces to escape. The log cabin on the site was the home of the Snodgrass family. **Lee and Gordon's Mill,** which alternated hands throughout the battle. At various times Confederate generals Bragg and Leonidas Polk and Union general Thomas Crittenden used it as a headquarters. The mill was rebuilt after it burned down in 1867. The **Gordon-Lee Mansion** is one of the few remaining structures from the time of the battle. It initially served as Rosecrans's headquarters, but was used as a hospital during the battle. There is a museum on the second floor.

Closer to Chattanooga, the Lookout Mountain Visitors Center at Point Park contains the famous James Walker painting of the *Battle Above the Clouds.* It also features an audio program discussing the work, and a bookstore. Around the center, three gun batteries mark a part of the Confederate siege lines that encircled Chattanooga, and the

Peace Monument—constructed from pink Massachusetts granite and Tennessee marble—shows a Union and a Confederate soldier shaking hands under one flag. A 500-foot trail leads down a set of stairs to the **Ochs Museum and Overlook,** and nearby is Umbrella Rock, where many Union soldiers had their pictures taken, including Grant. To the left of the Ochs museum is a trail to the **Cravens House,** a Confederate headquarters and the site of the fiercest fighting on Lookout Mountain. Sometimes fog will roll in and give the visitor an appreciation for the Battle Above the Clouds.

Missionary Ridge Reservations

The 20-mile-long Missionary Ridge runs east of the city of Chattanooga. A series of military reservations with monuments, cannons, and explanatory tablets marks significant spots on the ridge. Of note are: The **Sherman Reservation,** the area where Sherman tried in vain to break through the right side of the Confederate lines at Tunnel Hill; the **Bragg Reservation,** the site of Bragg's headquarters before he fled in the face of Thomas's attack. The monument on this spot honors Illinois troops.

Separate is **Orchard Knob Reservation,** the site of Grant's headquarters during the Union assaults of Missionary Ridge, where Grant and Thomas watched in stunned consternation as Union troops—without orders—charged up Missionary Ridge and carried the day.

Visitor Information

706-866-9241; www.nps.gov/chch
Hours: Both visitors centers, daily, 8 a.m. until 4:45 p.m.; extended summer hours from Memorial Day to Labor Day, 8 a.m. until 5:45 p.m.; closed December 25. Call Visitor Information for current Cravens House tour schedule.
Admission: There is a small daily admission charge to Cravens House and Point Park. National Parks Pass, Golden Eagle, Golden Age, and Golden Access are honored.
Accessibility: Wheelchairs are available for use at both visitors centers. Video tours are available of nonaccessible areas of the park. TDD is available for calls at the Chickamauga Battlefield Visitor Center. Parking spaces for the disabled are located at both visitors center parking lots. Be prepared to climb many steps at Point Park.

A Civil War ordnance rifle near the Brotherton Cabin. Longstreet's rout began at a gap in the Union lines nearby.

Special Events: The Battle of Chickamauga Anniversary Commemoration and the Battles for Chattanooga Anniversary Commemoration occur on the weekends closest to the anniversary to the battles (except on Thanksgiving weekend). Additionally, tours of Point Park and the Cravens House are available during the summer months. The summer walking tours from Point Park often include living-history demonstrations of rifle battles and of signaling, which was crucial in this battle spread over so much area. During some summer weekends, encampments of regiments from various states provide living-history demonstrations of a Civil War soldier's life.

Getting There: The Chickamauga Battlefield is nine miles south of Chattanooga on U.S. 27. The Visitor Center is located just south of Fort Oglethorpe, Georgia, one mile south of the intersection of Georgia highway 2 (Battlefield Parkway) and U.S. 27. Public transportation to Chickamauga Battlefield is not available.

Lookout Mountain Battlefield Visitor Center/Point Park. From Chattanooga, take U.S. 41 to Tennessee highway 148, then to the top of Lookout Mountain and right on East Brow Road.

Visitors may also visit the park on the St. Elmo buses from Chattanooga, which connect with the Lookout Mountain Incline Railway at the foot of the mountain. The top of the incline is within a short walking distance of the Point Park entrance.

Orchard Knob is in Chattanooga on Orchard Knob Avenue near McCallie Avenue (U.S. Routes 11 and 64).

From the Chickamauga Battlefield, to reach Missionary Ridge drive north three miles toward Chattanooga on U.S. 27 to Crest Road. Crest Road runs the entire length of the line occupied by the Confederates during the Battle of Missionary Ridge.

The Battle for Fort McAllister

At the outbreak of the Civil War, it was clear that the port of Savannah, Georgia, would be vital to the South. The Confederacy quickly built a four-gun earth fortification at Genesis Point—which lies at the entrance to the Ogeechee River—in order to guard the river, Savannah's southern flank, and an important railroad trestle upstream. The fortification was named Fort McAllister after the owner of the land.

Savannah was threatened early in the war when the Union occupied Tybee Island, just outside the harbor, and used the new rifled cannons to wreck and take Fort Pulaski in 1862. As a result, Fort McAllister gradually added more guns, a dry moat, and bombproof shelters.

The Earthen Fort Prevails

In July 1862, the C.S.S. *Nashville*, a 1221-ton side-wheel steamer, slipped through the Union blockade and anchored in the Ogeechee River, where it was protected by Fort McAllister. The ship underwent two name changes while it sat in the river, finally emerging in November 1862 as the privateer *Rattlesnake*.

Several Union wooden warships came after the raider, but the guns of Fort McAllister kept them at bay. The fort's sand-and-mud walls also proved an advantage against the Union's new rifled shells, because the shells simply dug into the earth instead of blasting it into pieces. In January 1863, new Union ironclads arrived outside the harbor. One of them, the *Montauk*, bombarded the fort on January 27 without effect. This was the first land shelling by an ironclad in naval history.

On February 27, the *Rattlesnake* tried to slip away, but she was detected and ran aground close to Fort McAllister as she withdrew. The next morning, the *Montauk* returned and began to leisurely shell the *Rattlesnake* until it caught fire and sank. The shells from Fort McAllister's guns bounced harmlessly off the ironclad, but the Confederates watched with considerable satisfaction when the *Montauk* hit a fixed torpedo as she left the harbor and had to run aground to keep from sinking. On March 3, three other monitors, the *Patapsco*, *Passaic*, and *Nahant*, attacked again, but after shelling the fort for eight hours without damaging it, the Union warships withdrew.

Fort McAllister Falls

Fort McAllister continued to guard the Ogeechee until late 1864 when General Sherman's army approached Savannah near the end of his famous March to the Sea. The fort was the last obstacle preventing Sherman from communicating with and being resupplied by the Union fleet, and controlling it was the key to Savannah. In early December, Sherman dispatched a Union division to take Fort McAllister and its 200-man garrison from the land

*A **Confederate gun** captured at Fort McAllister by General William T. Sherman's troops on December 13, 1864, awaits dismantling and shipment to nearby Fort Pulaski.*

side, since the naval attacks had been unsuccessful. The Confederates placed land mines on the approaches, but while the mines resulted in many casualties, Fort McAllister fell in less than half an hour on the afternoon of December 13, 1864. The Union soldiers used the Confederate prisoners to remove the remaining land mines, and Savannah became Sherman's Christmas present to Lincoln.

Fort McAllister State Historic Park

The 1724-acre park contains well-preserved earthwork fortifications. The Visitors Center has a small museum, gift shop, and a 17-minute video about the naval and land attacks on the fort. The museum's interior is designed to resemble a bombproof shelter and contains

numerous artifacts from the fort. There is a self-guided trail through the fort, and along the path visitors can see the remains of the C.S.S. *Nashville.* The fort also includes several cannons and a mortar battery. A visit to the fort takes 1 to 1 1/2 hours.

Visitor Information

912-727-2339;
www.fortmcallister.org/;
www.cr.nps.gov/goldcres/sites/
ftmac.htm

Hours: Park open 7 a.m. until 10 p.m.; office open 8 a.m. until 5 p.m.; historic site open Tuesday through Saturday 9 a.m. until 5 p.m. and Sunday 2 p.m. until 5:30 p.m.; closed Mondays (except legal holidays), Thanksgiving, and December 25.

Admission: Minimal charge for adults and children over 5; group rates available.

Accessibility: The fort is not handicapped accessible; the museum, two campsites, and restroom facility are accessible.

Special Events: Programs on the Fourth of July and the Saturdays before Memorial Day and Labor Day.

Getting There: Take I-95 to Georgia exit 90 (south of Savannah). Drive east on Georgia Route 144 through Richmond Hill, for just over six miles. Turn left at the state park sign onto Fort McAllister Road. The park is four miles ahead.

*The **privateer** Rattlesnake burning after being shelled by the monitor U.S.S. Montauk, in the Ogeechee River, Georgia, as the U.S. Navy gunboats Wissahickon, Seneca, and Dawn provide supporting fire. Fort McAllister is seen in the right-center background under heavy cannon smoke.*

Battle for Fort Pulaski

After the British attacked Washington and Baltimore in the War of 1812, the United States decided to build 200 forts along the East Coast called the Third System. Due to money problems, only 30 were completed—Fort Pulaski being the last. Completed in 1846, the fort was named after the Revolutionary War hero Count Casimir Pulaski. Coincidentally, Second Lieutenant Robert E. Lee's first assignment after graduating from West Point was at Fort Pulaski, when construction began there in 1830.

Fort Pulaski is located about 15 miles from Savannah, Georgia, on Cockspur Island. The island sits in a strategic location where the Savannah River divides into northern and southern channels. Two earlier forts were built on the same location but fared badly. Fort George, built by the English, was destroyed by colonists during the Revolutionary War. Its American replacement, Fort Greene, was completed in 1796 and destroyed by a hurricane only eight years later.

The two-tiered, pentagon-shaped fort's seven-and-a-half-foot-thick brick walls rose 25 feet out of a surrounding moat. Twenty-five million bricks, many specially hardened, were brought to the island a million at a time for the construction.

Fort Pulaski Is Put to the Test

After its completion, Fort Pulaski fell into disrepair because of financial problems. Just before the Civil War, troops from the state of Georgia occupied the fort and turned it over to the newly formed Confederate government. The Confederates quickly refurbished the fort and equipped it with 48 cannons.

Toward the end of 1861, operating under General Winfield Scott's "Anaconda Plan" (*see* sidebar, page 117), Union forces captured Beaufort, South Carolina, only 30 miles away from Savannah. In late November 1861, they landed on Big Tybee Island, just across the channel south of Fort Pulaski. This gave the Federals a forward staging area to organize their forces while monitoring the fort and the water passages to Savannah.

In early 1862, a Union engineer, Captain Quincy A. Gillmore, was given command of the troops in the area and ordered to capture Fort Pulaski. By February, Union forces had cut the telegraph wires to the fort, and Union artillery controlled both channels, cutting off resupply boats. The only way the Confederate commander, Colonel Charles Olmstead, and his 384 men could communicate with the outside world was through boatmen who crossed the marshes at night.

Actually capturing Fort Pulaski was quite daunting, though. Engineers were able to make very precise calculations about how long it would take to reduce a brick fort with cannon fire; given the size of Fort Pulaski's walls, their calculations indicated that normal shellfire would cause little damage unless fired from less than half a mile. Even with the walls battered down, invading troops would still have to land on open marsh, cross the moat, then fight their way across a wide inner courtyard, under fire the entire time.

Captain Gillmore's plan to capture the fort required complete stealth. His men built a road from a landing area to a point on the north end of

Under heavy bombardment, top, Fort Pulaski held out until Federal rifled-cannon fire breached two of the fort's casemates, left. These open gaps in the brick walls soon endangered the powder magazines, which eventually led to the fort's surrender.

Big Tybee Island opposite the fort. Operating quietly at night and speaking only in whispers, they moved cannons, ammunition, and other siege equipment into position and encamped there. The task took eight weeks. Finally, on April 9, 1862, Gillmore was ready. Union guns, still undetected by the Confederates, lined the northern end of Big Tybee, the farthest less than two miles from the fort and four of the batteries less than a mile away. Ten new rifled cannons—five large James rifles (two 84-pounders, two 64-pounders, and one 48-pounder) and five smaller 30-pounder Parrott rifles—were in the closest batteries, but they were still almost a mile from the fort. The rest of the weapons were large smooth bores—eight heavy mortars and six heavy Columbiads.

Early on the morning of April 10, Gillmore sent a small boat under a flag of truce to Colonel Olmstead to demand surrender. Olmstead, not surprisingly, refused. At ten minutes after eight a.m., April 10, the large mortars began to fire, but missed badly because of a strong easterly wind. These winds were to play havoc with the slow-flying, high-trajectory mortar rounds for the rest of the siege, which resulted in less than 10 percent of the mortar rounds fired hitting the fort.

The cannons were more effective. Throughout the day, Union cannon fire became increasingly accurate, and their rate of fire steadily increased. The next morning, the accurate James rifles began to concentrate their fire on the 19 Confederate barbette cannons trained on Big Tybee and soon wrecked most of the guns. The James rifles then knocked down two of the casemates on the southeast corner of the fort, and shells began whistling through these breaches to the other side of the fort, pounding the shielding of the fort's north powder magazine. Twenty tons of powder was stored in the magazine, and Olmstead realized it was only a matter of time before it exploded and demolished the inside of the fort, wiping out most of his soldiers. Olmstead surrendered at two thirty that afternoon. Union forces occupied Fort Pulaski, and soon its cannons made the port of Savannah practically useless to the Confederacy. Later in the war, the fort was used as a prison for captured Confederate officers.

The Federals looked carefully at the results of the bombardment, and found that the rifled cannons had been much more effective than the large Columbiad smoothbores against the walls. While the Columbiads' shot penetrated only 10 inches, the James and Parrott rifles' solid shot penetrated from 20 to 25 inches of brick with each hit and breached the wall with less than 2300 rounds. Gillmore also noted that the James and Parrott rifles could have been in place in less than a week, rendering the other guns practically useless. It was stunningly clear that just a few large rifled cannons could quickly knock down any brick fort. This fact dramatically changed the nature of fortifications from then on.

A James shell similar to the type used to bombard Fort Pulaski into submission. When fired, gases entered the base, passed through the vertical openings, and expanded a lead sabot into the cannon's rifling to rotate the shell.

cannon, dramatically illustrating the difficulty an invading force might have had. On the inside walls of the fort are the prison cells and living quarters of the soldiers, many restored to their Civil War configuration, with graffiti scrawled by the soldiers still visible on the walls. Stairs lead to the top of the fort, where visitors can walk the gun deck and see several cannons along the walls. Looking across to Big Tybee Island where the Union batteries were located gives the visitor an acute appreciation of the accuracy of Civil War cannons.

The visitor can also enter the northwest powder magazine. It was the fear that a magazine might blow up that drove the Confederate commander, Colonel Olmstead, to surrender. There is a path around the outside walls of the fort, where the visitor can see the pockmarks and embedded shells remaining from the bombardment.

Fort Pulaski National Monument

Established by presidential proclamation in 1924, the site includes the well-preserved fort and 5000 acres of salt marsh. The Visitors Center regularly shows a 20-minute film, *The Battle for Fort Pulaski*. There is also a small museum with weapons, uniforms, pictures, letters, and other artifacts linked to the battle. Audiocassettes and tape players are available on request for use at stations around the fort, and written audio station transcripts are available in English and Braille. Park rangers are available to answer questions.

A path leads from the Visitors Center to the fort's entrance—a drawbridge across the moat. Crossing the bridge and entering the fort, the visitor comes face to face with a

Visitor Information

912-786-5787; www.nps.gov/fopu/
Hours: Visitors Center and fort are open daily, 8:30 a.m. until 5 p.m., with extended hours in the summer; closed Thanksgiving and December 25; call for information.
Admission: Moderate fee for adults 17 and over; National Parks Pass, Golden Eagle, Golden Age, and Golden Access are honored.
Accessibility: Visitors Center parking, restrooms, and exhibits, picnic area parking and restrooms, and fort lower level and restrooms are wheelchair accessible. Audio transcripts are available in English and Braille. Audiocassettes and tape players are loaned upon request. The orientation film is captioned, and brochures are available in English, German, Polish, Japanese, French, and Spanish.
Getting There: Interstate highways 95 and 16 cross about 15 miles west of Savannah. From I-16, take U.S. 80 east. Follow signs for Fort Pulaski, Tybee Island, and beaches. A long narrow two-lane road crosses over a bridge and leads to the Visitors Center.

SIEGE AND COASTAL ARTILLERY

Cannons have been used to reduce and defend castles, fortresses, and other strong points since the Middle Ages, and this continued in the Civil War. Siege and coastal artillery was the loose term applied to artillery pieces used in this role. These pieces were of three types—guns, mortars, and Columbiads. They were too large to be moved easily, and since mobility was not an issue, they could be made very large. Nevertheless, siege artillery had to be moved to the place under siege, so they were usually mounted on some form of wheeled wooden carriage. Coastal artillery pieces were mounted in fixed fortifications on carriages of heavy timber or iron.

Guns

Guns were scaled-up versions of the battlefield weapons and were used for long-range, relatively low-trajectory fire. Three English rifled guns—the Whitworth, Armstrong, and Blakely—were used in the Civil War. Rifling involved cutting spiral grooves inside a gun barrel that caused the shell to spin out of the gun, making it fly farther, faster, and with much greater accuracy. Such guns made old brick and stone forts obsolete, and smoothbore siege guns were rapidly replaced or rifled.

While the British were far ahead in rifled-cannon development, in America, Robert Parrott introduced a new rifled-gun design, the Parrott rifle, using a cast-iron barrel with a wrought-iron reinforcing band shrunk around the breech to strengthen it. The Parrott rifle would become the most common rifled gun of the war and was used as field artillery, as well as in much larger siege and garrison guns. Parrott rifles forced the surrender of Fort Pulaski and reduced many other stone forts to rubble, though the rifles never overcame their reputation for bursting at the breech. During the siege of Charleston, an 8-inch, 200-pounder Parrott siege gun fired 35 rounds in two days. It exploded upon firing the 36th round.

The Confederates had to import most of their rifled cannons, but they also built their own rifled guns by rifling the barrels of smoothbore 32-pounders. This increased their range and accuracy and allowed the modified cannons to fire much larger elongated rifled projectiles. The Confederates also developed their own version of the Parrott rifle, the Brooke rifle. It was similar to the Parrott gun, with a cast-iron barrel

The Parrott rifle christened the Swamp Angel was sited on Morris Island at the entrance to Charleston Harbor. It was capable of firing a 200-pound projectile the 7900 yards to the heart of Charleston. On the last discharge, the gun burst, the breech being blown out of its jacket, below. The physical damage to Charleston was minimal, and its citizens remained defiant.

reinforced by single, double, or triple wrought-iron bands shrunk around the breech. While effective against wooden Union warships, it had problems, mainly caused by poor manufacturing.

The attack on Fort Fisher in late December 1864 was a classic example of the problems of rifled cannons. Two 7-inch Confederate Brooke rifles burst at the breech, decimating their crews. On the Union side, bursting 100-pound Parrott rifles caused more casualties than Confederate return fire.

The English guns, all superior to the Parrott, made up a large part of the Confederate big-gun inventory. The 8-inch English Blakelys were imported for use in the coastal defenses in South Carolina. The Blakely's barrel was cast iron strengthened with steel, and was effective when used with English ammunition. Its performance deteriorated when firing shells of Confederate manufacture.

The Armstrong rifle looked like a collapsible telescope. It was a very effective gun and was made in both muzzle-loading and breech-loading models. Whitworth rifles were also used in various sizes, and were unique in firing a hexagonal bolt that produced a distinctive whistle in flight.

Mortars

Mortars were short, stubby smoothbore pieces used for lobbing shells into the air at a high angle, to drop inside a protected target. They were solid and reliable weapons with virtually no tendency to burst. As with other heavy artillery, mortars were classed as siege and seacoast. Siege mortars were light enough to be transported by an army on the march and used from trenches during sieges and to defend fortifications. The Model 1841 8- and 10-inch siege models were much heavier mortars than the light Coehorn mortars carried by infantry, so they had to be transported on mortar wagons. In 1861 they were augmented by the large 10- and even more massive 13-inch mortars, and these longer and heavier models were classified as seacoast because they were so difficult to move. They were usually mounted on the decks of ships, on special barges, or on railroad flatcars.

Mortars typically used spherical shells with both timed and percussion fuses. They were extremely effective in a siege, especially when normal guns, with their flatter trajectory, could not penetrate the defensive works. They were especially helpful late in the war in the siege of Petersburg, when the Union

The 13-inch seacoast mortar weighed over 17,000 pounds and was made portable by being mounted on a railroad car, specially strengthened with extra beams and iron rods to withstand the strain of firing. The mortar threw a 218-pound shell about 2 1/2 miles with a charge of 20 pounds of powder.

Battery Rodgers was constructed to guard the southern approaches to the U.S. capital. The fort boasted two 15-inch Rodmans, each weighing in at 25 tons. Forty pounds of powder could send a 440-pound round shot over 5000 yards. The Rodmans could do major damage to a wooden sailing ship of war, and at close range even the ironclads were not safe from these massive weapons.

crews began to use timed fuses to explode mortar rounds loaded with canister over Confederate artillery and infantry positions.

The most famous mortar used during the war was the Dictator, a 13-inch Model 1861 seacoast mortar weighing over 17,000 pounds. It was used at the siege of Petersburg in 1864, mounted on a specially reinforced railroad car. It could fire a 220-pound projectile 4325 yards at a 45-degree elevation, and could crush a Confederate bunker. The 13-inch mortars were also widely used in mortar boats on the Mississippi River.

Columbiads

The largest guns of the war were the Columbiads—huge, heavy, large-caliber iron smoothbores with a distinctive "soda bottle" appearance. The Columbiad was an attempt to produce a versatile weapon that combined the characteristics of both high trajectory and flat trajectory weapons. They were virtually always classified as seacoast weapons because of their size.

Columbiads were not considered important until the late 1850s, when Lieutenant Thomas J. Rodman of the U.S. Ordnance Department produced a prototype Columbiad using a special casting method he had developed. Rodman had been traumatized in 1844 when he saw the U.S. Secretary of State, the Secretary of the Navy, a Congressman, and two others killed aboard the U.S.S. *Princeton* when a 12-inch gun exploded during a routine demonstration, and he was deter-mined to improve the strength of the cannon barrel. He knew that the normal method of casting large iron cannons began at the outer surface and progressed toward the interior, leaving the finished gun vulnerable to pressure from the inside when the gun was fired. Rodman left the gun hollow on the inside when he cast it, and then ran water into the barrel as it cooled. This made the gun cool from the inside out, giving it greater strength and making it less likely to develop cracks or explode. Rodman's process made it possible to build very reliable large-bore cannons. During the Civil War, Rodmans, as they were called, were the largest cannons in the U.S. arsenal, produced in 8-, 10-, 12-, 13-, and 15-inch models. Even two 20-inch guns were made. They were primarily smooth-bore, though a few rifled models were produced.

A 10-inch Rodman Columbiad was about 10 feet long, 2 1/2 feet in diameter, and weighed about 16,000 pounds. It could fire a 10-inch, 128-pound cannonball over three miles. A 15-incher could fire a 300-pound cannonball almost three miles at high elevation, and a 428-pound shell almost four miles firing at lower elevation. They were never intended to be mobile, and were mounted in open earth or masonry forts on special wrought-iron mounts. The government purchased 322 of the Model 1861 15-inch Rodman Columbiads between 1861 and 1871, and the huge pieces became the primary weapon of American coastal defense for over 30 years.

The Battle of Kennesaw Mountain

In May 1864, Union general William Tecumseh Sherman began the campaign that would eventually become his famous—or notorious—March to the Sea. Sherman's 100,000 men outnumbered the forces of his Confederate counterpart, General Joseph E. Johnston, by almost two to one. In order to offset Sherman's numerical superiority, Johnston's troops were forced to dig fixed positions; but each time they did so, Sherman outflanked them. Sherman's only frontal assault during his advance, which roughly followed the Western & Atlantic railroad line through Georgia toward Atlanta, took place at the battle of Kennesaw Mountain—one of the worst Union defeats during this campaign.

For over a month, Johnston and Sherman danced around one another—Johnston's forces entrenched themselves, and Sherman took his troops around—until, in mid-June, Johnston dug in on a string of peaks north and west of Atlanta, just west of the town of Marietta, Georgia. Johnston's defense line stretched unbroken for 12 miles, from the 691-foot Kennesaw Mountain in the north to three smaller rises in the south—Little Kennesaw, Pigeon Hill, and a southernmost rise that later became known as Cheatham Hill. The Confederate artillerymen placed cannons on and between the high points, while the infantry dug trenches and cut down trees to strengthen the line.

Sherman's Frontal Assault

During Sherman's operations around Kennesaw Mountain, the weather conspired against him. It rained almost continuously, making Johnston's task of entrenching easier while hindering Sherman's ability to maneuver along the muddy roads. The creeks overflowed their banks and turned what were already narrow paths through the woods into slippery, muddy quagmires that promised to make a frontal attack—if necessary—even more onerous than usual.

Confronted by the weather and Johnston's formidable defenses, Sherman made one last attempt to outflank the Confederate forces and

William Tecumseh Sherman

William T. Sherman was one of the most famous generals in United States history. He was also one of the most reviled figures ever in Georgia for his 1864 March to the Sea, which culminated in the fall of Savannah and cut the Confederacy in half, directly leading to the end of the Civil War.

While Sherman's early military career and subsequent business ventures were undistinguished, his record after returning to the armed services in 1861 was more noteworthy. He impressed Ulysses S. Grant with his solid performance at Shiloh, leading to a long-lasting alliance between the two. In 1869, then-president Grant promoted Sherman to General in Chief.

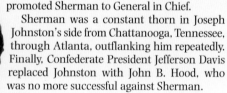

Sherman was a constant thorn in Joseph Johnston's side from Chattanooga, Tennessee, through Atlanta, outflanking him repeatedly. Finally, Confederate President Jefferson Davis replaced Johnston with John B. Hood, who was no more successful against Sherman.

Sherman's strategic use of psychological warfare in his March to the Sea is the primary reason for his ruthless reputation, but he believed that targeting supplies and property was the most expedient way to end the war with the loss of the fewest lives. He disproved his reputation for callousness both by agreeing to lenient surrender terms from Johnston and by urging mild Reconstruction terms after the war.

The Federal entrenchments *at the foot of Kennesaw Mountain. Sherman later recalled, "The summits were crowned with batteries, and the spurs were alive with men busy in felling trees, digging pits, and preparing for the grand struggle impending."*

cut Johnston off. But Sherman's maneuvers were easily visible from the Kennesaw peaks, and the Union probes were unsuccessful after a skirmish at Kolb's Farm.

Feeling pressure to advance quickly, both from his immediate superior, General Ulysses S. Grant, and from President Abraham Lincoln, Sherman decided against more flanking movements. Still pounded by rain, on June 24 Sherman ordered a frontal assault on the Confederate lines to begin on June 27.

Sherman planned to send out two diversionary forces against Johnston—General John McPherson's Army of the Tennessee to the north and General John Schofield's Army of the Ohio to the south. But the main thrust was to be made by General George Thomas's Army of the Cumberland directly up the middle, into the teeth of the Confederate defenses. One corps, led by General John Logan, would attack south of Kennesaw Mountain between Little Kennesaw and Pigeon Hill, while a larger force would attack the southernmost rise. Confederate lines took an angle at this point, making it vulnerable to attack from two sides. Meanwhile, the rain continued, so the Union forces were unable to carefully reconnoiter the Confederate positions.

The rain had stopped the morning of June 27, but the ground was still very muddy on what Confederate survivor Sam Watkins recalled as "one of the hottest and longest days of the year." Union cannons unleashed a 15-minute artillery barrage from over 200 guns at eight a.m.; and 15 minutes later, as scheduled, Logan began his attack on Pigeon Hill. The attack was three pronged, and some of the attacks made small gains, but none moved the Confederate line.

An hour later, at nine a.m., two more Union divisions began the main assault on the southernmost rise. The 8000 men spread across a front less than a mile wide, with some of the Union units moving in tight formation as they fought their way through the underbrush.

Hidden cannons and well-protected firing positions full of Confederate soldiers cut the Union infantry to pieces, and soon most of the attackers were pinned down. The rise was later named Cheatham Hill after the Confederate general, Benjamin Cheatham, who defended it.

While Union forces tried to attack the vulnerable angle, they were stopped short. In less than two hours, the Union units lost more than 1000 men, mostly from Illinois and Ohio, while the Confederates lost only one third as many. Both sides would later name the spot the Dead Angle because so many men were killed there, including Union

After days of artillery barrages, Sherman was frustrated with the slow progress of his armies and attempted a frontal assault on Johnston's positions, hoping to crush the Confederate center. By noon, the Federal army had lost 3000, including seven regimental and two brigade commanders, while the Confederates had lost only 800.

colonel Daniel McCook, who died later from his wounds sustained there. However, the Confederate lines had been set back too far off a rise in the ground, leaving a blind spot that could not be reached by defensive fire. Some of the Union soldiers made it to this safe area and took cover less than 100 feet below the Confederate lines. Using whatever entrenching tools they had, including their tin mess cups, they began to dig in.

By noon Sherman realized that the battle was over, for all practical purposes, and he had been defeated. He had lost about 3000 men while the Confederates lost only about 800, many from forward units overwhelmed at the beginning of the attack. Even though there were still Union troops taking cover in the blind spot, Sherman began to plan his next move.

A Standoff and Resolution

That night, Union soldiers in the blind spot began to deeply entrench themselves using shovels and other tools brought to them under cover of darkness. It was a bizarre situation—even though the two opposing forces were within yards of each other, each was so well dug in that any attack on the other brought the

prospect of fearful casualties. There was a brief truce two days later, on the 29th, to remove the dead, and then the stalemate continued. Meanwhile, Union soldiers began to tunnel under the Confederate works, intending to plant explosives that would blow the defenses open. The blast was set, appropriately, for July 4.

It was not to be. With dry weather finally arriving, Sherman reverted to his flanking maneuvers, sending his troops south on July 1. Johnston was forced to abandon the Kennesaw Mountain defenses, and moved to block the Union forces. On July 2, the Confederates quietly evacuated Cheatham Hill, leaving the Union soldiers with a partially completed tunnel. The dance began anew, but Sherman would never again attempt a frontal assault on a prepared position.

Kennesaw Mountain National Battlefield Park

In 1899, an agent for a veterans group, the Kennesaw Memorial Association, purchased a small tract of land near the Dead Angle to build a memorial honoring the 500 men from Illinois lost there. The Illinois Monument was completed in 1914,

the 1930s, a Civilian Conservation Corps (CCC) camp was established near Big Kennesaw and workers from this camp made many improvements, including the 2-, 5-, 10-, and 16-mile (round-trip) hiking trails they built over the entire length of the park.

Visitors can reach the battlefield sites at Pigeon Hill, Cheatham Hill, and Kolb's Farm (where the Union forces were repulsed during their last flanking maneuver before resorting to the failed frontal assault) by hiking or driving. The newly renovated Visitors Center includes a historical museum, which is unique because virtually all the displays—uniforms, small arms, cannons, and other items—have a direct connection to the campaign. Maps of the park locating the battle-field sites are available at the front desk. Every half hour there is a 20-minute film presenting an overview of the battle. The gift shop has a number of books on the battle, the Atlanta Campaign, and the Civil War, as well as a wide selection of Civil War prints by Alfred R. Waud and Thure de Thulstrup.

The most popular trail, which may be hiked or driven, starts next to

and some of the survivors attended the dedication. In 1917, the War Department took over management of the land and expanded the park to today's almost 2900 acres. During

---

Joseph Eggleston Johnston

Joe Johnston was well liked by his men and was arguably one of the Confederacy's ablest generals, yet his military philosophy and lack of humility was not appreciated by his superiors.

Johnston was the most senior officer to resign from the U.S. Army to serve the Confederacy; but due to a technicality, he was considered fourth in seniority by Confederate President Jefferson Davis—the start of Johnston's pique with Davis and their mutual lack of trust.

As commander of the Army of the Valley, Johnston's insight into the Union strategy at First Bull Run (Manassas) was instrumental in the Confederacy's victory, though he didn't receive popular recognition for his role there. After a disappointing result on the Virginia Peninsula, an injury forced Johnston to relinquish his command to Robert E. Lee.

By December 1863, Johnston had regained a command—of the Army of the Tennessee—and William T. Sherman began a long series of engagements and flanking maneuvers against him. Strategically, Johnston believed that he was better off with Sherman on the offensive because he would lose proportionally more troops than the Confederates did. While this plan may have been working, Davis lost patience and in July 1864 replaced Johnston with John Bell Hood.

Back in control of the Army of the Tennessee, Johnston surrendered to Sherman on April 26, 1865. Ironically, 26 years later Johnston died from a cold he caught at Sherman's funeral.

the Visitors Center and goes up to the top of Kennesaw Mountain. On the right-hand side of the road near the Visitors Center is the Georgia Monument, dedicated to all Georgians who fought in the war. Along the trail are entrenchments and views of the Kennesaw-area battlefield to the west and Atlanta to the east. There is a parking lot at the top, and from there a hiking trail runs about 150 yards to the summit of Kennesaw Mountain. The summit provides fine views of Atlanta and the surrounding area. One of the more interesting sites is the Western & Atlantic Railroad, which still runs just below the northern side of the mountain.

While touring the main battle sites, the visitor may be struck by the dense underbrush and thick trees and wonder how the soldiers could see well enough to fight. In fact, the ecology of the area has changed and the vegetation is much thicker today than it was at the time of the battle. In addition, soldiers cleared many trees to improve their field of fire, and exploding cannon shells leveled the ground further.

Moving south from the Visitors Center, the first battle site is Pigeon Hill, named because it was a rest stop for migrating passenger pigeons. A fairly steep but short foot trail runs up the side of the hill to a series of trenches from the battle, and there are many fine views to the west from the trail.

Farther south is a larger site that encompasses Cheatham Hill and the Dead Angle, where the most intense fighting took place. A well-marked turnoff leads to a parking area. On the road to the parking is the granite Texas Monument, dedicated to Texans who fought at Kennesaw Mountain, as well as a plaque describing the actions of a Confederate colonel from Arkansas who allowed Union soldiers to rescue their wounded from a fire caused by the fighting. From the parking lot, the visitor can follow the Cheatham Hill Loop Trail, which is well marked with signs, markers, and monuments. On the trail are parts of the interlocking defenses with an explanation of the design of the fortifications. Other highlights include the large Illinois Monument that was the genesis of the park, an embankment of cannon, and the grave of a soldier who died during the battle. Perhaps the most interesting spot is the Dead Angle, where the Union

and Confederate soldiers spent seven days separated by only a few hundred feet. The visitor can clearly see how the two sides were shielded by the curvature of the hill. Nearby is the Tunnel Monument that marks the spot where Federal soldiers tried to burrow under the entrenched Confederates and blow up the fortifications. Up the hill is a granite monument to Sherman's law colleague, Union general Daniel McCook, who was promoted from colonel just before his death after the battle at the Dead Angle.

The southernmost site is Kolb's Farm, where the first part of the battle was fought. The farmhouse was built in 1836 and is the only building within the park boundary from the time of the battle. It has been restored to its battlefield appearance and offers a fine view of the terrain to the west where the initial clashes took place.

There is a designated picnic area at the Visitors Center, and another on Cheatham Hill Road. Camping is not permitted in the park.

Visitor Information

770-427-4686;
www.nps.gov/kemo/

Hours: The Visitors Center is open daily, 8:30 a.m. until 5 p.m.; closed December 25. Seasonal hours for the park are posted, as are opening and closing times for the tour sites.

Admission: No charge.

Accessibility: The Visitors Center is fully accessible.

Special Events: In the summer, Civil War reenactors and park officials give living-history demonstrations.

Getting There: Kennesaw Mountain National Battlefield Park is about a 30-minute drive from Atlanta.

From I-75, take exit 269 and drive 2.1 miles west on Barrett Parkway. Turn left onto Old 41 Highway and go 1.2 miles to Stilesboro Road (the first traffic light after entering the well-marked park boundary). Turn right on Stilesboro Road, then left onto Kennesaw Mountain Drive. The Visitors Center is clearly visible on the left.

Private vehicles are allowed on the road to the summit next to the Visitors Center only on weekdays. On weekends there is a shuttle bus that regularly leaves for the summit.

Nearly 225 feet long and 54 feet wide, the C.S.S. Jackson was one of the largest of the ironclads built in the South. It burned to the waterline when nearly complete.

The National Civil War Naval Museum and Port Columbus Civil War Naval Center

Many modern techniques enhance visitors' experiences at the National Civil War Naval Museum, which was completed in 2001. The first exhibit is the most spectacular—a "ghost model" of the 225-foot Confederate ironclad C.S.S. *Jackson*. The white metal frame outline stands over the hulk of the massive *Jackson*, one of the largest of the Confederate ironclads. This gallery's specially designed lighting simulates underwater light and lends to the "ghostly" effect. The *Jackson* was under construction in the Columbus Naval Shipyard in 1865 when the Union forces arrived. They torched the ship and set it adrift in the Columbus River, where it floated downstream, burning until it sank. In the early 1960s, the hulk was recovered, and it forms the basis for this exhibit. The *Jackson*, like most Confederate ironclads, resembles the famous C.S.S. *Virginia (Merrimack)*, and this display gives a feeling for the size of that vessel.

Other artifacts in the museum include part of the hulk of the C.S.S. *Chattahoochee*, a Confederate gunboat scuttled in the Columbus River; a hull plate from the U.S.S. *Monitor* recovered in the Atlantic off the coast of North Carolina; and a huge flag from the C.S.S. *Arkansas*, taken by a Union sailor during a futile attack on the Confederate warship. A replica of part of Union admiral David Farragut's flagship, the U.S.S. *Hartford*, provides a display of living conditions on period warships. There is also a full-scale replica of the U.S.S. *Monitor*'s gun turret.

Another innovative exhibit is the full-size interior of

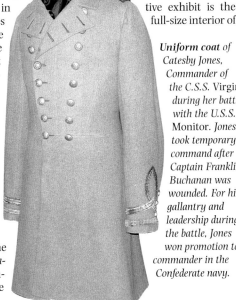

Uniform coat of Catesby Jones, Commander of the C.S.S. Virginia *during her battle with the U.S.S.* Monitor. *Jones took temporary command after Captain Franklin Buchanan was wounded. For his gallantry and leadership during the battle, Jones won promotion to commander in the Confederate navy.*

Commissioned in 1864, the C.S.S. Albemarle, *right, was 122 feet long, covered by two layers of 2-inch iron plating and armed with two 8-inch guns, one forward, the other aft, behind iron shutters. On the night of October 27 she was attacked by a Federal spar-torpedo boat that made "a hole in her bottom big enough to drive a wagon in." Following the Union recapture of the town, the* Albemarle *was refloated.*

the C.S.S. *Albemarle*, including the gun layout and pilothouse. This exhibit also contains an "ironclad simulator," which provides an absorbing audiovisual crew's-eye view of a naval battle, complete with sound effects. The display clearly shows how little a gun crew could see out of their gun ports, and leaves the visitor wondering what it would have been like in such a ship during combat, with shells bursting all around but little sense of how the overall battle was progressing.

In addition to the large artifacts and exhibits, there are several interesting wall displays. An extensive timeline takes the visitor through the naval history of the Civil War and is illustrated by many smaller artifacts, including the uniform of Catesby Jones, the commander of the C.S.S. *Virginia (Merrimack)* during its historic battle with the U.S.S. *Monitor.* Of special note are the three spectacular wall murals in the center gallery depicting all types of Confederate and Union combat vessels, including submersibles and balloon carriers. The left mural shows the river warships, the center mural the ships that fought the coastal battles, and the right mural oceangoing ships, including blockade runners.

A three-minute audiovisual presentation begins the self-guided tours through the museum. The museum's gift shop specializes in Civil War naval history books.

Visitor Information
706-327-9798;
www.portcolumbus.org
Hours: Daily, 9 a.m. until 5 p.m.; closed December 25.
Special Events: During the summer, the museum offers living-history programs and throughout the year offers a variety of speakers, including a Civil War Naval Archaeology Lecture Series. The museum's quarterly newsletter highlights upcoming events.
Admission: There is a minimal charge for adults, with discounts for students, seniors, and active-duty military personnel.
Accessibility: Handicapped accessible, with one wheelchair and one motorized scooter available to borrow.
Getting There: The museum is located in Columbus, Georgia, about 123 miles south of Atlanta. The square, reddish colored building is clearly visible from Victory Drive (U.S. highways 27 and 280). There is ample free parking.

The Battle of Pickett's Mill

In mid-May of 1864, during the push toward Atlanta, Union commander William T. Sherman left his main supply route, the Western & Atlantic Railroad, and moved south to try to turn the Confederate line. Sherman ordered General George H. Thomas, commanding the Army of the Cumberland, to outflank the Confederate army under General Joseph E. Johnston. In turn, Thomas selected General Oliver O. Howard's 4th Army Corps to lead the move on the Confederate right flank.

However, Johnston learned of this maneuver and shifted his troops' location. One of his divisions, commanded by Major General Patrick R. Cleburne, positioned itself on a hilltop overlooking Benjamin and Malachi Pickett's farm and gristmill, a small settlement known as Pickett's Mill.

Howard's 14,000 Union soldiers started moving west early in the morning of May 27. After a five-hour march through dense woods, Howard decided to attack what appeared to be the flank or rear of the Confederate line at Pickett's Mill. The message he sent to Thomas at about 3:30 p.m. said, "I am now turning the enemy's right flank, I think."

He was mistaken. Howard was looking at a point in the Confederate line where it turned and bent back, following the ridgeline overlooking a steep, overgrown ravine. On the ridgeline, Cleburne's 10,000 seasoned veterans were positioned in two lines, the first behind earthworks and the second line held back in reserve. The earthworks were along the edge of a large, deep ravine. On one side of it, Cleburne placed 12-pounder howitzers that could fire in front of his line of trenches. To reach this position, Union troops would have to cross the ravine and climb up, all the while in clear view and under fire from above and from one side by Confederate infantry and cannons.

Howard formed his three infantry brigades in columns, one behind the other, to penetrate the dense underbrush. His leading brigade commander, Brigadier General William B. Hazen, knew the attack was a "criminal blunder," but said nothing. As soon as the troops began to move, serious problems developed. One unit failed to show up, and the others found it extremely difficult to maneuver in the tangled underbrush. One of Hazen's officers

recalled the move as "a swarm of men struggling through the undergrowth of the forest, pushing and crowding."

Initially, Hazen's brigade drove away the Confederate pickets and dismounted cavalry, then pushed across the open ground upward to what they thought was an undefended ridgeline. As they moved into the ravine, the Confederates stood up behind their fortified line and began firing point blank. At the same time, the two Confederate cannons, loaded with canister and grapeshot, bombarded the mass of troops. The Union soldiers were quickly jammed together; they had no artillery support, and the ravine became a charnel house. Hazen's men tried to push up the sides of the ridge, but finally were forced to retreat after suffering about 500 casualties in the open ravine.

Meanwhile, the Confederates repositioned two more brigades to the far right of the line to prevent any possibility of being outflanked. At six p.m., Union general Thomas J. Wood ordered a second attack by Colonel William H. Gibson's brigade over nearly the same ground. Gibson's brigade lasted about 45 minutes and took almost 700 additional casualties.

At ten p.m., when the Union attacks had ended, the Confederates, with fixed bayonets, moved to sweep out the Union soldiers in front of their positions. The charge forward killed or captured many of the remaining Union troops in the ravine, while the rest quickly withdrew. By the end of the battle, the Union had lost 1600 men, the Confederates about 500. One of Hazen's staff bitterly noted after the war, "[The battle] is ignored by General Sherman in his memoirs, yet Sherman ordered it. General Howard wrote an account of the campaign of which it was an incident, and dismissed it in a single sentence."

The following day, May 28, 1864, Sherman realized that he had to return to the railroad to supply his army. He ordered a gradual shifting motion of the line back eastward to the railroad, and prepared for his next move, on Marietta.

Pickett's Mill State Historic Site

The Pickett's Mill Battlefield historic site consists of 765 acres in north-

Reenactors participating in the annual battle commemoration adhere to site rules prescribing the appropriate dress, armament, and behavior—all intended to enhance a visitor's experience.

ern Georgia. It is one of the best preserved Civil War battlefields in the nation, and is much the same today as it was on the day of the battle.

The park opened in May 1990, on the 125th anniversary of the Battle of Pickett's Mill. Today the park features a Visitors Center with a 15-minute video presentation on the battle, as well as an extensive interactive museum on the Atlanta campaign, including a computer game allowing the visitor to refight the battle. There are three color-coded walking tours highlighting the areas of major engagements. Free maps are available at the Visitors Center.

Visitor Information

770-443-7850;
www.ngeorgia.com/parks/
picketts.html

Hours: Tuesday through Friday, 9 a.m. until 5 p.m.; Sundays, 12 p.m. until 5 p.m.; closed national holidays.
Admission: Minimal charge for adults; discounted admission for seniors and children ages 6 to 18.
Accessibility: The park is handicapped accessible.
Special Events: The anniversary of the battle in late May is commemorated with a living-history weekend. There are candlelight tours where volunteers recreate the battle. The guided tours include several reenactments. There is also an annual Dallas Line Ghost Walk, usually in late May or early June. Call for details.
Getting There: The Visitors Center is located at 4432 Mount Tabor Church Road in Dallas, Georgia.

From Atlanta, from I-75 north: Take exit 277 (Acworth). Turn left on state highway 92 south, and follow it for 11 miles. At the four-way stop, continue straight ahead; 92 becomes 381, the Dallas–Acworth Road. Follow it two miles, then turn left on Mount Tabor Church Road. The entrance is one mile farther on the left.

From Atlanta, from I-20: Take exit 44. Turn right onto Thornton Road West, which becomes 278. Follow it to state highway 92 in Hiram. Turn right onto 92 north and go six miles, then turn left on Due West Road. Turn right on Mount Tabor Road. The entrance is less than 1/2 mile on the right (watch for brown directional signs).

From Chattanooga or northern Georgia: Take I-75 south to exit 123. Turn right onto Red Top Mountain Road, which dead-ends at U.S. 41. Turn left onto 41 south and travel until the first traffic light. Make a right turn onto state highway 92 south for approximately five miles, to a four-way stop. Continue onto state highway 381 for two miles, then make a left turn onto Mount Tabor Church Road. The entrance is 1 1/2 miles on the left.

From Carrolton: Go north on state highway 61 through Villa Rica toward Dallas. Cross four-lane U.S. 278, go over an overpass and stop at a traffic light (Business 6). Turn left, go about one mile to Legion Drive (the first road on the right). Turn right, continue to the dead end, and then turn right onto Dallas–Acworth Road. After about four miles, turn right onto Mount Tabor Church Road. The entrance is 1 1/2 miles on the left.

Southern Museum of Civil War and Locomotive History

One of the most daring escapades of the Civil War took place on April 12, 1862, when Union special agent James J. Andrews and a group of 21 Union soldiers boarded a Confederate train in Marietta, Georgia. While the passengers and crew were eating breakfast in the Lacy Hotel in Big Shanty, Georgia (today called Kennesaw), Andrews and his men absconded with the train and its locomotive, the *General*. They cut the local telegraph wires so the stationmaster would not be able to send the news up the line, and then started northwest, intending to wreck the Western & Atlantic Railroad line between Atlanta and Chattanooga. By tearing up track, burning the bridges, and destroying tunnels, they hoped to choke off Confederate supplies to Chattanooga just as the Union army was planning to attack

(that attack actually took place late in 1863).

But the Confederate conductor of the *General*, William Fuller, and two members of his crew pursued their stolen train, first on foot, then by handcar, and finally in a locomotive they appropriated, the *Texas* (which today sits nearby in Atlanta's Cyclorama). Fuller had to drive the *Texas* in reverse, but he and his men followed Andrews so closely that the Union men never had time to stop and do major damage to the railroad line. Later that day, Fuller and a force of Confederate cavalry ran them aground, and all 22 of Andrews's men were captured. Eight men including Andrews were hanged, eight others escaped, and six were paroled. When Congress created the Congressional Medal of Honor, the first ones were presented to several of the raiders

The **General,** *now restored, was nearly destroyed in the Union razing of Atlanta. Top, a Congressional Medal of Honor awarded to John Scott, one of Andrews's Raiders. The medal was awarded posthumously, as Scott was hanged soon after the chase.*

Sherman neckties was the name given to the twisted steel rails left in the wake of William T. Sherman's destructive campaign through the Confederate south.

(but not Andrews—as a civilian, he was ineligible). The Medal of Honor given to John Scott is on display in the museum, one of the few existing examples of this early decoration.

For many years, the small Big Shanty Museum, later called the Kennesaw Civil War Museum, was home to the *General* and the Great Locomotive Chase artifacts. In the mid-1990s, the city of Kennesaw acquired the Glover Steam Locomotive Collection, and in 1998 the city decided to combine the Glover Collection with the *General.* The new Southern Museum of Civil War and Locomotive History was built around the old museum, and opened in the spring of 2003. The museum is a member of the Smithsonian Affiliations program, making it eligible to host traveling Smithsonian exhibits, bring in Smithsonian historians for lectures, and display Smithsonian artifacts in its permanent collections.

The overall focus of the museum is the vital role of railroads in the Civil War, the first war in which railroads were integral to the war effort. The railroad's contributions to war efforts are interpreted with photographs and artifacts. Also highlighted are the attempts by both sides to destroy the other's railroads. One exhibit features the preeminent example of this destruction, showing how Union forces heated the rails and then twisted them around a support into what was known as a Sherman necktie. Other exhibits include collections of a wide variety of weapons and personal items, including an interesting group of sniper, or sharpshooter, rifles.

The second part of the museum focuses on the Glover Machine Works, which played a significant role in industrializing the South after the Civil War. It includes a reproduction of the Glover factory, featuring original machining equipment and two restored Glover locomotives in the process of being assembled.

Past the Glover exhibit is the General Theater, which shows a 30-minute movie about the chase every half hour. From the theater, visitors can then see other exhibits devoted to the story of each of the raiders, pictures of the chase, and a room that displays the well-restored *General* itself, as well as a wide variety of popular culture artifacts celebrating the *General* and the events of the Great Locomotive Chase.

The daring April 12 chase even inspired two movies—*The Great Locomotive Chase* by Walt Disney in 1956 and Buster Keaton's 1927 movie, *The General.*

Visitor Information

770-427-2117;
www.thegeneral.org/index.html
Hours: Monday to Saturday, 9:30 a.m. until 5 p.m.; Sunday, noon until 5 p.m.; closed Easter, Thanksgiving, December 25, and New Year's Day.
Admission: Moderate charge for adults and children 6 to 12; free for children 5 and under.
Special Events: As a Smithsonian Affiliate, the museum hosts a variety of traveling exhibitions; call for details.
Accessibility: The museum and exhibits are fully accessible.
Getting There: Kennesaw is located about 30 minutes from downtown Atlanta, 45 minutes from Hartsfield Atlanta International Airport, and 10 minutes from Marietta, Georgia.

From I-75 northbound or I-575 northbound or southbound: Take the Chastain Road exit (#271 on I-75 or #3 on I-575) and go west (Chastain Road will become McCollum Parkway). Pass the airport and turn right on South Main Street, then make a right on Sardis. The museum parking lot is on the left.

From I-75 southbound: Take the Wade Green Road exit (#273) and make a right. Wade Green Road will turn into Cherokee Street, and the museum is on the right just before the railroad tracks.

From U.S. 41: Turn on Watts Drive going east. Turn left on Main Street, then right on Cherokee Street. The museum is on the left.

Fort Scott

In the early 1850s, the frontier military post of Fort Scott, Kansas, was abandoned, but a town of the same name had grown in its place. While most residents of the town were proslavery, many "Free-Soilers" lived on its outskirts, and occasional clashes between the sides erupted during the political turmoil of the late 1850s popularly referred to as Bleeding Kansas. At this time, the Kansas Territory was focused on whether the future state would become a free or a slave state; and since that was to be decided by "popular sovereignty," people from both sides of the issue inundated the land, establishing residency there so they could vote on the issue. The town of Fort Scott eventually became neutral territory for both sides, and the site of the former fort embodied this coexistence—inside the fort in a former officers quarters was the Free-State Hotel, while across the parade ground a former infantry barracks served as the "Western" or Pro-Slavery Hotel. From time to time, violence brought the army back to restore order, until Kansas entered the Union as a free state in 1861.

At the outset of the Civil War, the Union army returned to Fort Scott and made it into a major logistical center for troops operating in the West. They expanded the fort into a huge facility—the largest in the state south of Fort Leavenworth—with a hospital, a military prison that housed Confederate prisoners of war and some of the many Southern sympathizers in the area,

and a training ground. During battles in Kansas and Missouri, or outbreaks of disease, there were so many patients in the fort's hospital that they overflowed into other buildings and even tents. Those that died were buried two miles away in the National Cemetery. The major supply depot also constructed there was crucial to the success of the Union campaigns in the region. It issued all rations, feed, horses, wagons, blankets, and equipment for troops in the surrounding areas.

Fort Scott was a tempting target to Confederate armies, and Confederate guerrillas constantly harassed the supply lines; but even though Confederate forces passed close to Fort Scott several times, it was never attacked. The forces assigned to protect the fort included several pathbreaking regiments—the 1st and 2nd Kansas Colored Volunteer Infantry regiments, the first African American troops from a Northern state; as well as the 1st, 2nd, and 3rd Indian Home Guards, the largest concentration of American Indians to serve in the U.S. Army during the Civil War. The fort was also the base for local Kansas regiments, as well as a temporary base for other units on their way to campaigns in Missouri, Arkansas, and the Indian Territory (now Oklahoma).

From the beginning of the war, Fort Scott provided a safe harbor for refugees. Initially, families fleeing the warfare in Missouri poured into Kansas and Fort Scott. Later, thousands of homeless people passed through from Arkansas and the Indian Territory. These included

Cavalry reenactors on parade. Troopers could cover some 35 miles in an eight-hour day under good conditions.

Troopers line up in formation on the parade ground. Military ceremonial functions including reviews, dress parades, band concerts, changing of the guards, and posting the colors for reveille and retreat were held on the parade ground.

hundreds of free blacks, escaped slaves, Indians, and pro-Union settlers.

As with many army towns, relations between the town's residents and the military could be tense. When the citizens of the town were evacuated because of the approach of Confederate troops, there was some looting by the troops left behind. Later, townspeople lynched two Union soldiers accused of raping a young girl.

After the Civil War ended in April 1865, the U.S. Army was quick to leave. Within six months, most of the buildings had been auctioned off and the army began to close the hospital. The troops, who had never been enamored of Fort Scott's isolation and harsh climate, gratefully went home.

Fort Scott National Historic Site

The Visitors Center contains a bookstore and regularly shows a 12-minute audiovisual program describing the fort's history. Inside the fort, 11 historic buildings containing 33 historically furnished rooms are open to the public. The site also contains three museums: the Infantry Barracks Museum explains the site's history, the Dragoon Barracks Museum depicts the life of a soldier stationed at the fort, and the Wilson-Goodlander House details the fort's construction and development. There is also a five-acre restored tallgrass prairie at the site. Visiting the site takes about an hour.

Visitor Information

620-223-0310; www.nps.gov/fosc

Hours: April to October, daily, 8 a.m. until 5 p.m.; November to March, daily, 9 a.m. until 5 p.m.; closed Thanksgiving, December 25, and New Year's Day.

Admission: Minimal charge for seven-day pass, free for children 16 and under; National Parks Pass, Golden Eagle, Golden Age, and Golden Access are honored.

Accessibility: Parking, restrooms, and most first-floor rooms are accessible to those in wheelchairs. The audiovisual program is accessible and is closed-captioned. A photo book and video tour are available for the mobility impaired. A wheelchair is available at the Visitors Center for onsite use.

Special Events: There is a Civil War Encampment each April and living-history programs on Memorial Day and Labor Day weekends. There are special programs on Armed Forces Day; and "Good Ol' Days" in early June, and on July 4. The fort hosts an American Indian Heritage Weekend in September and a Frontier Candlelight Tour of the fort in early December (reservations for the candlelight tour go on sale the last Saturday of October).

Getting There: Fort Scott National Historic Site is located in downtown Fort Scott, Kansas, 90 miles south of Kansas City, 60 miles north of Joplin, Missouri, and four miles from the Kansas-Missouri border. U.S. Routes 69 and 54 intersect here. Approaches from all directions are clearly marked with highway signs.

Old Bardstown Village Civil War Museum of the Western Theater and Women of the Civil War Museum

Although Kentucky was a slave state, it did not secede during the Civil War (though it was allotted a star on the Confederate battle flag). Its citizens were split, and by the end of the war 40,000 Kentuckians had gone to fight for the Confederacy and 90,000 for the Union. Most of these soldiers fought in the region, and their experiences form the main focus of the Old Bardstown Village Civil War Museum. It concentrates on the Civil War in the West, especially in Kentucky, telling its history in geographic and chronological groupings.

The Civil War Museum of the Western Theater features a diorama of the action at the Battle of Perryville on October 8, 1862, which took place just a short distance from the museum, as well as exhibits of other Western battles such as Stones River and Vicksburg. On display is an excellent collection of officers' uniforms, both Confederate and Union, representing all branches of service, including both navies. Other artifacts include the flag of the 2nd Kentucky Cavalry, captured near New Lisbon, Ohio, during Confederate brigadier general John Hunt Morgan's raid.

Personal items exhibited include Union major general Alexander M. McCook's uniform from the Battle of Perryville, Confederate cavalry brigadier general Tom Harrison's equipment and Sharps carbine, the sword of Confederate brigadier general Lloyd Tilghman (killed in the Battle of Champion Hill), and Confederate brigadier general John C. Breckinridge's silver flask. There are numerous items used by all soldiers, including lap desks, shaving kits, and a button clamp used to protect uniforms while the soldier shined his brass buttons. The exhibit also features letters, diaries, and other materials from soldiers, telling their own stories.

The separate Cavalry Room houses a model of a cavalryman's horse loaded with his full kit, including canteen, rifle, pistol, sword, letter pouch, and sleeping blanket. A room devoted exclusively to artillery contains eight cannons, including a unique one-pounder smoothbore cannon used in combat by Mosby's Raiders. The small cannon was made at the Tredegar Iron Works in Richmond, Virginia, and could be taken apart and transported on horseback to give the Confederate riders extra "punch" in their attacks behind Union lines. Other weapons include a 3-inch Ordnance Rifle and Mountain Howitzers, one belonging to Eli Lilly's 18th Indiana artillery.

The medical collection includes two complete amputation kits, and the nearby music collection displays a variety of violins, fifes, piccolos, clarinets, and regimental drums, along with a drummer boy's boots and uniform jacket and a description of such children's lives in the army.

Next door, in the Wright Talbott House, is the Women of the Civil War Museum, the first museum dedicated to the full story of women's involvement in the Civil War. Through exhibits of period clothing, paintings, and personal artifacts, it describes women's roles, including plantation and factory workers, nurses, and spies, as well as the over 400 women known to have disguised themselves as men to become combat soldiers during the Civil War.

Visitor Information

502-349-0291;
www.bardstown.com/~civilwar/

Hours: March 1 to December 15, Monday to Saturday, 10 a.m. until 5 p.m.; Sunday, noon until 5 p.m.; December 16 to February, Saturday, 10 a.m. until 5 p.m.; Sunday, noon until 5 p.m.

Special Events: In early August, Bardstown hosts a Living History and Civil War Celebration, which includes competitions and drills between "Union" and "Confederate" forces. Soldiers in full uniforms and ladies in period costumes explain life at that time.

Getting There: The museum is located at 310 East Broadway, Bardstown, in central Kentucky (about 80 miles southwest of Lexington and 40 miles southeast of Louisville) east of I-65, just off the Bluegrass Parkway.

From Lexington: Take U.S. 60 to the Bluegrass Parkway. Continue on the Bluegrass to exit 25. Take a right at the exit and follow the road into Bardstown.

From Louisville: Take I-65 south to exit 112, and turn left at the exit. Follow this road about 16 miles into Bardstown.

The Confederate Museum

Also known as Memorial Hall, this New Orleans museum was created by the 56,000 Louisiana Confederate Civil War veterans and their families in 1891 as a repository for their Civil War memorabilia.

Louisiana was the sixth state to secede from the Union, although it had hoped to remain neutral in the event of a war, in large part because New Orleans was the South's largest and richest city and served as an international port. But when South Carolina seceded, secessionism took hold and Louisiana seceded too, on January 26, 1861. Memorial Hall displays include several artifacts from the era of secession, including a Louisiana secession badge, an original copy of the Louisiana Ordinance of Secession, photographs of soldiers and citizens, and uniforms and accoutrements used by militia soldiers at the outbreak of the war.

The museum's collection includes more than 125 original Southern battle flags including the flag of Dreux's Battalion, commanded by Colonel Charles Dreux, the first Louisianian killed in the war; uniforms of famous Confederate officers

Louisiana-born
General P.G.T. Beauregard's elegant frock coat was made in Charleston, site of his first victory for the Confederacy when he forced the surrender of Fort Sumter.

like generals P.G.T. Beauregard and Braxton Bragg; and Confederate swords made by Louisiana manufacturers Dufilho, Thomas Griswald, and Praedel; as well as an exhibit of rare Confederate firearms, including those made by LeMat, Cook & Brother, and Tarpley.

The visual arts section of the museum displays more than 500 rare photographic images, including tintypes, ambrotypes, daguerreotypes, cartes de visite (small portraits the size of business cards), and albumens, as well as thematic paintings by such Southern artists as William Buck, George Coulon, Ellsworth Woodward, Blanche Blanchard, and Achille Perelli.

In addition to the artifacts listed above, there are some unique displays. One is devoted to New Orleans's population of well-educated free African Americans, called "free people of color," which included many skilled artisans and professionals. On January 8, 1862, this free black community formed a regiment of Confederate soldiers called the Native Guard. Although racial prejudice and fear prevented their use in combat, they dug and manned the

The main hall *of the museum exhibits some of the 125 Southern battle flags in the collection. The seven-star national flag, far left, was adopted in March 1861 to represent the original seven states of secession. By the end of that year, the flag held 13 stars.*

various entrenchments around the city. When the Crescent City fell into Union hands in April 1862, many of these soldiers chose to reorganize and volunteer for the Union army. Union "Native Guard" soldiers from New Orleans were the first black troops to see major battle action in the Civil War, fighting heroically at the battle of Port Hudson. The exhibit shows rare photographs of these African Americans in Confederate uniforms as well as pictures of their Union commanders at Port Hudson and a Native Guard canteen.

There is a most interesting tension between two of the other exhibits—the Jefferson Davis Stage and the display devoted to Union general Benjamin Franklin Butler, known to New Orleanians as "Silver Spoons" or "Beast." The Davis Stage honors the President of the Confederacy, who died in New Orleans in 1889. Davis lay in state at Memorial Hall, and more than 60,000 people came to pay their respects before the body was moved to his burial site in Richmond. Davis's wife, Varina,

donated many of her family's belongings and mementos to Memorial Hall, and the exhibit includes Davis's evening clothes, top hat, cane, saddle, Bible, and a crown of thorns given to him by Pope Pius IX. It also houses the Mardi Gras jewels and dress of their daughter, Winnie, who was often referred to as the Daughter of the Confederacy because she was born during the Civil War.

General Butler's exhibit strikes an entirely different tone. Butler was sent to New Orleans to oversee the Union occupation of the city, and for the next eight months he governed the unruly city with such an iron hand that he became its most infamous and hated citizen. The legend of the "Beast" was created by Butler's Martial Law orders and General Orders, No. 28 (the infamous "woman order," which stated that any woman who insulted Federal troops would be treated as though she were an active prostitute); by the hanging of the Confederate activist William Mumford, who had defaced the U.S. flag; and by his alleged pilfering of the city's assets. The display—which contains a piece of the U.S. flag torn down by Mumford, a set of silver spoons allegedly stolen by Butler (thus his other nickname), and political cartoons of the general—reflects the city's disdain for him. It also houses a rare lithograph of Fleurs du Sud (Flowers of the South) artwork with an arrangement of strategically positioned flowers in the likeness of the first Confederate national flag. This popular work was an attempt by New Orleanians to covertly display their Confederate patriotism within their federally occupied city.

Allow about an hour and a half to complete a self-guided tour of the museum.

For researchers, 90,000 war-related documents from the veterans and their families are on permanent loan to Tulane University in Uptown New Orleans and are available for research purposes.

Visitor Information

504-523-4522;
www.confederatemuseum.com
Hours: Monday to Saturday, 10 a.m. until 4 p.m.; closed Sundays, Mardi Gras Day, July 4, Labor Day, Thanksgiving, December 24 and 25, and New Year's Day.

> **Head-Quarters, Department of the Gulf, New Orleans, May 15, 1862.**
>
> ## General Orders, No. 28.
>
> As the Officers and Soldiers of the United States have been subject to repeated insults from the women calling themselves ladies of New Orleans, in return for the most scrupulous non-interference and courtesy on our part, it is ordered that hereafter when any Female shall, by word, gesture, or movement, insult or show contempt for any officer or soldier of the United States, she shall be regarded and held liable to be treated as a woman of the town plying her avocation.
>
> By command of Maj.-Gen. BUTLER,
> GEORGE C. STRONG,
> A. A. G. Chief of Staff.

Benjamin Butler's infamous order issued to prevent the insults his soldiers endured from patriotic Confederate women.

Admission: Moderate charge for adults; minimal charge for children 12 and under.

Getting There: The Confederate Museum at 929 Camp Street in New Orleans is easily accessible from the St. Charles Avenue "street car" (trolley) which travels from Canal Street (with a stop next to the French Quarter) through the city. The museum's stop is Lee Circle, and Memorial Hall is almost next to the D-Day Museum in the New Orleans Warehouse District. It is nine blocks (a very long walk in New Orleans heat) from the French Quarter.

Note: At publication the museum is awaiting decision regarding a possible relocation of the museum's collection, so it's best to check the Web site for up-to-date information: www.confederatemuseum.com.

***Confederate cavalrymen** from Louisiana rarely had uniforms or specialized equipment. Accustomed to riding since youth, most were rugged farmers who knew nothing about military tactics but who possessed, as one general observed, "every quality but discipline."*

INFANTRY TACTICS

At the beginning of the Civil War, grand strategy was dominated by the idea, carried over from Napoleon's time, that a single battle could decide a war.

Many of the Civil War military commanders were veterans of the Mexican War; their experiences there shaped their thinking about infantry tactics. During that war, infantry fought with smoothbore muskets and bayonets, and victories were won by frontal assaults ending in bayonet charges. An advantage in numbers, even a modest one, was considered sufficient to assure victory to an able, aggressive commander. Additionally, U.S. troops were able to overcome Mexican fortifications with little difficulty and came out of the war with little faith in the ability of defensive entrenchments to stop determined, aggressive offensive action.

Tactics were based on moving massed formations of soldiers in good order to a place where they could fire and advance, and all the officers' experience and training were based on the shorter range of the smoothbores—about 50 yards. The safest way to attack a position held by infantry was to send cavalry forward to scout, then to march a large group of infantry to a point 100 yards in front of the defensive position. Artillery was moved up to a few hundred yards from the enemy position and the attackers, supported by artillery, would march forward in close-packed ranks. The defenders could not fire effectively until attackers came within 50 yards, and at that range, both sides exchanged volleys. The surviving attackers then finished the attack with a bayonet charge while the defenders reloaded. If enough attackers survived the opening volley to outnumber the defenders when they reached the defensive line, the defenders usually broke and ran rather than face the bayonet charge. (This was a common phenomenon, and most bayonet wounds were in the back.) Cavalry would then swoop down and, using sabers, attack the fleeing defenders and force a rout.

New Technology and Tactics
In the period between the Mexican War and the Civil War, technical revolutions in infantry war—the rifled musket and the minié ball—increased the range and accuracy of the infantry musket, and changed how wars would be fought.

Therefore, the previous experience of officers and the soldiers' training based on the shorter range of the smoothbores were useless. From 1850 on, many tacticians recognized the problem presented by the rifled musket, called it "crossing the deadly ground," and tried to solve it. Some military professionals also realized that the rifled musket would be a tremendous asset to entrenched troops and might change the balance of the offense and defense.

However, there were no obvious answers to the problems the new weapon presented. Technology had stepped ahead of the tactics and experience of the officers of both sides, and they were slow to catch up. Once the Civil War began, battles were fought with new weapons but old tactics.

The training of both Union and Confederate soldiers showed the commanders' lack of understanding of the new battlefield. The armies on both sides emphasized marching in closed, disciplined formation. Infantry units drilled in complicated maneuvers that would ultimately lead to a frontal attack, in loading quickly and firing on command, and in bayonet training. The armies never seemed to realize the importance of training to provide aimed, accurate fire. Very little time was spent on target practice, which would have been much more useful than close-order drill.

The rifled musket also changed the roles of artillery and cavalry. In Mexico, artillery outranged the smoothbore muskets and could move close to the battle line to support an attack. Now artillery crews (and the horses they used to move their pieces) were vulnerable to long-range rifle fire, so they could not move forward close to the defensive positions and support an attack. At the same time, defenders' artillery could be dug in and protected against musket fire, so artillery became very effective in the defensive role, especially firing canister at short range—adding to the problems of the frontal attack.

The rifled muskets also circumscribed the cavalry's battlefield actions against infantry. Riders and horses were large, easy targets and could no longer approach the enemy's front lines in a scouting role. After a victory, they could not come crashing down on retreating troops as they had in the past, because the rifled

INFANTRY TACTICS *(continued)*

musket could pick them off at long range.

Despite the emphasis on offense, successful offensive actions were extremely difficult in the Civil War. Maneuvering large formations of troops required training and discipline, which was severely lacking early in the war. The problem was not only with the troops. The officers on both sides were not trained to command large numbers of men, to anticipate the unexpected, and to react to the increased strength of the defense. Commanders resorted to frontal engagements in part because of the difficulties of maneuvering undisciplined troops. Inexperienced troops also had to be kept close together so they could hear their commander's orders, and these close formations made fine targets for rifled muskets.

Most Civil War frontal assaults failed; they might create a breach, but rarely was a successful assault exploited. This required that enough troops be available to follow and exploit the breakthrough; but due to communication failures, command problems, or simply not expecting a breakthrough, extra troops usually could not be moved to where they were needed. Even when a successful assault overwhelmed the defending line and forced some units to retreat, the sheer size of armies, and the impact of long-range weapons ruled

out the possibility of destroying the enemy army in just one battle. In the end, the Civil War was decided not by one victory but by a series of them.

At First Bull Run (Manassas) and Antietam, soldiers on both sides carried out face-to-face standing firefights, but as the war progressed, there was increased reliance on field fortifications. Under threat of attack, infantry quickly dug in and erected light field fortifications—trees, earth, and rocks—to strengthen their defensive positions. The advantage quickly moved to the defense, and soon it became clear that for an attack to succeed against an entrenched enemy, at least a three-to-one numerical advantage was needed. Nevertheless, commanders spent much of the war ignoring this, and frontal attacks continued.

Gradually the situation changed. By 1864, the field armies were made up of experienced officers and disciplined troops able to conduct large-unit maneuvers. Both sides began to move their infantry to seize key points or to attack the flanks of the enemy instead of using costly head-on attacks. William T. Sherman advanced to Atlanta and beyond using flanking maneuvers, and Ulysses S. Grant used them at times during his advance toward Richmond and later Petersburg.

Once a battle was under way, the front lines took casualties, which slowed down the following troops. This brought confusion to the attack and allowed entrenched defenders to inflict further damage.

Organization

The commanding general of a Civil War field army concentrated on strategic planning for battle, since he could not directly control his widely dispersed forces. The movement of troops to the battlefield and leadership of troops in battle were the responsibilities of subordinate officers. The more heavily wooded American terrain also affected tactical control and tended to force it to low-level units.

Corps commanders handled "grand tactics," that is, translating the army commander's plan into battlefield tactics. They set up their corps's divisions just outside the battlefield and moved them onto the field. Once on the field, corps commanders provided overall tactical direction, but in fact the largest practical units of tactical maneuver were divisions. Often even smaller units, brigades and even regiments, were responsible for their own tactical maneuvers.

The following is a rough idea of how infantry were organized.

A company consisted of 100 men and was commanded by a captain.

A regiment was formed by combining 10 to 16 companies, about 1000 to 1600 men, and was commanded by a colonel. Larger regiments might be divided into two equal-size battalions.

A brigade consisted of three to six regiments, about 4000 men, and was commanded by a brigadier general.

A division was composed of two to six brigades, about 12,000 men, and was commanded by a major general. Union divisions usually had three or four brigades, Confederate divisions normally four to six. Artillery and/or cavalry units might be attached.

A corps was composed of two to four divisions, about 36,000 men, and was commanded by a major general (Union) or a lieutenant general (Confederate). The Union tended to have two or three divisions in a corps, the Confederates three or four.

An army was composed of corps within a geographic area. The number of corps in an army could vary considerably, from one to eight. Armies were commanded by major generals in the North, and usually by full generals in the South.

Formation Variations

There are basically two ways for a large military force to move forward in an orderly fashion—in line-abreast formation or in a column. Normally, Civil War troops marched from place to place in columns, and then, when they were ready to fight, deployed into line-abreast battle formations.

The standard battle formations

were the line, the column, the line and column, and open-order—a strung-out, irregular single line or series of lines. Attackers usually sought an opportunity to flank and "roll up" battle lines lengthwise, while defenses tried to protect these flanks with impassable terrain features.

As an army prepared to attack, it would send out one or two companies from each regiment, or sometimes whole regiments, as skirmishers. Skirmishers played the role that cavalry had taken before the rifled musket made men on horseback too vulnerable. They advanced several hundred yards ahead of the main line of battle and spread out, under cover if possible, to locate enemy positions and disrupt or delay enemy advances. As the battle developed, skirmishers either fell back or stayed and joined an attack.

The line was the most common formation for both offense and defense because it delivered the greatest volume of fire across the widest front. Civil War armies typically attacked in the two-line formation. In each line, the soldiers were lined up tightly, elbow to elbow. The second line would march 150 to 200 yards behind the first. Spacing was considered critical in line attacks. Generally, officers marched in front of each line. If the distance between the lines was too close, the second line would become mixed with the first.

The problem was that when the front line came under fire and took casualties, it slowed. The following line then merged with it, bunching the whole assault force into a disorganized mass. This brought confusion instead of strength to the attack, and the defenses could cut it to pieces. This tendency of assaulting troops to stall and lose momentum was of great concern during the Civil War. Commanders attempted to solve the bunching problem by better discipline, and attacking in a succession of lines continued to be widely used throughout the war. In fact, there was simply no way to organize attackers to overcome a defensive rifle line in a frontal attack unless the attackers hugely outnumbered the defenders. Theoretically, one way to avoid this bunching of

Corps badges were used to help commanders identify their units in the field. Originally cut from colored cloth, they were generally attached to the top of forage caps. These insignias, left, represent the 1st, 2nd, 3rd, 5th, 9th, and 20th Corps.

troops was to attack in column.

A column was one or more companies wide and eight or more ranks deep. Like the line, the column was a close-order formation, but the distance between ranks was six paces, about five yards. The idea was that men in a column were able to move faster than line formations, and, with more penetrating power, it could overwhelm defenders with superior numbers at the point of impact.

However, the column's narrow front in comparison to an enemy line made it an easy target for artillery and infantry fire on its flanks.

Attacks in column during the Civil War were relatively rare. Overall, they were the most ineffective of all offensive formations and almost assured heavy casualties for the attackers, since they could be fired on from both the flanks and the front.

The line-and-column was a combination of the two formations, but many commanders felt it combined the worst qualities of each.

Open-order attacks were another alternative, and were the only practical way to attack in heavily wooded areas like the Wilderness. In many cases, attackers began to employ larger skirmish lines to advance against enemy defenses. Supported by cover fire from the skirmishers, attackers would advance in smaller groups in rushes, lie down and fire, then rush forward again, repeating the process until the lines were close enough to attack the defensive line. However, skirmishers had problems effectively suppressing the enemy's fire when they were outnumbered. There were attempts to solve this by deploying more skirmishers, but Civil War commanders valued control and mass over all. Too many skirmishers sacrificed cohesion, and demanded more training of a kind the armies were unable to provide. Thus, while open order was often used, it was often not acknowledged as a "real" formation.

The Battle of Antietam (Sharpsburg)

On June 1, 1862, Robert E. Lee took command of the Confederate army in Virginia and renamed it the Army of Northern Virginia. From late June through early September 1862, Lee's newly christened army dominated the Federals, driving Union troops away from Richmond and inflicting a brutal defeat on Union forces at the Battle of Second Bull Run (Second Manassas) in August. The Confederacy's military successes meant they could reasonably hope for diplomatic recognition by England and France. They also hoped their military victories would cast doubt on Lincoln's ability to win the war, and thus influence Northern public opinion to vote for antiwar candidates in the upcoming November congressional elections. It was the quest for more politically significant military victories, as well as the desire to keep Union armies from occupying Virginia during the harvest season, that led Lee to invade Maryland in September 1862, resulting in the bloodiest day of the war and in American history.

On September 4, the Confederate army crossed the Potomac River at White's Ford near Leesburg, Virginia, and moved to Frederick, Maryland. Lee, believing the Union forces were discouraged and disorganized after Second Bull Run (Second Manassas), took a gamble and split his army into four parts, sending three of the sections under the command of General "Stonewall" Jackson to seize the Federal arsenal at Harpers Ferry, Virginia (*see* Harpers Ferry, page 307). Lee sent his plans to his commanders on September 9 in Special Orders, 191 (*see* sidebar).

On September 10, Union soldiers made a stunning discovery—an envelope with a copy of these Special Orders wrapped around three cigars, apparently dropped by a Confederate officer. When Union general George McClellan saw the Special Orders and realized how thin Lee had spread his army, McClellan foolishly announced to Lincoln he would "cut the enemy in two and beat him in detail."

A Confederate sympathizer rushed the news to Lee that McClellan had the Special Orders, but it was too late to recall Jackson's columns. Lee sent word to Jackson to return as soon as he had captured Harpers Ferry, and in the meantime, Lee prepared what was left of his army for an attack by McClellan. McClellan began to move on September 14, but Confederate general D. H. Hill held the Union forces at bay long enough for Lee to form a defensive position at Sharpsburg, Maryland.

On September 15—the same day that Harpers Ferry surrendered—McClellan found Lee's army outside Sharpsburg. Jackson, with most of the Confederate units, immediately turned north to aid Lee. On September 16, McClellan's 60,000 Union troops were in place against the vastly outnumbered Confederate army of about 18,000 led by Lee. But McClellan, always inclined to overestimate his enemy, did not attack and spent most of the day planning and reconnoitering. That afternoon he sent Union general Hooker with 12,000 men north of Sharpsburg with instructions to attack Lee's left flank the next morning.

Lee was taking a real chance, forming up his battle line with its

---

Special Orders, 191

According to the records, a Union division was bivouacked about a mile southeast of Frederick, Maryland, on a meadow occupied the day before by Confederate General D. H. Hill's command. Around ten a.m. on the 13th of September, 1862, Private Barton W. Mitchell of the 27th Indiana, along with Sergeant John M. Bloss, discovered an envelope lying in the grass. The document inside was a copy of Confederate general Robert E. Lee's orders for the invasion of Maryland, addressed to Confederate general Hill. Passed up through the chain of command, the captured order gave Union general George B. McClellan advance notice of his enemy's movements. Holding the paper, McClellan exclaimed, "Here is a paper with which, if I cannot whip Bobby Lee, I will be willing to go home."

The orders were not left as a Confederate plant to feed the Union false information, nor did the lucky officers who found the document consider that possibility. It was just a piece of remarkable good luck for the Union.

back to the Potomac, preventing a rapid withdrawal if necessary. But he was gambling that Jackson would return in time—and he did. Meanwhile, Lee chose his ground wisely for a defensive action. The Confederates were arrayed on top of a low ridge that runs north and south of Sharpsburg. They set up guns in the north on what was known as Nicodemus Heights, on the high ground in front of the Dunker Church (ironically the home of a small sect of pacifists), and on a ridge just east of Sharpsburg. East and south of Sharpsburg, Antietam Creek forms a natural boundary. Lee only had to defend one bridge, called the Lower Bridge, and he placed cannons and about 500 Georgia infantrymen above it. Confederate infantry filled in between these points, including a low lane known as the Sunken Road.

North of Sharpsburg, where the battle began, was the North Woods, the West Woods, and the East Woods, arranged in a rough U shape with Miller's cornfield in the middle. At the south end of the West Woods was the Dunker Church.

Fighting throughout the day on September 17 involved four waves and came within a hairsbreadth of ending the war, but all ended in bloody stalemate. The day began with a Union charge through what the Federals thought was an uninhabited cornfield, followed by a Union attack on the West Woods. Later, the Union attack at Sunken Road resulted in a Confederate blunder that nearly ended the war. The final attack of the day took place at the Lower Bridge.

Bloodshed in the Cornfield

Early in the morning, Hooker sent 10 brigades south toward Sharpsburg from the North Woods. Unaware that Confederate troops were hiding behind the tall corn, the Union troops began marching through Miller's cornfield. Then Brigadier General A. R. Lawton's troops stood up and opened fire, catching the Federals by surprise and decimating the first wave. Hooker quickly turned his artillery from the East Woods on the cornfield, slaughtering at close range the Confederates there. One Texas regiment lost 186 of its 226 soldiers, including two companies that were wiped out to the last man.

The Confederates retreated, still raked by Union cannons, as Union troops charged through the cornfield. Jackson, who had returned from Harpers Ferry and was now commanding troops forming a line in front of the Dunker Church, waited until the Union reserve brigades moved forward to take advantage of the breakthrough, then his Confederates launched a desperate counterattack. They pushed the Union troops back to the cornfield, but pointblank fire from Union cannons stopped the Confederate advance.

At seven thirty a.m., 7200 fresh Union troops from Union general Joseph Mansfield's XII Corps came in from the north. When Mansfield advanced to review the situation, Confederate fire cut him down. He was the first of six generals killed that day. Mansfield's deputy, Brigadier General Alphesus Williams, took over and began an attack, but

Hooker's I Corps charges Confederate artillerymen. The advance was repulsed before they reached the Dunker Church, right, with heavy casualties on both sides.

the Confederate fire stopped them. Some of Williams's men reached the Dunker Church, where they took cover and waited for support to renew their attack.

Walking into a Trap
At nine a.m., General Edwin Sumner led two divisions from his II Corps to attack the Confederates in the West Woods. Major General John Sedgwick's division led the attack, with Brigadier General William French's division following. Sumner thought a sudden attack by his 5400 men might carry the day for the Union.

However, the Union commanders made a series of tactical mistakes. They did not send skirmishers ahead of the main force into the West Woods to reconnoiter. The Union troops advanced in long lines close together, with one line only 75 yards behind the other. The first line could fire, but the following lines could not without hitting their own men. Finally, no one was responsible for ensuring that French's division was still following—but in fact, French's men had drifted to the south and lost contact with Sedgwick.

When Jackson saw Sumner's troops on the move, he rushed reinforcements to the West Woods, while Lee sent two brigades from the Lower Bridge to help. As the Confederates arrived, they slid in behind the rocks and trees on the edge of the woods, gradually forming a semicircle of about 10,000 men. When the unsuspecting Union soldiers came

within range, the Confederates began to fire from three sides. Most of Sumner's men had no chance. In less than 20 minutes, about 2200 Union soldiers were killed or wounded. Return fire was impossible. Union troops trailing the initial assault had to hold their fire to keep from shooting their own men in the back. Both Sumner and Sedgwick were wounded, and a Union colonel later wrote that he lost 60 men before his soldiers could get off a single shot. Jackson's troops then tried an ill-advised counterattack, but Union cannons broke it up.

By nine thirty a.m. neither side had gained ground, even though 12,000 men lay dead or wounded. Lee was moving troops back and forth, meeting the piecemeal Federal thrusts, but the attacks had pulled most of his army north of Sharpsburg. Lee now had two separate lines—the main one facing northeast toward Hooker and the East Woods, and a small force guarding the Lower Bridge.

The Bloody Lane
After getting separated from Sumner, French's division moved toward the center of the Confederate line a mile south of the cornfield where D. H. Hill's 2600 troops were manning a strong defensive position on a ridge above the Sunken Road, a hard clay road worn down through the years by rain and heavy wagons. Fence rails lined the twisting, half-mile-long road. While Hill's troops were adding more fence rails to the ridge, they saw French's division coming down a ravine toward them.

The rebels dropped behind their defenses, and their withering fire cut down charge after Union charge with heavy casualties. But Union major general Israel "Fighting Dick" Richardson's division arrived and attacked the vulnerable Confederate right flank. Lee ordered his last reserves forward, but the Confederate counteroffensive sputtered. Then, in the heat of the battle, a disastrously misunderstood order led them to abandon part of the Sunken Road. Seeing the gap open, Union colonel Francis Barlow sent the 61st and 64th New York regiments to the crest of a hill at the eastern end of the Sunken Road. His forces began firing repeated volleys down the trench. Confederate dead piled up, soon lying three deep for half a mile. The Sunken Road became "Bloody Lane."

The 800-yard-long road later called Bloody Lane had been worn down over the years by heavy farm wagons taking grain to the nearby mill. By one p.m. about 5500 dead and wounded troops from both sides lay along and in front of this lane.

About 300 Confederates surrendered, while the rest rushed to escape from the trench. The Union soldiers moved forward, stepping over the dead Confederates along the way. Now there was a great opening in the center of Lee's line. "The end of the Confederacy was in sight," one Confederate officer later wrote.

The Civil War might have ended there. Another attack would have crushed the Confederate center, but McClellan refused to commit his reserve corps, and his caution left the breakthrough stillborn.

Attack at the Lower Bridge

While McClellan hesitated, Lee faced another threat to the south. Four divisions of Major General Ambrose Burnside's IX Corps attacked the Lower Bridge, which was defended by less than 500 Georgia Confederates under Brigadier General Robert Toombs. Toombs's position was almost unassailable. The road to the bridge plunges into a depression a few hundred yards before the bridge, and the Confederates were poised behind trees and boulders on a steep wooded bluff overlooking it.

Just after nine a.m., Burnside sent his troops marching into this funnel. The road and the long, narrow stone bridge proved a perfect killing zone for Toombs's sharpshooting Georgians. After an hour of futile attacks, Burnside sent his forces to find other crossings. Union soldiers found Snavely's Ford, about a mile south of

the bridge, and began to pour across the stream. As they began to drive against the right flank of the Georgians guarding the bridge, another Union force crossed at a second ford a few hundred yards above the bridge and mounted artillery on the high ground. The Confederates were now under attack from both flanks, and at one p.m. two Union regiments rushed across the bridge, brushing aside the depleted ranks in the rifle pits above the bridge. Then, once again, Burnside paused. He took two hours to regroup his troops and march across the hills toward Sharpsburg to cut off Lee's line of retreat across the Potomac. Lee saw Burnside's men approaching out of the valley at Antietam Creek and moved all his available artillery southward. Once again, the battle appeared to be lost.

Still, Lee had hope. Just before Burnside crossed the Lower Bridge, General A. P. Hill, wearing his trademark red flannel shirt, arrived with some of his artillery. He also had 3000 of his men crossing the Potomac about three miles away.

About three p.m., Lee saw troops on the move to the south. One of his staff looked at the force with his binoculars and reported happily "they are carrying Confederate flags." Hill's Light Division had arrived. At three forty p.m. Hill's men drove into Burnside's unprotected left flank, forcing the Union troops back to the heights near the bridge. The attack across the Lower Bridge and Hill's counterattack cost the two sides 3470 casualties—twice as many Union as Confederate.

The Bloodiest Day Ends

General McClellan still had 20,000 men in reserve who had seen little or no action. He considered having them attack the weakest part of the enemy line, but after some hesitation, he decided against it.

By five thirty the battle was over. Both sides, exhausted, settled in as night fell. They tried to sleep while listening to the cries of the wounded.

The next day, September 18, both sides called a truce to retrieve their dead and wounded. Lee's forces were too weak to attack again, but Lee did not retreat. McClellan received more reinforcements, but he still hesitated. He decided to attack again on September 19, but on the evening of September 18 Lee and his army slipped across the Potomac River and escaped. The Confederacy's first invasion of the North was over.

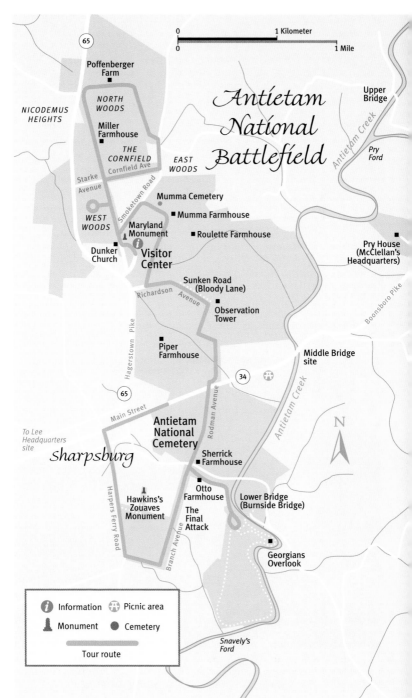

McClellan did not pursue as Lee's army withdrew into the Shenandoah Valley. An impatient President Lincoln visited McClellan at Antietam on October 1, telling him to go after Lee. McClellan refused, saying his army needed to reorganize and reequip.

The Results

In many ways, Antietam (Sharpsburg) was one of the Confederate army's great victories. Vastly outnumbered, they came out with a draw and inflicted more casualties on the Union forces. However, it was a strategic failure, perhaps the most significant one of the war. In the next weeks, the Confederacy would lose major battles at Corinth, Mississippi, and Perryville, Tennessee. In the east, the Union troops moved back into Virginia and prevented the local farmers from sharing their harvest with the Confederate armies. The Federals realized how close they had come to victory, and their confidence was restored.

The political significance of the battle was even greater than the strategic significance. Antietam caused Great Britain to postpone recognition of the Confederate government. Then, on September 22, President Abraham Lincoln issued the Preliminary Emancipation Proclamation, saying that on January 1, 1863, all slaves in states still in rebellion against the United States would be legally free. England and France, wanting to avoid the moral issue of slavery, quietly but completely dropped any consideration of recognizing the Confederacy.

Once it was clear that the North had no need to fear an invasion, Lincoln's Republican party won a significant victory in the congressional elections. It was also clear that McClellan's style was more cautious than Lincoln felt was warranted, and Lincoln replaced McClellan with Burnside on November 7.

Antietam National Battlefield and Cemetery

Antietam was the bloodiest day in American history. Troops numbering 5110 were killed, and almost 18,000 more were wounded or missing. To put the losses in perspective, there were four times as many American casualties at Antietam as there were on D-Day. It took about a week to bury all of the dead.

After the war, the state of Maryland donated 11 acres for a cemetery for 4776 dead. In July 1877, the first marker was installed, the Private Soldiers Monument (now known as "Old Simon"). The site was so significant that when the War Department began to buy major battlefields in 1890, Antietam was the first. The state of Maryland and several local farmers donated land to the project. State monument commissions began to erect monuments and markers on the battlefield to commemorate where their soldiers

General Burnside *has been criticized for his decision to have his troops charge across the bridge rather than simply ford the stream. The chief obstacle to crossing the creek was the steep banks on either side. These would have severely disrupted any battle line, particularly on the far side, where the soldiers would have had difficulty clambering out.*

In the days immediately after the battle, Lincoln became distressed at General McClellan's failure to pursue Lee's retreating army. In early October 1862, Lincoln visited McClellan at Antietam to urge him personally to attack. This photograph of Lincoln with McClellan is a rare view of Lincoln at the front.

fought, and today there are over 100 monuments on the park's 3365 acres.

In 1933 the battlefield was turned over to the National Park Service, which began to restore it to its 1862 appearance. Some of the major landmarks, such as Bloody Lane and the Lower Bridge (now called Burnside Bridge) were restored, and the Dunker Church, which had been destroyed by a storm in 1921, was rebuilt in 1962.

The Antietam National Battlefield and Cemetery Visitors Center includes a museum, an observation room, a store, a theater, and a research library. The award-winning film *Antietam Visit* is shown every half hour, except at noon and 12:30 p.m. This 26-minute movie recreates the battle and President Lincoln's subsequent visit to McClellan there. At noon the theater shows the one-hour *Antietam Documentary,* narrated by James Earl Jones. An observation tower near Bloody Lane gives another perspective.

Starting at the Visitors Center is an 11-stop, 8.5-mile self-guided tour of the battlefield, which can be taken by car, bike, or on foot. The stops include all of the main sites of the fighting, including the three woods, Miller's cornfield, the Sunken Road, and Burnside Bridge. Audiotapes to accompany the tour can be bought or rented at the Visitors Center. There are 300 plaques scattered throughout the battlefield detailing troop movements and other activities, as well as the monuments and 500 cannons. Three Union and three Confederate generals were killed or mortally wounded during the battle, and a "Mortuary Cannon"—a cannon tube, muzzle down in a block of stone—marks the spot where each of the six was killed. Going through the Visitors Center and taking the full driving tour takes about four hours.

Visitor Information

301-432-5124; www.nps.gov/anti/

Hours: Battlefield and cemetery open daily, June to August, 8 a.m. until 6 p.m.; September to May, 8:30 a.m. until 5 p.m.; closed Thanksgiving, December 25, and New Year's Day.

Admission: There is a minimal all-inclusive park entrance fee per adult or per family. Children 16 and under are free. National Parks Pass, Golden Eagle, Golden Age, and Golden Access are honored.

Accessibility: Most of the Visitors Center is accessible, including the observation room, restrooms, and water fountains. There is an elevator to the lower museum level. The film *Antietam Visit* can be captioned on request. Most of the stops on the battlefield driving tour are accessible except the Burnside Bridge overlook, but there are two handicapped parking spaces at the bottom of the hill that offer visitors access to the bridge along a gravel path. The cemetery has wide grass-covered paths, and its restrooms are not handicapped accessible.

Special Events: Rangers or costumed interpreters give talks, and enactors demonstrate tactics daily during the summer. Call to request a schedule. Special services are held on the days of the battle, September 17–18.

Getting There: The Antietam National Battlefield and Cemetery Visitors Center is located on Maryland highway 65, 1 mile north of Sharpsburg and 10 miles south of Hagerstown.

From the south or east: Take I-70 to Frederick. Take exit 29 onto state highway 65, Hagerstown Pike. Follow highway 65 for 10 miles and turn right at the park entrance.

From the north or west: Take I-81 or I-68 to I-70 toward Hagerstown. Follow I-70 to exit 29A. Take state highway 65 south for 10 miles to the park entrance.

The Baltimore Riots

When the Civil War began, Maryland, though a slave state, did not secede from the Union. However, its largest city, Baltimore, had extremely divided loyalties and was considering secession. It was an important part of the Underground Railroad, which helped slaves escape to freedom in the North, but it was also a hotbed of secessionist sympathy. Things were so bad there that in March, president-elect Abraham Lincoln had to slip through the city in the middle of the night because of the threat of assassination.

When Fort Sumter in South Carolina was fired upon and Lincoln called for troops, secessionist animosity in Baltimore reached critical mass and led to riots. On April 19, 1861, a week after the attack on Fort Sumter, the 6th Massachusetts Volunteer Militia Regiment arrived by train at Baltimore's President Street Station on its way south. The President Street Station was the southern end of the Philadelphia, Wilmington & Baltimore Railroad line, but because the rail line did not pass through the city, horse-drawn cars had to take the Massachusetts infantrymen to the other end of town, to the B&O's Camden Station,

to continue their journey south. As the regiment's cars moved along Pratt Street, an angry mob of Southern sympathizers blocked several of the vehicles, placed an anchor across the train track, and then began to break the windows. The rioters managed to trap about 200 Union soldiers and forced them out of the cars and onto the street. As the soldiers proceeded to march to Camden Station, the mob followed and continued to throw bricks and stones. The inexperienced soldiers panicked, fired into the crowd, and then fled, abandoning much of their equipment and deserting their marching band.

The mob then returned to the President Street Station, where they found another Union unit, Pennsylvania's Washington Brigade, which had just arrived unarmed and in civilian clothes. As the mob attacked, a local pro-Union group, mostly antislavery Irish and German immigrants, joined the fight against the secessionists. In the end, about a half dozen soldiers and at least 11 civilians died in the riots.

Maryland officials demanded that no more Federal troops be sent through the state. Secessionist groups tore down telegraph wires to

Washington and Baltimore. Mayor George W. Brown and Police Marshall George P. Kane (both Confederate sympathizers) ordered the destruction of key rail bridges to prevent Union troops from entering the city.

Lincoln would have none of this. Baltimore was a vital East Coast railway hub for the Union, and he acted to quell this disturbance to the Union rear. On May 13, Federal troops occupied the city and martial law was declared, outlawing support for secession and the Confederacy. Mayor Brown, Police Marshall Kane, members of the House of Delegates, a U.S. congressman, and other prominent Maryland citizens were taken to Fort McHenry and imprisoned, many for the duration of the war. Ironically, Francis Scott Key's grandson was one of the detainees.

The Baltimore Civil War Museum– President Street Station

The Baltimore Civil War Museum is located in Baltimore's Inner Harbor East, in the restored old President Street train station. The current building is only part of the original station, which was gutted by two fires in 1978 and sat abandoned for

more than a decade until the Friends of President Street Station was formed and saved the building. The April 19 riots took place just outside the museum on President Street and along nearby Pratt Street.

The permanent exhibition covers the history of Baltimore during the Civil War and the President Street Station's role in the Underground Railroad for slaves escaping to the North. This includes the fascinating story of Henry "Box" Brown, an escaped slave who was put in a shipping crate and literally mailed North, passing through the President Street Station during his unique escape. The compact museum uses panels and wall maps to explain Maryland's physical and philosophical position between the North and South and to describe the riots.

Visitor Information

410-385-5188;
www.mdhs.org/explore/
baltcivilwar.html

Hours: Daily, 10 a.m. until 5 p.m.
Admission: Minimal charge for adults and children ages 13 to 17.
Special Events: Guided tours of the route of the 6th Massachusetts Volunteer Militia Regiment are offered at 1 p.m. on weekends. There is an Annual Remembrance of the Pratt Street Riot event in early April when Civil War reenactors and the Friends of President Street Station honor the first casualties of the riot. There is also a regular evening Civil War Lecture Series. Call for dates and times.
Accessibility: The museum is accessible in all areas.
Getting There: From the Inner Harbor, the museum is located at the corner of President and Fleet Streets, just east of the Pier 6 Concert Pavilion and adjacent to the Marriott Inner Harbor East. It is an easy walk from the National Aquarium and other Inner Harbor attractions.

From the north or south via I-95: Take exit 55 and follow signs to downtown. Turn right on Pratt Street and then make another right on President Street and follow it to Fleet Street.

From the north via I-83: Follow I-83 to its end, where it becomes President Street. Follow President to Fleet Street.

Secessionists battle troops from the 6th Massachusetts Volunteer Militia Regiment.

Fort Washington Park

The first fort built on this site, 12 miles down the Potomac from Washington, D.C., in Maryland was known as Fort Warburton. It was destroyed by its own garrison in 1814 to prevent the British from capturing it as they moved upriver to take the capital. The fort was rebuilt in 1824 as Fort Washington, part of the Third System seacoast five-sided masonry forts commissioned after the War of 1812 to protect America's coastline. Fort Washington was intended to guard against enemy ships coming up the Potomac.

When the Civil War began, Fort Washington was the only fort that protected the capital. After First Bull Run (First Manassas), a circle of forts was built around the city, and Fort Washington became part of the outer defense line. After the war, the fort was abandoned until 1886, when it was reactivated and a battery of rifled steel guns was mounted there. Later, Fort Washington was a staging area for troops going to France in World War I, and it housed the U.S. Army's Adjutant General's School during World War II.

Today the fort, preserved in its Civil War form, sits in a 341-acre park on a high bluff across the Potomac River from George Washington's home in Mount Vernon, Virginia. The park has a picturesque lighthouse on the wharf, and the Visitors Center is located on the hill directly in front of the fort. Inside the center are exhibits and artifacts from Fort Washington's history and a bookstore, as well as an audiovisual program and special exhibits depicting elements of the park's history. The fort has a fine collection of Civil War cannons of various ages and sizes: At the park entrance are two 4.5-inch and two 3-inch ordnance rifles, all 1861 Models, mounted upright in concrete. In various locations at the fort are four unmounted 1844 Model 24-pounder flank howitzers and a mounted Model 1819 24-pounder siege gun, as well as two unmounted 1841 Model 6-pounder bronze field guns.

Visitor Information:

301-763-4600; www.nps.gov/fowa

Hours: Park grounds, 8 a.m. until sunset; fort and Visitors Center, April 1 to September 30, 9 a.m. until 5 p.m., and October 1 to March 31, 9 a.m. until 4:30 p.m.; the Visitors Center is closed from noon until 2 p.m. daily, and may be closed periodically without notice; the bookstore is open only on weekends; closed Thanksgiving, December 25, and New Year's Day.

Admission: Moderate per-vehicle charge or minimal individual charge. National Parks Pass, Golden Eagle, Golden Age, and Golden Access are honored.

Accessibility: The Visitors Center is wheelchair accessible; access is limited in certain areas of the fort.

Special Events: There are regular live-fire Civil War artillery demonstrations at the park. During the summer months there are also living-history programs. Guided tours of the fort are given on Saturday and Sunday at 2 p.m., 3 p.m., and 4 p.m.

Getting There: Fort Washington is located just outside Washington, D.C. From Washington, D.C., take the Capital Beltway (I-495) to exit 3A (Indian Head Highway or Maryland Route 210) and go to Fort Washington Road. Turn right and continue to the park entrance.

Battle of Monocacy

After the Union defeat at the first Battle of Bull Run (Manassas), the possibility of the Confederate army capturing the defenseless Union capital of Washington, D.C., became very real. When Union general George McClellan took over the army, he built a system of forts that arched around the city to hold back an assault by a field army and to defeat guerilla raids. By early 1864, the threat of invasion had diminished and the city's fortifications were so strong that General Ulysses S. Grant took most of the men in the forts with him for his campaign against Richmond and Petersburg.

In the summer of 1864, the Confederacy was fighting a holding action, hoping they could prevent any major Union victories before the presidential election of 1864. Even after their 1863 defeats at Gettysburg and Vicksburg, the Confederates still held Atlanta, Richmond, and Petersburg, and dissatisfaction with the war was rising in the North. Lincoln was facing the possibility that he might be defeated in the November elections by a peace candidate.

Confederate general Robert E. Lee and his Army of Northern Virginia were under heavy pressure from Grant at Petersburg, so Lee sent Lieutenant General Jubal A. Early north with orders to cross the Potomac River into Maryland and threaten either Baltimore or Washington. Lee anticipated that this diversion would pull some of Grant's troops from around Petersburg back to Washington.

Early exceeded all expectations. On June 17, his Army of the Valley set out by train to Lynchburg, Virginia, and moved quickly north, capturing large amounts of Union supplies along the way. On July 2, the Union army chief of staff, General Henry Halleck, and Grant heard that Early was approaching western Maryland, but they lacked firm Union intelligence.

The Union commander of the area, known as the Middle Department, was an Indiana lawyer, General Lewis "Lew" Wallace. He had been promoted to brigadier general in early September 1861, had fought well at Fort Donelson in February 1862, then had been promoted to major general on March 21, 1862 (at 34, the youngest man at that time to hold that rank). He was given command of a division, but a month later, in April 1862 at the Battle of Shiloh, things went awry for him. Wallace was relieved of his command and plummeted out of favor with the Union hierarchy. Wallace had some later success in the West, and in March 1864 he took command of the Middle Department, an area that included Delaware and Maryland west to the Monocacy River. Wallace's forces comprised a somewhat motley collection of recruits, garrison troops, unseasoned militia, and convalescents, their main role being to suppress Maryland secessionists.

When Wallace heard about Early's sortie, he decided to travel west to assess the situation firsthand. On July 5, Wallace left Baltimore with about 2500 men—mostly inexperienced soldiers of the Potomac Home Brigade and Ohio militia—for Monocacy Junction, about three miles southeast of Frederick Town, Maryland. When he arrived there, Wallace learned that Early's Army of the Valley had bypassed the Union garrison at Harpers Ferry and crossed the Potomac River at Shepherdstown into Maryland. Early forced the city of Hagerstown to pay him $20,000 to keep him from burning the town down, and was now marching toward Baltimore and Washington, D.C. Wallace was facing a veteran battle-hardened Confederate force that vastly outnumbered his cobbled-together units. He telegraphed Halleck and Grant with the news and asked for reinforcements. News of the Confederates' approach put Washington into a state of panic, and Grant, perhaps reflecting on how he had stripped Washington's defenses, immediately dispatched General Horatio G. Wright's corps to Washington. The first two brigades of the corps, under Brigadier General James B. Ricketts, were to arrive in a few days.

Still uncertain as to whether the Confederates' objective was Baltimore or Washington, Wallace decided to make a stand at Monocacy Junction. Both the major roads—Georgetown Pike, which ran to Washington, and the Baltimore Pike (National Road) to Baltimore—crossed the Monocacy River there, as did the B&O Railroad. Wallace's small force could cover the two roads and rail bridges, as well as several fords, but they would be stretched very thin. At Monocacy on July 6, Wallace was joined by Lieutenant Colonel David Clendenin and his

Confederate general Jubal A. Early, left, and his exhausted troops reached the outskirts of Washington on July 11, 1864. Turned back the next day by veteran Union troops that had reinforced the city's defenses at the last moment, Early abandoned any thought of taking the city. "We didn't take Washington," Early told his staff officers, "but we scared Abe Lincoln like Hell." Above, artillery at Fort Stevens.

squadron of 8th Illinois Cavalry. Wallace sent Clendenin and his cavalry to the mountains west of Frederick to try to locate the Confederate force.

On the morning of July 7, the Union forces heard cannon fire coming from Frederick Town. An hour later, Wallace received word that Clendenin had been pushed back by a superior force. On July 7 and 8, there were skirmishes as the Confederates advanced through Frederick Town. Once again, they were paid by the city not to burn the town down—this time $200,000.

After the skirmishes around Frederick, Wallace estimated that Early's forces numbered somewhere between 15,000 and 18,000 men and decided the Confederate objective was Washington. Wallace was cheered to hear that the first elements of Ricketts's troops had arrived in Baltimore, and on July 8 they arrived by train at Monocacy, with the rest of the division.

Wallace now had about 6000 men to hold the line against Early's army. He deployed his forces along a three-mile stretch of the east bank of the Monocacy River, hoping to delay Early long enough for the rest of Wright's corps to reach Washington. The Monocacy's high east bank was a natural fortification, and Union troops also occupied blockhouses and trenches along the riverbank. Wallace sent his own inexperienced troops to his right, along the Baltimore Pike and away from the

road to Washington, where he expected the main Confederate attack to come. He ordered Ricketts's more experienced veterans to cover the Georgetown Pike, the most direct road to Washington, holding a line from a covered bridge south to an area known as Worthington's Farm.

The battle began at sunrise on the morning of July 9. By eight a.m. the Confederates had gradually pushed the Union skirmishers down Georgetown Pike toward the covered bridge across the river, while more Confederates attacked Wallace's inexperienced troops along the Baltimore Pike. Early arrived from Frederick to survey the battlefield and quickly realized a frontal assault across the Monocacy River would be too costly. He sent a force of Confederate cavalry to find a ford for a flanking attack on the Union left side.

Around eleven a.m., about a mile south of the covered wooden bridge, the cavalry crossed the Monocacy to attack the Union left. The dismounted Confederate cavalry moved through a cornfield right into Ricketts's veterans, who cut them down. They were driven back two more times with heavy losses and forced to wait for reinforcements. Around two thirty that afternoon, three brigades of Confederate general John B. Gordon's division forded the river and attacked the Union left again. Ricketts's men held again and inflicted heavy casualties on the attacking Confederates. Gordon pulled back, regrouped, and attacked again at three thirty. The Confederates broke the Union line, but Gordon's division paid a heavy price.

One third of his division were killed or wounded, and both colonels of the 61st Georgia Brigade were killed.

With the Confederate breakthrough on his left, Wallace's forces—outnumbered and running low on ammunition—began to pull back. At four thirty, Wallace withdrew toward Baltimore, hoping he had held Early's Confederates long enough for reinforcements to arrive in Washington. During the retreat, Clendenin's 8th Illinois Cavalry moved through the community of Urbana and took up positions on a hill outside of the town. From there, they saw Confederate troopers dismount and begin looting the village. The dauntless Clendenin led his men back into the hamlet, surprising the Confederates. They captured the regimental colors of the 17th Virginia Cavalry and mortally wounded one of the company commanders.

Early's exhausted men rested that night, and the next day they continued their march toward Washington unimpeded. By July 11, Early and his men moved to within four miles of Georgetown with their battle flags flying. The advance cavalry of Early's army reached the outer defenses of Washington at Fort Stevens, but it was sheer bravado. By then, the remainder of Wright's corps and three additional brigades had reached Washington.

Early noted the reinforcements, and found the defenses "very strong . . . a circle of enclosed forts, connected by breast-works, with ditches, palisades . . . [and] every approach swept by a cross-fire of artillery." He realized that any attempt to capture the city was futile, and after some brief skirmishing around Fort Stevens (where Confederates whizzed bullets by the head of President Abraham Lincoln, who had come to the fort to observe the situation), Early retreated back through Maryland. His main mission—forcing Grant to move troops from Petersburg back to Washington—had been spectacularly successful. While Monocacy was later hailed as The Battle That Saved Washington, it is doubtful that Early and his Confederates could have ever breached Washington's defenses and then escaped, even if reinforcements had not arrived. Still, if Early had been able to approach close enough to force the evacuation of the city, it would have presented the Confederacy with an incalculable psychological victory.

Wallace had lost the battle but achieved his primary goal—he delayed Early long enough to allow reinforcements to reach Washington. After the battle, Wallace was criticized for not defeating Early, but gradually he was given credit by both Union and Confederate generals for "saving Washington." Wallace achieved more fame later in his life when he wrote the novel *Ben-Hur.*

Monocacy National Battlefield

The exhibit area in the Gambrill Mill Visitors Center includes an electric orientation map, interactive computer program, artifacts, interpretive displays of the battle, and a small bookstore. There are no formal trails through the battlefield, but the center provides maps and interpretive brochures for the park trails and an automobile tour of the battlefield area, with directions to the battlefield's five monuments.

In early 2004, the Visitors Center is scheduled to move from Gambrill Mill to the Best Farm, 1.5 miles closer to Frederick, off Route 355. Gambrill Mill will be converted to an unstaffed interpretive display detailing its use as an aid station after the July 1864 battle.

Visitor Information

301-662-3515; www.nps.gov/mono
Hours: The Visitors Center is open daily, Labor Day to Memorial Day, 8 a.m. until 4:30 p.m., Memorial Day to Labor Day, 8:30 a.m. until 5 p.m.; closed Thanksgiving, December 25, and New Year's Day.
Admission: Free.
Accessibility: The Visitors Center is wheelchair accessible, and the electric map has a written script for the hearing impaired.
Special Events: Programs vary throughout the year. Park Rangers offer programs and special events in coordination with living-history volunteers.
Getting There: The battlefield is about six miles southeast of Frederick, Maryland.

From I-270: Take exit 26 at Urbana. Follow state highway 80 east 0.2 miles to a stop sign. Turn left onto state highway 355 north and go 3.7 miles to the battlefield on the right.

From I-70: Take exit 54 (Market Street, Routes 85 and 355). Follow state highway 355 south 3.75 miles to the battlefield on the left.

The Gambrill Mill Visitors Center is 0.1 miles on the left past the

The National Museum of Civil War Medicine

The unusual National Museum of Civil War Medicine documents what Walt Whitman called the "real war." It is the only museum devoted exclusively to the subject of Civil War medicine and the story of the major medical advances during the conflict—advances that changed medicine forever.

During the war, there were significant advances in the use of anesthesia, evacuation of the wounded, hospitals, nursing, surgery, and sanitation. The museum also tells the story of the dedication and innovation of the medical personnel and support staff on both sides who brought about extraordinary changes to the medical community by reforming organizations and administration to meet the emergency.

The museum houses a collection of over 1500 artifacts relating to medical care during the Civil War—either donated or on long-term loan from private collectors and other museums. Well over half of the museum's collection is attributed to the generosity of its founder and chairman, Gordon E. Dammann, D.D.S. Dr. Dammann has collected Civil War medical artifacts for over 30 years and has amassed one of the finest collections in the world. Among the many artifacts currently on display are surgical instruments used by Union and Confederate medical staff, medical knapsacks and panniers, stretchers and litters, prosthetic devices, a table used for amputations at a field hospital during the battle of Cedar Creek, and the only known surviving surgeon's tent from the Civil War, used by surgeon John Wiley of the 6th New Jersey.

The museum is located in Frederick, Maryland, near many Civil War battlefields. (Frederick's historic buildings survived only because the town paid a $200,000 ransom to Confederate general Jubal A. Early to prevent him from razing the town.) During the war, 38 of Frederick's buildings, including nine churches, were converted into hospitals. Several times the city was overwhelmed with huge numbers of casualties from nearby battles. Before the Civil War, the museum's antebellum brick building housed a lumberyard and furniture shop; but during the war, the company made caskets and grave markers for General Hospital #1 across the street. Part of the building was also used as an embalming station for soldiers whose families could afford to have their sons' bodies preserved for shipment home after the battles of South Mountain and Antietam.

The 7000-square-foot museum's nine galleries describe different

Field dressing stations, *located close to the fighting, offered bandages for wounds, whiskey for shock, and morphine for pain. Here, Union medical personnel attend to a wounded Confederate soldier—a common occurrence during the war.*

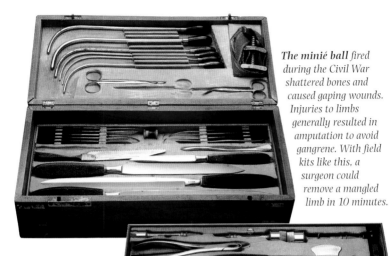

The minié ball fired during the Civil War shattered bones and caused gaping wounds. Injuries to limbs generally resulted in amputation to avoid gangrene. With field kits like this, a surgeon could remove a mangled limb in 10 minutes.

facets of how the sick and wounded were cared for, told in vignettes by individual physicians, nurses, and other caregivers. Panels in the galleries quote the words and war experiences of Union private Peleg Bradford, a member of the 1st Maine Heavy Artillery, who was hospitalized several times during the war for various illnesses and ultimately lost a leg after being shot in the knee.

The displays begin by describing the inadequacy of medical training. At the time, medical school consisted only of two six-month terms of lectures, and the average medical student in the United States received practically no clinical or laboratory experience. Many of the older American doctors hadn't even gone to medical school, but had apprenticed instead.

The museum's galleries then progress to the recruiting process, which often consisted of only a cursory exam that frequently ignored diseases and severe physical defects, and then describe soldiers' camp-life experiences, including a typical morning sick call.

Six of the galleries are "full immersion" exhibits that contain a central tableau, such as a surgeon and his assistants preparing to perform an amputation. When the visitor enters these exhibits, a recorded conversation between the participants begins, providing a gripping and graphic description of the scene.

Some of these immersion galleries follow what happened when soldiers were wounded—how they were evacuated, taken to a field dressing station, then to a field hospital for surgery, and finally to a pavilion hospital for longer-term care. One features Union and Confederate stretchers and depicts members of the ambulance corps loading the wounded into four-wheeled ambulances—an important innovation, given that at the beginning of the Civil War there was no established system to transport wounded soldiers from the front lines to the field hospitals in the rear. Another depicts Union medical personnel attending to a wounded Confederate soldier at a field dressing station modeled after the 32nd Massachusetts Infantry's station near the Wheatfield at Gettysburg.

One room vividly depicts an amputation in a Confederate field hospital located in a barn. The terrible injuries from minié balls and the number of wounded needing immediate treatment were the main causes of the large numbers of amputations during the war. Surgeons often operated for days at a time without a break, and as one witness described the scene, "The surgeons and their assistants, stripped to the waist and bespattered with blood, stood around, some holding the poor fellows while others, armed with long, bloody knives and saws, cut and sawed away with frightful rapidity, throwing the mangled limbs on a pile of amputated limbs as soon as removed."

Before the Civil War, systematic hospitalization was practically unknown. After the first battles produced a large number of wounded and sick needing long-term care, both the North and the South constructed large, clean, well-ventilated, and relatively efficient pavilion-style hospitals. As the war

Confederate wounded await transportation under makeshift tents. Smith's barn, far right, was used as a makeshift hospital during and after the Battle of Antietam.

continued, the quality of care that the patients received improved dramatically and pavilion hospitals had only an 8 percent mortality rate for all patients. Here a gallery depicts the Union's Hammond Hospital in Point Lookout, Maryland.

The last gallery depicts a variety of subjects relating to Civil War medicine, including dental care, death and embalming, and the hospitals in Frederick after the battle of Antietam. The gallery features an elaborate coffin with drawers and drains for ice and adjustable viewing ports whose positioning depended on the condition of the body. The embalmers attached directions for the undertaker who would remove the coffin for burial.

The museum's Dispensary Museum Store offers a unique selection of items relating to Civil War medicine, including books, prints, videos, CDs, and reproduction Civil War medical instruments.

Visitor Information

301-695-1864;
www.civilwarmed.org/
Hours: Monday to Saturday, 10 a.m. until 5 p.m.; Sunday 11 a.m. until 5 p.m.; November 15 to March 15, open until 4 p.m.; closed Easter, Thanksgiving, December 25 and 26, and January 1 and 2.
Admission: Moderate charge for adults, college students, and children ages 10 to 16.
Accessibility: All areas are accessible to the physically challenged.
Special Events: The museum sponsors an annual conference on Civil War medicine the first weekend of August. Docent-guided tours are available for all age groups of 10 or more. They can be arranged Monday through Saturday, 10 a.m. until 3:30 p.m. and Sunday 11 a.m. until 3:30 p.m. (2:30 during winter hours). A $25 deposit for groups of

25 or more must be received two weeks in advance to reserve a tour.
Getting There: The museum is located at 48 East Patrick Street in downtown Frederick, Maryland. It is 37 miles from Gettysburg, Pennsylvania, 23 miles from Antietam, Maryland, 20 miles from Harpers Ferry, West Virginia, and 55 miles from Washington, D.C. There is a public parking garage on the left just past the museum.

I-70 from Baltimore: Take exit 56, state highway 144 west (E. Patrick Street). Proceed 1.6 miles to the museum on the left.

I-70 from Hagerstown: Take exit 54, and go north on Route 355. Turn right on E. South Street, left on S. Carroll Street, and left on E. Patrick Street. The museum is 1 1/2 blocks on the left.

I-270 from Washington, D.C.: Take I-270 north to U.S. 15 north at the 15/I-70 split. Take the South Jefferson Street exit (U.S. 340 east), and proceed about 0.7 miles on S. Jefferson Street. Turn right on W. South Street, left on S. Carroll Street, and left on E. Patrick Street. The museum is 1 1/2 blocks on the left.

U.S. 15 from Gettysburg: Take U.S. 15 south to exit 13A (state route 144 east, Patrick Street). Proceed about 0.4 miles on route 144 east, which becomes W. South Street. Make a left on S. Carroll Street, and left on E. Patrick Street. The museum is 1 1/2 blocks on the left.

U.S. Routes 15/340 from Harpers Ferry and Leesburg: Take U.S. 15 north/340 east toward Frederick. Once in Frederick, do not turn off for Route 15 north, but continue into town on Jefferson Street. Proceed about 0.7 miles on Jefferson Street, turn right on W. South Street, left on S. Carroll Street, and left on E. Patrick Street. The museum is 1 1/2 blocks on the left.

MEDICINE

If the Civil War was militarily the first modern war, medically it was a war fought at the end of the medical Middle Ages. Civil War doctors were woefully unable to treat the widespread disease and battle injuries. One of the many tragedies of the war was that the medical knowledge of the early 1860s did not include sterile dressings, antiseptics and antiseptic surgery, or an understanding of the importance of sanitation and hygiene in preventing disease.

Organization

At the beginning of the Civil War, the medical corps of both sides were underqualified, understaffed, and undersupplied. Few doctors were experienced in surgery or in dealing with large-scale medical and logistical problems.

The Union army medical department was totally unprepared for war. It consisted of 71 surgeons and assistant surgeons (doctors in those days were all called surgeons), of whom many were political appointees and a few were quacks. Of 11,000 physicians in the Union, only 500 had ever performed surgery.

Fortunately for the Union, William A. Hammond was appointed Surgeon General in 1862. Hammond added several hundred surgeons to the army, and he instituted a number of reforms, including appointing medical inspectors and moving makeshift general hospitals into buildings designed specifically as hospitals. But in many areas, Hammond was frustrated. Lincoln's Secretary of War, Edwin M. Stanton, did not always approve Hammond's recommendations. In 1864, Hammond was court-martialed on a petty charge and dismissed from the army, but after the war he was exonerated and reinstated.

The Confederate army's medical department was in better shape organizationally. In July 1862, Samuel Preston Moore took over as the Confederate Surgeon General. Shortly after he resigned his commission as a medical officer in the U.S. Army, he took charge of the Confederate medical organization, which consisted of only 23 other members who had left the Union Medical Department.

Moore had much greater authority than his Union counterpart did, and his orders usually were quickly obeyed. There was nothing he could do about a shortage of surgeons, though. There were just 3000 physicians in the Confederacy, and only 27 had performed surgery.

The outbreak of the war brought in a vast number of medical men on both sides, many of them well-known surgeons. Their presence gave powerful incentive to others, and younger medical men quickly joined.

Hospitals

When the battles started, doctors took over houses, churches, schools, even barns for hospitals. As the number of wounded grew, these buildings were thought to breed and spread disease because of inadequate plumbing and bad ventilation. In 1862 both the North and South began to build "pavilion" hospitals—long, wooden buildings with ample ventilation and ample bed space. By 1865, there were 204 Union general hospitals, while the Confederacy had 154 hospitals.

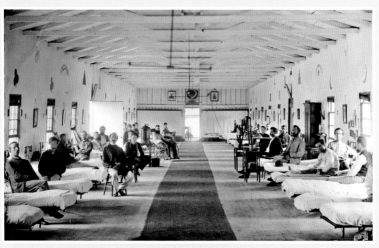

A patient ward at Armory Square Hospital in Washington, D.C.

Battle

Each regiment was assigned a surgeon and an assistant surgeon. During a battle, the assistant surgeon and one or more other men would establish an advance medical station just beyond musket range, with lint, bandages, opium pills, morphine, and whiskey. Stretcher-

A surgeon about to perform an amputation in the field.

bearers went forward to find the wounded and, if the latter could not walk, to carry them to the dressing station. After doing immediate triage, the surgeons usually gave the soldier an opium pill or rubbed morphine into the wound and then sent him to a field hospital.

The most important weapon of the war was the .58-caliber minié ball. The wounds it produced differed in an important way from the gunshot wounds of preceding wars. The old low-velocity round ball caused many fractures in bones of the extremities, but it never produced the shattering bone destruction the minié ball did. The long-range, slow-moving, heavy, conical-shaped, soft lead minié ball distorted on impact, causing large gaping wounds filled with dirt and pieces of clothing. When it hit the torso, it tended to tear internal organs in ways the smoothbore musket ball did not, and its abdomen and head wounds were nearly always fatal.

Field hospitals were located about one half to one mile behind the line of battle, preferably in a sheltered spot behind a hill or in a ravine, marked with a yellow flag with a green H. Amputations, resections of bone, ligatures of arteries, removals of foreign bodies, adjusting and permanently fixing fractures, and all minor and major operations and dressings were done here.

Every effort was made to treat wounded men within 48 hours. The surgeons used a crude system of triage, and tried to pass over both the slightly wounded and the mortally wounded in the interest of saving as many lives as possible. Special attention was given to arm and leg wounds. Amputation was often the "treatment." Of the approximately 175,000 wounds to the extremities received among Union troops, about 30,000 led to amputation.

The Confederate army had roughly the same proportion.

Most amputations were performed with an anesthetic—usually chloroform. A good, capable surgeon could amputate a limb in 10 minutes. The closer to the body the amputation was done, the greater the risk it would be fatal.

The cleanliness of wounds was considered unimportant, and surgeons often went days without washing their hands or instruments, thereby passing germs from one patient to another. Amazingly, about 75 percent of amputees on both sides survived.

As soon as possible after the permanent dressings were applied, the wounded were transported by river or railroad to more permanent hospitals in villages, towns, and cities some miles distant. Cavalrymen never bothered these hospital transport trains, which were identified by a scarlet locomotive and a string of three red lanterns burning on the front at night.

Disease

Approximately 620,000 men died in the Civil War. About three of five Northern deaths and two of three Southern deaths were due to disease. Typhoid, dysentery, and pneumonia were the three leading killers. Typhoid fever is estimated to have caused one quarter of noncombatant Confederate deaths, and dysentery probably cost the Union army 50,000 deaths—more men than the Confederate army killed.

Both armies faced the same basic problems—diseases caused by overcrowded and unsanitary conditions, mosquitoes, and lice. Lack of shoes and proper clothing, especially on the Confederate side, exacerbated minor ailments. Poor diet was a problem for both armies. Fresh fruits and vegetables were rarely available.

But the main cause of disease was the filth of the army camps. To try to remedy this, the Union government created the U.S. Sanitary Commission in June 1861, directed by Frederick Law Olmsted (the landscape architect of Central Park in New York and many other famous parks). For the rest of the war, the commission successfully pressured the army Medical Department to improve sanitation and provide clean water, good food, and fresh air in the camps, to build large, well-ventilated hospitals, and to encourage women to join the newly created nursing corps.

Drugs

Drugs were a constant problem for the Confederacy. Confederate Surgeon General Moore foresaw shortages in drugs, surgical instruments, and hospital supplies; but there were really only two sources of supply at his disposal—capture and blockade running. Despite frequent shortages of some drugs, the Confederate record for providing the necessary medicine to its soldiers was a good one.

Nurses

Early in the war, the staff nurses were mainly convalescing patients, who were often weak, unpleasant, and did not like the dirty work. The Union soon decided that a corps of female nurses should be added to the army, and eventually thousands of women served as volunteer nurses in military hospitals.

Dorothea Dix, widely known as a reformer of jails and as the "founder" of several state mental hospitals, was appointed Superintendent of the United States Nursing Corps, and the idea of professional nursing was born. Initially, it did not work well. Dix had extremely Victorian tastes, insisting that her nurses be at least 30 and dress in drab clothing. They could not socialize with either surgeons or patients, and they had to insist upon their rights as the senior attendants in the wards. Many surgeons disliked Miss Dix's nurses, not the least because most had no nursing training, tended to use their own home remedies instead of the prescribed drugs, and tried to interfere with operations they did not feel were necessary. The situation slowly reached equilibrium as younger and more flexible nurses began to appear in the army.

The Confederacy believed that a military hospital was no place for a lady, though in Richmond there were significant numbers of women working in the city's many hospitals. Both Confederate and Union medical staffs used small groups of Catholic nuns in certain general hospitals, and they were well regarded.

The female nurses provided solace beyond their numbers, and proved an invaluable aid to the sick and wounded soldiers and medical authorities on both sides. More than 4000 women served as nurses in Union hospitals, and respect for the role of women in medicine rose considerably among both patients and doctors.

The hospital ship Red Rover—*a converted Confederate transport—helped in the fight against fever and dysentery during the Union's Mississippi campaign.*

Point Lookout State Park

Point Lookout, Maryland, is located at the extreme tip of St. Mary's County, on a peninsula formed by the joining of the Chesapeake Bay and the Potomac River. In 1830, the Federal government erected a lighthouse there. Before the Civil War, Point Lookout was a resort community; but in 1862, when it became clear that the Civil War would not end quickly, the Hammond Hospital was built at the tip of the Point, along with a supply depot for the Army of the Potomac—both were convenient to the battlefields in the East.

This proximity to the battlefields also made Point Lookout a suitable location for a prisoner-of-war camp, known as Camp Hoffman, for enlisted Confederate soldiers and for Maryland's Southern sympathizers. The new POW camp was surrounded by water on three sides, making it difficult to escape. But conditions at the camp were terrible; there were no trees or shrubs for shelter, the camp was only a few feet above sea level, drainage was poor, and the camp was damp year round.

As the early war "parole" system ended, Point Lookout became the largest Union prisoner-of-war camp in the country. Soon there were over 20,000 Confederates in two wooden-walled prisoner pens. One pen was about 30 acres and the other about 10 acres, each sited on flat sand and surrounded by a fence 15 feet high.

Although the prison camp was "designed"—a very loose term—for 10,000 prisoners, during most of its existence it held from 12,600 to 20,000 prisoners, both military and civilian. More than 52,000 were held there at one time or another. The prisoners were provided with tents for shelter, but after large battles an influx of new prisoners often meant there were not enough tents to go around. The extreme overcrowding, Maryland's freezing temperatures, shortages of firewood for heat, polluted water, and low food rations took their toll. The camp was in operation for less than two years, from August 1863 until June 1865, and nearly 4000 prisoners died there. However, the 8 percent death rate was actually less than half the death rate among soldiers who were in the field with their own armies.

Among the guards at Point Lookout were African American soldiers of the U.S. Colored Troops (USCT) regiments. In a few cases these soldiers guarded their former masters. During their incarceration, a number of the Confederate prisoners defected to the Union side. The 1st and 4th Regiments, U.S. Volunteers, were organized from these Confederate prisoners and sent west to fight Indians. The camp's most unusual "prisoner" was Sergeant Sarah "Jane" A. Perkins, a soldier with the Confederate Pittsylvania Artillery. After she was captured at the Battle of Spotsylvania, she was sent to the Point Lookout POW Camp. Two months later she gave birth to a baby boy. She was then sent to Old Capitol Prison in Washington, D.C., and finally to Fitzburg Prison.

In 1864, as part of General Jubal Early's raid into Maryland, the Confederates planned a raid on Point Lookout, hoping to free the prisoners, arm them, and have them march on Washington. However, Union officers learned of the planned attack and the raid was aborted.

Today Point Lookout State Park features a restored Civil War fort and a visitors center with a museum displaying exhibits about the prison. Most of the prison pen site is under water now, but the Friends of Point Lookout have recreated a section of the wall, as well as the barracks and officer quarters. Visitors can also still see

the remains of the open graves of the Confederate dead who were removed to the Point Lookout Cemetery. The lighthouse, owned by the U.S. Navy, is still at the tip of the Point, though not in use.

The Point Lookout Cemetery holds 3384 Confederate soldiers in a mass grave. An 85-foot granite monument—the first Confederate monument erected after the Civil War—rises over the area, with large bronze tablets containing the names of the prisoners at its base. There is also a smaller memorial monument erected by the state of Maryland.

Visitor Information

301-872-5688;
www.dnr.state.md.us/publiclands/
southern/pointlookout.html
Hours: The park and Fort Lincoln are open daily, 6 a.m. until 8 p.m.; the Visitors Center is open daily, 8 a.m. until 6 p.m.
Admission: Minimal per person fee to enter the park on weekends and holidays.
Accessibility: The Visitors Center and fort area are handicapped accessible, but the individual buildings within the fort area are not; that area is not paved, but is mostly flat and grassy.
Special Events: Point Lookout sponsors historic programs and demonstrations throughout the year. Popular annual festivities include: Blue and Gray Day in May, featuring artillery and infantry demonstrations; dress parade and evening pro-

grams; and a Confederate Memorial Service, usually the second weekend in June, when descendants of the Confederate POWs gather to honor their ancestors. Additional living-history character portrayals of Confederate Civil War soldiers are featured throughout the summer. Call for dates and times.
Getting There: The park is at the southern tip of St. Mary's County, at the junction of the Potomac River and the Chesapeake Bay.

From Baltimore: Take I-695 to route I-97 south to Maryland Route 3 south (Route 3 will turn into Route 301). Follow Route 301 south to state highway 4 south in Upper Marlboro. Follow highway 4 south all the way across the Solomons Island Bridge. After the bridge, turn left at the first traffic light, which will be state highway 235 south, and follow it to the town of Ridge (at a blinking red light). Turn left onto state highway 5 south, and follow it to the end (approximately seven miles) to Point Lookout.

From Washington, D.C.: Take I-495 to route 4/Pennsylvania Avenue, then south to Upper Marlboro, then as above.

From the south: Take U.S. 301 north across the Potomac River, then turn east and south on state highway 234 toward Leonardtown. At the end of highway 234, turn right onto state highway 5. Follow highway 5 south all the way into Point Lookout.

An 1864 lithograph, left, shows the Federal hospital at the tip of the peninsula and an idealized view of the prison camp, top right. Union troop quarters surrounded the prison on three sides, with Chesapeake Bay guarding the fourth. Below, Confederate prisoners take the oath of allegiance before being paroled at the end of the war.

The Battle of Brices Cross Roads

In the spring of 1864, General William T. Sherman led more than 100,000 Union soldiers into northern Georgia to capture Atlanta. Sherman's supply lines through Tennessee were long and vulnerable, especially his single railroad link—the one-track Nashville & Chattanooga Railroad. To protect these supply lines, Sherman sent Brigadier General Samuel D. Sturgis south to eliminate the threat from Confederate major general Nathan Bedford Forrest's cavalry units, which specialized in harassing Union lines of communication.

Sturgis marched south with 8000 Union soldiers, more than 20 cannons, and 250 wagons carrying supplies. In fact, Forrest was just then in northern Alabama planning an attack on Sherman's rail link, but he hurried back to intercept Sturgis close to the town of Baldwyn, Mississippi, at a spot known as Brices Cross Roads. On the night of June 9, as the two units prepared to face each other, torrential rains poured down.

Forrest's plan was simple. "Their cavalry will move out ahead of their infantry and should reach the cross roads three hours in advance. We can whip their cavalry in that time. As soon as the fight opens they will send back to have the infantry hurried up, and coming at a run for five or six miles the infantry will be so tired we will run right over them."

Before dawn the next morning, Forrest moved out with 1500 men and two batteries of cannon, followed a few hours later by 3300 more men. Forrest's troops met the Union cavalry a mile east of Brices Cross Roads, and by taking advantage of the terrain, the outnumbered Confederates held Sturgis's men back. Meanwhile, Union infantrymen, who had set out two hours later than the cavalry, heard the sounds of the fighting ahead. In the sweltering heat, their officers drove the troops forward at a rapid trot, but nearly impassable muddy roads and their long supply train slowed their progress. When they finally arrived at Brices Cross Roads, they were—as Forrest expected—overheated, exhausted, and in no condition to fight a tough battle. By midafternoon the Union lines had been pushed back to Brices Cross Roads and the Confederates were in control of the battle. Sturgis tried a careful withdrawal across the Tishomingo Creek Bridge, but a wagon overturned on the bridge. Pounded by cannons, the Union troops broke ranks to ford the creek and began to flee down the road, with Forrest in hot pursuit.

Eight miles farther down the road, more Union soldiers panicked when they tried to ford the deep mud of the Hatchie River. The retreat became a rout. Sturgis's two Union colored-troop regiments fought furiously (many refused to surrender because

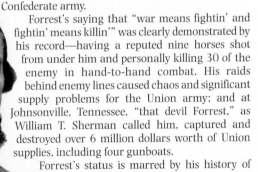

Nathan Bedford Forrest

Nathan Forrest, though uneducated, was a great military tactician and cavalryman. A self-made man, he became one of the wealthiest men in the South by the time of the Civil War, through his plantation and slave trade, and he rose from private to lieutenant general in the Confederate army.

Forrest's saying that "war means fightin' and fightin' means killin'" was clearly demonstrated by his record—having a reputed nine horses shot from under him and personally killing 30 of the enemy in hand-to-hand combat. His raids behind enemy lines caused chaos and significant supply problems for the Union army; and at Johnsonville, Tennessee, "that devil Forrest," as William T. Sherman called him, captured and destroyed over 6 million dollars worth of Union supplies, including four gunboats.

Forrest's status is marred by his history of racism—from his early slave trade to a possible massacre of U.S. Colored Troops at Fort Pillow, Tennessee, and his brief association with the Ku Klux Klan after the war (though he tried to have the organization disbanded in 1869).

A monument dedicated to both Union and Confederate dead is flanked by a Civil War–era cannon.

The center includes many interactive exhibits, including flip cards with questions and answers about the battle, a diorama playing various bugle calls from Civil War times, and a display of a soldier's uniform and gear in which visitors can feel the gum blanket or raincoat worn by soldiers at the battle—on a hot, muggy June day.

Brices Cross Roads National Battlefield Site

Congress made Brices Cross Roads a National Battlefield Site in 1929 after much lobbying by the United Daughters of the Confederacy and local organizations. The site has a monument to the battle, two artillery pieces, and an interpretive wayside. In 1994, the Brices Cross Roads National Battlefield Commission purchased 800 acres of the original battlefield for preservation.

Visitor Information

For the Visitor and Interpretive Center: 662-365-3969; www.brices-crossroads.com. For the battlefield: 662-680-4025 or 1-800-305-7417; www.nps.gov/brcr/

Hours: The Interpretive Center is open Tuesday–Saturday, 9 a.m. until 5 p.m.; Sunday, 12:30 p.m. until 5 p.m.; closed Monday. The national battlefield can be visited at any time.

Admission: Minimal fee for admission to the Interpretive Center; National Parks Pass, Golden Eagle, Golden Age, and Golden Access are honored at the battlefield.

Accessibility: The Interpretive Center is fully accessible; the battlefield is not.

Getting There: Brices Cross Roads Visitor and Interpretive Center is next to the town of Baldwyn in extreme northeast Mississippi, about nine miles from Tupelo. Take U.S. 78 to Tupelo, then U.S. 45 north to Baldwyn 15 miles. The national battlefield is four miles west of Baldwyn on state Route 370. Baldwyn is 113 miles from Memphis, Tennessee, and 160 miles from Birmingham, Alabama.

they expected to be killed if they were captured) but to no avail.

More rain fell that night, further slowing the Union retreat. Harried by Forrest's cavalry, most of the Union artillery and wagons bogged down on the muddy roads and had to be abandoned.

When the debacle ended, Sturgis had lost 2240 men. Over 1600 were captured, along with at least 16 guns, 1500 small arms, 176 large six-horse wagons, including five ambulances, and immense quantities of other equipment and supplies including medicine. Forrest had fewer than 500 casualties.

Brices Cross Roads Visitor and Interpretive Center

Baldwyn resident Claude Gentry, known as Mr. Claude, took a great interest in the battle and collected a large number of artifacts from the battlefield. When Gentry died, his grandson turned the collection over to the city. These artifacts are housed in the Brices Cross Roads Visitors and Interpretive Center in the town of Baldwyn, four miles east of the site of the battle. There is a 22-minute video detailing the battle, a bookstore, and a gift shop that offers period gifts and resource material about the Civil War. The permanent exhibits include a flag carried by the U.S. Colored Troops during the battle and a lighted outdoor exhibit flying the flags of the 10 Northern states and five Southern states whose soldiers fought in the battle.

The Battle of Tupelo

Confederate general Nathan Bedford Forrest's virtual destruction of a Union force at Brices Cross Roads in June 1864 did not deter Union general William T. Sherman from sending another force into Mississippi almost immediately to try to destroy the Confederate cavalrymen. Forrest had become Sherman's personal nemesis, and the Union general said his forces would "follow Forrest to the death if it cost 10,000 lives and breaks the treasury. There never will be peace in Tennessee until Forrest is dead." To achieve that end, Sherman sent Major General A. J. Smith and a force of over 14,000 men from Memphis into Mississippi. Forrest was concerned because he had both personnel and health problems. He only had about 7500 men, mainly cavalry, of whom 20 to 25 percent would be out of action holding the horses during a battle. On June 28, he telegraphed his superior, General Stephen Lee, to join him: "I am suffering from boils. If enemy should move out I desire you to take command of the forces. Our force is insufficient to meet this command. Can't you get help?"

Smith's large Union force advanced south slowly and deliberately so as not to make the mistake the Union forces had made at Brices Cross Roads, where they were caught and defeated before they could form their defenses. As they moved, Confederate cavalry nipped at their heels and even briefly captured the Union supply train. However, these forays did not stop Smith, and he and his forces continued to march, burning the surrounding countryside as they moved. On July 13, the Union forces dug in for the night at Harrisonburg, just outside of Tupelo, on a strong defensive line set on a small ridge gradually sloping toward what was mainly open ground.

Forrest and Stephen Lee decided to attack, despite scouting reports from their subordinate commanders that "we are going to be badly whipped." To add to the problems, the hot weather and rapid marches were taking a toll on their men and Forrest was ill. Even though most of the troops were his, he pressed the higher-ranked Lee to take command. Lee protested, but finally agreed.

At seven thirty in the morning on July 14, the Confederates, although outnumbered two to one, attacked. It was an uncoordinated disaster. As the Confederates advanced slowly, a Kentucky brigade raced forward and outdistanced the rest of the troops, allowing entrenched Union forces to concentrate their fire on the single brigade and decimate it.

It was so hot that many of the already weary Confederates fainted during the advance, and this, combined with the heavy losses, collapsed the attack. The Confederates fell back and dug in, expecting Smith to follow, but Smith, not wanting to be lured into an ambush, stayed in place. The next morning, the Union forces turned north back to Memphis. Forrest and his cavalry followed them, but the Confederate attacks petered out after Union soldiers wounded Forrest in a skirmish at Town Creek.

Smith had inflicted a stinging defeat on Forrest and the Confederates, but his superiors criticized him for not continuing his attack with his vastly superior force. This was probably unjustified. Smith's forces had wounded Forrest, inflicted twice as many casualties as they suffered (wounding three Confederate brigade commanders and almost every field and line officer of the 38th Mississippi) and had caused a great deal of damage to the Confederate infrastructure. Forrest was still on the loose, but he never again seriously threatened Sherman's supply lines.

Tupelo National Battlefield

In 1925, the Brices Cross Roads–Tupelo Battlefield Association, working with the United Daughters of the Confederacy, began to lobby for the two battlefields to be designated National Battlefield sites. Both received that designation on February 21, 1929, and a monument was erected on each site. The Tupelo site became part of the National Park Service in 1933, and in 1942 the two cannons that stand there today were mounted. It was designated a National Battlefield on August 10, 1961.

Visitor Information

800-305-7417; www.nps.gov/tupe/
Admission: Free.
Accessibility: There is no designated parking for the site.
Getting There: The small one-acre site is within the city limits of Tupelo, Mississippi, about 1.3 miles west of U.S. 45 and one mile east of the Natchez Trace Parkway.

BALLOONS

The first hot-air balloon was launched in France in 1783. The balloons were first used regularly for military purposes during the Civil War. In early 1861, a number of well-known balloonists approached the U.S. War Department, suggesting the establishment of a balloon corps to provide aerial reconnaissance for the Union armies from stationary balloons. The most prominent of the balloonists were Thaddeus S. C. Lowe and John LaMountain.

Lowe met with President Abraham Lincoln, and on July 17, 1861, Lowe went up in a balloon on a simulated reconnaissance mission and sent telegrams while floating 500 feet above Washington. Lincoln—duly impressed—established the Balloon Corps, with Lowe as commander. The first U.S. balloon designed for military use, the *Union*, was ready on August 28. However, because Lowe had not completed a portable gas generator to inflate the balloon, he could use it only in the Washington area, where he had access to the municipal gas lines.

Secretary of War Simon Cameron ordered Lowe to build six more balloons, made of silk coated with linseed oil, and the Balloon Corps began to operate. On September 24, 1861, Lowe ascended, and telegraphed intelligence on Confederate troops located at Falls Church, Virginia, more than three miles away. Based on this information, Union guns fired—the first time in the history of warfare that troops were fired on with an aerial spotter.

On July 25, 1861, while Lowe was campaigning in Washington, another balloonist, John LaMountain, demonstrated his balloon to Major General Benjamin F. Butler, the commander of the Union forces at Fortress Monroe in Virginia. During the demonstration, LaMountain made the first aerial reconnaissance of the Civil War, surveying Confederate encampments around Newmarket Bridge, Virginia, and the James River north of Newport News. However, despite Butler's support, LaMountain had difficulty getting equipment. Lowe refused to cooperate with him, and animosity developed. LaMountain had few allies, and finally General George McClellan dismissed him.

Lowe's balloons became much more tactically useful when he produced a gas generator to fit in the back of a standard army wagon, so the balloons could be moved to a battle area and inflated there. Lowe's balloons became popular with senior officers, and several went aloft with Lowe. Two of Lowe's gas balloons were launched almost daily to observe Confederate positions dur-

*The balloon **Intrepid** being inflated to reconnoiter enemy positions at the Battle of Fair Oaks. Thaddeus Lowe is standing to the right of the* Intrepid, *with his hand resting on the netting while measuring the amount of gas already in the balloon.*

Thaddeus Lowe ascending in the Intrepid *at the Battle of Fair Oaks. As soon as the balloon passed the treetops, Confederate batteries opened fire until he rose beyond their reach. Years later he wrote, "It was my night observations that gave the primary knowledge which saved the Federal army at the battle of Fair Oaks."*

BALLOONS *(continued)*

ing the Warwick–Yorktown siege of April and May 1862, where observer Lieutenant George Armstrong Custer first saw the Confederate evacuation. To try to stop these intrusions, the Confederates introduced antiaircraft guns. Confederate major E. P. Alexander fired his artillery at the balloons, but the guns could not be elevated high enough. Still, the artillery could reach it while it was being raised or lowered. No hits were scored, but this may have discouraged some high-ranking Union officers from using the balloons.

Observation balloons had several drawbacks. They could be used only on calm, clear days, and anything more than a gentle wind would buffet the balloon, making accurate observations impossible and perhaps driving it to the ground. Often the movement of the balloon tore loose the telegraph wires that connected the balloon's machine with one on the ground, thus making the balloon useless for relaying information. There was also the problem of gathering useful information, which required having a military man in the balloon.

Lowe provided tactical reports to the Union troops during the Battle of Fair Oaks, when he was able to continually transmit information on Confederate troop positions.

Despite their utility, the balloons never became universally popular among the Union commanders. Six weeks after Fredericksburg, the Army of the Potomac's new commander, General Joseph Hooker, cut Lowe's pay and reduced his staff. After much acrimony, Lowe resigned his position on May 8, 1863. By August, the Balloon Corps had disbanded and aerial observation by the Union army ended.

The Confederate army also had a small balloon corps. In the spring of 1862, Captain John Randolph Bryan built a balloon consisting of a cotton envelope coated with varnish and filled with hot air. On his second flight, he was fired on by Confederate troops—clearly not expecting the Confederacy to have such cutting-edge technology—but Bryan escaped and landed safely. The other two Confederate balloons were "silk-dress balloons," made of multi colored patches of silk, but both were captured by the Union.

The Siege of Vicksburg

In late March 1863, Union general Ulysses S. Grant tried to capture Vicksburg, Mississippi—known to the Confederates as the "Gibraltar of the Mississippi," and which President Abraham Lincoln called "the key!" He exhorted Grant to capture the city quickly, saying, "The war can never be brought to a close until that key is in our pocket." The campaign would take over three months and several major battles in west-central Mississippi, concluding with a 47-day siege of the city.

Control over Vicksburg was the final obstacle to Union control of the Mississippi River, which was a vital part of the Union's "Anaconda Plan" (*see* sidebar, below) for winning the war. It would divide the Confederacy in two and sever its supply lines, while also providing the Union access to those same supply lines and transportation and trade routes.

Capturing Vicksburg was not easy. It sat on the Mississippi riverbank, high on bluffs where its guns and fortifications dominated the waterway. Grant and his subordinate, General William T. Sherman, had tried and failed to take Vicksburg in late December 1862 with a frontal land assault.

This time, Grant planned to attack from the south and east, and took a risk by cutting his forces loose from their normal long, continuous supply lines so they could advance quickly. Grant began by marching the main body of his forces down the west side of the river past Vicksburg to the river port at Hard Times, Louisiana, where he met Union rear admiral David D. Porter's fleet of seven ironclad gunboats, a ram, and three transports. After moving Grant's troops across the Mississippi, Porter attacked Confederate batteries south of Vicksburg at Grand Gulf. Meanwhile, other Union troops moved through Mississippi on raids, further diverting Confederate units from Vicksburg's 40,000-strong forces, led by Lieutenant General John C. Pemberton, one of Grant's old friends.

By May 1, Vicksburg defenders were scattered throughout the area, and Grant defeated a vastly outnum-

The Anaconda Plan

The Anaconda Plan was one of the Union's first attempts to devise a strategy to win the war with a minimum of casualties and bitterness. Union general-in-chief Winfield Scott proposed to strangle the South (thus the name Anaconda, bestowed by Union newspapers) by blockading the more than 3500 miles of Southern coastline and sending 60,000 troops down the Mississippi with gunboats to take the river from Illinois to the Gulf of Mexico.

While the plan had merit, it ignored a number of realities. First, it would be several years before the United States Navy would have enough ships to execute an effective blockade. Second, the longer the Confederacy existed, the better its chances for diplomatic recognition and economic support from European countries. Third, the Anaconda Plan did not guarantee the South would ever surrender. Fourth—and perhaps most important—Northerners and Southerners alike did not want a long war. Instead, they wanted immediate action in the misguided belief that one battle would end the war. While the Anaconda Plan was never officially adopted, it was a basic Union strategy, supplemented by aggressive (and, for most of the war, futile) attempts to destroy Lee's Army of Northern Virginia and capture Richmond, the Confederate capital.

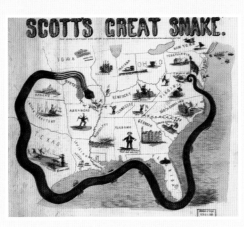

Coehorn 13-inch mortars used at Vicksburg could lob a 200-pound explosive shell about two miles.

he could help Pemberton at Vicksburg. The two Confederate generals began to try to work their way out of their dilemma, but as early as May 13, Johnston telegraphed Richmond ominously, "I arrived this evening, finding the enemy in force between this place and General Pemberton. I am too late."

Grant then turned west toward Vicksburg. On May 16, he smashed through Champion's Hill and the Black River Bridge, forcing Pemberton back toward the defenses of Vicksburg. By May 18, Union forces began to arrive at Vicksburg from the east and northeast. Sherman went north to take the hills overlooking the Yazoo River, where he had suffered a major defeat the previous year, and from that point was able to reconnect and protect the Union supply lines. Grant's gamble had paid off.

bered Confederate force at a hard fought battle at Port Gibson, Mississippi, south of Vicksburg. Pemberton assumed that Grant would turn north toward Vicksburg, so he moved his own troops north toward the city to cut off the Union forces. Instead, Grant first turned northeast toward Jackson to eliminate the Confederate forces there before they could reinforce the Vicksburg troops.

Grant joined up with the forces of Union general Sherman, Major General John A. McClernand, and Major General James B. McPherson in a well-planned maneuver that put their troops between Pemberton's forces in Vicksburg and the Confederate force in Jackson. When the newly arrived Confederate general Joseph E. Johnston heard that Grant was approaching, Johnston hastily abandoned the city of Jackson, eliminating any hope that

By May 19, Vicksburg was surrounded. From Jackson, Johnston had earlier suggested to Pemberton that he try to escape with his forces and leave the city to Grant, but Pemberton chose to fall behind Vicksburg's defenses. He sent a message to Johnston saying, "I have decided to hold Vicksburg as long as possible. I still conceive it to be the most important point in the Confederacy."

Illuminated by burning buildings and barrels of pitch ignited by Confederate defenders, Federal gunboats and transports carry troops and supplies for General Grant's offensive.

Civilian Life Under Siege

During the 47-day siege of Vicksburg, the Union forces shelled the city regularly, driving many civilians from their homes and into about 500 overcrowded underground caves. Children trying to play outside the entrances were dragged in anytime a shell exploded nearby, and occasionally one would hit directly above a cave, trapping or killing all inside. Dogs ran wild, occasionally attacking people in the streets or raiding campfires when food was cooking.

Union sharpshooters also kept up a constant drizzle of small-arms fire on the area. The hospitals ran short of medicine, and the constant influx of wounded made them hellish even by Civil War standards.

As food became scarce, soldiers received only two biscuits, two slices of bacon, a few peas, and a spoonful of rice a day. Some of Vicksburg's citizens took advantage of the battle by selling food to the highest bidder. A Confederate soldier reported, "Molasses was ten dollars a gallon, flour five dollars a pound, and corn meal one hundred forty dollars a bushel." On July 4, 1863, over 29,500 Confederates surrendered. To the disgust of the residents, the Union troops marched in with "flying banners & joyful music"; but the atmosphere changed as the victors passed out "sugar, whisky and fresh fruit in great abundance" and a dozen steamers arrived "loaded down with provisions of every kind."

Grant immediately sent Union troops to attack Vicksburg's defenses. He ordered General Francis P. Blair's division to attack Stockade Redan, a Confederate fort guarding one of the approaches to the city. However, Southern troops had cut down dozens of trees to block the approach, and Blair's three brigades were cut to pieces.

Grant then tried another massive attack along the three separate roads that led to the Great Redoubt—a four-sided, rectangular fortress that, with the Third Louisiana Redan, guarded the road between Jackson and Vicksburg. Union forces were able to get close enough to plant flags on the walls, but were finally forced back.

After that failure, Grant decided not to risk more of his troops and began a classic siege of the city. Union forces surrounded the city with fortifications to cut it off from the outside world. At the same time, Union engineers and sappers began to dig trenches up to several of the most important Confederate fortifications, then planned to tunnel under them and mine the tunnel with huge quantities of black powder charges. When detonated, the explosions would rip holes in the fortifications from below, through which Union troops could storm.

In Vicksburg, the rapid arrival of the Union forces caught the citizens by surprise, but their reaction was defiant. They had been bombarded earlier in the war but had refused to surrender; but time would reveal that they were not well prepared for a siege. For the rest of May, the only encouraging note for the population was when Confederate batteries sank the Union gunboat *Cincinnati* on May 26. Even this proved a mixed blessing. Union sailors unloaded the cannons from the gunboat on the opposite shore and joined in the general bombardment.

The situation inside the city rapidly deteriorated. The Union forces used huge Coehorn mortars to lob explosive shells weighing up to 200 pounds into the city. The mortars had a significant impact on the population, and one Vicksburg resident noted, "If any one of them was silent from the beginning of the siege until the white flag was raised any longer than was necessary to cool and load it, I fail to recall the occasion."

While the citizens retrieved their water from Vicksburg's cisterns, the soldiers in the fortifications outside the city had to rely on water taken straight from the muddy Mississippi. Soon disease began to take a toll on the Confederate soldiers. Throughout June, Pemberton and Johnston kept up a steady stream of messages trying to coordinate a relief effort or a breakout, but it came to nothing.

Meanwhile, Union trenches moved inexorably toward the Confederate fortifications. "Pioneer" battalions of 150 men would work all day on the trenches, and a second shift replaced them at night. Despite heavy Confederate fire and attempts to countermine, on June 24, 1863, the Union forces completed a tunnel 40 feet under the Third Louisiana Redan. The next morning, the miners loaded it with 2200 pounds of black powder. At three thirty that afternoon, Union engineers detonated the charges. The whole fort and connecting outworks seemed to begin a leisurely upward movement, gradually breaking into fragments through which could occasionally be caught a glimpse of some dark items—men, gun carriages, and other solid objects. The Union artillery and infantry began to fire, and the first column of volunteers from the 31st and 45th Illinois Infantry began the assault.

The explosion blew a huge crater into the works—over 10 feet deep and over 30 feet wide—but the Confederates quickly moved up on the far side. As the Union troops tried

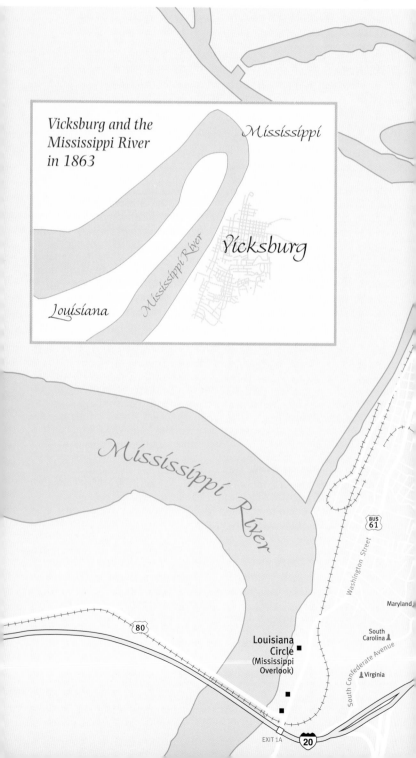

Vicksburg and the
Mississippi River
in 1863

Mississippi

Vicksburg

Mississippi River

Louisiana

to move out of the crater, they were mowed down, and finally had to fall back.

On July 1, the Union engineers detonated a second mine, wrecking the fortifications, but an infantry assault proved to be unnecessary. By July 3, starvation, daily bombardments, and the hopelessness of the situation drove Pemberton to ask for surrender terms. However, he refused Grant's demand for unconditional surrender. That evening Grant, overruling his staff's objections, offered Pemberton terms that would allow his men to be paroled over their signatures and to keep their private possessions. Pemberton accepted the next day, July 4. Grant supplied food to the Confederate soldiers and the citizens of Vicksburg for the next five days while the paperwork was completed.

Thus ended the Vicksburg Campaign. The day before, Robert E. Lee had been defeated at Gettysburg,

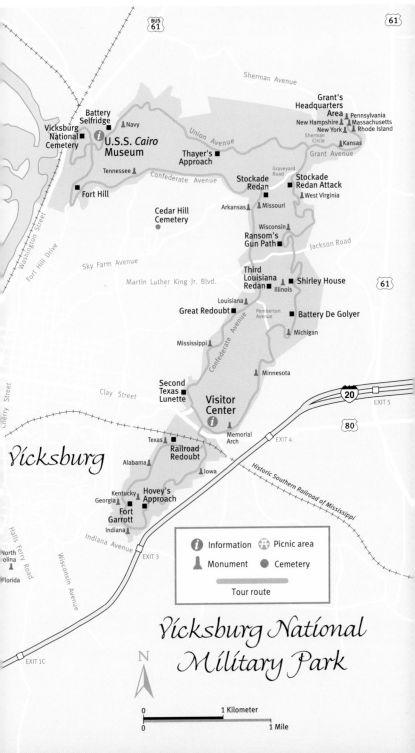

Vicksburg National Military Park

The U.S.S. Cairo was one of seven ironclad river gunboats, called Pook Turtles after their designer, Samuel M. Pook. The gunboat was a flat-bottomed, light-draft stern-wheeler, measuring 175 feet in length with a 6-foot draft. Its original armament of 13 guns included 8-inch guns, 32-pounders, 42-pounders, and one 12-pounder howitzer.

and the double defeats ended any realistic Confederate hopes of a military victory.

Vicksburg National Military Park

The 1800-acre park, established in 1899 by Congress, commemorates the campaign, siege, and defense of Vicksburg, as well as its history under Union occupation during the Civil War and Reconstruction. It includes a collection of over 1320 historic monuments, markers, tablets, and plaques that make the park the largest collection of outdoor sculpture in the southeastern United States. There are 20 miles of reconstructed trenches, earthworks, approaches, and parallels; nine fortifications; a 16-mile tour road; five historic buildings (including an antebellum home); and over 140 cannons. The area also includes the Vicksburg National Cemetery and a museum that houses the restored Union gunboat U.S.S. Cairo.

Vicksburg National Cemetery is the final resting place of 17,000 Civil War soldiers, more than in any other national cemetery in the United States. After the conclusion of the Civil War, the U.S. Army located and exhumed the remains of 300,000 Union veterans buried in the South, then reinterred them in national cemeteries. Approximately 75 percent of the Civil War dead at Vicksburg are unidentified; their graves are marked by square blocks and a grave number. Upright headstones with rounded tops mark the graves of known soldiers. Originally the cemetery was intended only for Union dead, but in the late 1860s two Confederates were mistakenly buried in Section B of the cemetery. Graves of 5000 Confederates who died in the campaign are located in what is today the Cedar Hill Cemetery (Vicksburg City Cemetery).

The centerpiece of the U.S.S. Cairo Museum is the namesake 175-foot Union ironclad gunboat, which was sunk north of Vicksburg by a Confederate mine. Designed to operate on the lower Mississippi River and overcome the strong Confederate defenses, it mounted 13 cannons and was clad in heavy armor. On the morning of December 12, 1862, the *Cairo* led a small flotilla up the Yazoo River. As they approached Vicksburg, two explosions under the gunboat tore open the hull, and the *Cairo* sank slowly. No crew members were lost, but the *Cairo* took its place in history as the first ship sunk by an electrically detonated mine. The *Cairo* was raised in 1964. The restored gunboat includes a reconstructed gun deck with cannons, the ship's engines and boilers, and the pilothouse. The museum also contains artifacts recovered from the vessel, including sailors' personal possessions, cookware, medical supplies, and weapons. A six-minute video tells the story of the sinking and recovery of the *Cairo.* The museum is located at milepost 7.8 along Park Tour Road.

The park Visitors Center offers general and historical information services, including an 18-minute orientation film, exhibits on the various topics of the Civil War period, a bookstore, and regional information. The exhibits inside the Center include a Hospital Room, Cave Life, and a variety of military artifacts.

Visitor Information
601-636-0583; www.nps.gov/vick/; *Cairo* Museum, 601-636-2199; www.nps.gov/vick/cairo/cairo.htm
Hours: Vicksburg Military Park and Cemetery, daily, 8 a.m. until 5 p.m.; Park and cemetery closed December 25; *Cairo* Museum, November to March, daily, 8:30 a.m. until 5 p.m.; April to October, daily, 9:30 a.m. until 6 p.m.
Admission: Small fee per vehicle; National Parks Pass, Golden Eagle, Golden Age, and Golden Access are honored.
Accessibility: The main park Visitors Center and the *Cairo* Museum are wheelchair accessible.
Special Events: Living-history demonstrations during the summer.
Getting There: From the east or west: Take I-20 to exit 4B at Vicksburg, Mississippi. Follow Clay Street (U.S. 80) west for less than 1/2 mile to the park entrance.

From the north: Take I-55 south to Jackson, Mississippi, then I-20 west to exit 4B at Vicksburg. Follow Clay Street (U.S. 80) west for less than 1/2 mile to the park entrance.

From the south: Take I-55 north or U.S. highway 49 to Jackson, Mississippi, then I-20 west to exit 4B at Vicksburg. Follow Clay Street (U.S. 80) west for less than 1/2 mile to the park entrance.

Vicksburg Battlefield Museum

The Vicksburg Battlefield Museum is home to the Gray & Blue Naval Society's collection of over 200 Civil War gunboat models, the largest collection of Civil War ship models in the world. These slab-sided steamboats with armor mounted on their sloping sides and heavy cannons firing broadside were the key to winning battles that took place along the United States rivers. The collection, all in the same 1-to-96 scale, gives the visitor the opportunity to compare and contrast the size, armament, and general appearance of these important vessels.

Other exhibits include a diorama of the siege of Vicksburg with over 2500 1-to-87-scale figures of soldiers. There are few trees displayed, only the terrain, making it easier to understand the battle. There are also models of other types of riverboats that plied the Mississippi, as well as models of U.S. Navy warships with Mississippi names, a collection of artifacts from the siege of Vicksburg, and original Civil War paintings by

Herb Mott. Every hour the museum presents a half-hour film, *The Vanishing Glory,* which tells the story of the siege of Vicksburg.

Visitor Information
601-638-6500; vicksburgbattlefieldmuseum.com
Hours: Labor Day to Memorial Day, daily, 9 a.m. until 5 p.m.; Memorial Day to Labor Day, daily, 8 a.m. until 8 p.m.
Admission: Moderate fee for adults and minimal fee for students.
Accessibility: Fully accessible.
Getting There: The museum is located in Vicksburg, Mississippi.

From the east or west: Take I-20 to Vicksburg, Mississippi, then take exit 4B to Frontage Road and turn right. The museum is next to the Battlefield Inn.

From the north or south: Take I-55 to Jackson, Mississippi, then take I-20 west approximately 40 miles to Vicksburg. Use exit 4B to Frontage Road and turn right. The museum is next to the Battlefield Inn.

"Fighting Tom" Sweeny and General Sweeny's Museum

General Thomas "Fighting Tom" Sweeny lost his right arm above the elbow during the Mexican-American War. He remained in the army during the 1850s, and in January 1861 he was promoted to captain and given command of the large St. Louis arsenal. In February 1861, he was replaced as commander by his friend, Captain Nathaniel Lyon, and Sweeny became Lyon's trusted deputy until the Battle of Wilson Creek in August 1862, where Lyon was killed and Sweeny was wounded.

In January 1863, Sweeny was given command of the 52nd Illinois Volunteer Infantry, and he commanded the 52nd at Shiloh in fighting near the "Hornet's Nest." Sweeny and his men fought well and Sweeny was wounded several times, including a serious wound in his good arm. He also led the regiment at the Battle of Corinth, where he was again slightly wounded in his left arm and had a horse shot out from under him. In March 1863 he was promoted to brigadier general, and in 1864 he joined Sherman's army as a division commander in the Atlanta campaign.

General Thomas Sweeny

During this campaign, he suffered a self-inflicted personal disaster. Sweeny has been described as a "hot tempered Irishman" not averse to having a drink; and having been a professional soldier before the outbreak of the Civil War, he did not gladly suffer "political generals"— those he thought achieved their rank by political connections and/or wealth. One of the political generals Sweeny disliked was Grenville Dodge, a former railroad official who was the commander of the XVI Corps and Sweeny's immediate commander during the Atlanta campaign. (In fact, Dodge was a fine commander who had been wounded at Pea Ridge.)

On July 22, 1864, Sweeny and the rest of Dodge's corps repulsed Confederate general John B. Hood at Atlanta. Three days later, Dodge and Colonel John W. Fuller, an upper-class English immigrant and one of Dodge's brigade commanders, were in Sweeny's tent, where an altercation broke out. Apparently, Sweeny (who had been drinking) was irritated that Dodge had given an order directly to one of his units during the battle. When Dodge told Sweeny that Fuller was to be promoted for heroism in the last battle, Sweeny's Irish nationalist dislike of Fuller exploded. He accused Fuller of cowardice, and Dodge called Sweeny a liar. Sweeny went Dodge one better, saying he was a "God-damned liar" and a "cowardly son of a bitch." Blows were exchanged; Sweeny apparently struck Dodge, then Fuller wrestled the one-armed Sweeny to the ground. Sweeny was arrested, but before the court-martial convened, Dodge received a head wound in battle. Sweeny was acquitted, but his serious military career was over. After a series of minor assignments, he was dismissed from the United States Army for being AWOL in December 1865. Dodge recovered from his wounds and went on to serve in the West, giving his name to the famous Dodge City in Kansas; then after the war he became the chief engineer for the transcontinental railroad.

However, Sweeny's army career was not over. He, like many Irishmen, was a member of the Fenian Brotherhood, a revolutionary group dedicated to the liberation of Ireland. After Sweeny left the army, the Fenian Senate, hoping to use his war experiences to fight for Irish freedom, appointed Sweeny as Secretary of War. Sweeny and one of the Fenian leaders, John O'Neill, planned an invasion of Canada with United States Army surplus rifles and ammunition, intending to hold the country hostage and exchange it for Irish freedom from Great Britain. On May 25, 1866, Sweeny, accompanied by O'Neill, took 600 men and crossed the Niagara River, then defeated a group of Canadian militiamen at the Battle of Limestone Ridge. They fled back to the United States, but the American government wanted no more of such high jinks. On June 5, 1866, President

The five red stars in the flag carried by the 1st Cherokee represent the five "Civilized Tribes"—Cherokee, Creek, Chickasaw, Choctaw, and Seminole.

Johnson sealed the border and Sweeny was arrested. He was soon released and then, for political reasons, brought back into the regular army, retiring in 1870.

General Sweeny's Museum of Civil War History

General Sweeny's Museum of Civil War History, overlooking the Wilson Creek National Battlefield in Republic, Missouri, is the only private museum in the United States that tells the story of the Civil War in the area west of the Mississippi River, known as the Trans-Mississippi. It is owned and operated by Dr. Tom Sweeny, a retired physician and a distant relative of General Sweeny's, and contains several thousand Civil War artifacts gathered by Dr. Sweeny over 40 years.

Of special interest are items from the nearby Battle of Wilson Creek consisting of weapons, a uniform, photographs of participants from both sides, and two of the five Congressional Medals of Honor awarded after the battle. General Sweeny's memorabilia include a Tiffany presentation sword and a pair of field glasses, given to him on October 27, 1862, by the officers of the 52nd Illinois "as a token of respect and confidence," as well as a captured Confederate flag and a belt plate from Shiloh. The museum also contains the sword belt and sash of Confederate general Patrick Cleburne, considered the best division commander in Tennessee and called by some the Stonewall Jackson of the West. The museum has a significant collection of small arms, as well as display cases devoted to Civil War medicine, and it includes a number of flags, such as a rare Cherokee Indian "Cherokee Braves" Confederate flag, carried by the troops of Brigadier General Stand Watie—the only Native American to become a general in the Confederate army.

Visitor Information:
417-732-1224; www.civilwarmuseum.com/index.html

Hours: March to October, Wednesday to Sunday, 10 a.m. until 5 p.m.; closed November to February.

Admission: There is a moderate charge for adults and for children five and over.

Accessibility: The museum is handicapped accessible.

Getting There: The museum is at 5228 South State Highway ZZ in the town of Republic, about 10 miles southwest of Springfield, Missouri, and just north of the Wilson Creek Battlefield Park.

From Springfield: Take U.S. 60 west to the highway FF exit and go south on highway FF to the intersection of highway M. Do not go straight through the intersection; instead, turn right on highway M and continue for about three miles to the intersection of highway ZZ. Turn left on highway ZZ and continue south almost one mile to the museum.

From I-44: Take exit 70 (highway MM) and continue south to the intersection of U.S. 60 at a traffic light. Go through the intersection, where highway MM will become highway M. Continue approximately 1/2 mile and turn right on highway ZZ. Continue south almost one mile to the museum.

North on U.S. Highway 65 (from Branson/Lakes area): Turn left (west) on state route 14 at Ozark and follow Route 14 about 10 miles to state highway ZZ. Turn right on ZZ and follow it north about seven miles to the museum.

The Battle of Wilson Creek

When the Civil War began, the allegiance of the state of Missouri became a key issue for both sides. Missouri held a strategic location on the Missouri and Mississippi Rivers, and its population was divided between Union and Confederate sympathizers. Though a state convention had voted not to secede, Missouri's governor, Claiborne F. Jackson, was a secessionist and wanted to bring Missouri into the Southern fold. In April 1861, Jackson rudely refused Lincoln's request to send troops for the Union army, calling it "diabolical." He also mobilized some of the state's militia units for "training" at Camp Jackson, near St. Louis, easy striking distance from the large United States armory in the city.

The arsenal's new commander, the fiery, irascible Captain Nathaniel Lyon from Connecticut, would have none of it. Lyon, a West Point graduate and a staunch Unionist, had replaced his old friend and fellow Unionist Captain Thomas "Fighting Tom" Sweeny, who had lost his right arm above the elbow in the Mexican-American War. Sweeny became Lyon's deputy, and the two set out to thwart Jackson's plans. On April 25, Lyon sent most of the armory's weapons to Illinois, where they would be safe from Southern sympathizers. On May 6, the irrepressible Lyon, dressed as a woman, walked inside the militia's Camp Jackson and analyzed its preparations. Four days later he sent troops to Camp Jackson and forced the militiamen to surrender. Unfortunately, a riot ensued shortly after, and dozens of the Southern sympathizers were killed, further heightening tensions.

Lyon Takes On the Confederates

Lyon, now promoted to brigadier general, assumed control of military affairs in Missouri. He captured the state capital at Jefferson City, then routed Jackson and his supporters in a battle outside of the town. Jackson fled to southwest Missouri with part of the State Guard, commanded by General (and former Missouri governor) Sterling "Old Pap" Price.

Lyon put a pro-Union state government in place in the capital, then gathered reinforcements and marched toward southwest Missouri to run the Confederates out of the state. Like a medieval warrior king, Lyon entered Springfield with a mounted personal escort of large, brutal-looking soldiers armed with heavy rifles and oversize swords. By July 13, 1861, Lyon had about 6000 soldiers camped at Springfield—regulars from Kansas, Iowa, and Missouri, three batteries of artillery, and Brigadier General Franz Sigel and his German Brigade, whose badly outnumbered force had just been mauled by Governor Jackson at Carthage. Lyon knew the Confederates had strong forces in the region, and he wrote to St. Louis and Washington demanding reinforcements. However, Union general John Frémont, the new commander of the Western department, offered no assistance. When he was told that Lyon wanted to fight at Springfield, Frémont—perhaps preoccupied with the defense of St. Louis—said it was Lyon's choice. Despite the rebuff, Lyon, Sigel, and Sweeny began to make plans to attack the Confederates in the Southwest.

Meanwhile, the Confederates were organizing. In late July, "Old Pap" Price went to Cassville, where his unkempt, undisciplined Missouri State Guard of 4500 armed and 2000 unarmed men were joined by Brigadier General Ben McCulloch's 3200 disciplined, well-armed Texans. General N. Bart Pearce's Arkansas brigade of 2500 troops was within 10 miles of Cassville, together with two batteries of artillery, so the combined Confederate force amounted to over 10,000 armed men, besides the 2000 unarmed Missourians.

Even though the three generals each had an independent command, they decided to march together on Springfield, 52 miles away, planning to destroy Lyon's army and regain control of the state.

On August 1, Lyon learned that McCulloch, Price, and Pearce had joined forces and were advancing on Springfield. Lyon was vastly outnumbered and again asked for reinforcements from Frémont, but was again refused. Now Lyon was forced to decide whether to fight or retreat. The only safe place to retreat to was Rolla, 125 miles away. The road there was through rough country, and McCulloch had a strong cavalry force that Lyon could not match. The prospect of retreating from a much larger enemy force while at the same time being harassed by cavalry was not enticing.

Lyon expected the three Confederate armies to come by different routes, so he decided to take the offensive, planning to surprise them and defeat one unit at a time. Lyon and his force of about 6000 men, infantry, cavalry, and 18 pieces of artillery started to march from Springfield. The next day, August 2, at about five p.m., they met a small Confederate advance guard under General James Rain about a mile south of Dug Springs. Lyon's men surprised and routed Rain's outnumbered forces, sending them scurrying back to the Confederate main force, where General McCulloch was dismayed at what he perceived to be Rain's lack of courage. McCulloch and the other two commanders organized their forces and prepared to advance.

By the next day, Lyon realized that the three Confederate armies were not separated and he was vastly outnumbered. He immediately retreated to Springfield, just missing a confrontation with the advancing enemy.

The Confederates then stopped at Wilson Creek, approximately 10 miles southwest of Springfield. The divided command was beginning to take a toll, and there were disputes among the commanders. Price was anxious to attack, but McCulloch refused to move unless he was given overall command of the combined army. Finally, after three days of wrangling, Price agreed and McCulloch took over command of the entire Confederate force. With the leadership issue settled, McCulloch ordered the army to be ready to move that night, August 9, to attack Springfield. However, a light rain began to fall, delaying them. Many of the Confederates, especially Price's poorly equipped Missourians, did not have waterproof cartridge boxes, so there was concern that their ammunition would be wet and useless if the rain fell harder. McCulloch reluctantly cancelled the march order.

Back in Springfield, Lyon was again torn about whether to retreat or stay and fight the much larger combined Confederate army. Many of his officers wanted to withdraw, but his fiery deputy, "Fighting Tom" Sweeny, pressed him onward. Lyon told his men, "There is a superior force of the enemy in front . . . [and] it is evident that we must retreat. . . . Shall we endeavor to retreat without giving the enemy battle before-hand . . . or shall we attack him in his position and endeavor to hurt him so that he cannot follow? I am decidedly in favor of the latter plan."

A Surprise Attack

Lyon planned a bold, early morning attack on the Confederates from two directions. Sigel would take a force of 1200 men and swing wide to the south around the right and behind the Confederates, while Lyon would lead the main attack from the north. Success would turn on the element of surprise, so Sigel was told not to attack until he had heard Lyon's cannons.

Late on the afternoon of August 9, Lyon left about 600 troops behind to guard the town and led 5400 soldiers in two groups out of Springfield. Lyon's group marched south most of the night, then before dawn rested within sight of the Confederate campfires. Sigel then took two regiments of infantry, six pieces of artillery, and two companies of cavalry and turned the right flank of the Confederates as planned. He mounted an artillery battery on a small hill within 500 yards of their camp, dispersed his men, and waited for Lyon to attack. Luck was with the Union forces. The night before, the Confederates had withdrawn their sentries in preparation for the planned attack on Springfield, and when it was cancelled, they were not sent out again.

At about five a.m. on August 10, Lyon began his assault, moving down the west side of the north–south running Wilson Creek while sending Captain Joseph B. Plummer's battalion to the opposite side of the creek near a point called Gibson's Mill. Plummer was to attack down the east side of the creek toward a farmhouse and cornfield owned by John Ray.

At daylight, Confederate general Rain, camped at Gibson's Mill, sensed something was wrong and sent a staff officer out to scout the countryside. The officer soon raced back and told him that a large enemy force was moving toward him. Rain instantly informed Price and hurriedly prepared to meet the attack. McCulloch was at Price's quarters, but McCulloch downplayed the intelligence because he had a low opinion of Rain after his defeat at Dug River. McCulloch was about to go look for himself when another messenger dashed up saying that Rain was falling back before a strong Union attack.

The Confederates heard Lyon's artillery to the north, followed a moment later by the roar of Sigel's guns from behind them. Confusion reigned as Sigel's fire crashed down on the Confederate cavalry camp. Sigel began to advance from the south behind the Confederate camp while Lyon's men rolled down from the north, overrunning several Confederate outposts. They scattered Price's Missouri State Guards and pushed them off the 150-foot high Oak Hill ridge. Fortunately for the Confederates, a battery of their cannons—the Pulaski Arkansas Battery from Little Rock—had set up on a high point of land overlooking Oak Hill from the east. When the Arkansans saw the Union attack, they opened fire on Lyon's troops, stopping their advance. Lyon then dug in on the Oak Hill heights, a naturally strong defensive position.

This gave Price the opportunity to gather his State Guard troops and form them into a battle line on the lower part of Oak Hill's south slope. Confederate cavalry attempted to aid the attack by moving around the Union left, but the Union artillery stopped them. Meanwhile, McCulloch galloped south to take command of the disorganized Confederates and try to stop Sigel's attack in the rear.

The battle lines were drawn on Oak Hill. In many places, the forces were less than 300 yards apart, but heavy undergrowth concealed them from each other. The heavy brush was helpful to Price's Missouri State Guards because it forced the fighting to close range, where their shotguns and other primitive weapons were not a disadvantage, and it allowed the untrained troops to attack with little maneuvering. The fight went on for hours. Price sent his men on at least three charges, but each time the Union lines held. Lyon could not retreat under such pressure, and the Confederates would not also.

East of Wilson Creek, Plummer's battalion drove the Confederates back to the Ray House and began to press the Arkansas battery that had stopped Lyon's attack. In Ray's cornfield, the Confederates counterattacked and drove back Plummer's troops, severely wounding Plummer.

A Case of Mistaken Identity

Meanwhile, Sigel, whose artillery fire from the rear had routed the Confederate cavalry, moved to a new position to intercept the Confederates retreating from Lyon's attack. His battery occupied a commanding position—his infantry was extended on both sides of the road, with a company of regular cavalry on each flank. Then McCulloch attacked, personally leading his troops. One of McCulloch's units, Hébert's 3rd Louisiana "Pelican Rifles," were wearing gray uniforms, uniforms that were almost identical to one of the Union units, the 1st Iowa, under Lyon's command. As they approached the Union lines, Sigel saw the gray uniforms and assumed that Lyon's men had arrived. Just as he told his men to hold their fire, the Louisianans opened fire at point-blank range, decimating Sigel's force. Then McCulloch and his battalions charged out of the brush, routing Sigel and his men. Now the entire Confederate force, which outnumbered the Union force two to one, was free to concentrate on Lyon and his troops on Oak Hill.

There the battle was raging. One of the Union commanders said later, "The engagement had become inconceivably fierce all along the entire line, the enemy appearing in front, often in three or four ranks, lying down, kneeling and standing, and the line often approaching to within thirty or forty yards, as the enemy would charge . . . and be driven back." Price was wounded slightly in the side, and Sweeny was severely wounded in the thigh. Lyon had been hit once in the leg already when he was grazed in the head by a bullet and his horse killed. Lyon mounted another horse, drew his sword, and called for a charge, but then a Confederate bullet hit him in the heart and he fell dead, making him the first Union general to be killed in the war.

Major Samuel Sturgis now took over command of the Federal army. At eleven thirty, the Confederates broke off the action and retreated down the hill for the fourth time. As they massed at the base of the hill for another attack, Sturgis saw that the Union situation was deteriorating. The Union troops were running low on ammunition, and when one of the Union reserve units refused to attack, Sturgis began to lose confidence in his exhausted troops. He conferred with his commanders, then ordered a withdrawal. While the order was controversial, it was probably a wise decision. Given more time, the Confederates had both the numbers and the cavalry to cut Sturgis off from Springfield. The battle for Oak Hill—known for posterity as Bloody Hill—had lasted for five hours, leaving the hillside piled with dead from both sides.

Led by General Nathaniel Lyon, men of the 1st Iowa Infantry Regiment charge the Confederate line at Wilson Creek. A bullet struck him dead shortly after, making him the first Union general killed in the war.

Sturgis retreated to Springfield, but the Confederates did not pursue. The next day Sturgis abandoned Springfield and retreated farther, to Rolla. The Union troops moved in a three-mile-long wagon train, loaded with over two million dollars in gold (used to pay the troops and for supplies, since paper money was worthless while the outcome of the war was uncertain), on the long and difficult road already crowded with hundreds of Union refugees. Price urged McCulloch to pursue the Union forces, but McCulloch declined. Price could have taken his Missouri State Guard and pursued on his own, but did not take advantage of the opportunity. When Price and the Confederates occupied Springfield, they arrested Union sympathizers and forced many blacks, both free men and former slaves, into Confederate army labor units.

The Aftermath

In the confused retreat from the battlefield, the Union soldiers left the body of General Lyon on Oak Hill. The next day, one of the Union's Missouri Volunteers, Dr. S. H. Melcher from Springfield, took the body back to Springfield. When the Union soldiers abandoned Springfield, the body was again left behind, but finally Mrs. John S. Phelps, the wife of a Congressman and Union army officer, took the body and buried it. It was later removed by Lyon's family members and reinterred in Connecticut. Lyon was highly praised after the battle, and it was said that General William T. Sherman blamed the next four years of conflict in Missouri on Lyon's death. On reflection, it seems that if blame were to be assessed, it would be more accurate to say that the next four years were the result of Frémont's failure to reinforce Lyon.

Two of the Confederate commanders, Price and McCulloch, were at odds at the end of the battle. McCulloch thought that Price's militiamen had not fought well, and by regular army standards he was probably correct. McCulloch also considered Price's men undisciplined and sloppy (also probably correct) and forbade his men to have anything to do with them after the battle. The two generals were forced to work together later at the battle of Pea Ridge, but only after Confederate President Jefferson Davis personally intervened and placed them under another commander, General Earl Van Dorn. Pea Ridge was a disaster, and McCulloch was killed there.

Although a relatively small engagement, the fighting at Wilson Creek was extraordinarily violent, and about 1300 of the 5400 Union soldiers and about 1200 of the almost 12,000 Confederates were casualties. This early in the war medical care was appalling, and many if not most of the wounded died. Many of the troops were buried in mass graves in the naturally occur-

Although close to the battle, the Ray House was never struck by musket or cannon fire. When the battle ended, the family, hiding in the cellar, emerged to find their farm house was now a hospital and began to assist medical personnel in treating the wounded and dying. Later, the body of General Nathaniel Lyon was brought to the house and examined before it was removed to Springfield under a flag of truce.

ring sinkholes in the area.

Shortly after Wilson Creek, Price and his Missouri State Guard captured the Union garrison at Lexington, but in early 1862 he and his men were driven into Arkansas. The Union victory at the Battle of Pea Ridge in March 1862 kept organized Confederate military forces out of Missouri for more than two years. For the next few years, Missouri was the scene of savage small-unit fighting and guerrilla warfare, with small bands of mounted raiders pillaging the countryside and destroying anything that might aid the enemy. In September 1864, Price returned to Missouri with an army of 12,000 men and raged through the state. By the time his campaign ended, he had marched nearly 1500 miles and destroyed an estimated ten million dollars worth of property.

The Union was forced to withdraw a large force from Georgia and send them back to deal with Price. At Westport, Missouri, on October 21–23, 1864, the largest battle fought west of the Mississippi pitted Price against Union general Samuel Curtis, who had defeated Price years earlier at the critical battle of Pea Ridge. Curtis thrashed Price again and forced him to retreat south, finally ending organized Confederate military operations in Missouri.

Wilson Creek National Battlefield

Wilson Creek was not declared a National Battlefield until 1960, and the Visitors Center was completed in 1982. With the exception of the vegetation, the 1750-acre battlefield has changed little from the time of the battle.

The battlefield can be toured by walking or driving. The Visitors Center offers a free park brochure with information about the battle and a 4.9-mile self-guided tour; or for a detailed narration, car tapes for the self-guided tour can be purchased. There are eight stops at significant points in the battle, as well as five walking trails off the paved tour road, each less than a mile long. There is also one monument on the battlefield, dedicated to the first Union general killed in the Civil War, Nathaniel Lyon.

At the time of the battle, eight families lived in the prairie and farm fields around the immediate battle site. The Ray House is the only house remaining on the battlefield from the time of the battle, and it served as a temporary field hospital for Confederate soldiers after the engagement. The house still contains original items, including the bed where General Lyon's body was examined after he was killed.

The Visitors Center features a 13-

minute video that gives a historical background to the battle, a six minute fiber-optics map program that shows how the battle developed and the troop movements, and a bookstore. Restrooms are located only at the Visitors Center.

The John K. and Ruth Hulston Civil War Research Library, next to the Visitors Center, is open from Tuesday to Saturday. Springfield attorney John K. Hulston and his wife Ruth donated most of the approximately 5500 volumes, which mainly focus on the Civil War period and the Civil War in the Trans-Mississippi Theater. The library's volumes are noncirculating, and there is no open stack or checkout policy, but they are available for use by serious scholars. Staff members can perform limited research for patrons if requested by regular mail, e-mail, telephone, or in person. More extensive research on a particular topic should be done in person.

Visitor Information

417-732-2662; www.nps.gov/wicr
Hours: Visitors Center, daily, 8 a.m. until 5 p.m.; closed Thanksgiving, December 25, and New Year's Day; Park open Memorial Day to Labor Day, 8 a.m. until 9 p.m.; April 1 to Memorial Day and Labor Day to October 31, 8 a.m. until 7 p.m.; November to March, 8 a.m. until 5 p.m.; the battlefield is closed on December 25, New Year's Day, and during periods of inclement weather; the Ray House is open on weekends Memorial Day to Labor Day, subject to staff and volunteer availability. Call for details.
Admission: Minimal charge per adult over 16 and per vehicle; National Parks Pass, Golden Eagle, Golden Age, and Golden Access are honored.
Special Programs: On August 10, the anniversary of the battle, there is a special program and ceremony during the morning. An annual candlelight tour is traditionally held in August and requires advance tickets not included as part of the regular admission charge. Living-history programs depicting Civil War soldier life, cavalry drills, musket firing, artillery demonstrations, Civil War medicine, and Civil War–era clothing are presented on Sunday afternoons from Memorial Day to Labor Day. During the summer, the Ray House has interpreters dressed in period clothing to explain the exhibits. Call for information.

Accessibility: All areas of the Visitors Center and Ray House are wheelchair accessible from the parking areas. A wheelchair is available in the Visitors Center. Interpretive stops along the tour road are wheelchair accessible, but trails off the tour road are not. Designated handicapped parking spaces are available at each of the parking areas.
Getting There: The battlefield is 10 miles southwest of Springfield, Missouri. Parking is available in the Visitors Center parking area as well as at each of the eight interpretive stops.

From I-44: Take exit 70 (highway MM) and continue south to the intersection of U.S. 60 at a traffic light. Go through the intersection, where highway MM will become highway M. Continue approximately 1/2 mile and turn right on highway ZZ. Continue south about one mile to Farm Road 182 (Elm Street) and turn left at the intersection. The entrance to the battlefield will be on the right.

South on U.S. highway 65: Exit on the James River Freeway (U.S. 60). Continue west on the James River Freeway to the state highway FF exit and continue south on highway FF to the intersection of highway M. Do not go straight through the intersection; instead, turn right on highway M and continue for about 3 miles to the intersection of highway ZZ. Turn left on highway ZZ and continue south about one mile to Farm Road 182 (Elm Street). Turn left at the intersection, and the entrance to the battlefield will be on the right.

North on U.S. highway 65 (from Branson/Lakes area): Turn left (west) on state Route 14 at Ozark and continue west on Highway 14 to state highway ZZ. Turn right on ZZ and follow it north to Farm Road 182 (Elm Street). Turn right at the intersection, and the entrance to the battlefield will be on the right.

South on state Route 13: (Note: Route 13 becomes the Kansas Expressway when entering Springfield.) Follow the Kansas Expressway south to U.S. Route 60. Go west on U.S. 60 to the intersection of state highway MM. Turn left on highway M. Continue approximately 1/2 mile to highway ZZ and turn right on ZZ. Continue south about one mile to Farm Road 182 (Elm Street) and turn left at the intersection. The entrance to the battlefield will be on the right.

New York State Military Museum and Veterans Research Center

It took 137 years for this impressive collection to find a permanent home, but it was well worth the wait. The massive Saratoga Springs Armory with its castle towers seems a very appropriate setting for the collection's more than 10,000 artifacts related to New York State's military forces and veterans.

These artifacts encompass the United States's military history, beginning with the Revolutionary War and continuing through Desert Storm in the early 1990s. Included are thousands of Civil War items, among them the largest collection of Civil War flags in the world.

History of the Museum

In 1865 the New York State Legislature passed a bill formally establishing the state's collection of military memorabilia as a way of honoring its veterans and preserving an important element of state history. The bill also called for the creation of a museum to house the collection.

For the next 100-plus years, the collection was the responsibility of the Division of Military and Naval Affairs, under whose auspices it became the largest such collection in the country even as its artifacts were being stored in various locations throughout the state. In the late 1980s these items were brought together at the Washington Avenue Armory in Albany, and 10 years later at the Watervliet Arsenal Museum.

In 2002 the decision was made to house the collection permanently in the 1889 Saratoga Springs, New York, armory designated a historic landmark on the National Historic Register.

In the next several years, it's expected that the design of the display area will continue to evolve as the museum adapts to its new home. In addition, the museum is developing its Web site as an important research tool, so that items such as newspaper clippings, photographs, and oral histories will be available online.

The Civil War Collection

Perhaps foremost among the museum's Civil War artifacts are the more than 1000 state regimental battle flags. These flags were not only a source of pride and identification for a regiment, but in an age of linear warfare, they helped maintain the line, with two flags in the middle and marker flags on either end. As early as 1863, as regiments began to be mustered out, they brought their flags back to the state capitol, where they eventually became part of this collection.

The museum's uniform collection contains two particularly important pieces. One is the bloodstained uniform of Colonel Elmer Ephraim Ellsworth, known as the first Union martyr. Ellsworth, a New York native, organized a group of cadets in Chicago and named them for the French Algerian infantrymen who were called Zouaves. He and his Chicago Zouaves, with their colorful uniforms, performed drills at the White House, and Ellsworth soon became one of President Lincoln's favorites.

In May of 1861, Ellsworth's company, part of a 130,000-man regiment, was sent to occupy Alexandria, Virginia, located directly across the Potomac River from the United States capital and known for its Southern sympathies. Walking past a hotel called the Marshall House, Ellsworth spied a large Confederate flag flying from the roof. In the process of capturing the flag, Ellsworth was shot dead. (The bullet hole is still visible in his uniform, despite the well-meaning efforts of someone who had the coat dry-cleaned in the 1960s.) His assailant

Colonel Elmer Ellsworth's frock coat, with the bullet hole made by the slug that killed him after he tore down a Confederate flag in Alexandria, Virginia.

was also killed, and both men soon became fallen heroes for their sides.

The 44th New York Regiment was formed in Ellsworth's honor, calling themselves Ellsworth's Avengers and adopting a ballad that included the stanza, "First to fall, thou youthful martyr, Hapless was thy fate; Hastened we, as thy avengers, From thy native state; Speed we on, from town and city, Not for wealth or fame, But because we love the Union, And our Ellsworth's name."

The other uniform of note was made for a child—Gustav Schurmann—who enlisted at the age of 12 in 1861 with his father as a member of the 40th New York Volunteers (known as the Mozart Regiment after Mozart Hall in New York City). Though his father soon returned home due to illness, Schurmann remained as a drummer boy, serving under four generals and in 10 major battles.

Schurmann learned 148 calls and tunes as a drummer boy. He eventually became a bugler (his bugle is on display here also) and learned 67 distinct calls used to orchestrate troop movements on the battlefield. His experiences were chronicled in a New York newspaper and he became well known among the troops. In April 1863, Schurmann accompanied General Daniel Sickles to the White House, where he spent the afternoon playing with the President's son Tad. After he mustered out of his regiment in 1863, Schurmann worked as a bookbinder and later a customs agent. He died of tuberculosis at the age of 56.

Among the weapons here are presentation and dress swords, Springfield rifles and handguns, a 13-inch coastal mortar that is comparable to the Union mortar called the Dictator—which had to be fired from a railroad flatcar because of its 17,000-pound mass—a collection of Napoleons, and two of the eight known Delafields still in existence.

The museum's Civil War photography collection consists of nearly 4000 photographs, 2300 of which are identified cartes de visite (small portraits the size of business cards). These are gradually being made available on the Web site. There are also several Mathew Brady photographs and many taken by local

Drummer boy
Gustav Schurmann served two years in the Union army and was present at 10 major battles—eventually becoming a bugler. His uniform and bugle are on display at the museum.

New York state photographers.

The Research Center has an impressive assembly of newspaper clippings, originally gathered by the Bureau of Military Statistics during the war, as well as soldiers' diaries and letters.

For those interested in a detailed history of New York's Civil War regiments, the museum has begun posting on its Web site unit histories, tables of battles fought and losses, and photographs of men in the units.

Visitor Information

518-583-0184;
www.dmna.state.ny.us/historic/
mil-hist.htm

Hours: The museum is open Tuesday to Saturday, 10 a.m. until 4 p.m. The research center is open Tuesday to Friday, 10 a.m. until 4 p.m. and by appointment on Saturday. Both are closed on major holidays.

Special Events: Civil War weekends with living-history presentations, artists, and authors; see the Web site.

Admission: Free for both.

Accessibility: The museum is completely accessible; the library is partially accessible.

Getting There: From the south: Take I-87 north from Albany to exit 13N and go north on U.S. 9. Turn right on state Route 29 (Lake Avenue) and proceed to the armory.

From the north: Take I-87 south to exit 15; proceed south on Route 50 and turn left on U.S. 9; proceed to state route 29 (Lake Avenue). Once on Lake Avenue, the museum is in the armory building, three blocks on the left.

United States Military Academy at West Point and the West Point Museum

Though far from the physical battles of the Civil War, the U.S. Military Academy at West Point could well be called the war's training ground, as it produced 450 of the conflict's generals and hundreds of its officers. Nearly all of the significant battles of the Civil War were commanded on both sides by former West Pointers, including the opening salvo at Fort Sumter, which pitted Confederate brigadier general P.G.T. Beauregard against Union major Robert Anderson, Beauregard's former artillery instructor at the Point.

Between 1825 and 1861, the years in which the war's future commanders (among them Robert E. Lee and Ulysses S. Grant) attended the Academy, the curriculum consisted mainly of mathematics, science, and engineering, with military strategy and tactics covered only in the final year.

The wife of an 1847 graduate described the Point as a place "where reality wears the gloss of romance, and military glory appears in the brightest holiday dress, accompanied by all the poetry of war." But the Point was also a place where the honor and duty of command were ingrained in every aspect of a cadet's education, so that while those who later fought in the war found neither poetry nor romance in its butchery, they could still call upon the lessons in leadership they had learned together at the Academy.

Other Civil War graduates include George Custer, Jubal Early, A. P. Hill, Stonewall Jackson, James Longstreet,

Philip Sheridan, William Tecumseh Sherman, and J.E.B. Stuart. Lewis Armistead, with whom Early served at Gettysburg, also attended, but he was dismissed for smashing a plate over Early's head during a mess hall disagreement.

The West Point Museum

The West Point Museum, founded in 1854, is the oldest and largest military museum in the country. The col-

George Armstrong Custer, *left, graduated in 1861, dead last in his class. Eventually rising to the rank of major general during the Civil War, he was interred at West Point after his death at Little Big Horn. The class of 1863, top, included John Rogers Meigs, who rose to the rank of brevet major serving as Phil Sheridan's chief of engineers.*

***Militia drill** scene by James Walker portrays the close formation marching used in battle that led to devastating casualties for both sides in the Civil War.*

lection was begun with material brought here following the British defeat at Saratoga in 1777, and its six galleries include an impressive range of Civil War memorabilia.

The subbasement and basement galleries feature small and large weapons—examples of how American industry focused its resources on developing effective armaments, a major by-product of the conflict. In the Large Weapons Gallery, visitors can examine such items as Civil War cannons, a Union rocket launcher, and a Confederate mountain rifle. The Small Weapons Gallery features small arms such as a Russian Lancer's lance used by a Pennsylvania regiment, a Spencer carbine, and one of the war's major refinements in rifled firearm bullets—a minié ball, which could kill at half a mile and was accurate at 300 yards.

The first floor's West Point Gallery exhibits artifacts and memorabilia from some of the Academy's most famous graduates, among them Lee and Grant. Also on the first floor is the History of Warfare Gallery, which is coordinated with the curriculum studied by current cadets in its depiction of warfare from ancient times to the present.

The second floor features the History of the U.S. Army Gallery, which explains why the Civil War is regarded as the first major war of the industrial era, as well as its significance for advancements in battlefield medicine. On the same floor is the American Wars Gallery. Its Civil War exhibit includes field glasses used in the battle of Gettysburg and a sharpshooter rifle used by Major General Hiram Berdan, considered the top rifle shot in America at the time and the inventor of a repeating rifle and a patented musket ball.

The Medal of Honor Wall, which can also be found on the second floor, commemorates Academy-graduate recipients of this award—created during the Civil War. Among the 25 names inscribed on the wall is that of Brigadier General Oliver Howard, who led the 61st New York Infantry at the Battle of Fair Oaks, Virginia, in 1862, and was twice severely wounded but still led the charge that resulted in the amputation of his right arm. The U.S. Army Center of Military History's Web site, www.army.mil/cmh-pg/moh1.htm, includes a complete listing of the names and citations of the more

The Battle Monument was dedicated in 1897 "in memory of the officers and men of the American Army who fell in battle," specifically the Regular Army casualties of the North during the Civil War. It was designed by a firm that included Stanford White, one of the nation's foremost architectural designers of the 19th century.

than 3400 Americans who have been awarded the Medal of Honor.

Located directly in front of the museum is the Visitors Center, which has informational videos and pamphlets about the Academy. The museum and Visitors Center are outside of the official West Point grounds, so visitors do not need to take a guided tour to view these areas.

West Point Cemetery and Trophy Point

West Point Cemetery sits on a promontory overlooking the Hudson River. Among the Civil War veterans buried here are Brigadier General Robert Anderson, Major General George Armstrong Custer, Brigadier General John Buford, Major General Daniel Butterfield, and Lieutenant General Winfield Scott. At the entrance to the cemetery stands the Old Cadet Chapel, a neoclassical structure built in 1836. It originally stood elsewhere on the grounds, and was dismantled and reconstructed stone by stone on the present site in 1910. This was the first place of worship built at the Academy, and it is one of the oldest buildings still in use here. The cemetery can be toured only by researchers who have received special permission from the PR office.

Visitors can tour the West Point grounds only with a guided tour, which includes Trophy Point. Located at the western edge of West Point, it has an impressive display of more than 60 Civil War cannons, including the 11 Confederate bronze field guns buried muzzle down that

surround the Battle Monument. The monument, considered the largest polished granite shaft in the Western Hemisphere, was dedicated in 1897 to the memory of those who died fighting for the Union in the Civil War. Upon it are inscribed 2230 names.

Visitor Information

845-938-2203;
www.usma.edu/Museum

Hours: Daily, 10:30 a.m. until 4:15 p.m.; closed Thanksgiving, December 25, and New Year's Day.

Admission: Free.

Accessibility: The museum, Visitors Center, cemetery, chapel, and Trophy Point are all accessible by wheelchair and stroller.

Getting There: The museum is located at 2110 New South Post Road in Highland Falls.

From the east or west: Take I-84 to exit 10 (U.S. 9W). Follow U.S. 9W south to the second West Point/Highland Falls exit. This will lead you into Highland Falls. Follow signs to the Visitors Center and museum.

From the south: Take the Palisades Interstate Parkway north to its end (Bear Mountain traffic circle). Follow signs for U.S. Route 9W north (3rd exit off traffic circle). Take the first West Point/Highland Falls exit. This will lead you into Highland Falls. Follow signs to the Visitors Center and museum.

From the north: Take the New York State Thruway (I-87) to exit 17 east. Take I-84 east for three miles to exit 10 (U.S. Route 9W). Then follow the directions for "From the east or west," above.

IRONCLADS

Although ironclad warships were well established in major world navies by 1861, the Civil War was witness to the first battle between ironclads. Nevertheless, the United States showed little interest in such ships, and when the war began it had only one ironclad under construction. Throughout the war, the vast majority of the Union navy ships were wooden, and it was those that kept the critical blockade. However, it was clear that ironclads would be needed for specific missions—to bombard heavily defended positions at close range and to counter the Confederate ironclads. The Union ironclads were not superior to their Confederate opponents, but they were hard to sink and had reliable engines, which the Confederate boats lacked.

The Union navy's Ironclad Board ordered four types of ironclads built—one original design and three more-or-less-conventional designs. The original design was the U.S.S. *Monitor*, designed by John Ericsson. The key to the *Monitor* was that it could be built quickly.

This was critical, because in July 1861 the Confederacy had decided to rebuild the captured Union 40-gun steam-frigate *Merrimack* as an ironclad. The *Merrimack* had been set on fire and scuttled in Norfolk Navy Yard in April, but her hull and machinery were intact. The Confederates renamed her the C.S.S. *Virginia*, cut down her hull, and mounted an armored casemate—a timber roof plated with three layers of iron. The *Virginia* was to carry two 7-inch Brooke Rifles forward, two 6-inch Brookes aft, and three 9-inch Dahlgren cannons on each side. She would be, by far, the most formidable warship in American waters.

The Union reply, the *Monitor*, was a totally new design. It had a single rotating cylindrical turret, 20 feet across and nine feet high, on a flat, low deck with few protrusions except stacks and a pilothouse. It had heavy armor—11 inches thick on the turret and nine inches on the pilothouse—and the turret mounted two 11-inch Dahlgren smoothbore cannons.

The race was on to complete construction first. On Saturday morning, March 8, 1862, the *Virginia* steamed down the Elizabeth River to Hampton Roads under the command of Captain Franklin Buchanan. The first Union warship that the *Virginia* encountered there was the anchored 24-gun sloop-of-war *Cumberland*, whose guns bounced off the *Virginia* "like so many peas." The *Virginia* opened fire and then rammed the *Cumberland*, sinking the Union ship with nearly 100 men.

The *Virginia*'s next target was the frigate *Congress*, whose captain had run her aground so she could not be sunk. From about 150 yards away, the *Virginia* fired "shot and shell into her with terrific effect, while the shot from the *Congress* glanced from her iron-plated sloping sides, without doing any apparent injury," according to a Union officer. In a few bloody minutes, over 100 of the *Congress*'s crew were killed or wounded. When the *Virginia* ceased firing, the *Congress* was afire, her captain was dead, and her crew was abandoning ship. The *Virginia* then turned to the steam frigate *Minnesota*, which had also been run aground, but the water was too shallow for the

U.S.S. **Cumberland** *sinks after being rammed by the ironclad C.S.S.* Virginia.

Rear Admiral John A. Dahlgren, the "father of American naval ordnance." The Dahlgren gun, a powerful class of smoothbore cannons, became the standard weapon on Union naval vessels after 1856.

IRONCLADS (continued)

Confederate vessel to close the range. The *Virginia* left about seven p.m., leaving the *Minnesota* still stuck on a mud bank.

While the *Virginia* was fighting the Union fleet, the *Monitor*, commanded by Lieutenant John Worden, approached. Three days at sea had worn out the *Monitor*'s crew. She was a terrible sea boat and had been tossed about by the waves, and when the rough seas swept over her deck they poured into the ventilation tubes, almost suffocating the men. Worden tied his vessel to the side of the *Minnesota*. Clearly, the *Virginia* was expecting to destroy the *Minnesota* the next day and eliminate the Union naval presence in Chesapeake Bay.

The next morning, the *Virginia* was commanded by Captain Catesby Jones, who had taken over after Buchanan was injured the previous day. As she approached the *Minnesota*, the *Monitor* intercepted the attacking ironclad.

Both ships had ordinance problems. The *Virginia* had fired most of her solid shot and would have to use hollow explosive shells, while the *Monitor* had been ordered to fire her powerful 11-inch Dahlgrens with only half their normal powder charge since a burst gun inside the turret would have disabled the *Monitor*, and that could not be risked. (The Dahlgrens were very reliable, though, and had she fired with a full powder charge the *Virginia* might have been destroyed.)

For the next four hours, the ironclads hammered away at each other

to no avail. The *Virginia*'s thin-skinned shells and the *Monitor*'s underpowered shot bounced off each other's thick iron armor. At one point the *Minnesota* added a broadside against the *Virginia*, but it did no damage, and the Confederate ship answered with a rifled shell through the *Minnesota*'s side that set her on fire.

Finally the *Virginia*'s gunners concentrated their fire on the *Monitor*'s pilothouse. A shell struck it and the blast through the viewing slit blinded Worden, forcing the *Monitor* to withdraw until he could be relieved. By the time she was ready to return to the fight, the tide had begun to go out and the *Virginia*, which drew 22 feet of water, had to turn away toward Norfolk. The battle was a draw, but it saved the Union navy in the area and was treated by Northern newspapers as a huge victory.

While the *Monitor* was one of the most overrated weapons of all time, the "victory" made it a political necessity for the U.S. Navy to purchase more. They quickly contracted for a class of 10, the Passaics, based on a modified *Monitor* plan. They were the first large class of ironclads to be built from one set of plans. The Passaics were larger and had heavier armament than the *Monitor* did, but retained all of her faults. They were followed by nine of the Canonicus class, and later by an even more advanced *Monitor*, the *Onondaga*.

The most important characteristic of the *Monitor* and her sisters was that they were highly damage resistant, though they were inferior warships in virtually every other way. The turret was the *Monitors'* main fault. While it was supposed to allow the guns to fire at nearly any angle, it was vulnerable to damage and rarely worked properly. A more serious problem was that the *Monitors'* guns were muzzle-loaders, and reloading them in the small turret was difficult and time consuming. *Monitors* also had a very low rate of fire, and they were slow and unseaworthy, which made them only suitable for inshore operations.

The first of the two conventional Union ironclad designs, the *New Ironsides,* was less well known but very successful. She was a standard 1850s' steam-and-sail warship with broadside guns and, for a time, a full sailing rig. She was large—232 feet—and heavily armed with two 150-pound Parrott rifles and fourteen 11-inch Dahlgren smoothbores and a belt of armor along the gun deck. While the *New Ironsides* seemed old-fashioned, she was probably the most well-liked ship in the U.S. Navy. Not the least of her charms was her durability—she was hit hundreds of times but was never disabled. She was also heavily armed and able to fire her extensive broadside much faster and with many more guns than a *Monitor*-type warship, so she was superb for bombarding land targets.

The second conventional design, the *Galena,* was a complete failure. A smaller steam-and-sail ironclad sloop, she had an unconventional—and ineffective—armor plating arrangement, a system of interlocked iron plates. After sustaining heavy battle damage in an engagement with the Confederate *Fort Darling* at Drewry's Bluff, the *Galena* ultimately had her armor removed.

The River Ironclads

These were the first ironclads designed and built in the Western Hemisphere and were arguably the most effective warships of the Civil War. In order for the Union to move down the Mississippi as planned, they needed ironclads to combat strong Confederate fortifications. In August 1861, naval constructor Samuel M. Pook and engine designer Thomas Merritt designed and constructed armored vessels to attack land positions on the inland rivers. The ships had to be armored and have the firepower to destroy or neutralize the forts. In addition, they could draw no more than 10 feet of water and had to be able to maneuver in narrow rivers. Pook developed

a class of casemate ironclad 512-ton paddle wheelers for the role. Called the City class, they were round-nosed, flat-bottomed, 175 feet long, and about 50 feet wide. Their casemates were protected by an iron plate, and armor was placed around the boilers, engines, and on the pilothouse. Each ship was armed with 13 smoothbore and rifled cannons. The Citys were powered by two high-compression steam engines. They were cheap to build, easy to maintain, could make five to nine miles an hour, and could run on other fuel besides coal. However, the high-pressure boilers were always in danger of exploding.

Confederate Secretary of the Navy Stephen Mallory said, "Inequality of numbers may be compensated by invulnerability," so the Confederate government quickly tried to acquire some ironclad warships. Eventually the Confederate government was able to purchase the French-built C.S.S. *Stonewall*—which didn't arrive until after the war was over.

Mallory was also determined to build his own ironclads, though the Southern states could not produce any significant part of an ironclad except the hull. The Confederate ironclads all had casemates with forward-, side-, and rear-firing cannons on a low-lying hull. Most Southern ironclads had strong, sharp bows to ram and sink enemy ships, so they were often simply called rams. Their engines were their Achilles heel—they were usually railroad engines, weak and unreliable. Many of the Confederate ironclads had very effective armor, several layers of iron plate over a solid wooden sheathing. The wood absorbed the shock and kept the relatively brittle iron plating from shattering. Had the South possessed enough iron and forging facilities to put six or more inches of plate over this wood bulkhead, the rams would have proved almost indestructible.

While the Confederate-built ironclads could not seriously challenge the Union blockade, their mere presence vastly complicated the Union navy's task. Tactically, the Confederacy used many of its ironclads to defend its harbors and rivers, since one ironclad could defeat several wooden warships—and most of the Union warships were wooden. However, this meant that Southern ironclads were rarely concentrated, and if the Union attacked one's home harbor, the single Confederate ironclad could be overwhelmed by a larger number of Union warships.

The C.S.S. *Neuse*

The twin-screw steamer C.S.S. *Neuse* was one of 22 ironclads ordered by Stephen R. Mallory, Secretary of the Navy for the Confederacy, who believed the Confederates needed ironclad warships to offset the Union navy's numbers. The Confederacy intended to build its ironclads near large seaports; but as Union forces captured the ports, the builders moved inland. Soon a "naval ship-yard" was any area located along a river (or even a large stream) with construction infrastructure available. Usually the ironclads built there were shallow-draft vessels with a few heavy guns and served as "point defense" weapons, protecting the areas around where they were built. Most of the ironclads had many long delays during their construction. The Confederate navy was given a low priority when it came to procuring scarce materials and to transporting them. Often the warships' equipment was delayed in transit because railroad lines were being used to move troops and supplies for the land forces.

On October 17, 1862, on the banks of the Neuse River at White Hall, North Carolina, the shipbuilding firm of Howard & Ellis began work on an armored gunboat that was to become the *Neuse.* Because the ironclad was a relatively simple flat-bottomed ship, similar to a barge, the carpenters did not require any special skills to build it. Her hull was made from local pine and water-proofed with oakum, a loosely twisted jute fiber impregnated with tar.

In December, raiding Union troops approached White Hall, where the *Neuse* was under construction. The Confederates burned down the local bridge, trapping the Union forces on the opposite bank, but the Union commander sent a volunteer, Henry Butler, of the 3rd New York Cavalry, to swim across the river and set the ironclad on fire. The courageous mission failed (Butler survived), and the frustrated Federals then tried artillery, but the shells only slightly damaged the *Neuse.* The Union forces left White Hall with the *Neuse* still intact.

In November of the next year, the still unarmored *Neuse* was slipped into the river. Workers using poles moved her 18 miles downstream to the Confederate "naval station" at Kinston, North Carolina, to transform the pine ship into an ironclad. She was moved into a site called the

cat hole, next to a steep riverbank that made it easier to load the ship's machinery and iron armor.

Still, it was not until January 1864 that machinery began to arrive. The steam engine came from a locomotive, probably from the Baltimore & Ohio No. 34, while the armor became a political issue. It was rolled into plate made from rail-road tracks that ran between Kinston and New Bern, and the state of North Carolina said that since the armor came from the state, the ship could only be used for the defense of the state!

Union commanders in the occupied port of New Bern viewed the *Neuse* as a threat, and monitored her construction by reports from spies and deserters. They were especially worried that the ironclad would be completed in time to attack New Bern on March 14, 1864, the second anniversary of its capture by Union forces. Their concern increased when, in March, two 68-pound Brooke rifles were mounted in the ironclad. In fact, General Robert E. Lee did want to use the ironclad to support a land attack on New Bern, but the delivery of the iron plate was agonizingly slow and there were pay disputes with the ship's carpenters. In the end, the *Neuse* was not ready in time for the attack.

Finally, on April 22, 1864, the *Neuse* steamed toward New Bern, but less than a half mile after she left her moorings, the ironclad ran hard aground on a sand bar. She was not able to float free until mid May, then was ordered to return to her moorings in Kinston. During the summer and the fall of 1864, the ironclad, now nicknamed the *Neuse*-ance, remained inactive. There were no ground troops to support her in an attack on New Bern, and low water made it hazardous to try to move again. By late November, the river had risen sufficiently to allow the *Neuse* to move, but there were still no Confederate troops available for any offensive action.

In early 1865, Union forces captured the port of Wilmington, North Carolina, and soon General Braxton Bragg, in charge of Confederate forces, ordered the evacuation of Kinston and the scuttling of the *Neuse*. On March 12, 1865, the *Neuse*'s last captain, Captain Joseph Price, ordered his crew to shell the advancing Union cavalry units. The warship finally had a chance to do what she was designed for, engage

The hull remnant of the C.S.S. Neuse, *above, on display at the site. The original configuration was similar in design to the ironclad C.S.S.* Albemarle, *inset.*

the enemy. Nevertheless, the Union forces continued to advance, and Price and his crew placed a dynamite charge under the *Neuse*'s bow. They then set fire to the ship, and while the *Neuse* was burning the charge went off and blew an eight-foot hole in her port bow. The *Neuse* sank and settled with her smokestack out of the water. Her crew of almost 100 men surrendered to the Union forces.

C.S.S. *Neuse* State Historic Site

For many years, the area where the *Neuse* sank was used as a river swimming hole for Kinston residents. Then in 1961, efforts were begun to raise the hulk. It was floated in 1963, and in 1964 was moved to its present location. It is one of three ironclads from the Civil War on display in the United States, the others being the U.S.S. *Cairo* in Vicksburg, Mississippi, and the C.S.S. *Jackson* in Columbus, Georgia.

The *Neuse* was an underwater archaeologist's dream; more than 15,000 artifacts were recovered from the ship. They make up the *Neuse* collection, part of which is on display at the Visitors Center. The center also contains a large-scale model of the ship, with a section cut away to show the *Neuse*'s interior

and armament. There's a video telling the history of the *Neuse* and its recovery.

A project was begun in 2002 to build a full-scale replica of the C.S.S. *Neuse* that will be mounted close to the river near the cat hole where the original *Neuse* was fitted out.

Visitor Information
252-522-2091;
www.ah.dcr.state.nc.us/sections/hs/neuse/neuse.htm
Hours: Tuesday to Saturday, 10 a.m. until 4 p.m.; closed Sunday and Monday.
Admission: Free; donations are accepted.
Special Events: In the fall, reenactors camp on the banks of the Neuse River and offer a living-history program to explain military life during the Civil War. Guided tours are available upon advance request. Call for information.
Accessibility: The center and tours are accessible to all visitors.
Getting There: Kinston is located about 80 miles southeast of Raleigh, North Carolina. From Raleigh, take I-40 south to U.S. 70 heading east (toward Goldsboro). In Kinston, exit on east U.S. 70 Business (West Vernon Avenue). The C.S.S. *Neuse* site is located approximately 1/2 mile ahead on the right.

The Battles for Fort Fisher

At the beginning of the Civil War, the Confederacy took control of a long, thin peninsula called Federal Point in southern North Carolina between the Atlantic Ocean and the mouth of the Cape Fear River. This strategic location controlled the entrance to Wilmington, one of the main ports for Confederate blockade runners. The Confederates quickly changed the name to Confederate Point and began construction of defensive works. In September 1861, the new post was named Fort Fisher, in honor of North Carolinian colonel Charles F. Fisher, killed at the first Battle of Bull Run (Manassas).

Despite the construction, when Colonel William Lamb arrived in July 1862 to take command, the fort was little more than several sand batteries mounting fewer than two dozen guns. Lamb recognized Fort Fisher's importance to the security of Wilmington and began to improve it. More guns were installed, and the last battery, the four-gun Battery Buchanan in the south, was completed in October 1864, transforming Fort Fisher into a massive, powerful edifice.

The fortifications were shaped like a 7, with the land defenses in the bar running across the peninsula and the shaft consisting of a mile of sea defenses running along the ocean-front and mounting 22 guns in 12-foot-high batteries with two larger batteries on the south end. The land defensive line was 682 yards long, with 25 guns mounted in fifteen 32-foot-high mounds. Some of the guns were improved by rifling machinery brought in from Charleston, South Carolina, which gave the guns much longer range and greater accuracy. As an added benefit, Fort Fisher was made mostly of earth and sand, which was ideal for absorbing the shock of heavy explosives from the new rifled projectiles.

In late December 1864, the Union launched a combined land-sea attack on Fort Fisher, commanded by Major General Benjamin Butler. After considerable weather delays, the attack was begun by a "powder boat," a gigantic floating bomb designed to be towed close to the fort and detonated, hopefully damaging the structure badly. The U.S.S. *Louisiana* was specially modified with 215 tons of powder, and towed into position off Fort Fisher a little after midnight on December 24, but the *Louisiana* was too far from the fort when it detonated, so it did little damage.

After the failure of the powder boat, the 64-ship Union armada moved to take the fort the old-fashioned way. They moved into position off Federal Point, and from one p.m.

until dark they pounded the fort with 10,000 rounds of solid shot and explosive shell from 600 guns. They wrecked many of the fort's buildings, but left the main systems untouched. The landing force commander, Major General Godfrey Weitzel, said, "I saw [Fort Fisher] had not been materially injured . . . it would be butchery to order an assault on that work under the circumstances."

On Christmas Day, the warships fired another 10,000 rounds at the fortifications, seemingly causing heavy damage, and at two in the afternoon Butler sent Weitzel's amphibious infantry assault force ashore at a beach north of Fort Fisher. They dug in and then began to advance at nightfall, expecting little opposition after the massive bombardment.

Instead, the Confederates moved out from inside their bombproof shelters, manned the battlements and berms, and mowed the Union troops down. There was panic and consternation in the Union ranks, and Butler lost his nerve. As the weather deteriorated, the shattered Union forces fled back to their landing area to be picked up and returned to the fleet. The commander of the 1st Brigade of the 117th New York, General N. Martin Curtis, was delayed, and by the time he reached the beach with more than 600 men and a number of Confederate prisoners, the weather was too bad to pick up his troops, so they were left stranded.

This success enhanced Fort Fisher's reputation for invulnerability, and the next day, December 26, Confederate general Braxton Bragg arrived from his headquarters across the bay at Wilmington and surveyed the victory with satisfaction. However, when the Confederate commanders asked permission to wipe out Curtis's vulnerable troops still on the beach, Bragg—who had a reputation for incompetence—refused to allow the attack. Curtis and his troops were rescued from the beach by the Union navy the following day.

Union general Ulysses S. Grant and Navy Secretary Gideon Welles were infuriated to learn of the expedition's failure to capture Fort Fisher. Grant said, "The Wilmington expedition has proven a gross and culpable failure," but insisted that the Union forces will "be back again with an increased force and without the former commander." Butler was relieved of command, and Major General Alfred Terry was assigned to lead the second expedition against Fort Fisher with a "provisional corps" of 10,000 men from the Federal Army of the James, including a division of U.S. Colored Troops. A fleet of 58 warships under Admiral David D. Porter would transport and support Terry's force.

Terry's Expedition

The armada arrived off Fort Fisher on January 12, 1865. A force of ironclad Union gunboats began to shell the selected landing zone, a point four miles north of Fort Fisher and about one mile north of the previous landing zone. Soon Union troops begin embarking from the transports. Short of troops, the Confederates decided not to challenge the Federal landing and allowed Terry's forces to dig a strong line of entrenchments across the peninsula.

At the same time, Confederate general W.H.C. Whiting, the planner and builder of the fort, had been unsuccessfully lobbying Bragg for reinforcements. Frustrated, he went

Confederate barracks photographed *after the Union capture in January 1865. Constructed of earth and sand supported by heavy timbers, these underground shelters survived the massive artillery barrage unleashed by the Federal gunboats.*

to Fort Fisher on the morning of January 13 and told Lamb, "My boy, I have come to share your fate. You and your garrison are to be sacrificed." When he surveyed the situation, Whiting found the Union fleet had destroyed every gun on the land face of Fort Fisher except for two, and he signaled Bragg, "Unless you drive that land force from its position I cannot answer for the security of this harbor."

On January 15, Terry launched a two-pronged attack, with his army force of 4200 men attacking the northwest side of the fortification line while 2261 of Admiral Porter's sailors and marines simultaneously attacked the northeast side of the fortifications.

Fleet Captain K. R. Breese commanded the naval shore contingent, but he began his attack without coordinating the assault with army infantry forces. The Confederates met the assault with massive fire from their fortifications, and the Union navy men, armed only with revolvers and cutlasses, were routed and forced back up the beach.

Before the Confederates could celebrate, though, Terry's army troops slammed into the western side of the fortifications. Under heavy fire, Union soldiers with axes chopped holes in the fort's palisades to make way for the infantry, who then began to pour through. The desperate Confederates began indiscriminate long-range firing from guns at Battery Buchanan, at the south end of the peninsula, hitting both Union and Confederate soldiers.

The Union troops gained a foothold inside the fort and battled their way from one gun emplacement to another as Union ironclad warships renewed their bombardment of Confederate-held portions of the fort's land face. The fort's commander, Colonel Lamb, gathered a group of wounded men and tried to take them back into the battle; but Lamb himself was seriously wounded just as he gave the order to charge, and this final counterattack was almost wiped out. The Union forces continued to attack, and the Confederates were gradually forced back down the peninsula.

Meanwhile, Bragg still believed in Fort Fisher's invulnerability. He was on the opposite shore and completely out of touch with the situation, but he dismissed reports that the Union forces were close to capturing

Confederate infantrymen fire on U.S. Navy sailors and marines, part of the two-pronged attack on the fort by Union forces. Moundlike earthen "traverses" protected the gun crews from enfilading fire.

marines were running about in the fort with torches, entering powder magazines, discharging firearms, and some were "searching for plunder in the main magazine some ten or fifteen minutes prior to the explosion." Their conclusion was that the explosion was "the result of carelessness on the part of persons unknown."

After the battle, Secretary of War Edwin Stanton told Lincoln that Union commanders Terry and Porter should be commended for the "perfect harmony and concert of action between land and naval forces." On the Confederate side, Bragg was roundly criticized for not sending reinforcements to the fort when they could have been helpful, and the fort's commander, Lamb, spent the rest of his life criticizing Bragg and lobbying for recognition of his garrison's gallantry.

Fort Fisher State Historic Site

The Visitors Center describes the importance of the fort and the battles that eventually resulted in its capture in January 1865. The centerpiece of the Civil War gallery exhibit is a 16-foot-long fiber-optic model that shows the Federal Point peninsula as it appeared in 1865, with three-dimensional models of Fort Fisher and Battery Buchanan. A narrator describes the events as 5000 colored moving lights show troop movements, battles, and naval engagements, and the strategy and tactics used by both the North and the South. It also shows the final hours of Fort Fisher, including the Union naval bombardment, the Union ground attack, and the final Confederate surrender at Battery Buchanan. Artifacts on display include a saber handed over to Union forces by the Confederates at the fort's formal surrender, a sword used by Charles Fisher, the fort's namesake, and a diamond-encrusted sword made by Tiffany and presented to one of the Union commanders by his men.

Only about 10 percent of the original fort remains—approximately 180 yards of the land face on the river side and 75 yards of the ocean side of the fort. A restored palisade

the peninsula, and he told President Jefferson Davis that afternoon that all was well at Fort Fisher. Incredibly, Bragg then decided to change the commander at the fort, and sent a general and three staff officers to row across the channel to Fort Fisher to take over. As the four arrived at the southern tip of the peninsula, Union infantry, including the 27th U.S. Colored Troops, approached, and Bragg's men had to row frantically back to the mainland.

At ten p.m., a gravely wounded Whiting surrendered to Terry, and Union forces set off fireworks to celebrate their victory. A few hours later, a shamefaced Bragg wired General Robert E. Lee and Davis: "I am mortified at having to report the unexpected capture of Fort Fisher, with most of its garrison, at about 10 o'clock to-night."

Then a stunning tragedy occurred. A little after dawn the next day, Fort Fisher's main magazine exploded, killing about 200 men from both sides. Though Confederate sabotage was suspected, an official court of inquiry found that the main magazine had no guards and that drunken soldiers, sailors, and

*A **shattered gun** and scattered debris show the effects of the massive bombardment unleashed on the fort by the Federal fleet on December 20, 1864. In spite of this barrage, the fort held on until January 15, 1865.*

fence and the partial remains of Battery Buchanan are at the southern end of Federal Point, just south of the ferry landing. The park includes a quarter-mile-long self-guided shady tour trail, which leads around the remains of the fort on the river side and to the rear of the fort. Many locations on the trail have wayside exhibits with photos and text that give historical context and details. A gun emplacement features a reconstructed, operational replica of a heavy seacoast 32-pounder cannon. The fort also has working reproductions of a Napoleon 12-pounder fieldpiece and a Coehorn mortar. All three cannon types were mounted at Fort Fisher.

A pavilion at the north end of the parking lot houses a display of underwater archaeology, "Hidden Beneath the Waves," featuring recovered and preserved artifacts from local shipwrecks, including sunken blockade runners. The North Carolina Underwater Archaeology headquarters is located on the property. Battle Acre, a monument to Confederate dead, is located on the ocean side of U.S. 421.

Visitor Information

910-458-5538;
www.stepintohistory.com/
states/NC/Ft_Fisher.htm and
www.ah.dcr.state.nc.us/sections/hs
/fisher/fisher.htm

Hours: April to October, Monday to Saturday, 9 a.m. until 5 p.m., Sunday 1 p.m. until 5 p.m.; November to March, Tuesday to Saturday, 10 a.m. until 4 p.m., Sunday 1 p.m. until 4 p.m.

Admission: Free; there is a suggested donation for some special events.

Accessibility: The Visitors Center and restrooms are fully accessible; the tour trail is accessible with assistance, but the restored gun emplacement is not.

Special Programs: Daily guided tours starting at the Visitors Center are available Monday to Saturday, 9:30 a.m., 11 a.m., 1:30 p.m., and 3 p.m. and Sunday, 1:30 p.m. and 3 p.m. (The 9:30 tour is available only from April through October.) Groups should make reservations in advance. Throughout the year, reenactors and guided tours explain the life of Confederate and Union soldiers, teach visitors to "drill" with wooden rifles and with a bronze 12-pounder cannon. Staff and volunteers also live fire the Napoleon 12-pounder and the 24-pounder Coehorn mortar throughout the year. There are special celebrations in May on Confederate Memorial Day, as well as spring artillery demonstrations. Call for details.

Getting There: Fort Fisher is 18 miles south of Wilmington, North Carolina.

From I-40: Take College Road (state highway 132) south through Wilmington to U.S. 421. Take U.S. 421 south through Carolina Beach and Kure Beach. Fort Fisher is on the right just south of Kure Beach.

From Southport: Take the Southport–Fort Fisher Ferry (Call 1-800-byferry). This 30-minute ride takes you to the end of Federal Point. Take U.S. 421 north for two miles. Fort Fisher is on the left.

SUBMARINES

Submarines had been used successfully since the early 17th century, and by the time of the Civil War, military submarine technology was well established. Submarines were propelled by either oars or a hand-cranked propeller, had some form of ballast control, a rudder, and some type of air supply. Later they either towed an explosive charge or carried one on a rod extending from the nose, called a spar torpedo.

Submarines were a curious phenomenon in the Civil War. While well over 20 were probably used, except for a few famous cases, hard data is difficult to find. Submarines were viewed as a formidable weapon, so information about them was carefully guarded, especially on the Confederate side, where they were part of the Secret Service, not the navy. Union officers had condemned submarines as "infernal machines" (along with mines), and there appears to have been some concern that they might violate the rules of war. Apparently for that reason, Confederate data was destroyed as the war ended. Little Union submarine-development data was publicly released, perhaps in part because they were reluctant to admit they had considered the use of such weapons.

Union submarines were intended for salvage, clearing, and perhaps mine laying, rather than attack operations. Just after the war began, a Frenchman, Brutus de Villeroi, obtained a contract from the Union navy to build a 46-foot-long submersible using an air-purifying device to supply air to the crew while underwater. The *Alligator*'s crew consisted of 16 oarsmen, a commanding officer/helmsman, and a diver who could do salvage operations or plant mines. This first submarine in the U.S. Navy was placed in service on June 13, 1862. It was intended to clear obstacles, and was towed from Philadelphia to the James River. The water proved too shallow for it to submerge fully, and when the Union army retreated from the Virginia peninsula, it was brought to Fortress Monroe and redesigned. In 1863 the *Alligator* sank in a storm without ever being used operationally.

The Confederates were much more interested in using submarines as attack boats to break through the Union blockade. Confederate submarines were reported as early as the fall of 1861, and there is a seemingly unlikely story that one was sabotaged and sunk at a dock in Tennessee in the fall of that year. Some were also reported in the ports of New Orleans, Mobile, and Savannah that year.

Before one rejects these reports out of hand, it should be noted that Confederate submarines (all built by private companies) were often very small, and a small submarine of the time was easy to build. One simply needed some type of propulsion system such as a hand-operated propeller, a pump system (to let the sub submerge and surface), and an air source, and to seal it all in a watertight hull, often a simple boiler. There was also great monetary motivation to build submarines because a Confederate law provided that "the inventor of a device by which a vessel of the enemy should be destroyed should receive 50 percent of the value of the vessel and [its] armament."

In the fall of 1861, a submarine built by engineer William Cheeney was tested in the James River off Richmond, Virginia. The boat (apparently unnamed) was a conventional submarine except that it towed an air hose on a flotation collar. While the hose solved the problem of air, it also served to mark the submarine's position. A Union spy reported that the submarine sank a target barge, and Union navy ships in the area rigged antisubmarine nets held up by poles around their ships to snare an approaching submarine or its spar torpedo.

Cheeney's submarine apparently attacked the U.S.S. *Minnesota* in October of 1861, but the antisubmarine net worked. The ship was unharmed, but the submarine escaped. It made another attack several weeks later, but a Union picketboat saw the air float and stopped the attack by simply cutting its air hose.

A consortium of designer James McClintock, his assistant Baxter Watson, and cotton broker and lawyer Horace L. Hunley—which had developed and launched the *Pioneer*, a 30-foot-long, three-man submarine in March 1862—joined with the Singer Torpedo Company that built most of the torpedoes (mines) used by the Confederate navy. With Singer, the group built and launched the *American Diver*, an improved *Pioneer*, in Mobile Bay. The *American Diver* was designed for an

During its operations in Charleston, the C.S.S. Hunley *was sketched and later paint-ed by Conrad Wise Chapman. The* Hunley's *sinking of the* Housatonic *affected Federal blockading strategies, which in the case of Charleston may have allowed a greater pos-sibility for blockade-runners to get through to that besieged port.*

SUBMARINES *(continued)*

electric motor, but nothing went right for the ship. The electric propulsion plant was too unreliable and the primitive electric batteries and motor were insufficient to power the boat. Steam power was tried unsuccessfully as well, and she was eventually converted to a manual-crank propeller. Awkward and diffi-cult to control in the water, *American Diver* sank in a storm in Mobile Bay in January 1863, though her crew was rescued.

Hunley's group's next effort was a larger submarine, 40 feet long. It was operated by eight men turning the propeller crank and one man to steer, control the diving planes, and maintain the ballast. Known as the *Fish*, it was considered quite safe when operated by an experienced crew in calm seas, but it was involved in several unfortunate accidents.

After successful test runs in Mobile, the *Fish* was offered to General P.G.T. Beauregard, com-mander of the port at Charleston. There, in August 1863, the crew took it out repeatedly but failed to attack an enemy ship. Then in late August a new volunteer crew mis-takenly caused the vessel to sub-merge with the hatch covers open. Five of the nine-man crew drowned.

In October 1863, while making a practice dive beneath a Confederate ship, the *Fish* sank again, plowing nose first into the sea bottom and drowning Hunley and his crew. Once again it was salvaged, and renamed the C.S.S. *Hunley* after its lost captain. After months of trials, in February 1864 the *Hunley* was ready for an attack mission.

By now, the Union ships close to Charleston, especially the ironclads,

were well prepared for the subma-rine threat. The new Hunley cap-tain, Lieutenant George E. Dixon, decided to attack one of the less well-prepared warships farther out. On the night of February 17, 1864, the *Hunley* headed for the sloop U.S.S. *Housatonic*, but was spotted by sen-tries aboard the Union ship, which opened fire. In response, the subma-rine rammed its torpedo into the *Houstanic's* hull. The *Housatonic* exploded and then sank slowly, the first warship ever sunk by a subma-rine. All but five of her crew were rescued. The *Hunley* sent a signal back to the shore that it had been successful; then it disappeared—until 1995, when it was found about a half mile from its victim. It is now being investigated by archaeologists at Charleston's Warren Lasch Conser-vation Center. On weekends, visitors can view the submarine in the con-servators' lab.*

The Singer Submarine Corps built several more submarines, four in Shreveport, Louisiana, and one in Galveston, Texas. Union forces were sent to capture them at the end of the war, but their crews scuttled them first. There is no record they were ever used operationally.

The Presbytere Museum in New Orleans offered an example of how secretive Confederate submarine activities were. For a long time, a classic Confederate Civil War sub-marine found in Lake Pontchartrain in 1878 sat outside the museum. Its hull plates are an unusual pattern, indicating it was built to be a subma-rine. Despite exhaustive research, its name, origin, and the fate of its crew remain a mystery. Today it has been removed from the front of the muse-um for further study.

*For more information, see www.hunley.org/main_index.asp?CONTENT=TOURS

The Battle of Fort Macon

Fort Macon was a part of the chain of defenses along the coast of the United States known as the Third System, built after the War of 1812. Fort Macon was built on the northeast end of the Bogue Banks barrier island to guard Beaufort Harbor, North Carolina's major deepwater ocean port.

On April 14, 1861—35 days before North Carolina seceded—secessionists took over the fort to keep it out of Federal control. The fort was in poor shape, and the Confederates hurriedly tried to make it combat ready to repel an expected attack on Beaufort Harbor. The Confederacy sent a number of medium-caliber and larger guns to Fort Macon, and Confederate infantry regiments were stationed in the immediate area to guard the island against an amphibious landing by Union forces.

In March 1862, the three infantry companies on Bogue Banks assigned to protect Fort Macon were stripped to protect New Bern, the second largest city in North Carolina, from an attack by Ambrose Burnside. After a sharp battle on March 14, Burnside's forces took New Bern. Since Fort Macon was the only major Confederate stronghold on the North Carolina coast north of Wilmington, Burnside's forces quickly moved to capture it.

Fort Macon was commanded by Mississippian colonel Moses J. White, a 27-year-old West Point graduate and a staff ordnance officer, who suffered from severe epilepsy. There were 441 men in the garrison, most from North Carolina. None had any combat experience.

The fort had 54 cannons, mostly smoothbore 24- and 32-pounders, but also 8-inch and 10-inch smoothbore Columbiads. Additionally, it had a 5.82-inch rifled Columbiad and four of its smoothbore 32-pounders had been converted into rifled cannons by a portable rifling machine. Once converted, the cannons fired elongated rifled projectiles weighing 50 to 64 pounds, rather than round 32-pounder cannonballs. These five rifled cannons, with long range and great accuracy, were the best guns the fort possessed.

The fort had provisions for seven months, but only enough gunpowder on hand for three days of sustained firing. Additionally, the gunpowder was not the best type for bursting charges that would explode over the enemy, or for explosive ammunition. However, there was a more serious problem—the lack of land defenses. The fort lacked the short, stubby mortars needed to lob explosive shells into entrenched enemy troops and artillery, because they had been considered redundant as long as Confederate infantry regiments guarded Bogue Banks. Now that the infantry had been transferred to New Bern, Fort Macon's land side was unprotected, and there was no way to acquire mortars.

On March 19, Burnside dispatched Brigadier General John G. Parke to capture Fort Macon. On March 23, Parke arrived in Carolina City, on Bogue Sound just across from Bogue Banks, and demanded the fort's surrender, but White politely refused.

From March 26, when Parke's forces occupied the town of Beaufort, until April 23, Parke continued to move troops, guns, and equipment over to Bogue Banks. Meanwhile, Parke's occupation of Beaufort put a huge emotional strain on the Confederate garrison, many of whom were from the local area. They were concerned about how their families were coping, and White had angered them when he said he would not hesitate to shell the town if Union forces attempted to place cannon batteries there.

These strains had practical consequences. When Union infantry units and a train with siege guns landed on Bogue Banks about five miles north of Fort Macon on March 29, some of White's men deserted and helped Union officers conduct a reconnaissance of the area. Over the days that followed, more and more of White's men deserted.

On April 24, Burnside—who had arrived to observe the operation and had brought along two floating batteries to support the attack—tried to persuade White to surrender without a fight, but White again refused. Burnside ordered the attack to begin.

The next morning, Fort Macon's garrison roll call showed 263 men present for duty out of 403. At five forty a.m. the Union batteries on Bogue Banks opened fire on Fort Macon, and about 20 minutes later the Confederates began to return fire with the fort's 21 guns that could bear on the Union land batteries.

During the morning, things went well for White and his men. Just before nine a.m., four Union gunboats joined in the action, and after less than an hour and a half of

Federal artillery bombard Fort Macon using their new rifled cannons. Eventually two of the fort's powder magazines were in danger of being hit and exploded by Federal shells. Rather than being blown up by their own gunpowder, the Confederates were forced to surrender.

rough treatment by the Confederate guns, the Union ships withdrew. At the same time, the two Union floating batteries were ineffective because of choppy seas that rolled the platforms and made their fire erratic. On the land side, the Union 10-inch mortar battery was hit several times by White's guns and temporarily silenced. Heavy smoke from the fort's guns kept the Union gunners from being able to see where their shells were falling, so they did not know that most of their rounds were overshooting the fort and landing in the water.

Then the battle turned. Union officers manning a signal station on the top story of the Atlantic Hotel in Beaufort found they were in a perfect position to spot the fall of the shots of the Union artillery, and they began to signal range corrections to the Union batteries. By noon, most Union rounds were hitting the fort or exploding over it, and the fort's gunners were under heavy fire. Without mortars to lob shells into the protected Union batteries and without the proper powder to detonate airburst or high-explosive shells from their own guns, the Confederate gunners were almost helpless. White, who had directed the battle all morning, had a physical break-

down and had to retire to his quarters. By two p.m., only two or three of the fort's guns were returning fire, and those only at five-minute intervals. About three thirty p.m., a last-ditch effort was made by the fort's garrison to return fire with all the guns that had not been knocked out, but by four p.m. most of the fort's guns were silent again.

The three Union 30-pounder Parrott rifle cannons were proving particularly accurate and destructive. Union gunners began concentrating their fire on the specific sections of the fort's walls that protected the gunpowder magazines, and by four thirty p.m., two of the fort's powder

A navy smoothbore 32-pounder rifled cannon, center picture, stands guard on the top of the fort. Above, the outer defensive wall is separated from the inner citadel by a ditch, or moat. Entrance to the citadel is by way of the sally port across the ditch.

magazines were in danger of being detonated by Federal shells. White's deputy met with the fort's officers to review the situation and found that many of the fort's most important guns had been knocked out, gun crews had been pulled back from the exposed batteries on the outer wall, and the garrison was exhausted. The wall next to the southwest gunpowder magazine was cracking and would soon be torn open, exposing the magazine and its five tons of powder to the enemy fire. The northeast powder magazine was also in danger of being pierced, and if either of these was hit, the resulting explosion could destroy the fort. Shortly after the meeting, the fort ran up a white flag, and at daylight White and Burnside formally drew up and signed surrender terms.

Of 1150 shots fired by the Union batteries, 560 were hits, badly damaging the walls and grounds. Seventeen of the fort's guns had been knocked out or damaged. Some of the Parrott projectiles had gone through two feet of solid masonry, and one passed through a solid stone staircase. But despite the physical damage, only seven Confederates had been killed and 18 wounded. One Union soldier was killed and three wounded.

This battle, along with the destruction of Fort Pulaski two weeks earlier, proved that rifled cannons had made masonry fortifications obsolete.

Fort Macon State Park

After its capture, Fort Macon was used on and off by the U.S. Army until 1903, when it was declared obsolete and abandoned. On June 4, 1924, the United States government sold the fort and surrounding reservation to the state of North Carolina for use as a public park. During 1934 and 1935, the Civilian Conservation Corps restored the fort and developed public recreational facilities. The U.S. Army again took control of the fort during World War II, and on October 1, 1946, the army returned the fort and park to the state. It is now the most visited park in North Carolina.

Fort Macon has an outer defensive wall about 24 feet high, separated from an inner citadel by a ditch, or moat. The main entrance to the citadel is by way of the sally port across the ditch. Through the sally port is the parade ground with two mortars, a cannon, and casemates (or chambers), on the side walls. To the left of the sally port are restored rooms duplicated from copies of the fort's original plans, and the Fort Macon Museum, with exhibits covering different periods of the fort's history.

The fort has 26 casemates that contain exhibits and displays. Of special interest are the gunpowder magazines under the stairways; restored enlisted men's and officers' quarters from the period; and a restored hot-shot furnace—to heat cannonballs, which were then used to set wooden warships on fire. There is also a replica brick baking oven, a restored cooking range, and a restored commissary storeroom.

Most of the fort's original cannon emplacements are still in place, and two full-size replicas of the navy smoothbore 32-pounder cannons that the Confederates converted into rifled cannons are mounted on the top of the fort. During the summer a staff member will answer questions.

Visitor Information
252-726-3775

Hours: The fort is open daily, from 9 a.m. until 5:30 p.m.; closed December 25. The park is open November to February, 8 a.m. until 6 p.m.; March and October, 8 a.m. until 7 p.m.; April, May, and September, 8 a.m. until 8 p.m.; June to August, 8 a.m. until 9 p.m.

Admission: Free.

Accessibility: The interior of the fort is accessible, as are picnic areas and swimming facilities.

Special Events: Historic reenactments are regularly held on the fort's parade ground. Friends of Fort Macon volunteer guides give daily tours from April to October at 10 and 11 in the morning, and at 12, 1, 2, and 3 in the afternoon, weather permitting. There are also musket- and cannon-firing demonstrations. The 1st North Carolina Volunteers present Civil War reenactments, usually in April, July, and September. There is a Concerts in the Fort series every other Friday in June and July at 7 p.m. Call 252-726-3775 for a schedule.

Getting There: Fort Macon State Park is located on the eastern end of Bogue Banks. From I-95, take U.S. 70 east to Morehead City, and then turn south on Atlantic Beach Causeway. Cross the bridge to Atlantic Beach and turn left on state highway 58. The fort is located at the tip of the island.

The Battle of Plymouth

On June 3, 1863, the Union navy received word that a new Confederate ironclad ram, the *Albemarle*, was being built at Edward's Ferry on North Carolina's Roanoke River. No Union ships could reach her because the water there was so shallow, so the navy recommended that the Union army send a force to burn her, but no force was ever sent.

The ram was built under the supervision of her first commanding officer-to-be, former U.S. Navy officer Commander J. W. Cooke, C.S.N. The main shipbuilder was 19-year-old Gilbert Elliot. Because of a lack of materials and workers, the *Albemarle* took over a year to finish even though she, like her sister ship the C.S.S. *Neuse*, was simply a steam-powered, flat-bottomed barge, sharp at both ends, with her casemates covered by railroad iron.

The biggest obstacle was finding iron. Confederate troops had to raid iron pots and farm implements from the local people, often at gunpoint, to be melted down for the ship. Most of the side armor was railroad iron rolled into two-inch-thick plates placed over four-inch-thick wood planking. Peter Evans Smith, a mechanical engineer and the owner of the plantation where the ironclad was being built, helped a great deal; he developed what would become the modern twist drill to speed up the drilling of holes in the two-inch iron plates. The new drill reduced the drilling time per hole from 20 minutes to only four.

When completed, the *Albemarle* was 158 feet long, including an axe-head-shape iron-plated oak ram in the bow. The ship was 35 feet and 3 inches at the beam, drew nine feet of water, and displaced 376 tons. Her two 200-horsepower steam engines (reportedly taken from a sawmill) gave the *Albemarle* a speed of five knots. Her 60-foot-long iron-covered casemate housed two slow-firing 8-inch Brooke rifled cannons, one fore and one aft, that could be pivoted 180 degrees to fire out of three different gunports, and the casemate had a 35-degree slope to deflect enemy rounds.

The *Albemarle* was only partially completed when Cooke was ordered to support an operation to try to retake Plymouth, North Carolina—a town that been occupied by the Union since 1862. Plymouth was close to the Wilmington & Weldon Railroad line from Wilmington, North Carolina, to Richmond, Virginia, on which Lee's Army of Northern Virginia depended to keep supplies flowing from Wilmington—the only major Southern port still open. The Union forces at Plymouth had become increasingly aggressive in trying to cut the line, especially at the critical Weldon Bridge. Cooke promised to be at Plymouth by April 18, even though workmen were still on the ship, the engines had not been tested, and her crew was untrained.

Late in the afternoon of April 17, 1864, 26-year-old Confederate brigadier general Robert F. Hoke launched his force of 7000 men against the forts at Plymouth. Plymouth was defended by about 2800 Union troops under the command of Brigadier General Henry Wessells, a 55-year-old West Point graduate. In addition, a strong Union naval force under the command of Lieutenant Commander Charles Flusser was in the Roanoke River. The Union fleet consisted of two 730-ton "double-ender" side-wheel gunboats, the *Miami* (Flusser's flagship) and the *Southfield*, each carrying one rifled 100-pounder and five large shell cannons. The rest of the force consisted of the side-wheel steam gunboat *Ceres* and two picketboats, the *Bombshell* and the *Whitehead*.

The Union ships pounded the attacking Confederates, and Wessells's men were well dug in at Plymouth's forts. The initial Confederate attacks made little progress, and by April 18 it was clear that the Confederates needed the *Albemarle*'s support.

A Victorious *Albemarle*

Meanwhile, the Confederate ironclad was slowly making her way down the river. The ship was still incomplete, and there were reports that her armor was being bolted on as she sailed toward Plymouth. Finally, about three a.m. on the 19th, the *Albemarle* arrived. Flusser had chained the *Miami* and *Southfield* together, hoping to trap the ironclad between them and board her, and the two ships steamed toward the *Albemarle*. The Union ships moved into close range and opened fire while trying to maneuver the Confederate ship between them. Almost immediately, one of the *Miami*'s 100-pounder shells bounded off the *Albemarle*'s sloped iron sides and back toward the Union ship, where it detonated. Several pieces of shrapnel struck

Flusser, killing him instantly.

The *Albemarle* tried to ram the *Miami*, but slid off and then rammed the *Southfield* in her engine room. The *Southfield* began to take on water and slowly sank, taking the *Albemarle* with her. Water was pouring into the forward gun ports before the Confederate ship was able to pull her ram free. As the *Albemarle* began to move again, the other Union ships, having lost their commanding officer and one of their main units, turned and fled down the river.

The *Albemarle* then turned her guns upon the Union troops. The Confederate forces moved into the town and, in house-to-house fighting, drove the Union defenders into their last stronghold, Fort Williams. The *Albemarle* anchored just offshore close to the fort and began shelling. Wessells's forces, surrounded now on land and water, held out until the next day, April 20, and then surrendered at ten a.m.

The Union Targets the *Albemarle*

The *Albemarle* returned to Plymouth so the work she needed could be completed. On May 5 she moved downriver toward New Bern to support a planned Confederate attack against the town. After traveling about 15 miles, she ran into a seven-ship Union fleet lying in wait for her. Though none of the Union ships were ironclads, they were heavily armed, and the *Albemarle* was too slow to ram them. As the battle raged, Union 100-pound rifled projectiles and the 9-inch solid shot made little impression on the Confederate ironclad, and she disabled the double-ended ram U.S.S. *Sassacus*. However, when the action ended at dark, the *Albemarle* had been rammed once and hit by at least 44 shells, and she limped back to Plymouth for repairs.

Finally, the Union decided to take drastic action against the *Albemarle*, and navy commander William Cushing was chosen for the job. Cushing was something of a wild man who had been expelled from Annapolis but had made a name for himself during the Civil War as a daring commander of what today would be called special operations. There was an element of personal revenge in this for Cushing, who had been a close friend of Flusser's, the commander of the Union fleet killed in the first engagement with the *Albemarle*. Cushing decided to take small steam launches and fit them with "torpedoes"—explosive charges —mounted at the end of a 14-foot spar. For this to work, Cushing would have to take the launch next to the *Albemarle*, push the torpedo under the ironclad, and then detonate it.

The night of October 27, Cushing took one of the modified launches, *Picketboat Number One*, with a crew of more than 20 officers and men up

*The U.S.S. **Sassacus** ramming the C.S.S.* Albemarle *during the Confederate ironclad's engagement with Federal gunboats. The* Sassacus *was hit in a boiler and disabled in this action; the* Albemarle *was not significantly damaged by the ramming or by gunfire.*

Lieutenant William B. Cushing and his crew leap from their sinking spar-torpedo boat after successfully attacking the C.S.S. Albemarle.

the Roanoke River to Plymouth to attack the *Albemarle.* Their stealthy approach was initially undetected, but as Cushing calmly circled the ironclad to set up his approach, the lookouts on the *Albemarle* detected them and opened fire. Cushing's boat had a small cannon on the bow, and he returned fire with a blast of grapeshot that "moderated their zeal," while lining up on the ironclad. Cushing then ran the launch over an antitorpedo boom of floating logs and exploded the torpedo under the ram's hull. At the same moment, a blast from the *Albemarle*'s main gun hit the launch. Cushing and his crew leapt or were thrown into the river. Some were killed and others captured; Cushing survived. The intrepid Union officer swam ashore and hid, overhearing Confederates saying that the *Albemarle* had sunk in eight feet of water, with her upper works above the surface. Cushing then stole a small boat, rowed down the river until he found a Union picket vessel, and reported his success to his superiors.

Without the *Albemarle*'s interference, Union troops were able to recapture the town four days later, on October 31, 1864. Plymouth remained in Union hands for the rest of the war.

Port O' Plymouth Museum

The Port O' Plymouth Museum is located on the Roanoke River in downtown Plymouth, North Carolina, in the town's old Atlantic Coastline Railroad station. Established in 1988 by the Washington County Historical Society, the museum is mainly devoted to the Civil War, including the Union occupation of Plymouth and the resulting Battle of Plymouth in April 1864. Special attention is paid to the Confederate ironclad ram C.S.S. *Albemarle*'s participation in the battle, its later successful exploits against the Union fleet, and its sinking October 27, 1864,

near Plymouth. There is a model of the *Albemarle,* and recovered cannonballs, bullets, guns, pictures, and many other battle artifacts are on display against the backdrop of a painting of the Plymouth waterfront in the 1860s. A full-time curator and staff give lectures and tours of the facility.

A 63-foot replica of the C.S.S. *Albemarle,* launched April 2002, is berthed in the Roanoke River behind the museum. In addition, a local shipbuilder has contracted to build a replica of Cushing's 30-foot spar torpedo launch, *Picketboat Number One,* which sank the *Albemarle* the night of October 27, 1864.

Visitor Information

252-793-1377;
www.livinghistoryweekend.com/
port_o.htm

Hours: In the winter, Monday to Saturday, 9 a.m. until 4 p.m.; in the summer, Tuesday to Saturday, 8 a.m. until 5 p.m.; openings and times vary on Sundays and Mondays depending on the availability of volunteers. Call for information.

Admission: Minimal fee for adults and children.

Special Events: The Battle of Plymouth Living History Weekend is held in late April and includes reenactors, cannon firings, the *Albemarle* replica in action, and a number of other events. On Saturday, there is a reenactment of the street fighting in the town that took place before the last fort fell. During the summer, the *Albemarle* replica cruises the river at noon for half an hour and fires her guns at noon and 12:30 p.m. Call for details.

Getting There: Plymouth is located in Washington County, North Carolina, on the south side of the Roanoke River about eight miles from Albemarle Sound. Take I-95 to U.S. 64 east (past Rocky Mount) toward the Outer Banks. Once in Plymouth, take Washington Street until it dead-ends at Water Street. Turn right, and the museum is on the left at the end of the business district.

Civil War Library and Museum

The oldest chartered Civil War institution in the country, founded in 1888, this Philadelphia museum has memorabilia from the conflict in seven galleries on three floors.

The most famous artifact is the stuffed head of Old Baldy, General George Meade's warhorse. Old Baldy was wounded at least 14 times during the war but survived to the age of 30, outliving Meade by 10 years. Other items relating to Meade include his distinctive slouch hat, a presentation sword made by Bailey & Co., and his boots with eagle-head spurs.

An entire room is devoted to General Ulysses S. Grant. It houses the original surrender document from Fort Donelson, Grant's field glasses, a presentation sword given to him after the Vicksburg victory, his death mask, and other items.

Additional exhibits include rifles and swords, uniforms, battle flags, plaster casts of President Abraham Lincoln's hands and face, Confederate President Jefferson Davis's smoking jacket, the first John Wilkes Booth wanted poster, and items from Civil War prison camps.

The library is noted for its research facilities and contains more than 12,000 volumes, 100 reels of microfilm, and nearly 5000 photographs.

Visitor Information

215-735-8196; www.netreach.net/~cwlm/

Hours: Thursday to Saturday, 11 a.m. until 4:30 p.m.; closed major holidays.

Admission: Moderate charge for adults and minimal charge for children 3 to 12.

Accessibility: The building is not handicapped accessible.

Special Events: The CWLM's Old Baldy Civil War Round Table meets the second Thursday of each month for discussion and to hear presentations by noted historians. The Round Table also sponsors the annual Mid-Atlantic Regional Conference of Civil War Round Tables and is very involved in Civil War–related preservation. Contact the museum to learn about its changing special exhibits.

Getting There: The museum is located in Philadelphia's Center City at 1805 Pine Street, between 18th and 19th Streets.

Grand Army of the Republic Civil War Library and Museum

This collection includes Civil War artifacts, war relics, personal memorabilia, paintings, documents, and photographs—many of them contributed by the veterans who founded GAR Post 2 soon after the war. Some of the notable items in the collection include tree stumps embedded with cannonballs fired on the Chickamauga battlefield, a portion of the stockade from Andersonville prison, the handcuffs that John Wilkes Booth intended to use if he kidnapped President Abraham Lincoln, and part of the blood-stained pillowcase from the Petersen House where Lincoln lay dying.

The museum is located in Ruan House, which is listed on the National Register of Historic Sites. Visitors are greeted by volunteers dressed in period clothing—men in blue Union uniforms, and women in hoop skirts. On the first Sunday of each month, the museum hosts an open house at one p.m. and three p.m. that includes a two-hour presentation by costumed docents relating a first-person perspective on the war.

Visitor Information

215-289-6484; www.garmuslib.org

Hours: First Sunday of each month for an open house, noon until 5 p.m.; Tuesdays and Wednesdays, 10 a.m. until 2 p.m. (call to confirm weekday hours); closed major holidays. The museum is also open by appointment for groups or researchers.

Admission: Free.

Accessibility: Partially handicapped accessible.

Getting There: The museum is located at 4278 Griscom Street in northeast Philadelphia, Pennsylvania.

From the south on I-95: Take exit 27 toward Bridge Street and merge onto Aramingo Avenue. After 1/2 mile, turn sharp left on Tacony Street. Go another 1/2 mile and turn right on Church Street, then left onto Griscom Street to the museum.

From the north on I-95: Take exit 27 and turn right on Bridge Street. Go 1/4 mile and turn left on Torresdale Avenue for about 3/4 mile. Turn right on Church Street. After less than 1/2 mile, turn left onto Griscom Street to the museum.

SMALL ARMS

Civil War soldiers used a variety of different firearms, such as muskets, carbines, rifles, and pistols. While field artillery caused massive devastation, small arms killed more soldiers.

A New Bullet

A small weapon revolutionized warfare during the Civil War. Casualties from the rifled minié ball and similar rounds exceeded those from any other weapon in that conflict. Some sources say as many as 90 percent of the battlefield wounds were caused by these rifled musket rounds, and as many as 234,000 men died from these wounds.

minié bullet

The minié ball's secret was that it was the first practical rifled round fired from a musket. The improved range and accuracy from a rifled bullet had been known as early as 1500, but the increased time it took to load a rifled bullet was too great a drawback for use in battle. Rifles had been used for hunting long before the Civil War. The principle was simple: Spiral grooves were cut into the inside of a gun barrel, and a bullet made to fit the grooves. When the gun was fired, the bullet gripped the grooves and exited in a tight spiral. The spin vastly increased the round's range and accuracy. For a hunter, the additional time and effort it took to ram the rifled bullet down the gun's barrel was a minor problem; but in battle, the need to fire rapidly outweighed the need for accuracy. In contrast, an unrifled musket ball was smaller than the barrel and could be loaded quickly.

In the mid-1800s a French army captain, Claude Minié, designed the first really practical solution. The minié round was smaller than the bore of the rifle and could be rammed down as easily as a smoothbore musket round, and thus it didn't slow the rate of fire. But when the rifle was fired, the minié ball expanded enough to fit into the rifled grooves, spinning as it exited the barrel. The improvement was dramatic: A smoothbore musket had an effective range of about 100 yards against a human-size target. With a minié ball, a rifled musket's accuracy was more than three times as great—over 300 yards.

Moreover, 300 yards was not the maximum range. Civil War rifled muskets firing minié balls could hit an infantry-company-size target (52 feet wide by 6 feet high) at 3000 feet—over half a mile! Now mass infantry charges across open fields would result in huge casualties, though it took Civil War commanders a long time to adjust to this new reality. The minié ball also made a whistling whine in flight, which had a disconcerting effect on experienced and inexperienced infantry alike.

Firing Shoulder Weapons

Civil War muskets did not use loose powder and shot. Instead, soldiers used a paper cylinder containing both the round and about 60 grains of black powder behind it. To fire, the soldier would tear off one end of the paper cylinder, pour the powder into the barrel, push the round out of the paper, and then use his ramrod to force the bullet down the barrel on top of the powder. Finally, he fitted a small percussion cap over a hollow tube under the musket's hammer. When he pulled the trigger, the hammer snapped down and exploded the cap, igniting the powder. This time-consuming process required disciplined troops to go through a complex loading sequence correctly and shoot accurately while all around them cannon shells exploded.

Effects of Small Arms

By modern standards, Civil War small-arms bullets were anything but small. The standard .58-caliber round was over a half inch in diameter. When it hit, the soft lead flattened and often broke up inside of the victim. Because the round traveled relatively slowly, it rarely went completely through the bone, instead splintering or shattering it. A hit in the abdomen or head generally meant death, and if a man was shot in the arm or leg, amputation was the norm.

Percussion Rifle Muskets

Most Civil War rifle muskets had very similar dimensions—about 56 inches long and about nine pounds in weight—but used different types of ammunition and had their own advantages and disadvantages.

The U.S. Musket 1842 (M1842) was the first American musket to use the percussion-cap system and was the predecessor to the rifled muskets that became the main armament of Civil War infantry. The M1842 went into production in 1844 at Harpers Ferry and initially used a .69-caliber smoothbore. After the successful testing of the minié ball, the U.S. Army began a program to rifle the smoothbore M1842s to accept the minié round. The bore on these rifled M1842s changed caliber from .69 to .58, which tests had shown to be the most effective size. Both sides used rifled M1842s, but because of a shortage of rifled muskets, the Confederates used unrifled M1842s until at least 1863.

The U.S. M1855 Rifle Musket was the first rifled musket produced in the U.S. The M1855 was unique because instead of a percussion cap it used a tape primer—very similar to a roll of caps children use in a cap gun. As in a cap gun, the tape moved automatically as the rifle was cocked. While sound in theory, the system proved troublesome in practice and was replaced by a percussion cap on later musket rifles.

The Springfield U.S. M1861 Rifle Musket was the most common weapon used by Civil War infantry. It was quite similar to the M1855 but used percussion caps instead of the tape primer.

The Richmond Confederate Rifle Musket was virtually identical to the M1855 but used percussion caps instead of the primer tape. These weapons often fired a unique Confederate-designed round, the Gardner insert, which was easier to use than the standard Union minié round.

The Enfield Rifle Musket was a very popular, well-built British rifle musket and probably the second most widely used rifled musket in the

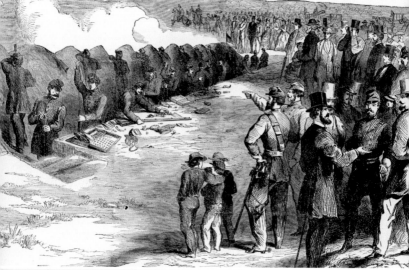

Hiram Berdan, a wealthy inventor and top rifle shot, sent agents all over the North to recruit the best marksmen in each state to form a unit of sharpshooters. They were to serve as snipers to demoralize the Confederate troops by picking off their officers and artillerymen at long range. Before being accepted, a recruit had to prove that he could shoot by putting 10 bullets within five inches of the center of a bull's-eye at 200 yards.

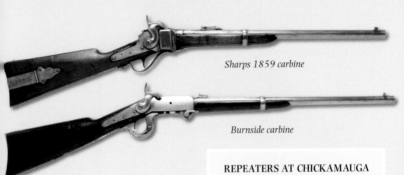

Sharps 1859 carbine

Burnside carbine

war after April 1862. The Enfield was considered more accurate than the M1861 or M1863 but it had a slower rate of fire, and it was more expensive than other rifled muskets.

Breech-Loading Carbines

One of the most pressing needs at the beginning of the Civil War was a practical weapon for the cavalry. The cavalry needed a short rifle that could be loaded from the rear—a breech-loader. They could also be fired two or three times as fast as muzzle-loaders. At the beginning of the war, there were two breech-loading carbines available to Union forces, the Sharps and the Burnside. Only one, the Maynard, was available to the Confederate forces, and it proved difficult to maintain.

The Sharps M1859 carbine was a .52-caliber single-shot breech-loader that was a little over three feet long and weighed less than eight pounds. The Sharps used a totally combustible linen or nitrate-treated paper cartridge ignited by percussion caps. It had a range of 400 yards, was very durable, easy to produce, and cheap, though it had problems with gas leakage from the breech lock when it was fired. As an added benefit, the Sharps could use the later metallic cartridges.

The Burnside carbine, designed by Union general Ambrose Burnside, was a .54-caliber, 40-inch, 7-pound carbine designed to use a special conical-shaped brass cartridge that was intended to solve the gas-leakage problem. Over 50,000 Burnside carbines were produced, third only behind the Spencer and Sharps. Nevertheless, they were not universally popular because they were fragile, and the unique cartridge tended to stick in the breech.

The Maynard carbine was a Confederate .50-caliber breech-loading carbine. It was small and light—37 inches, 6 pounds—and fired metallic cartridges. In service, it was considered an excellent weapon,

especially noted for its long-range accuracy.

Rapid-Fire Small Arms

As the war progressed, the Union capitalized on a breakthrough in cartridge design, the internally primed metal cartridge. The internal priming eliminated the need for a percussion cap, and the strength and stability of the metal cartridges allowed them to be loaded in a magazine. The size, ease of use, and rapid rate of fire of the carbines made them very popular weapons. By the end of the war, the Union cavalry was more than equal to the Confederate cavalry, mainly because of these rapid-fire carbines.

The most important rapid-fire rifle was the **Spencer carbine,** perhaps the most popular weapon used in the Civil War. It was a standard size—39 inches, 8 1/4 pounds, .52-caliber—lever-action breech-loader, but it carried seven of the new internally primed metal cartridges in a magazine. To fire again, the rifleman simply had to pull the trigger, lower the trigger guard lever to eject the spent cartridge, cock the hammer, and then fire again. The Spencer fired 21 rounds a minute at a time when three rounds a minute was considered good for a muzzle-loading percussion musket. It was first delivered

> ### REPEATERS AT CHICKAMAUGA
> "I found the 39th Indiana regiment coming from a crossroad,—a full, fresh regiment, armed with Spencer's repeating-rifles. . . . its commander . . . dismounting his men, dashed at the enemy in a most effective charge. [Colonel John T.] Wilder, coming up on our right, also attacked . . . with the same repeating-rifles. They did splendid work. [Confederate general James] Longstreet told Wilder after the war that the steady and continued racket of these guns led him to think an army corps had attacked his left flank."
> —*Union officer Gates P. Thruston*

*A **Union** cavalry-man armed with two Colt Army revolvers. In the Union army, handguns were issued only to the cavalry and mounted light artillery.*

Colt Model 1851 Navy pistol

SMALL ARMS *(continued)*

to Union forces in October 1863 and was also produced as a 47-inch, 10-pound rifle.

The Henry rifle was by far the most advanced rifle used in the Civil War. It had a 15-shot magazine and a lever-action cocking mechanism that allowed it to fire more than twice as fast as the Spencer. It was reliable and accurate, but it fired relatively small .44-caliber, copper-cased cartridges not used by any other weapon. It was also more expensive and more difficult and time consuming to produce than the Spencer.

Pistols

Most pistols used during the Civil War were multishot revolvers, either single action (the hammer had to be manually cocked before firing) or, later, double action (a trigger pull would fire the weapon). While revolvers were unreliable and inaccurate except at very short distances, they were popular because they could fire a number of bullets quickly.

The Colt Model 1851 Navy pistol and **Colt Model 1860 Army pistol** were the most widely used handguns on both sides. Both were six-shot, single-action, percussion revolvers, but the "Army" and

"Navy" designations had nothing to do with the services that used them. Instead, they designated different calibers—.44 for the Army and .36 for the Navy. Other than the different calibers, the two weapons were practically identical, weighing a little less than three pounds and measuring 13 to 14 inches.

The Remington New Model 1861 Army and **1861 Navy revolvers** were the second most widely used pistols in the war. Roughly the same size as the Colt, they also used the same caliber designations. The Remington was less expensive and easier to manufacture than the Colt. It was also sturdier. As a result, Remington pistols replaced the Colt in the Union army after November 1863.

The LeMat Revolver was a unique pistol made in Europe but invented by a New Orleanian, Jean LeMat. The LeMat revolver held nine conventional .40-caliber bullets and also had a large center barrel that fired an 18-gauge shotgun shell.

The Starr Army Revolver .44-caliber came in either single action or double action and was issued mainly to Union cavalry. Next to the Remington and the Colt, the Starr was the most widely produced Civil War pistol.

The Battle of Gettysburg

In June 1863, after his victory at Chancellorsville, Confederate general Robert E. Lee resisted efforts by some in the Confederate political leadership to send part of his army west to help defend Vicksburg. Instead, he proposed to once again invade the North. Lee's aims were much the same as his 1862 invasion that Union forces stopped at Antietam. He hoped to relieve the economic pressure on Confederate supporters in northern Virginia, to threaten Washington, D.C., and other Union strongholds, and to reenergize the debate in Europe over recognizing the Confederacy. Lee also felt that he had advantages that he did not have in September 1862. Now his soldiers were rested, reasonably well equipped, and flushed with victory.

In late June, Lee moved across Maryland and headed toward Harrisburg, Pennsylvania. He divided his 80,000 men into three infantry corps, led by Lieutenant General James Longstreet; Lieutenant General Richard Ewell, who had been newly promoted to replace Stonewall Jackson, killed two months earlier at Chancellorsville; and another new lieutenant general, A. P. Hill. (Hill's timely arrival had saved Lee at Antietam.) Ewell's corps led the way, well ahead of the rest of the force.

While he moved through Pennsylvania, Lee allowed Major General J.E.B. Stuart to take his cavalry and move east, essentially on his own, expecting Stuart to find and report the location of the Army of the Potomac. Stuart moved well behind the Union lines, where he successfully harassed Union supply trains, but these maneuvers left him out of touch with Lee. With little specific information about his enemy's location and strength, Lee became more and more nervous, constantly pressing his subordinates for news of Stuart's whereabouts.

On the Union side, General Joe Hooker, commander of the Army of the Potomac, had been relieved at his own request—a result of frustrations with the War Department. General George Meade replaced him on June 28. Meade knew of Lee's invasion and moved the Army of the Potomac out to fight, hoping to engage Lee from strong defensive positions near Pipe Creek, Maryland. Lee learned from a spy that Meade had replaced Hooker and that the Army of the Potomac had moved into Maryland with 95,000 men in pursuit of the Confederates. Lee called back Ewell so Meade would not catch him with his army separated, then turned to meet the Union army. Lee planned to collect his forces in the mountains between Chambersburg and Gettysburg, a small college town located at the intersection of 10 roads. Since Lee was moving in the direction of Gettysburg, on June 30 Hill allowed a division to do some foraging. After warning them that Union cavalry might be in the area, Hill allowed the division to go to Gettysburg in search of supplies.

The report was accurate. One of Meade's forward elements, two brigades of Union cavalry commanded by Brigadier General John Buford, had moved into Gettysburg the day before. The next morning, July 1, when Buford saw Confederate infantry approaching, he sent word back to his commander, General John F. Reynolds, who was close behind him. Buford recognized the importance of Gettysburg's massive complex of roads, so he decided to stay and fight dismounted on the high ground of Seminary Ridge. His units were armed with the latest in weapons technology, the breech-loading seven-shot Spencer carbines, and the outnumbered Union force stopped the Confederate division cold (*see* Small Arms sidebar, page 157).

Gettysburg as a Battleground

General Reynolds brought part of his corps up to reinforce Buford on Seminary Ridge, but Reynolds was shot and killed by a Confederate sharpshooter almost immediately after he arrived. Union major general Oliver Howard took command of the overall effort. Some forces deployed along ridges to the northwest of the town while other Union divisions moved into town. Almost by accident, the battle was starting. Gettysburg was neither side's first choice of a battlefield, but both were willing to fight there.

Union forces pushed the Confederates back to the west of the town until Ewell's and Hill's Confederate reinforcements arrived. They soon flanked and overwhelmed the Union forces, causing almost 10,000 casualties. The Confederates had also taken heavy losses, but they were jubilant as they drove the Union forces through the town and out to high ground to the east and south, known as Cemetery Ridge.

Howard had placed forces on Cemetery Ridge with orders to hold it at all costs, and the Union forces that fell back rallied there. Lee realized that if he struck quickly he might be able to force the Union forces off the heights and carry the day. However, except for Ewell's corps, most of his troops were out of position or exhausted from the day's fighting. Lee politely suggested to Ewell that he try to force Cemetery Ridge. Ewell hesitated, and then decided against such a move. This hesitation served the Union well. There is little doubt the aggressive Jackson would have pressed ahead, but Ewell was not confident enough to try. In fairness, even if Ewell had attacked, there is no guarantee that he would have been able to dislodge the well-dug-in Union forces.

Meanwhile, Meade began to move his entire army toward Gettysburg. The Union's defensive position was set up on the high ground in the general shape of an upside down J. The shank consisted of Cemetery Ridge with Cemetery Hill at the north end and a thickly vegetated hill called Big Round Top at its southern end. A smaller, less overgrown hill, Little Round Top, stood between Cemetery Ridge and Big Round Top, and Union forces set up a lookout station there. The hook of the Union "J" turned northeast from Cemetery Hill around the ridge to Culp's Hill in the southeast. The shape of the Union defenses allowed troops to be moved back and forth quickly.

Longstreet thought the Union defensive positions were unassailable. He urged Lee not to attack but instead to flank the defenses and reposition his troops between the Army of the Potomac and Washington, D.C., which would force the Union to attack the Confederates in defensive positions. Lee declined, unwilling to give up the momentum he had built. He ordered Longstreet to attack the southern part of Cemetery Ridge the next morning with two of his divisions and one of Hill's, while Ewell's corps would threaten Union positions on the north side of the line. Lee told Ewell to attack if Meade pulled troops from positions in the north to reinforce the south.

The next day, July 2, both sides made their final preparations. Meade assigned Union general Daniel Sickles's corps to take two divisions and cover the Union southern flank

at the south end of Cemetery Ridge. When Sickles arrived, he decided that his assigned position was too low. Without telling Meade, he moved his troops into position along higher ground overlooking the Emmitsburg Road. While this seemed to put Sickles in a better position, he had inadvertently broken the Union line, isolating his corps from other Union units. To make matters worse, Buford's Union cavalry units, who had engaged the Confederates the previous day, were now supposed to be protecting Sickles's flanks. Buford had received permission to go to the rear so his men could rest and tend to their mounts, but through an oversight, his cavalry was not replaced, nor was Sickles notified that he'd be without Buford's men.

This was the area that Longstreet had been ordered to attack, but Longstreet had problems of his own. To preserve the element of surprise, his forces had to take a long, round-about detour behind ridgelines to avoid being seen by the Union lookouts on Little Round Top, and he did not get into position until four p.m.

Meade's Planning Pays Off

When Meade heard Longstreet's artillery firing from the south, he rode down to inspect Sickles's defenses. He was stunned to find Sickles out of position, leaving a gap that threatened the entire Union line as well as leaving the Round Tops unprotected. Meade called for reinforcements, but it was too late. Longstreet sent one division to press Sickles on the center, attacking

Little Round Top, left background, and Big Round Top, center, were the object of Longstreet's corps's advance, foreground. They came close to seizing the Federal positions until driven back by General Samuel Crawford's Pennsylvania Reserve Division.

through a peach grove and a wheat field, now called the Peach Orchard and the Wheatfield respectively. At the same time, Confederate general J. B. Hood's division moved south around Sickles. Some of Hood's men engaged the Union forces in a rough, boulder-strewn area known as Devil's Den, but when Hood saw that the two Round Tops were unoccupied, he disobeyed his orders and took some of his forces to capture the heights. Hood was wounded in the attack, but his men made the steep climb and took Big Round Top. After a brief rest, they scrambled north down a valley and across to Little Round Top. Once there, they could sweep up behind the Union line on Cemetery Ridge and decide the battle.

Just at that moment Union reinforcements arrived, brought to the battle by an unlikely hero, Brigadier General Gouverneur K. Warren, Meade's chief engineer. He had been on an observation tour when he saw that there were no Union troops occupying the critical heights of Little Round Top. Warren took over a brigade and ordered it to Little

Round Top. The Union forces arrived just before the Confederates. There was a sharp, desperate fight between them and the 20th Maine, commanded by Colonel Joshua Chamberlain. After several hours of close combat, the men from Maine, almost out of ammunition, won the day with a bayonet charge.

While the battle for Little Round Top raged, Meade poured in reinforcements to help Sickles, but despite the support, the Union troops were slowly forced back to Cemetery Ridge. At the same time, a Confederate attack against the center of the ridge threatened to break

Joshua Chamberlain was awarded the Medal of Honor for gallantry at Gettysburg—but not until 1893. At war's end, Grant promoted him to brevet brigadier general for his bravery at Petersburg and selected him to receive the formal surrender of arms and colors at Appomattox.

through, but a desperate charge by the 1st Minnesota delayed it, an attack that cost the unit 82 percent casualties. By the time the Confederates regrouped, Union reinforcements had arrived.

To the north, Hill saw an opening when Meade moved forces from Culp's Hill south to help Sickles. There was only one Union brigade holding the hill, but Ewell's attack was too late. His men were able to occupy some Union trenches at the lower part of Culp's Hill but could not break through before reinforcements arrived. Other Confederate forces tried for Cemetery Hill, but it took them an hour under heavy cannon fire to cross the rough ground at the base of the hill. They were able to fight their way up and into some Union batteries, but they were also forced back by Union reinforcements. Meade's tight defensive position that allowed him to move troops rapidly to counter Confederate attacks was paying dividends.

That night the Union commanders met to plan the next day. The atmosphere was tense. Meade was a brand-new commander, facing the acknowledged genius of Lee and the other seasoned Southern generals, but the Union forces had held and their position had solidified. After the near disasters of the afternoon, they were now solidly in control of their defensive line from Little Round Top along Cemetery Ridge, and they held most of Cemetery Hill and Culp's Hill. After some discussion, Meade decided to stand and fight, and as the meeting broke up, with great foresight he predicted that the Confederate attack would come across the open ground in the center of the Union line at Cemetery Ridge. He was assured that the troops would be ready.

On the Confederate side, J.E.B. Stuart and his cavalry had finally arrived, and Lee, both ill and excited by the knowledge that he had almost carried the day, was determined to attack. Now he had two fresh units that had not been in combat, General George E. Pickett's division and Stuart's cavalry, and he felt that with these units he could overpower "those people," as he called the Union army. Lee ordered Ewell to make an early morning attack on the northern part of the Union line. This would be followed by a massive artillery barrage against the Union center, and then Longstreet's I Corps would make a frontal charge with General Pickett's three fresh brigades, as well as six brigades from A. P. Hill's corps. At the same time, he would send Stuart's cavalry around the Union rear to attack Meade from behind.

Early the next morning, Lee met with Longstreet to outline the battle plan. Longstreet still argued against a frontal assault against the entrenched Union forces and once again advised Lee to simply outflank the defenses. Lee refused, and ignored Longstreet's plea not to send Pickett and the other Confederate units in a frontal attack.

While Lee and Longstreet were conferring, the battle began along Culp's Hill, as Union forces tried to take back the positions they had given up the day before. After six hours of fierce back-and-forth fighting, the Union forces succeeded in retaking the positions.

Pickett's Fateful Charge

Now an eerie quiet settled over the area. The Confederates were busy preparing for their next attack, and the Union forces could do nothing but wait. Two hours later, at one p.m., the Confederate artillery opened fire in the center with over 150 guns, to prepare the way for the frontal assault. The Union guns responded, and for the next hour and a half a brisk exchange took place. The Confederate fire was effective, but many of the rounds went high over the Union infantry positions, hitting the forces behind the lines (including Meade's headquarters) but causing relatively little damage to the Union front lines. Gradually return fire from Union cannons died down and some Union cannons began to pull back, leading the Confederates to believe that they had withdrawn. Longstreet reluctantly approved the final assault, and at three p.m. about 14,000 Confederates began to advance. The front of the well-disciplined formation stretched for over a mile. The line consisted of three of Pickett's brigades in the south, a gap, then six brigades from Hill's division to the north. With their 27 regimental battle flags waving as if they were on parade, the Confederates began to advance toward the Union positions almost a mile away. At the point of attack, the Union infantry was outnumbered almost three to one, but they were well dug in behind stone walls and other fortifications.

It was a massacre. The Confederates had to cross open fields, and at their slow pace it took them almost 15 minutes to cover the distance to the enemy lines. In actuality, the Union cannons had not withdrawn, only slowed their firing to save ammunition and let the barrels cool before the assault they knew was coming. The cannons the Confederates had seen being pulled back were damaged, but now new ones were wheeled in to take their place.

The Union artillery resumed fire not only from the front but also from both flanks. The Confederates moved across the Emmitsburg Road taking casualties as they went. Pickett's brigades saw the gap between themselves and the other Confederate forces and maneuvered to close it, which not only slowed their forward movement but also shrank the line to a front only a half mile wide, making them easier targets. As the Confederates closed to within 400 yards of the Union lines, Federal cannons opened fire with canister, tearing even greater holes in the Confederate ranks. As the gray lines approached, a Union gunner remembered, "When I saw this mass of men approaching . . . knowing we only had one thin line of infantry to oppose them, I thought our chances for kingdom come were very good. We [were] loaded with canister and bided our time. When we commenced to fire . . . the slaughter was dreadful. Never was there a better target for light artillery."

The Union rifled muskets now came into play. Some units opened fire while the Confederates were 200 yards away—others waited until they were much closer and delivered a full volley at short range, where they could not miss. As the Confederates passed inside the south flank of the Union lines, some Union infantry units swung down like a gate closing around the end of the enemy line and began to fire, so the Confederates were being hit from two sides.

A small number of Confederates, led by General Lewis A. Armistead, reached the first rank of the Union lines in the center and threatened a breakthrough, but Union reinforcements rushed forward and plugged the gap. Armistead was killed and most of the rest of the Confederates died with him or were taken prisoner.

As Union fire continued to cut them down, the Confederates finally broke, turned, and poured back across the Emmitsburg Road to safety. As the remnants of his once magnificent Confederate force returned, Lee spoke to them encouragingly, "All this will come out right in the end . . . in the meantime, all good men must rally." When he saw Pickett (whose whereabouts during the advance are a mystery to this day), Lee told him to regroup his division. Pickett, who had lost all 15 of his regimental commanders and over half his men, looked at his leader in disbelief and said, "General Lee, I have no division now." In less than an hour, the Confederates had lost over 5500 men, along with their hopes for victory in the war. The Union lost a little over 1000 men.

While Pickett's men and the other Confederate units were charging into history, Stuart and his cavalry were trying to come around behind the Union forces, and Union cavalry intercepted Stuart a few miles east of Gettysburg. The two forces joined in a rousing seesaw battle that saw both mounted charges and dismounted combat, but the clash ended in a draw.

As the Confederates in front of Cemetery Ridge retreated, the Union forces began to celebrate. Union officers rode up and down Cemetery Ridge dragging Confederate flags through the dust in front of their cheering troops. As Meade moved along the line, he was greeted by a band playing "Hail to the Chief."

Meade Declines to Attack

Then both sides began to get back to business. Lee and Longstreet started to dig in, anticipating that Meade would follow the victory with a strong counterattack. A Union force from Little Round Top was foolishly ordered to charge strong Confederate positions—it was chewed to pieces and its commander killed. This sounded a cautionary note for Meade, who was not sure where Stuart and his formidable cavalry force were. (It was not until later in the day that he heard Stuart had been defeated.) Some of his generals

Long after the war ended, Confederate raider John Singleton Mosby wrote of General George Pickett's last encounter with General Lee in Richmond. Lee treated Pickett, left, with icy civility. After leaving Lee's presence, Pickett spoke bitterly of him to Mosby saying, "That old man had my division massacred at Gettysburg." Mosby replied, "Well, it made you immortal."

urged him to attack with the 16,000 fresh troops and over 100 cannons that had been held in reserve. Meade demurred.

While Meade was later criticized for not attacking, his caution is understandable. The Union victory appeared complete. He had been in command of the Army of the Potomac for less than a week, and in those few days had convincingly defeated the seemingly invincible Lee. He may have considered himself lucky, and he would have been understandably reluctant to risk his victory by being led into a trap.

Lee remained across the field from Meade the next day, July 4, while he sent his thousands of wounded men to the rear in a wagon train estimated at 19 miles long. That night a torrential rain pounded the area, and Lee began his retreat.

As Lee retreated, Meade followed slowly and seemed to miss at least one opportunity to dramatically shorten the war. Union cavalry behind Lee's retreat destroyed the pontoon bridge crossing the Potomac at Fallen Waters, Maryland. Lee's tired force was trapped against the swollen river while Confederate engineers tried desperately to build a new bridge. Meade approached, but perhaps influenced by false reports that Lee was spoiling for a fight, put off an attack planned for July 12. The next day, Lee and his army escaped across the river, leaving Meade only a few trailing units to capture. The battle was over, but as one contemporary writer said, it "offered greater temptations to ifs and might-have-beens than any other battle fought on this planet."

The might-have-beens started immediately. Lincoln, who had been "impatient" with Meade's failure to advance immediately after the battle, was beside himself. A few days later he wrote a letter to Meade thanking him for the "magnificent success," while at the same time complaining that "Lee . . . was within your easy grasp, and to have closed on him . . . would have ended the war. As it is, the war will be prolonged indefinitely." Wisely, given the public reaction to Meade's victory, Lincoln had second thoughts and did not send the letter. However, Meade never received the credit he felt he deserved for the victory. He had enemies in the military, the Congress, and the press, and they constantly harped on his failure to pursue Lee. After the war, Meade

noted sadly in a letter, "I suppose after a while it will be discovered I was not at Gettysburg at all."

The news of the victory at Gettysburg made the Fourth of July a happy one in the North. Walt Whitman noted that the newspaper headlines screamed, "Glorious Victory for Union Troops" and that reporters compared the battle to Waterloo. Not only was the public thrilled with Lee's defeat, it had profound political consequences. The Confederate Vice President, Alexander Stephens, had hoped to use a victory by Lee to negotiate for a peace agreement; but after the dual victories at Gettysburg and Vicksburg, Lincoln did not even allow him to enter Union territory. The defeats also ended any faint hope the Confederacy had for diplomatic recognition by European countries.

Gettysburg National Military Park and Gettysburg National Cemetery

A little less than a year after the battle, a Gettysburg resident purchased some of the land where the most important fighting took place. The Gettysburg Battlefield Memorial Association was founded to manage this land as a memorial to the Union victory. In 1880 the Grand Army of the Republic took over the Association, and on February 11, 1895, Congress established Gettysburg National Military Park as a memorial dedicated to the armies that fought the battle. At that time, there were already about 17 miles of roads, preserved fortifications, and numerous markers on the battlefield. Today Gettysburg National Military Park covers nearly 6000 acres with over 1400 monuments, markers, memorials, and cannons, as well as about 90 period buildings. Gettysburg is the largest preserved battlefield in the United States, and each year nearly two million people come to visit the park and cemetery.

The park contains more than 26 miles of paved roads for private vehicles, and visitors can tour using a self-guided map in the "Gettysburg National Military Park" brochure available at the Visitors Center. The 18-mile, 16-stop tour includes all of the major sites and wayside exhibits. Audio programs are available at specified stops. A driving tour of the battlefield takes about three hours. Licensed Battlefield Guides are avail-

Lincoln's Gettysburg Address

On November 19, 1863, the Gettysburg National Cemetery was dedicated by a long list of dignitaries and a crowd of 15,000. After a two-hour oration by Edward Everett, President Abraham Lincoln delivered a two-minute, 272-word prose poem that was in some sense as important as the battle.

Lincoln's address answered the question, "Why are we fighting this war?" Before the Civil War, there had been a debate in the United States about which took precedence, the Constitution, which permitted slavery, or the Declaration of Independence, which proclaimed, "all men are created equal." Lincoln made it clear that the ideas in the Declaration were the core of what made America unique in the world. He also made it clear that he believed that the Union had to fight to keep the country together lest it fall prey to the centrifugal forces that had destroyed other republics. It was a question of whether a minority had the right to break up the country if they disagreed with it. Lincoln clearly believed they did not have that right. That was what the war was about.

There are five known drafts of the Gettysburg address, of which Lincoln's actual reading copy was either the "Nicolay draft" or the "Hay draft." The Nicolay draft may have been the one Lincoln removed from his coat pocket and read at the ceremony. However, this copy is missing certain words and phrases that contemporary accounts reported in the speech, and Lincoln rarely departed from his written text in speeches, therefore supporting the opposing theory that the Hay draft was actually the reading copy. The Nicolay draft follows.

Four score and seven years ago our fathers brought forth, upon this continent, a new nation, conceived in liberty, and dedicated to the proposition that "all men are created equal."

Now we are engaged in a great civil war, testing whether that nation, or any nation so conceived, and so dedicated, can long endure. We are met on a great battle field of that war. We have come to dedicate a portion of it as a final resting place for those who died here, that the nation might live. This we may, in all propriety do. But, in a larger sense, we can not dedicate—we can not consecrate—we can not hallow, this ground. The brave men, living and dead, who struggled here, have hallowed it far above our poor power to add or detract. The world will little note, nor long remember, what we say here; while it can never forget what they did here.

It is rather for us, the living, we here be dedicated to the great task remaining before us—that, from these honored dead we take increased devotion to that cause for which they here, gave the last full measure of devotion—that we here highly resolve these dead shall not have died in vain; that the nation shall have a new birth of freedom, and that government of the people, by the people, for the people, shall not perish from the earth.

able for a fee, and audio tours are available commercially.

The Visitors Center includes a museum that features the George Rosensteel Collection of artifacts, uniforms, and weapons of the Civil War, considered by many to be the finest collection of Civil War artifacts in the world. The center also contains a large bookstore and an "electric map"—an audiovisual presentation on a giant relief map of the battlefield. There is a minimal fee charged for the 30-minute program, which gives visitors a brief overview of the three days of the battle and the major personalities.

Shortly after the battle, a Soldiers Cemetery was established on the battleground near the center of the Union line to properly bury the Union soldiers who died there. Pennsylvania governor Andrew Curtin used state funds to purchase the 17 acres of cemetery grounds and pay for the reinterment of Union dead from a number of small gravesites that covered the battlefield. The Gettysburg National Cemetery is best known for the immortal Gettysburg Address that President Abraham Lincoln delivered at the cemetery's dedication on November 19, 1863.

At the time of the dedication, less than half the Union battle dead had been reinterred, and it was several more years before the bodies of the more than 3500 Union soldiers killed in the battle were moved into the cemetery. After the war, the remains of more than 3300 Confederate soldiers were removed from the battlefield and reinterred in cemeteries in the South. The Gettysburg National Cemetery was completed in 1872 and turned over to the War Department, and in 1933 it was transferred to the National Park Service.

Today the cemetery contains the graves of over 6000 honorably discharged servicemen and their dependents from the Civil War, Spanish-American War, World War I, World War II, and the Vietnam War.

The Gettysburg Cyclorama Center is adjacent to the Visitors Center and is open daily from 9 a.m. until 5 p.m. It contains exhibits, paintings, and the Gettysburg Cyclorama, a huge, 360-degree painting of Pickett's Charge by Paul Philippoteaux. The program lasts 20 minutes.

Visitor Information
717-334-1124;
www.nps.gov/gett/
Hours: Park grounds and roads are open daily, 6 a.m. until 10 p.m.; Gettysburg National Cemetery is open daily from dawn to sunset; the Visitors Center is open daily in the summer, 8 a.m. until 6 p.m., and 8 a.m. until 5 p.m. the rest of the year; park buildings are closed Thanksgiving Day, December 25, and New Year's Day.
Admission: Free for the park, cemetery, and park buildings; there is a minimal charge for the cyclorama for adults and children ages 6 to 16.

Accessibility: The Visitors Center and Cyclorama are wheelchair accessible with at least one wheelchair available per building. Handicapped parking is available at both buildings and on the park avenues. Much of the grounds and many buildings are accessible to mobility-, sight-, and hearing-impaired visitors. Detailed information is available on the Web site, and an accessibility brochure for the park is available at the information desk.

Special Events: Annual events include a Memorial Day ceremony in the National Cemetery, special activities known as Gettysburg Civil War Heritage Days on the battle anniversary, ceremonies on the anniversary of the Gettysburg Address (November 19) and Remembrance Day (the Saturday closest to November 19). The park draws large numbers of reenactors and is host to regular living-history weekends featuring history camps and programs by park volunteers. During the summer, there are events virtually every weekend. Contact the park for exact dates and times.

Getting There: From Washington, D.C. (77 miles) take I-495 to I-270 to U.S. Route 15 through Frederick, Maryland. Follow park signs to the Visitors Center.

From Baltimore (60 miles): Take I-695 to I-795, then to MD Route 140 to U.S. 15 through Westminster and Emmitsburg, Maryland. Follow park signs to the Visitors Center.

From I-76 at Harrisburg, Pennsylvania (30 miles): Take U.S. 15 south to Gettysburg and follow signs to the Visitors Center.

Harvest of Death, *a photograph by Timothy O'Sullivan, was made one day after the battle ended. It shows two dozen of the 43,000 casualties of the battle, hours after General Lee's retreat. None of the bodies wear any shoes or boots. They were stolen by retreating Confederates who desperately needed footwear.*

National Civil War Museum

During the Civil War, Harrisburg, Pennsylvania, was the home of the largest Union training base in the country, Camp Curtin, where over 300,000 soldiers were trained. Today Harrisburg is the home of the comprehensive National Civil War Museum, a museum that explores the issues of the conflict from all sides. Built on the high point of the city's Reservoir Park, the two-story museum is modeled after mid-1800s buildings found in Pennsylvania's Cumberland Valley and Virginia's Shenandoah Valley, complete with a brick façade, plazas, overlooks, and an 80-foot-high cupola. The museum includes exhibit areas, a gift shop, meeting room, public auditorium, a library, and 27,000 square feet of exhibition space. Over 850 artifacts (about one quarter of the collection) are displayed in a dozen galleries, along with life-size dioramas and video presentations. The museum houses the country's largest collection of

artifacts that once belonged to the controversial Confederate general George Pickett, best known as the commander of the futile charge at Gettysburg.

The museum deliberately puts a great deal of emphasis on personal experiences, from the common soldiers to the men and women on the home front, as well as the varied conditions of African Americans, who were both slaves and soldiers. The military sections include all aspects of the soldiers' experiences, including time away from battle, wounds, disease, and prisoner-of-war experiences, as well as the emotional impact of combat—what might today be called posttraumatic stress disorders.

Each gallery helps narrate the

The "Weapons and Equipment" exhibit continues the theme of how the armies were created, using the museum's world-class collection of firearms; swords; accoutrements; ammunition; and uniforms of the Union and Confederate infantry, cavalry, artillery, and navy.

The raising of the stars and bars, left, after the Confederate capture of Fort Sumter opens the "First Shots" exhibit.

story of the war, starting with "A House Divided," which provides a timeline of incidents and issues in United States history before the Civil War. A high-definition video, *We the People,* introduces visitors to a number of Americans—Northerners and Southerners, men and women, white and black, military and civilian—whose lives would be changed in major ways by the war. As the visitor moves through the exhibits, the words of these Americans interpret the events from their unique points of view. The displays analyze the nature and depth of the sectional controversies from both military and civilian viewpoints.

Other galleries depict the emotionalism of those who supported and opposed the "peculiar institution" of slavery, complete with numerous prewar slavery artifacts including metal neck collars, a cat-o'-nine-tails whip, handcuffs, and pictures of abused slaves.

Life-size dioramas and accompanying background music are used throughout the museum to bring to life the sights and sounds associated with the war. The various dioramas include a slave auction, showing mannequins standing on the auction block set against the sounds of the auction and spirituals, soldiers' activities at Camp Curtin, and a graphic view of surgeons preparing to amputate a soldier's leg.

Galleries featuring the military aspect of the war include the firing on Fort Sumter, as well as interpreting the war aims of the North and South and describing how unprepared each was for war—tactics, strategies, and logistics of the widespread battles at New Orleans, Shiloh, the Peninsula, Antietam, and Fredericksburg; Grant's capture of Forts Henry and Donelson; and the disastrous Union attacks at Fredericksburg. Also explained are the varied motivations of soldiers, and the exploits of the 200,000 African American soldiers and sailors who fought for their race's freedom on the Federal side. There were over 160 African American regiments in all branches, which had the lowest desertion rates and the highest mortality rates in the Union army.

The "Civil War Music" gallery offers personal audio devices that allow the visitor to listen to a selection of Northern and Southern spirituals, popular songs, and bugle calls. Also on display are army band instruments and sheet music from the war. Elsewhere, set against the roar of artillery at the first shots of the war, the visitor can hear outraged Union cries of "On to Richmond."

Various battle maps are accompanied by a video narration by noted author and Civil War historian Dr. James I. "Bud" Robertson, Jr., and videos show a vivid picture of Civil War battles as well as how artillery and muskets were loaded and fired.

Social aspects of the war highlighted in the exhibits include an especially poignant letter started

Camp Curtin, *located in Harrisburg, Pennsylvania, was the largest Union training camp of the Civil War, with over 300,000 men passing through its gates. The largest diorama in the museum presents a picture of how soldiers passed the time in camp.*

from a hospital by a wounded soldier to his mother and father. Gradually the letters falter, and the penmanship changes. It was finished by a nurse, who wrote to the parents that their son had died. Another gallery considers the roles of women, including factory workers, nurses, farmhands, and even the occasional spy and soldier.

The final room houses a single exhibit, "Lincoln: War & Remembrance," focusing on the Civil War's impact—amendments to the Constitution, Reconstruction, and rapid westward expansion unhindered by the political question of slave versus free states. The museum theater offers a 16-minute video, *A Nation Endures*, that shows the events and emotions following the surrender of Lee's Army of Northern Virginia and Lincoln's assassination. The original group from the *We the People* video give their final thoughts, and the video closes with newsreel footage of Civil War veterans meeting on battlefields in friendship long after the end of the war.

Visitor Information

717-260-1861;
www.nationalcivilwarmuseum.org/
Hours: Monday to Saturday, 10 a.m. until 5 p.m.; Sunday, noon until 5 p.m.; closed Easter, Thanksgiving, December 25, New Year's Day, and all U.S. government holidays except July 4 and the day after Thanksgiving.
Admission: Moderate charge for adults and students; family passes are available.

Accessibility: The museum is fully accessible.
Special Events: There are numerous special events, especially in the summer. The annual Harrisburg Pipes and Drums Festival takes place in May, and other recent programs have included a living-history "Life on the Home Front" interpretation, as well as numerous encampments showing how soldiers on both sides lived in the field. On Veterans Day, reenactors and living historians display equipment and artifacts and talk about the life of soldiers and civilians during the Civil War. In late November or early December, the museum hosts "A Civil War Christmas." Call for details.
Getting There: The National Civil War Museum is on the eastern edge of Harrisburg, Pennsylvania, in Reservoir Park.

From I-83: At exit 50 (Progress exit & U.S. Route 22/Walnut Street), take U.S. 22 west (Walnut Street) toward downtown for 2.5 miles to the Parkside Cafe. (Where Route 22 bears right, stay on Walnut.) Turn left at the Parkside Cafe into the entrance to Reservoir Park and proceed up the hill to the parking area.

From I-81: Take the North Progress Avenue exit, and then take Progress Avenue south to Walnut Street (U.S. 22). Turn right on Walnut Street (U.S. 22 west) and follow it toward downtown for 2.5 miles to the Parkside Cafe. (Where Route 22 bears right, stay on Walnut.) Turn left at the Parkside Cafe into the entrance to Reservoir Park and proceed up the hill to the parking area.

The Battles for Fort Sumter

Fort Sumter, built in the center of the shipping channel in Charleston Bay, South Carolina, was another in the series of Third System seacoast five-sided masonry forts commissioned after the War of 1812. Construction progressed very slowly, and it was still not complete in December 1860. Nevertheless, it was a formidable edifice, with three levels of guns behind five-foot-thick walls towering almost 50 feet above the water. Fort Sumter had an additional advantage—it was built on an artificial island of rubble and granite, so it was not surrounded by beaches where boats could land. To capture it, an invading force would have to bring boats alongside and either breach the walls or scale them.

As tensions between the North and South increased after Abraham Lincoln's election, it was clear that South Carolina might secede, and control of the forts in that state became hotly contested. South Carolina's governor, Francis Pickens, wanted to control Forts Moultrie and Sumter and Castle Pinckney, and he sent negotiators to Washington to try to secure the forts through peaceful means.

Fort Sumter was unmanned in December 1860, but Union major Robert Anderson commanded a small garrison at another Charleston installation, Fort Moultrie. He was the son of Major Richard Anderson, the American officer who had commanded Fort Moultrie in 1780. On December 11, 1860 Anderson received instructions from the War Department "to defend yourself to the last extremity" in the event of hostilities.

Anderson was a Southerner but a Union loyalist, and when South Carolina seceded on December 20, he realized he had to act. On December 26, while Pickens's negotiators were in Washington, he quietly moved his force of 84 officers and men from the vulnerable Fort Moultrie to Fort Sumter. Reaction was immediate. In the North, Anderson's move was hailed as "bold and patriotic," but the South condemned it as provocative.

While President James Buchanan had officially authorized Anderson's move to Fort Sumter, Buchanan hadn't done so intentionally; he had approved a recommendation to that effect without reading it thoroughly. Now that Anderson had occupied Fort Sumter and was requesting reinforcements, Buchanan had to decide how to proceed. There was considerable debate in the Cabinet, with the opposition led primarily by Virginian John Floyd, the Secretary of War. But during this crisis Floyd resigned, and his replacement, Joseph Holt, recommended holding Sumter. Outgoing President Buchanan finally agreed to send a relief expedition to reinforce Anderson. The merchant ship *Star of the West*, loaded with men, ammunition, and several months' provisions, was sent to Fort Sumter, accompanied by the warship U.S.S. *Brooklyn*. When the *Star of the West* attempted to reach the fort on January 9, 1861, Confederate batteries manned by military cadets from the Citadel fired on the merchantman, and it withdrew.

Meanwhile, Anderson prepared to defend the fort, moving and mounting its 66 cannons. At the same time, the Confederates also prepared their batteries to bombard the fort if ordered. In the process, the Confederates deployed a new weapon, a small (12-pound) Blakely rifled gun from England, the forerunner of the powerful rifled guns that would ultimately make masonry forts obsolete.

The tense stalemate continued until March 5, the day after Lincoln's inauguration, when Anderson sent a message to Washington saying his garrison was running low on food. By the end of the month, Lincoln decided to resupply Fort Sumter. The South was outraged. On April 10, the Confederate Secretary of War, Leroy Walker, ordered the commander of the forces facing Fort Sumter, General P. G. T. Beauregard, to demand that Anderson and his troops evacuate the fort. (Ironically, Beauregard had been one of Anderson's artillery students at West Point.)

On April 11, Beauregard sent a contingent to demand Sumter's surrender. Anderson refused but said that his food was nearly gone and he would evacuate the fort at noon on April 15. (In fact, he was hoping that the relief expedition would arrive beforehand.)

But the Confederates refused to delay further and at four thirty a.m., April 12, a signal shell exploded over Fort Sumter and the bombardment began. Within a few minutes, Confederate guns and mortars ringing the fort opened fire.

Major Anderson held fire until it was light, about seven o'clock in the morning, and then responded slowly. While he had ammunition for his big guns, he lacked some mundane items like friction primers—the small brass tubes filled with gunpowder used to ignite the powder in the cannons. To add to his difficulties, most of Fort Sumter's heaviest guns were on the unprotected top level of the fort. Anderson ordered these abandoned to minimize casualties.

The bombardment continued into the dark, rainy night as Charleston watched from the harbor or the rooftops. The next morning, heated shot from Confederate guns set fire to the officers' quarters in the fort, and soon the powder magazines were in danger. About one thirty in the afternoon, the Union flag was shot down, and a short time later a Confederate representative, Louis Wigfall, rowed to the fort and demanded its surrender. (Wigfall was not an authorized representative of Beauregard, although he suggested the terms that Anderson agreed to and that Beauregard ultimately approved.) After some negotiations, Anderson agreed to surrender the fort, with the provisos that he and his men be allowed to salute the United States flag as it was lowered and that they be evacuated to a Northern port. By early evening, the siege had officially ended. During the 33-hour bombardment, more than 3000 shells had been fired at Fort Sumter, but it had stood up well. Only a few Union soldiers had been wounded.

As the Union forces prepared to withdraw on Sunday, April 14, they fired a cannon salute to the United States flag. There was an accidental explosion with one of the guns, and Union private Daniel Hough was killed, the first casualty of the Civil War. The following day, April 15, 1861, Abraham Lincoln issued a call for 75,000 militia. Major Anderson and four of the Union soldiers released from Fort Sumter would eventually become Union generals including Abner Doubleday, who reportedly had fired the first Union shot of the battle.

Under the Stars and Bars

The Confederates rebuilt Fort Sumter into a formidable citadel armed with about 95 guns and a 500-man garrison. The fort, along with Fort Wagner on Morris Island to the south and Fort Moultrie on Sullivan's Island to the north, became the primary defenses of the port of Charleston. The port soon became a major haven for Confederate blockade runners and a huge thorn in the Union's side.

In June 1862, Union forces tried but failed to capture Charleston from the landward side. Ten months later, they decided to try to destroy Charleston's defenses with the Union's new ironclad warships, equipped with rifled cannons. On April 5, 1863, nine Federal ironclads arrived outside Charleston, and two days later they moved slowly, in single file, up the narrow main ship channel

*A **Confederate battery** fires on Fort Sumter in this contemporary wood engraving.*

between Morris Island and Fort Sumter to bombard the Confederate fortifications. The Confederate batteries, firing from fixed positions and using buoys to determine the range of the Union ships, dominated the fight. The forts fired more than 2000 rounds in the two-and-a-half-hour battle and disabled five ironclads, one of which, the *Keokuk*, sank the following morning. The ironclads fired about 150 rounds, and only about 35 hit the Confederate fortifications.

Union commanders then tried to capture Fort Wagner on Morris Island with the intention of shelling Fort Sumter into submission from there. On July 10, 1863, Union forces landed on Morris Island and moved forward to attack Fort Wagner. The attack was repulsed. Then, from July 16 to 18, Fort Wagner was pounded by over 40 Union cannons and mortars in preparation for another attack. On July 18, more than 5000 Union troops attacked again, led by the African American troops from the 54th Massachusetts. The battle—made famous by the 1989 film *Glory*—raged much of the day, but the well-entrenched Confederates again pushed the Union forces back, inflicting 1500 casualties while losing less than 200 of their own.

After this failure, Union forces blockading Fort Wagner ferried eight batteries of long-range rifled heavy cannons across to Morris Island and set them up west of Fort Wagner. Brigadier General Quincy Gillmore, who had commanded the Union batteries that had destroyed Fort Pulaski near Savannah, now commanded these guns on Morris Island, from which they shelled Fort Wagner. On August 17, 1863, they began the bombardment of Fort Sumter in earnest. Nearly 1000 shells were fired at the fort the first day, while the fort could not reply because its guns did not have the range of the Union's rifled cannons. By August 24, over 6000 rounds had been fired, leaving only one of Fort Sumter's guns operational. The fort's walls were shattered, the left face breached, and enough debris had fallen into the water to provide a sloping avenue for a land assault. In early September, Union ironclads returned to shell Fort Sumter again, and on September 6, the Confederate garrisons evacuated Morris Island after a long siege. Now Union cannons could be placed just three quarters of a mile away from the still-defiant Fort Sumter.

Union admiral John Dahlgren decided to try to capture Fort Sumter with a small-boat assault, and on the night of September 8–9, 400 Union sailors and marines tried to take the fort. However, while the fort had been reduced to rubble and its cannons knocked out, the debris was a perfect hiding place for riflemen. The Confederates remained quiet until the first troops were leaving the boats—then they opened fire. Only a few of the boats even made it to shore, and in the melee the Union forces lost about 125 men and five of their small boats before they pulled back. After this defeat, Admiral Dahlgren lost interest in trying to capture Fort Sumter. With Morris Island in Union hands, he controlled Charleston harbor and could prevent any blockade runners from entering or leaving.

General Gillmore's batteries continued to fire at the fort and soon reduced the seaward side of Sumter to a pile of debris, but caused few casualties to the well-entrenched Confederates. On December 5, the

bombardment stopped—there seemed to be no reason to continue.

General Gillmore left in May of 1864 and was replaced by Major General J. G. Foster, who developed a series of ambitious plans to capture the fort. On July 7, 1864, he began shelling it again, but by August, with Union cannons running low on ammunition, the War Department ordered Foster not to try an invasion. The Union forces continued to fire sporadically at the fort, piling rubble on rubble, but Fort Sumter held out. It was not until Union forces under General William T. Sherman approached in 1865 that it was abandoned. If Fort Pulaski had showed the power of the new rifled siege artillery, 22 months of futile shelling of Fort Sumter showed their limitations.

On April 14, 1865, four years after Fort Sumter had initially surrendered, Robert Anderson, now a retired brigadier general, returned. As Union warships in the harbor fired salutes, he raised the same flag he had lowered four

years before. That same night, Abraham Lincoln was assassinated.

Visitor Information

843-883-3123; www.nps.gov/fosu
Hours: Museum and park open daily, 10 a.m. until 5:30 p.m. April to Labor Day, and 10 a.m. until 4 p.m. in March and from September to November. Hours at other times vary and can be obtained from the park. Closed December 25 and New Year's Day.

Special Events: There are special events on April 12 and 13. Interpretive signs for self-guided tours are spread throughout the fort. National Park Service historians explain the history of Fort Sumter and role in

Union artillery destroyed the eastern barracks during the bombardment of September 8–9, 1863. The bake oven, center, was frequently used to heat solid shot red hot—an effective way to set wooden ships on fire.

This American flag flew over Fort Sumter throughout most of the 33-hour bombardment in 1861. After the surrender, it was replaced by the Confederate Stars and Bars, left, until retired Brigadier General Robert Anderson raised this same American flag again over the recaptured fort on April 14, 1865.

the Civil War to boat-tour groups.

The Fort Sumter Visitor Education Center is located next to Liberty Square at the corner of Concord and Calhoun Streets in Charleston and features a number of exhibits, including the 33-star American flag that Major Anderson flew over the fort from December 1860 until he was forced to strike it in April 1861.

Admission: High daily fee for adults and moderate daily fee for children ages 6 to 11 for the boat ride. The 2 hour, 15 minute tour consists of approximately 1 hour at Fort Sumter, then a 1 hour and 15 minute cruise around Charleston Harbor. For more information call Fort Sumter Tours, 843-722-2628.

Accessibility: Accessibility is limited. At Fort Sumter, three elevators give access to the upper levels of the fort. A wheelchair is available.

Getting There: Fort Sumter is located a little over three miles from Charleston at the harbor entrance, and it requires a boat trip to visit. Concession tour boats leave from Patriots' Point in Mount Pleasant and the Fort Sumter Visitor Education Center next to Liberty Square at the corner of Concord and Calhoun Streets in Charleston.

Of Note: Fort Moultrie is across the bay from Fort Sumter on Sullivan's Island.

Fort Moultrie

Fort Moultrie has been overshadowed in Civil War history by the two other forts defending the Charleston, South Carolina, harbor—Fort Sumter and Fort Wagner. In fact, Fort Moultrie played a significant role both in the beginning of the Civil War and in the later defense of Charleston.

The Civil War was the second time that Fort Moultrie defended Charleston Harbor. During the Revolutionary War, the harbor was guarded by Fort Sullivan, a log fort commanded by William Moultrie. The fort was still incomplete when a British fleet attacked Charleston on June 28, 1776. Fort Sullivan's wooden walls absorbed the British cannon balls while the fort's cannons hammered away at the British ships. After a nine-hour battle, the British withdrew. The fort was later renamed Fort Moultrie in honor of its commander.

In 1809, a new Fort Moultrie was built on roughly the same spot, on the southern tip of Sullivan's Island, one mile northeast of what was to become Fort Sumter. It was not a powerful fort, and the weaknesses of American forts like Fort Moultrie were exposed by the British navy in the War of 1812. In 1816 the United States began construction of a whole new type of coastal forts, called the Third System. Fort Sumter, in Charleston Bay, was one of these new forts; but as the memory of the War of 1812 faded, interest dropped off and funding for the forts dried up. In December 1860, when the Civil War storm was gathering, Fort Sumter was still not complete.

That December, the Union garrison protecting Charleston harbor consisted of more than 80 men under the command of Major Robert Anderson. They were stationed at Fort Moultrie, which, while obsolete, had been improved over the

Fort Moultrie helped protect Fort Sumter from Union ironclads in 1863. Almost a century before, guns at an earlier fort here helped repel the British fleet during the Revolution.

years. The fort was now adjoined by the town of Moultrieville, and given the logistics and isolation of living on Fort Sumter Island, Fort Moultrie was not an unattractive location. However, as the situation in South Carolina deteriorated, Anderson realized that Fort Moultrie would be impossible to hold. It sat low on Sullivan's Island and its walls were only 11 feet high. That, plus its lack of shore-facing cannons, made it practically indefensible from a land-side attack. On December 26, 1860, Anderson and his forces famously decamped for Fort Sumter. The Confederates quickly took over Fort Moultrie, and the guns from the fort actively participated in the bombardment of Fort Sumter.

After Fort Sumter was captured on April 14, 1861, the Confederates moved to strengthen Fort Moultrie and the other forts around Charleston. Fort Moultrie received new cannons, and her masonry and palmetto-log walls were strengthened. By mid-1863, the fort was occupied by the 300 men of the 1st South Carolina Infantry (Regular). They manned a formidable array of cannons—nine 8-inch Columbiads, five 64-pound James rifles, as well as 32 smoothbore cannons and two 10-inch mortars. Similar improvements had been made at Fort Sumter and Fort Wagner. The Confederates had made other sophisticated preparations in Charleston Harbor. They laid "torpedoes" (moored mines) in the channels, and artillery specialists placed range buoys in the water at precise distances from the forts, so it was easy for the gunners to make the critical range calculations on attacking ships. (Distance is very difficult to judge over water.)

When a fleet of Union ironclads approached Charleston to bombard Fort Sumter on August 17, 1863, these preparations paid dividends. Fire from Fort Sumter and Fort Moultrie quickly hit five of the Union's nine attacking ironclads, sinking one, and the Union ships withdrew after less than an hour of combat. When the Union forces attacked again, they avoided Fort Moultrie and instead landed on Morris Island to the south of the bay. Fort Moultrie was not abandoned until Charleston surrendered in February 1865.

Fort Moultrie National Monument

The Fort Moultrie Visitors Center is located across the street from the fort, next to the parking lot, and includes restrooms, first aid, park literature, and a bookstore. The Visitors Center also contains museum exhibits and shows a 22-minute film on the fort's history every hour and a half. Ranger programs and guided tours are also presented at various times. A park brochure for visitors to use on a self-guided tour is available here as well.

Fort Moultrie has been laid out to show two centuries of seacoast defense in a single location. Five sections of the fort and two outlying areas have been restored, each representing a different period in the fort's history, with typical weapons from that time, including 19 Civil War cannons. Interpretive signs posted throughout the fort allow visitors to follow the fort's history as they walk.

The tomb of Seminole chief Osceola is in the fort as well. Osceola was captured by American forces in Florida in 1837 while carrying a white flag of truce and was imprisoned along with 200 other Seminoles in Fort Moultrie. Three months later, in January 1838, he died there of malaria.

Visitor Information
843-883-3123; www.nps.gov/fomo
Hours: Daily, 9 a.m. until 5 p.m.; closed December 25 and New Year's Day.
Admission: Minimal charge for adults 16 and over or per family; National Parks Pass, Golden Eagle, Golden Age, and Golden Access are honored.

Special Events: There are special programs on April 12 and 13, the anniversary of the attack on Fort Sumter; and on June 28, Carolina Day, celebrating the defeat of the British in 1776.
Accessibility: The Visitors Center and most of the fort is accessible by wheelchair. A wheelchair can be borrowed from the Visitors Center.
Getting There: Fort Moultrie is located in Charleston, South Carolina. Take I-26 or I-526 to U.S. 17. Take U.S. 17 to Mt. Pleasant and turn onto SC Route 703. At the first stoplight on Sullivan's Island, turn right onto Middle Street. The fort is 1.5 miles down Middle Street.

The Battles for Chattanooga Museum

For a description of the Battles of Chattanooga, see "Chickamauga & Chattanooga National Military Park," Page 54.

The main attraction of this museum is a three-dimensional electronic battle map of the major battles fought around Chattanooga in late 1863. The electronic battlefield display includes 5000 miniature soldiers, 650 lights, and extensive sound effects, bringing significant military conflicts to life. Some of the engagements depicted are Brown's Ferry and Wauhatchie, when Union forces gained control over critical supply routes into the city; Lookout Mountain, famous as the "Battle Above the Clouds"; and Grant's attack on Missionary Ridge, directed from Orchard Knob, one of the most famous and effective charges in the Civil War (though Grant did not order it or expect it).

Originally built in 1957, this museum was known as the Confederama. By the early 1990s, the museum was in danger of closing, but local businessmen helped save what they considered a landmark. A new owner renamed it The Battles for Chattanooga Electric Map and Museum, refurbished and rewired the displays, and recorded a new digital soundtrack. The museum also includes an artifact and weapons collection and a gift shop.

Visitor Information
423-821-2812;
www.battlesforchattanooga.com/
Hours: Daily, 10 a.m. until 5 p.m.; summer hours, daily, 9 a.m. until 6:30 p.m.

Admission: Moderate charge for adults and children three and older.
Accessibility: The museum is handicapped accessible.
Getting There: The museum is in Lookout Mountain, Tennessee, adjacent to Chattanooga.

From Georgia: Take I-75. Approaching Chattanooga, take the I-24 (west) split toward downtown Chattanooga. Take exit 178 (Lookout Mountain/South Market Street) and follow the Lookout Mountain ramp. Proceed through the next two stoplights, then turn left on Broad Street South, which becomes U.S. 41. Continue on U.S. 41 about a half mile to the "Ruby Falls" ramp on the left side of the highway. Continue past Ruby Falls and to the top of Lookout Mountain. At the top of the mountain, take a sharp right onto East Brow Road and follow the directional signs to the end of the road, where you will find the museum and Point Park.

From Knoxville: Take I-75 south to Chattanooga. Near Chattanooga, take the I-24 (west) split, then proceed as above.

From Nashville: Take I-24 east toward downtown Chattanooga. Take exit 174 and turn right on U.S. 41 (Cummings Highway). Follow the directional signs and "Ruby Falls" signs, continue past Ruby Falls, then proceed as above.

From Alabama: Take I-59 to the merge with I-24 east, then follow the Nashville directions above.

From Chattanooga: Take Broad Street South, which becomes U.S. 41, and continue on U.S. 41 about a half mile to the "Ruby Falls" ramp on the left side of the highway. Proceed as in the Georgia directions.

The Battle for Fort Donelson

When General Albert Sidney Johnston took command of the Confederacy's Western Department in mid-September 1861, he faced a host of problems. One of the most critical was how to control the Cumberland and Tennessee rivers, which traveled deep into Confederate territory. The Cumberland, especially, was vital. It flowed past Nashville, Johnston's supply hub, and the large ironworks at Clarksville, Tennessee. Controlling the river also meant preventing Union gunboats from moving up and down the rivers, harassing Confederate forces and destroying critical bridges. To protect the rivers, the Confederates quickly built Fort Henry on the Tennessee River and Fort Donelson on the Cumberland River, at a point where the two rivers were only 12 miles apart.

On October 12, 1861, unbeknownst to Johnston, his problems increased exponentially. That day a new type of Union warship, an ironclad steamer named the U.S.S. *St. Louis* (later renamed *De Kalb*), was launched from a shipyard in Missouri onto the Mississippi River. Over the next three months, Union shipyards on western rivers launched six more ironclads. The slope-sided steamers bore a vague resemblance to the later C.S.S. *Virginia (Merrimack)*, and carried 122 tons of armor, but only drew six feet of water so they could easily navigate shallow rivers. They were heavily armed, most with three 7-inch rifled cannon, three 8-inch smoothbores, six 32-pound smoothbores, and a 30-pound Parrott rifle. By mid January 1862, they were ready to fight, and they were immediately put to use by Union general Ulysses S. Grant and Union commodore Andrew Foote.

Fort Henry was the first target of the new fleet. Although it was well fortified with 17 guns, it was built on such low ground that it flooded easily (the highest point of the fort was actually lower than the river's high water mark). Grant anticipated from his scouts' reports that the low-lying fort would be an easy target for the new Union gunboats, and he expected Foote's ironclad fleet to make short work of it. Grant ordered his infantry to be used only to cut off the anticipated retreat of the garrison to Fort Donelson.

Confederate brigadier general Lloyd Tilghman, commander of Fort Henry, knew he could not defend the fort, and when he heard that Grant's arrival was imminent, on February 5 he withdrew most of his 2600 men and sent them overland to Fort Donelson. Tilghman stayed behind with 70 men to man the guns and pin Grant down.

Foote's gunboats moved to attack at eleven a.m. on February 6, and less than two hours later Fort Henry surrendered. However, while the weather had been unseasonably mild, it had rained constantly, slowing Grant's infantry just enough so they could not block the enemy troops moving to Fort Donelson. After Fort Henry surrendered, Grant sent Foote's gunboats upstream to destroy the Memphis & Ohio Railway bridge over the Tennessee, cutting

The U.S.S. St. Louis, left, a 512-ton Cairo-class ironclad river gunboat. She was badly hit and disabled by Confederate cannon fire during the action at Fort Donelson.

one of Johnston's main lines of communication. Although Grant wanted to advance on Fort Donelson, now the only fortified position between the Union army and the undefended city of Nashville, he had to wait. The weather was still rainy, his troops needed supplies, and he wanted Foote to return to provide him with naval gunfire support.

The ease with which the Union gunboat flotilla and Grant's small army picked off Fort Henry sent shock waves through the Confederates in Tennessee. Johnston responded by unwisely attempting to both withdraw his forces all along the line and to fight Grant at Fort Donelson. Rather than go personally to Fort Donelson with a large force to fight Grant, Johnston retreated toward Nashville with much of his army. He sent Brigadier General John B. Floyd to take command of the fort, along with 12,000 men. Floyd, a former U.S. Secretary of War under President Buchanan, had little experience as a field commander.

However, Fort Donelson was much stronger than Fort Henry. It was located high off the river, its outer fortifications were over two miles long, and it had two strong artillery batteries on the river. The high battery was over 100 feet above the water and contained a rifled Columbiad protected by two

"Unconditional Surrender" Grant

Ulysses Simpson Grant (born Hiram Ulysses Grant) was arguably the greatest Union general, and one of the best in the history of the American military. Appointed general-in-chief in March 1864, he won the war for the Union, became the first American officer to receive a four-star ranking (July 25, 1866), and served two terms as President of the United States.

Though he was trained at West Point, his record there and in the Mexican War was fairly mediocre. Thereafter, he left the army, tried his hand at a series of unsuccessful business ventures, and ended up a reluctant employee of his father's tannery. During the Civil War, though, he came into his own, learning from his experience and mistakes, never looking back, and always certain he could succeed. Grant forged a trusting relationship with President Abraham Lincoln that

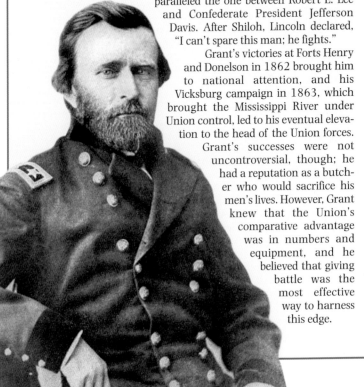

paralleled the one between Robert E. Lee and Confederate President Jefferson Davis. After Shiloh, Lincoln declared, "I can't spare this man; he fights."

Grant's victories at Forts Henry and Donelson in 1862 brought him to national attention, and his Vicksburg campaign in 1863, which brought the Mississippi River under Union control, led to his eventual elevation to the head of the Union forces.

Grant's successes were not uncontroversial, though; he had a reputation as a butcher who would sacrifice his men's lives. However, Grant knew that the Union's comparative advantage was in numbers and equipment, and he believed that giving battle was the most effective way to harness this edge.

32-pounder cannons. The lower battery was just above the river level and had nine 32-pounders and one 10-inch Columbiad. The fort itself was at the top of the bluffs, surrounded by rifle pits. An attack from the land side had to pass through thick woods and a line of Confederate rifle pits that surrounded the fort. After breaking through the line of rifle pits, the assault force would then have to climb the 80-foot ridge to the fort.

On February 12, Grant, reinforced with a new division, moved on Fort Donelson. Floyd had not yet arrived at Donelson, and the acting commander was General Gideon J. Pillow, a rather lazy Mexican War veteran best known for rancorous conflicts with his superior officers. Pillow's deputy was the competent Brigadier General Simon B. Buckner, ironically an old friend of Grant's. Buckner viewed Pillow as incompetent and was quickly proved correct. Pillow refused to interfere with Grant's march through the collection of hills, marshes, and broken country between the forts, even though the rough terrain would have provided excellent defensive positions for the Confederates.

The Confederates built upper and lower river batteries in an attempt to defend the strategic transportation and supply routes provided by the Cumberland River and protect major supply bases in Tennessee. Armed with heavy seacoast artillery, the batteries inflicted serious damage to Union gunboats during the battle. The roar of the land and naval battle was heard 35 miles away.

On February 13, Floyd arrived at Fort Donelson and took command. The Confederates now had 15,000 troops, almost the same number as Grant, but Admiral Foote and his fleet arrived with 12,000 reinforcements for Grant, bringing the total Union strength to about 27,000. One of Foote's gunboats moved close to the fort to divert the Confederates while Grant dug in around the fort, but the gunboat, the U.S.S. *Carondelet*, was knocked around by the fort's cannons at long range and quickly fell back. It was a cautionary note for Foote, but he ignored it.

During the night, the unseasonably mild weather changed. The temperature dropped to 10 degrees, two inches of snow fell, and a strong

The bombardment of Fort Donelson by Federal warships. From left to right, timberclad Tyler; *ironclads* Carondelet *(partially obscured),* Pittsburg, Louisville, *and* St. Louis. *Many of the ships were damaged in this action.*

wind lashed the miserable troops on both sides. At dawn on February 14, Grant's troops stood outside their fortifications around Fort Donelson to see if Admiral Foote could repeat the success he found at Fort Henry. But what they saw was a bloody shambles for the Union fleet. The fort's upper battery subjected Foote's ironclads to long-range fire as they approached. The Confederate shells were falling downward (known as "plunging fire") when they hit Foote's ships, and easily penetrated the thin decks. The shells also struck the sloping side armor of the ironclads at an almost perpendicular angle, thus penetrating the armor more easily.

As Foote's fleet moved closer, the low-lying battery began to inflict a different type of damage. The Confederates skipped their cannon balls across the water, hitting the ironclads at the waterline. Other shells bounced through the open gun ports on the ships, decapitating the gun crews. Some Union ships had their steering shot away and rammed other ships, several cannons burst, and the battle line became a confused jumble. One by one, the Union warships were disabled and withdrew downriver. Foote was wounded twice, while his gunners did not

After Confederate generals *Floyd and Pillow turned command of Fort Donelson over to General Buckner and slipped away to Nashville with about 2000 men, Buckner asked General Grant for terms. Grant's answer was short and direct, "No terms except unconditional and immediate surrender can be accepted." Buckner surrendered.*

inflict a single casualty on the Confederates.

There was little ground action that day and Grant, sobered by the experience with the gunboats, settled in for a siege. Grant extended the Union right to hem in the Confederates, but left a 400-yard gap on his right flank. He was more concerned about the welfare of his men. It was still windy and well below zero, and his troops needed food and winter clothing.

Floyd placed most of his Confederate troops in trenches along a ridgeline facing the Union army, backed up by artillery. Buckner was on the right of the Confederate line and Pillow on the left. However, Floyd was not a confident commander, and despite the victory over the gunboats, he overestimated the Union strength. That night, he told Pillow and Buckner that he wanted to abandon Fort Donelson, break through the Union lines, and retreat to Nashville.

However, Grant did not expect the Confederates to try to break out, and early the next morning he rode downstream to visit the wounded Foote aboard his flagship. Before departing, he told his division commanders not to attack but to stay in place and hold their positions.

He did not have a second in command, nor did he designate an acting commander.

Soon after Grant departed, Pillow smashed into the Union right. He was immediately successful, aided considerably by the gap on the Union right flank and confusion in the leaderless Union ranks. After several hours of hard fighting, Pillow broke the Union line and pushed it back, and by noon he had opened an escape route. Buckner's fresh troops then moved up and were in position to cover the evacuation of the Confederate forces from the fort.

At this point, a tragicomedy of errors began for the Confederates. Pillow dashed off a triumphant telegram to General Johnston announcing his victory, and then inexplicably felt he was threatened from behind. He told Buckner to fall back, but Buckner realized the breakout was almost complete and refused. The two argued while Floyd, the overall commander, dithered and refused to make a final decision.

While the Confederate leadership self-destructed, Grant returned to learn that his right was under fierce attack. He organized his forces to cut off the Confederate advance, while at the same time attacking the right side of the enemy lines that had been weakened to support the attack.

Floyd finally gave up trying to arbitrate the dispute between his subordinates and let Pillow order the Confederate troops back to Fort Donelson. Meanwhile, the Union troops had succeeded in capturing the outer line of Confederate defenses. They were on the verge of capturing the entire fort when Buckner returned with his men and drove them back.

By nightfall, the Confederates were back where they had started, and Floyd called another meeting of the commanders. Over Buckner's objections, Floyd and Pillow decided to surrender, but neither wanted to turn himself over to the Union forces or to accept the responsibility for the surrender. Floyd passed the command of the garrison to Pillow, who in turn passed it to Buckner, who accepted and sent for "a pen, paper, and a bugler." While Buckner wrote a message to Grant asking for surrender terms, Floyd and a number of Union troops escaped upriver on two steamers, while Pillow crossed the river in a small, flat-bottomed boat. Nathan Bedford Forrest, the commander of the Confederate cavalry, disgustedly took off on his own and rode to freedom on a flooded road next to the river. Each of his cavalrymen carried a Confederate infantryman behind him on the back of his horse. Fifteen minutes after Forrest passed, Union forces cut off the road.

When Grant received Buckner's note asking for terms on February 16, Grant famously replied, "No terms except unconditional and immediate surrender can be accepted." His old friend Buckner thought this was "ungracious," but had to accept.

With the surrender of Forts Henry and Donelson, Nashville was doomed, and the Union had a new hero—U. S. "Unconditional Surrender" Grant.

Fort Donelson National Battlefield

The 536-acre Fort Donelson National Battlefield includes the earthen fort, upper and lower batteries, and approximately two miles of earthworks. It also includes a Visitors Center, the Dover Hotel (also known as the Surrender House), and the Fort Donelson National Cemetery. Approximately 20 percent of the battlefield is within the park. There are five miles of walking trails, as well as several short foot trails along the auto-tour route. The Donelson Trail is a little over three miles long, and begins and ends at the Visitors Center. The optional Cemetery Spur Trail increases the length of the Donelson Trail to almost six miles. The River Circle Trail begins and ends at the Lower River Battery and is almost two miles long.

The Visitors Center has an information desk, auditorium, a bookstore, and a museum. The exhibits include an audiovisual slide program about the battle. A brochure and an audiocassette tape for a self-guided automobile tour of the battlefield are available here.

The Dover Hotel (Surrender House) is an adaptive restoration of the historic building where Buckner surrendered to Grant.

The Fort Donelson National Cemetery was established in 1867 for the Union soldiers killed at Fort Donelson. In 1933, responsibility for the cemetery was transferred from the War Department to the National Park Service. Today the site is the burial place of American veterans representing seven wars.

Visitor Information

931-232-5706; www.nps.gov/fodo
Hours: Visitors Center daily, 8 a.m. until 4:30 p.m.; closed December 25. Dover Hotel (Surrender House), Memorial Day to Labor Day, noon until 4 p.m.; the hours depend on the availability of volunteers. Call for exact times.
Admission: Free.
Accessibility: A captioned version of the Visitors Center slide program is available upon request. Restrooms are accessible to visitors using wheelchairs. Trails are not handicapped accessible.
Special Programs: From June to August, costumed living-history demonstrations are conducted daily. The park staff also conducts a variety of interpretive programs at the Visitors Center. Call for times.
Getting There: The battlefield is located off U.S. Route 79, which passes through Dover, Tennessee. Dover is approximately 90 miles west of Nashville and 30 miles west of Clarksville, Tennessee.

From the east: Take I-40 to I-24, then U.S. 79 to Dover.

From the north and south: Take I-65 to I-24, then U.S. 79 to Dover.

From the west: Take I-40 to U.S. 45E at Jackson, U.S. 45E to U.S. 79 to Dover.

FIELD ARTILLERY

The wheeled field artillery pieces that dot Civil War battlefields and memorials today were one of the most important components of the Civil War armies. Yet the Union forces began the war with only about 160 field artillery pieces, and the Confederate armies had even less. Northern foundries quickly began to produce more, and the Union did import a few pieces—especially British ones that were generally superior to the American. The South had a much more limited manufacturing capability, and depended far more on British imports and captured weapons.

Pound versus Bore

The size of Civil War field artillery was measured in two ways, by "pound" or by "bore diameter," and some pieces used both. For smoothbore field artillery, pound—derived from the weight of a solid shot, or cannon ball—was the most common measurement. For example, a 12-pounder (commonly designated 12-pdr) fired a 12-pound cannon ball. By the time of the Civil War, the pounder designation had been standardized with the bore diameter on smoothbore field artillery pieces. Six-pounders had a 3.67-inch bore, 12-pounders a 4.62-inch bore, and 24-pounders a 5.82-inch bore.

Most rifled field artillery used the same system, but the solid shot of a rifled field gun, or the pointed cylinder called a bolt, was longer than and roughly twice as heavy as a spherical cannon ball of the same diameter, so a rifled cannon had a larger "pounder" designation than a smoothbore cannon with the same bore size.

Field Guns and Howitzers

Field guns and howitzers were similar pieces of equipment, but a howitzer fired its round with a smaller charge and at a higher trajectory than a field gun. This allowed the howitzer to be made shorter and lighter than a field gun of the same pound designation/muzzle bore. Therefore, howitzers were more mobile, an important consideration in a fast-moving battle. Also, field guns fired conventional solid-shot cannonballs, while howitzers fired shells, also spherical but filled with explosives. These shells had a time fuse that, in theory, would detonate as the shell hit the ground.

However, howitzers' effectiveness depended heavily on experienced operators. They had to be aimed more accurately than field guns since the thin-walled shells, unlike cannonballs, could not be aimed short and bounced across the ground to the target.

Smoothbore versus Rifled Pieces

The attraction of rifled artillery was

obvious. Rifled cannons had a much longer range, fired a heavier round, and were significantly more accurate than bronze smoothbores of the same size. In long-range engagements, the rifled pieces were supreme; but throughout the war, the smoothbores also had their place in the battle, since they had subtle advantages that sometimes loomed large in combat.

The foliage and terrain of many Civil War battles often constrained the effective range of cannons to a mile or less, putting a premium on rate of fire, and smoothbores could fire faster than rifled pieces. Additionally, at close range the round of choice for field artillery was canister, a thin iron cylinder filled with small (1- to 1 1/2-inch) iron balls. The thin cylinder fragmented when fired, filling the air with the balls, much as a giant shotgun shell would. At 200 yards, a round of canister from a smoothbore covered an area of about 20 yards, and canister was effective out to 400 yards. Firing canister from rifled weapons was much less effective than from a smoothbore. The spin imparted on the canister from the rifling produced centrifugal force on the small balls, and rather than scattering in a uniform pattern they left a large "doughnut hole" in the center of their coverage.

Rifling bronze smoothbores offered the promise of doubling the weight of the round they could fire, as well as increasing their range and accuracy. Union general Charles James developed a rifled projectile early in the war and rebored some 6-pounders for the new shell. Unfortunately, James's rifled shells quickly wore down the soft bronze inner lining of the cannons, and the project was abandoned.

DEATH FOUR RANKS DEEP

As we returned a Yankee battery of eight guns had full play on us in the field, and our line became a little confused; we halted, every man instantly turned and faced the battery. As we did so, I heard a thud on my right, as if one had been struck with a heavy fist. Looking around I saw a man at my side standing erect, with his head off, a stream of blood spurting a foot or more from his neck. As I turned farther around, I saw three others lying on the ground, all killed by this cannon shot. . . This was the second time I saw four men killed by one shot.

—From the diary of Private John H. Worsham, 21st Virginia

Field Artillery in Battle

Wheeled field artillery was designed to be light and maneuverable. It was organized into batteries, usually consisting of six guns for Union forces and four for the Confederates.

Accompanying each two-wheeled gun carriage was a two-wheeled vehicle known as a limber, with a caisson (chest) to hold ammunition, fuses, and other necessities. Every gun had a six-man crew with two more to man the limber and four to six horses to move the pair, and a full battery could consist of over 100 men and horses. On good roads a battery could cover two and a half miles an hour.

The ability to set up and fire quickly and accurately was the most important asset of field artillery. A good smoothbore crew could set up and fire in under a minute and could fire two rounds a minute of shot or shell. This could be increased to four rounds a minute with canister.

Bronze Smoothbore Artillery

At the beginning of the war, virtually all the field artillery pieces in both armies were bronze smoothbores

Ammunition

Artillery ammunition included **solid shot, shell, chain shot, canister,** and **grape shot,** each of which came in any of the nine common artillery calibers. **Solid shot** and **shell** were used against long-range, fixed targets such as fortifications; **chain shot,** consisting of two balls connected by a chain, was used primarily against masts and rigging of ships. Very frequently used was **canister,** consisting of small iron balls encased in a container. **Grapeshot** was usually wrapped in a cloth or canvas covering and tied with string, which made it look like a bunch of grapes.

Shell

Solid shot

Canister

Canister shot packed in sawdust.

with a green patina. There were five main types:

The Model 1841 6-pdr/3.67″ field gun was the main U.S. Army field artillery piece prior to the war, but its short range and small round made it obsolete at the beginning of the war. Both sides replaced these as quickly as possible, but because the Confederates had an overall shortage of cannons, they had to keep the model in service longer than the Union forces.

The Model 1841 12-pdr/4.62″ field gun was more useful than the 6-pounder, but it was rather heavy, weighing almost a ton. It was replaced by the more versatile and lighter Napoleon.

The Model 1841 12-pdr/4.62″ howitzer was light (less than 800 pounds) and highly mobile. But it had a range of less than 1000 yards, and was vulnerable to counterfire from field guns, iron rifled field guns, and even shoulder-fired small arms.

The Model 1841 24-pdr/5.82″ howitzer fired a large shell, but its relatively short range (about 1300 yards) and weight (over 1300 pounds) somewhat offset these advantages.

The Model 1857 Light 12-pdr/ 4.62″ or "Napoleon" field-gun howitzer combined all the best attributes of a bronze smoothbore. It was relatively light (about 1200 pounds) had a long range of over 1600 yards, and could fire virtually every type of ammunition—shot, shell, and canister. It was developed in France under the instructions of Emperor Napoleon III and was ordered by U.S. Army officers who saw it in action during a visit to Europe. The Napoleon was popular with both sides. Union factories produced 1200 and the Confederates made 500 to 600 of their own version.

Rifled Field Artillery Pieces

After James's failed attempt to rebore bronze smoothbores, it was clear that rifled weapons would have to be made of iron. Experiments with cast-iron cannons showed that they burst when fired because of the internal pressure, which was much greater with rifled cannons than with smoothbores. James Parrott, a former U.S. Army officer, tried to create a usable cast-iron cannon by adding a reinforcing band of wrought iron around the breech, where the pressure was greatest. Parrott was successful to a degree. His cannons became an early mainstay of the

THE TOOLS OF A WELL-DRILLED TEAM

On the command "Load," crewman Number 1 sponges the bore as 2 receives the round from 5 and places it in the muzzle. Number 3 closes the vent as 1 rams the round home. The gunner (the corporal who aims the gun) steps to the breech to sight the piece, while 3 drops back to the trail handspike and shifts the gun according to the gunner's directions.

Number 5, meanwhile, returns to the limber and gets a new round from 6 and 7, who have cut the fuse according to the gunner's shouted orders. When the gun is aimed, the gunner steps back to observe the effects of the shot and commands "Ready."

At this point, 1 and 2 stand clear. Number 3 shoves the pick through the vent and into the powder bag. Then number 4 hooks a friction primer to the lanyard and inserts the primer in the vent. Number 3 holds the primer, while 4 steps back, holding the lanyard slack.

Now the gunner commands "Fire." Number 3 steps back from the wheel, and 4 pulls the lanyard, firing the piece. At the same time, Number 5 delivers the next round to 2. When the gun has recoiled, the crew pushes it back into position, and the sequence begins again with the command "Load."

Union artillery, and one of the first Parrotts was sold to the Commonwealth of Virginia in the summer of 1860. The Virginia Military Institute instructor of artillery, Professor Thomas J. Jackson, later known as Stonewall, liked the Parrott. Later in the war, the Confederates made their own copies of the piece.

There were two main types of rifled field artillery:

The Model 1861 10-pdr/2.9″ Parrott rifle was developed between 1859 and 1860. It was the first workable American rifled gun available to either side, and its range

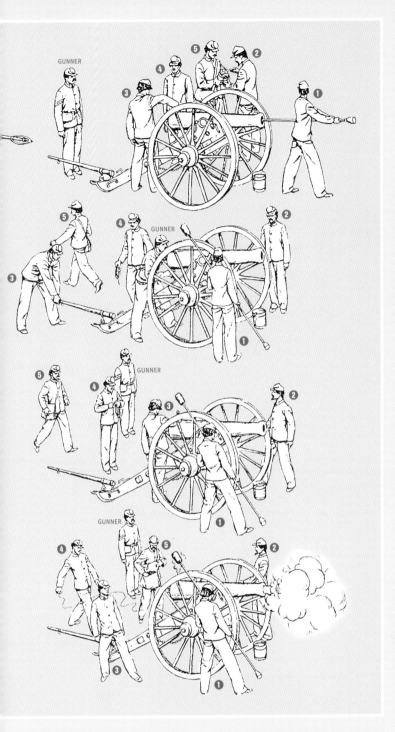

and accuracy made it a formidable force on the battlefield. However, like earlier cast-iron pieces, the Parrotts occasionally burst without warning. The problem was uneven, though, and many Parrotts fired several thousand rounds without a difficulty.

The Model 1863 3″ Parrott rifle was made with improvements specifically intended to alleviate the bursting problem.

The 20-pdr/3.67″ Parrott rifle was a heavier version of the Parrott 10-pounder, with the same reputation for bursting unexpectedly. The Parrotts were gradually phased out

as Ordnance Rifles became available.

The Model 1861 3″ Ordnance wrought-iron rifle was adopted in 1861 and was generally considered to be the finest field artillery piece of the war. The patented wrought-iron weapon was virtually immune from bursting, was 100 pounds lighter than the Parrott, and was accurate out to a range of 2000 yards, slightly more than the Parrott. At ranges under a mile it was considered deadly accurate. About 1000 of these fine pieces were produced for the Union army, but they were expensive and slow to produce.

The Battle of Shiloh

Following the losses of Forts Henry and Donelson in the winter of 1862, Confederate general Albert Sidney Johnston and his forces were forced to fall back and abandon Kentucky, as well as much of western and middle Tennessee. Johnston established a new defensive line that protected the Memphis & Charleston Railroad, the direct route from the Mississippi River to the eastern part of the Confederacy. General P.G.T. Beauregard, the hero of Fort Sumter and First Bull Run (Manassas), was sent to assist Johnston as his second in command. Beauregard and Johnston met at Corinth, Mississippi, a railroad junction just south of the Mississippi–Tennessee border.

On the Union side, on March 11, 1862, President Abraham Lincoln unified all the western armies in the Knoxville–Missouri River area under Major General Henry "Old Brains" Halleck, giving him command of four armies—Major General Don Carlos Buell's Army of the Ohio, Major General C. F. Smith's Army of the Tennessee, Major General Samuel Curtis's Army of the Southwest in Missouri and Arkansas, and Major General John Pope's Army of the Mississippi. Major General Ulysses S. Grant had been commander of the Army of the Tennessee, but Halleck had replaced him with Smith, perhaps because Halleck was jealous of Grant's popular acclaim after his capture of Fort Donelson.

The Union Plans a First Strike

The Confederate retreat was an unexpected favor to Halleck. He ordered Smith to meet Buell's forces at Savannah, Tennessee, and then together attack the Confederates at Corinth. Buell left Nashville on March 16 but proceeded south in a leisurely fashion. This lack of urgency almost led to a major Union defeat. Meanwhile, Smith and six divisions—40,000 men—floated down the Tennessee River to Pittsburg Landing on the west bank, nine miles south of Savannah, and their arrival was reported back to Beauregard.

When Smith was seriously injured stepping off a boat on March 17, Grant resumed command of the Army of the Tennessee but was ordered not to attack the Confederates until Buell's 20,000 troops arrived. Grant set up his headquarters in Savannah and stationed his men around Shiloh Church, a meetinghouse southwest of Pittsburg Landing. The nine miles between the headquarters and the front line units would deprive the Union forces of Grant's leadership during the important first hours of the battle.

While Johnston marched his army toward Corinth, Beauregard gathered General Braxton Bragg's and General Leonidas Polk's forces in Corinth from all around the South. Their almost 18,000 troops joined with Johnston's men, creating a Confederate army of almost 49,000 men—one of the largest military forces ever assembled west of the Appalachians. While the force was large, it was almost completely lacking in combat experience. But Grant's troops were equally raw.

When Johnston arrived at Corinth on March 22, Beauregard told him that the combined Confederate forces needed to stop the Union advance down the Tennessee River.

Federal ironclads bombard Fort Henry on February 6, 1862, as Union forces begin their Southern drive along the Tennessee River to gain control of the Mississippi Valley.

Grant was the ideal target, isolated well forward in a poor tactical position, but the Confederates had to strike before Buell's army joined Grant.

Beauregard showed his mastery of strategic and administrative tasks by coordinating the converging forces of Johnston, Polk, and Bragg. This suited Johnston, who told Beauregard to command the operation from the rear. Johnston would lead his units at the point of battle, as he preferred. By the beginning of April, Johnston's army was in place, with four corps and a number of independent cavalry regiments that would accompany the army to Shiloh.

Muddy Approach to Shiloh

On April 3, Johnston's forces began to advance north toward Grant's position. The Confederate troops had done little drilling, and their commanders had no experience coordinating this type of movement. There were only two roads through the swampy, dense woods, and when it began to rain heavily on April 4, the artillery and wagons bogged down in the mud. Poor coordination caused gridlock between units that met on the roads, and the move sputtered. The attack was originally planned for April 4, but the exhausted Confederate troops did not arrive around Shiloh until late afternoon on April 5, making an attack before April 6 impossible.

Now Beauregard began to lose his nerve and recommended canceling the attack, afraid that Grant knew the Confederates were in the area after the disorganized, noisy advance. Johnston insisted that the attack proceed as planned. He was concerned about the negative effect a retreat might have on his green but aggressive troops, and he may have viewed this as his chance to redeem his reputation after the recent losses of Forts Henry and Donelson.

Grant's Army of the Tennessee was formed into six divisions, each with its own cavalry regiment and artillery batteries. On April 5, five of the divisions were in the area from Shiloh Church north toward Pittsburg Landing, while one—Major General Lew Wallace's—was at Crump's Landing, five miles north, to protect Savannah. That evening when General William "Bull" Nelson, leading the first division of Buell's Army of the Ohio, arrived in Savannah, Grant told him to camp on the other side of the river, since he thought there would be no fighting until Buell arrived.

Around Shiloh, Grant's troops were camped in an area bounded by the Tennessee River on to the east and Owl Creek to the west. The Hamburg–Savannah Road ran basically north–south between the two, with a major spur running east to Pittsburg Landing. The highest terrain was a ridge running generally east to west, 200 feet above the river just south of Pittsburg Landing. To the south of the ridge, Dill Creek created a ravine from the Tennessee River inland. Pittsburg Landing was the critical point, because Grant depended on the Tennessee River for reinforcements and supplies. Grant's army erected tent cities and waited for Buell to arrive and then move on Corinth.

General William T. Sherman's and Brigadier General Benjamin M. Prentiss's divisions were the southernmost of the Union units, camped around Shiloh Church, an area full of dense woods cut by ravines. Aside from a dozen or so fields scattered throughout the woods, the ground was difficult for horsemen. There were few roads in the area, but many winding trails, which made it hard for spread-out units to stay in touch with each other.

On the Confederate side, Johnston had a simple battle plan. He wanted to break through the Union left and drive along the Tennessee toward Pittsburg Landing, forcing Grant to retreat away from the river and possible reinforcements. Since he was attacking with inexperienced troops and commanders, Beauregard, with Johnston's approval, had set up a formation that emphasized numbers over maneuverability. The four corps were placed close behind one another, and the divisions inside the corps were then placed side by side, forming long lines abreast. Such a formation was fine for a straight-ahead attack in open country, but in broken country it could not be controlled and would cause huge problems as the day went on. Additionally, the plan did not put any extra forces on the Confederate right, where Johnston wanted to break through.

Johnston would lead the brigades personally and control specific portions of the battlefield. Beauregard was left to direct reinforcements and supplies from the rear. Johnston's primary objective, to cut Grant off from Pittsburg Landing, seems to have been given little emphasis.

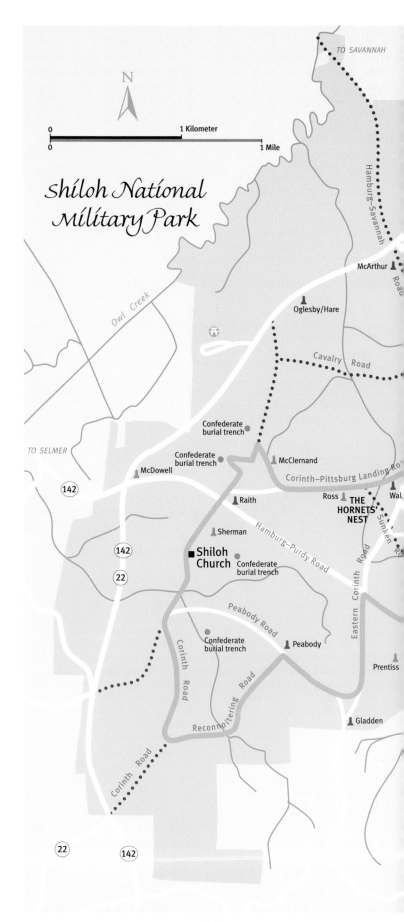

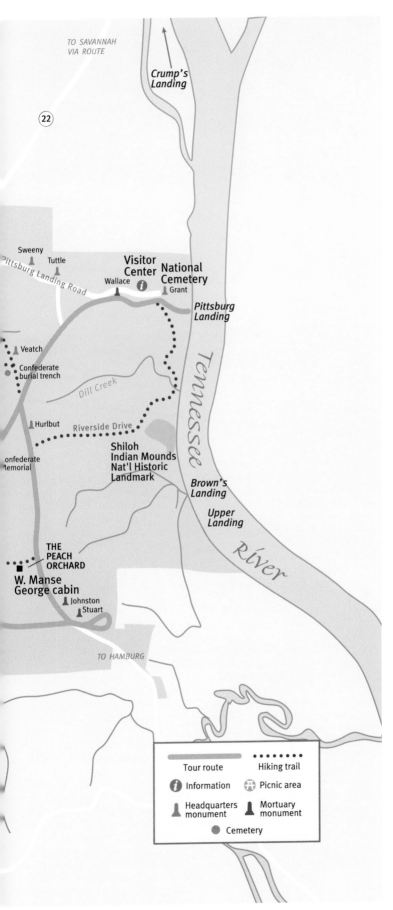

TO SAVANNAH
VIA ROUTE

Crump's Landing

22

Sweeny

Tuttle

Pittsburg Landing Road

Wallace

Visitor Center

i

National Cemetery

Grant

Pittsburg Landing

Veatch

Confederate burial trench

Dill Creek

Hurlbut

Riverside Drive

Tennessee

Confederate Memorial

Shiloh Indian Mounds Nat'l Historic Landmark

Brown's Landing

Upper Landing

THE PEACH ORCHARD

W. Manse George cabin

Johnston

Stuart

River

TO HAMBURG

Tour route

Hiking trail

i Information

Picnic area

Headquarters monument

Mortuary monument

Cemetery

Instead, the Confederate commanders were given a basic guideline: march toward the sound of the heaviest fighting.

On the Union side, the easy victories in the West seem to have made the commanders overconfident. On April 5, Sherman wrote Grant that he did not expect an attack, and Grant told Halleck that while he did not expect one, he "will be prepared should such a thing take place."

He was not. There was almost no security for his units, and no forces were sent out for distant patrolling or reconnaissance. The evening of April 5, Union leaders were completely unaware that a Confederate army of almost 49,000 men was two miles away, preparing to attack the next morning. The unsuspecting Grant had about the same number of Union troops, but they were scattered, with more than 9000 of them five miles away at Crump's Landing.

A Surprise Attack

Before dawn on April 6, Prentiss, whose division was closest to the Confederate lines, sent out a large patrol to scout in front of the Union picket line. Behind Prentiss, the rest of the Union army was slowly beginning to awaken, starting fires for breakfast. The troops had their arms stacked and anticipated another routine day in camp. Near Shiloh Church the patrol became involved

in a firefight with what they thought were Confederate outposts. Suddenly they found themselves in the middle of Johnston's full-scale attack and fell back rapidly. The Confederates surged forward, and later Confederate general Beauregard commented that the Union got "the most surprising surprise."

Thanks to Prentiss's patrol, Prentiss and Sherman—who heard the fighting—had a few minutes to prepare their divisions for the onslaught. They scrambled to set up positions in front of their bases before the Confederates arrived; but the Union camps were out of sight of each other, which made a coordinated defense impossible. As the violent Confederate attack broke over them, Union units tried to set up defensive positions, but the Confederate army flowed around each pocket of resistance. In some places, Union soldiers were actually fighting from between their tents, while some simply broke and ran to the safety of Pittsburg Landing.

As the Confederates advanced, many of the Union regiments fought stubbornly and yielded ground slowly, even holding in spots. The Confederates pressed all along the line, and when they broke through against one Union unit, the others on the line had to fall back to keep from being outflanked as they were slowly pushed back toward Pittsburg Land-

Confederates capture General John Alexander McClernand's headquarters at Pittsburg Landing.

attack had lost focus. The first three corps had become intermingled into a broad line. Commanders had lost track of their own men and could only control those in front of them. The attack degenerated into a frontal assault, trying to turn both Union flanks and to penetrate the center, with no emphasis on any point.

Still, the Confederates were advancing rapidly, and when Grant stepped off the boat, he saw hundreds of Union stragglers who had thrown down their arms and hurried to the Landing for safety. Grant formed a line of cavalry to stop the stragglers, with instructions that after they had recovered from their fright, they should be sent to reinforce some part of the line as needed. Next, he sent word to Wallace to march his division to Pittsburg Landing, and he sent a force to secure the bridges that Wallace's division would have to cross as it marched from Crump's Landing. Thus, by about nine thirty, Grant thought that in a few hours two divisions would join him around Shiloh. He then went forward to tour the battlefield and talk with his division commanders, but the situation was so chaotic it took him several hours to make sense of it.

On the Union right, Sherman had

ing. By midmorning, entire Union divisions were isolated, but they were fighting hard and making the Confederates pay for their gains.

At his headquarters in Savannah, Grant heard gunfire to the south at about six thirty, leapt up from the breakfast table, and headed for the river to take a boat to Pittsburg Landing. Before leaving Savannah, he ordered General Nelson to take his newly arrived division and march down to a point opposite Pittsburg Landing.

By nine a.m., as Grant neared Pittsburg Landing, the Confederate

Grant's headquarters in Savannah was transferred to the Tennessee River boat Tigress, below center, as soon as the cannonade announced the start of the battle. Later, these ships transported reinforcements and supplies.

managed to regroup his men, and he held a line in front of Shiloh Church for several hours after most of his division's camps were overrun. Before the morning was out, he was wounded and several horses had been shot out from under him. Finally, Sherman's forces broke; but as he fell back, Union reinforcements temporarily stabilized the position.

In the center, Prentiss's troops caught the brunt of the Confederate attack. By nine a.m. his division was cut to pieces and he was forced back. As he retreated, Prentiss managed to scrape together a small fraction of his division—about 1000 men— and form a line with another division.

Johnston was leading the Confederate assault personally. His strength was inspiring leadership, and he knew his green troops and their commanders needed this in the heat of their first battle. Nevertheless, as the Confederates advanced, their inexperience and lack of discipline showed and they became increasingly disorganized. Some men broke ranks to loot the newly captured Yankee camps or stopped to eat the Union troops' breakfast. Others dropped out of the battle because of fear. The terrain, full of dense woods and winding ravines, confused them, and the sheer speed of the advance mixed their units. The Confederate commanders, often equally confused about their position, simply tried to move forward.

By late morning, Grant was trying to stabilize a line that would protect Pittsburg Landing and the Hamburg–Savannah Road that Wallace's division was supposed to use. In the center, the Union now held an excellent defensive position, a sunken road in a dense wood on higher ground that ran eastward from an open field. Grant saw how strong the position was and told Prentiss, "Maintain that position at all hazards," which Prentiss did. A Confederate later noted, "Behind a dense thicket on the crest of a hill was posted a strong force of hardy troops as ever fought . . . [They] put forth a murderous storm of shot and shell and musketry fire which no living thing could quell or even withstand." Before the day was over, the sunken road the Union occupied at Shiloh was to become as famous as other sunken road defensive positions at Antietam and Marye's Heights at Fredericksburg. The unique whine of the minié balls coming out of and going into the sunken road led to the area's later being dubbed the Hornets' Nest.

By noon, the Union right was folding. However, the Union left, under the command of W.H.L. Wallace (not to be confused with Lew Wallace), had held close to the Tennessee River. The Confederates were now wheeling from the left to the right along the battlefield. General Johnston was on the right side, where he knew the battle would

Under the command of Captain Andrew Hickenlooper, the 5th Ohio Light Artillery Battery defends the Hornets' Nest against repeated Confederate assaults. Massing 62 guns against the defense, the Confederates eventually won out.

They would still have to be ferried across when they arrived. Additionally, Lew Wallace's division had become lost on the five-mile march from Crump's Landing and was wandering through the woods well north of the fighting.

On Grant's right flank, Sherman continued to be pushed back slowly, but the center of the Union line was solid now where they were burrowed into the sunken road. Next to the road was a peach orchard in full bloom. As bullets zipped through the trees, petals rained down on the soldiers lying below, giving some the impression of falling snow.

Confederate general Bragg launched several vigorous but uncoordinated assaults on the Union line; but each time, the Union defenders held their ground, forcing the Southerners to re-form and charge again.

As Bragg regrouped for another attempt on the Hornets' Nest, General Johnston saw an opportunity to win the battle by moving forward on Pittsburg Landing. He sent a brigade to the extreme end of the battlefield near the Tennessee River and told them to turn north to Pittsburg Landing. When the brigade moved forward seemingly unopposed, Johnston said, "We've checkmated them."

Union Flanks Finally Collapse

Johnston returned to observe Bragg's next assault on the Hornets' Nest but got too close. Johnston was hit three times and seemed to be only lightly wounded. He dismounted under a nearby tree. There it was discovered that a ball had gone through his boot into the calf of the right leg, where it severed an artery. Johnston soon lost consciousness and died. As the second highest officer in the Confederate army, he was the highest ranking general on either side to die in battle. With Johnston went the Confederates' hope of victory, because only he had been focused on the need to capture Pittsburg Landing, and only he was close enough to the front to control his disorganized forces.

Beauregard now assumed command. He knew what was happen-

be decided. He roamed the front, moving units, ordering attacks, and directing artillery fire. All the while, he moved to his right trying to push toward Pittsburg Landing and force the Union troops off the river. Beauregard now sent most of the Confederate reserves directly to Johnston on the right.

However, while Johnston knew how he wanted the battle to develop, he made little effort to ensure that his corps commanders were following the battle plan. In fact, now his corps commanders began to improvise. Their forces were so mixed that each general agreed to command only the troops in the immediate third of the battle line in front of him. And although Johnston had driven the Army of the Tennessee back and was steadily advancing, the Union lines were stiffening. The Confederates had committed all their forces to battle but had not achieved a decisive victory, and now they had no reserves to take advantage of a breakthrough.

On the Union side, Grant thought that large numbers of Union reinforcements were within a few miles of the battlefield, but he was in for a nasty surprise. For some reason, General Nelson's division, which Grant had told to move at six thirty, did not leave Savannah until one thirty p.m., and their lead units were still several miles away from Pittsburg Landing and marching down the opposite side of the river.

ing on the field, but the battle had a life of its own and was beyond his control. The generals simply attacked where they saw an opportunity.

Grant saw Prentiss in the afternoon and told him to hold on "as cool as if expecting victory," and Prentiss, W.H.L. Wallace, and their men in the center of the line were doing just that. Each time the Rebels advanced, they were repulsed. As the battle raged, parts of the nearby woods caught fire. The screams of wounded men being incinerated in the burning woods could be heard above the roar of gunfire and the other sounds of the battle.

Gradually Prentiss's determined resistance began to have an unexpected consequence. Each time a Confederate unit broke through the Union line, it turned to the sound of the fight at the Hornets' Nest instead of moving to Pittsburg Landing. About three thirty, the Confederates began collecting all the artillery they could find, and they amassed the largest concentration of artillery yet assembled in North America, 62 cannons, and began to pound the Union position at the Hornets' Nest. At first, Union batteries that had supported the Union defensive line fired back, but soon the superior numbers took effect and the Union batteries began to move out. Still, Prentiss and Wallace held on.

Shortly after four p.m., Sherman fell back on the Union right for the last time. The Union forces set up on the Hamburg–Savannah Road, the route Lew Wallace's division was expected to use; but only part of the Confederate units followed. The rest swung to the right and came up behind the rear of the Hornets' Nest. Once again, the Hornets' Nest drew Confederate forces onto itself and away from their main objective.

W.H.L. Wallace and Prentiss had held their ground for five hours against 12 separate assaults, but now they were surrounded by the bulk of the Confederate army. Wallace's regiments turned to the rear and some fought their way out, but Wallace was killed. Prentiss saw his position was hopeless and ordered a withdrawal, but his troops were cut off as Confederates closed from both sides. After saving the day for the Union, at five thirty Prentiss finally surrendered.

As the Union flanks collapsed in midafternoon, Colonel Joseph D. Webster, Grant's chief of staff, received Grant's permission to

Confederate general *Albert Sidney Johnston was the highest ranking officer to die in battle during the war.*

assemble artillery on the ridge overlooking the approaches to Pittsburg Landing. By the time Prentiss surrendered, the remnants of the Union right, including Sherman's forces, anchored the line on the Hamburg–Savannah Road. From there to the Tennessee River on the Dill Creek ravine there was virtually no organized Union infantry, but Webster now had 50 guns in position on the north ridge of the ravine about half a mile south of Pittsburg Landing. There were also two Union gunboats, the *Tyler* and the *Lexington*, in the river. As the early spring twilight approached, Grant was ready for the South's final assault of the day. He knew that Lew Wallace's and Nelson's divisions would arrive at some point, but he had to hold until they did.

After Prentiss's surrender, Bragg, who had spent the afternoon directing disorganized charges against Prentiss at the Hornets' Nest, was eager to seize Pittsburg Landing. However, Beauregard had no reserves to send forward, and so he sent orders to Bragg and his other commanders to suspend attacks all along the line. Bragg either did not receive or disregarded the orders. He only had about 2000 men in two under strength brigades, one of which was out of ammunition. Nevertheless, at about six p.m. Bragg ordered an attack across the Dill Creek ravine into the teeth of the Union artillery. The Confederates were ripped by Union cannons until they were under the bluffs where the Union line was established, but the ravine ran straight to the river where the Union gunboats were anchored. The gunboats' cannons had a clear shot down the ravine and raked the Confederate line. Despite their officers' exhortations, the Confederate troops refused to move up the bluffs, and finally they withdrew.

As night fell, Beauregard's original force of 44,000 Confederates had shrunk to half that size. Nevertheless, Beauregard was sure the Union was in much worse shape, and he thought Grant would retreat back to Savannah. Beauregard was so sure he had won a major victory that he sent this news, suitably embellished, to Richmond. He then went to sleep.

He was wrong. Grant's army was badly mauled but intact. Later Sherman and Grant met at Pittsburg Landing and Sherman said, "Well, Grant, we've had the devil's own day, haven't we." Grant reflected on the reinforcements that would be coming in and responded, "Yep. Lick 'em tomorrow, though."

Finally, General Lew Wallace arrived with his division, along with Nelson and the rest of Buell's Army of the Ohio. As Buell's 20,000 men crossed the river under the cover of fire from the Union gunboats, to meet up with the rest of the reinforcements, they were shocked at the sight of the thousands of stragglers that still crowded the riverside.

As night came, a new nightmare began on the battlefield. Thousands of wounded soldiers covered the ground, groaning and crying for help. Around midnight, a huge thunderstorm moved in and rain came pelting down. The combination of the wounded crying for help, the roar of the rain and thunder, and the flashes of lightning gave those who saw it a glimpse of hell.

General Beauregard did not know that Buell had arrived with reinforcements, and though most of the Confederate units were low on ammunition, there was little attempt to bring supplies forward or make other preparations for a second day of battle. In any event, there was not much the Confederates could do, because few commanders knew where all of their units were.

A New Day Turns the Tide

By contrast, the next morning, April 7, the Union forces were ready to attack. Buell was assigned the Union left flank, and about five a.m. he sent one division forward; then Buell stopped to allow more divisions to move into line for a full-scale attack. On the other flank, Grant sent forward Lew Wallace's division, supported by Sherman and other Union units that had borne the brunt of the fighting the day before. At nine a.m., the advance resumed across the entire front.

Beauregard launched a counterattack, which stopped the Union advance at first, but the Union troops held and began forcing the Confederates back. The force of the attack, stoked by the 25,000 fresh troops, was too much for Beauregard's tired, outnumbered defenders. The fighting was heavy, but the Confederates were steadily pushed back. Shortly after noon, Beauregard realized he could not hold. He ordered a retreat back to Corinth despite opposition from some of his commanders, especially Bragg.

The Union army did not pursue the Confederates past the original Union camps. Grant's men were exhausted, while Buell had little cavalry and knew virtually nothing about the terrain. The inexperienced troops were also disturbed by what they had seen when they disembarked and what they saw on the battlefield. Not only were there dead and wounded everywhere, but some passed a pond, later called Bloody Pond, that had been turned bright red by the blood of the wounded and dead. Ambrose Bierce described a part of the battlefield: "The woods had caught fire and the bodies had been cremated . . . some were swollen to double girth, others shriveled to manikins." Thus the Battle of Shiloh, the second great battle of the Civil War, ended.

Aftermath

After the battle, a large tent hospital was set up to treat the wounded from both sides. It was the first attempt to concentrate medical facilities in one area, and became the prototype for both Union and Confederate Civil War hospitals for the rest of the war.

The day after the Battle of Shiloh, the Confederates were handed another defeat when Union general Pope and Commodore Andrew H. Foote took Island No. 10, a Confederate outpost on the Tennessee River, capturing 7000 Confederates and opening the Mississippi as far as Memphis. The Confederates' extensive fortifications near Memphis and along the upper Mississippi were now useless and were soon abandoned.

On April 8, Grant sent troops to pursue Beauregard. They ran into a Confederate rearguard at Fallen

Timbers, which forced the Union troops back to Pittsburg Landing.

The losses at Shiloh had a huge impact on the civilian population on both sides. The total Union casualties were well over 13,000, while the Confederates lost around 11,000 (Grant later said the Confederate figures were much too low). These losses made Shiloh the bloodiest battle of the war up to that time, the ninth costliest battle of the Civil War, and almost as controversial as the later battles of Antietam and Gettysburg. Grant, whose earlier victories had aroused a great deal of jealousy among his contemporaries, was brutally attacked by politicians and the press in the North. The governor of Ohio, who lost many men from his state in the battle, said that Grant should be "court-martialed or shot" for "criminal negligence." Grant's friend Sherman noted later, "It was publicly asserted in the North that our army was taken completely by surprise; that the rebels caught us in our tents; bayoneted the men in their beds; that General Grant was drunk. . . . The controversy was started and kept up, mostly to the personal prejudice of General Grant." President Lincoln, who knew what it meant to be criticized, did not take any of the complaints to heart. He stood by Grant, famously saying, "I can't spare this man; he fights."

Nevertheless, Grant, who was certainly not drunk, was removed from command and became Halleck's administrative subordinate. He considered resigning, but Sherman convinced him to stay in the army. On July 11, Halleck was sent to Washington and Grant returned to command.

On the Confederate side, Shiloh shook the leadership beyond Johnston's death. Bragg began what was to become a pattern, exploiting his friendship with Jefferson Davis while intriguing against Beauregard. He also criticized his fellow officers, saying the defeat at Shiloh was the result of "a want of discipline and a want of officers." A short time later, after controversially evacuating Corinth, Beauregard was relieved of his command. With the dismissal of Beauregard and the death of Johnston, Bragg became the Confederates' leading western general. Davis and the Confederacy would pay dearly for that choice.

Shiloh was a great opportunity for the Confederacy to annihilate a sizable Northern army deep in Southern territory, and the South never again came close to such a victory against a large Union force. The first day of Shiloh was one of the few times the Confederates outnumbered the Union in numbers of artillery and troops. Had they destroyed Grant's force, after the Union defeat at First Bull Run (Manassas), it might have changed the course of the war. Instead, Shiloh added to the momentum of earlier Union victories in the west.

The true importance of Shiloh was its effects on Grant and Sherman. Grant had felt the war would end quickly after his easy victories at Forts Henry and Donelson, but now he realized it would be a long, bitter struggle. It was also the beginning of the partnership of Sherman and Grant, a partnership that would eventually doom the rebellion. They were a superb complement to one another, and Sherman would fondly say later, "He stood by me when I was crazy and I stood by him when he was drunk."

Shiloh National Military Park

The first official recognition of the Shiloh battlefield was in 1866, when the federal government established the 10-acre Shiloh Military Cemetery to bury Union soldiers. In 1893 a group of Union veterans visited Shiloh and founded the Shiloh Battlefield Association, and were soon joined by Confederate veterans and their families. At one time the association included former generals Buell, Prentiss, and Lew Wallace, as well as William Johnston, son of the Confederate commander killed at the battle. The association bought up small parcels of land until Congress established Shiloh National Military Park on December 27, 1894, as one of the first five Civil War Military Parks.

In 1901 the Shiloh Park Commission, made up of many of the members of the original association, established a number of historical plaques, monuments, and troop-position markers. Many states worked with the commission to develop and place monuments to their troops. By 1927, 12 states had erected 117 memorials. In 1909 a tornado struck the area and destroyed or damaged many of the memorials, but the park was rebuilt in less than two years.

Today the park encompasses almost 4000 acres on the west bank

Federal troops *formed a defensive line along a sunken road and a wooded thicket subsequently known as the Bloody Lane and the Hornets' Nest. The monument honors the men of the 1st Minnesota Battery that helped defend the Hornets' Nest.*

of the Tennessee River and is considered one of the best-preserved Civil War battlefields. The park contains over 90 percent of the most contested areas of the battlefield, as well as over 60 percent of the troop-movement areas. It now has over 500 markers, over 200 cannons, and more than 150 monuments. The monuments are divided into several different sections, including state monuments, regimental monuments, and headquarters and mortuary monuments. The park is also home to the Shiloh National Cemetery.

The Visitors Center, near Pittsburg Landing, contains a museum with artifacts, a movie theater that shows a 25-minute film interpreting the battle, as well as a bookstore and gift shop. The Visitors Center provides free literature about the park, the Battle of Shiloh, and current and upcoming park activities, as well as a self-guided auto-tour map. An audiotape tour of the battlefield is available in the bookstore.

The 10-mile self-guided tour stops at 14 wayside exhibits, including a reconstruction of the Shiloh Church, the Hornets' Nest, the Peach Orchard, and the Bloody Pond.

Additionally, Shiloh National Military Park has a "monument location system" that allows visitors to locate quickly any of the hundreds of commemorative features on the battlefield. Civil War Battlefield Series Map #102 shows all current monuments and is available from the bookstore.

Visitor Information

731-689-5696; www.nps.gov/shil

Hours: The park is open daily, 8 a.m. until dusk; the Visitors Center is open daily from 8 a.m. until 5 p.m.; both are closed December 25.

Admission: Minimal individual or per-vehicle weekly fee; National Parks Pass, Golden Eagle, Golden Age, and Golden Access are honored.

Accessibility: The Visitors Center is wheelchair accessible, and one wheelchair is available upon request. Parking spaces for those with disabilities are located at the Visitors Center parking lot.

Special Events: There are living-history demonstrations on the weekend closest to the Shiloh anniversary dates. There are also Memorial Day programs each year. From Memorial Day through Labor Day there are a variety of programs, including guided tours, live-fire artillery demonstrations, and reenactors in Civil War uniforms around military camps. Call for details.

Getting There: The park is about 110 miles from Memphis and about 150 miles from Nashville in Hardin County, Tennessee, on the west bank of the Tennessee River about 9 miles south of Savannah, Tennessee.

From I-40: Take the Lexington, Tennessee, exit at state highway 22 and go south about 50 miles.

From Memphis, Tennessee: Take U.S. 72 to state highway 57 east approximately 100 miles, and then state highway 22 north.

The Visitors Center is located on Pittsburg Landing Road, about two miles north of the intersection of state highways 22 and 142.

The Battle of Stones River (Murfreesboro)

Following the Union victory at Perryville, Kentucky, in early October 1862, both the North and the South made changes in their military organizations. General Joseph E. Johnston was sent to command all of the Confederate armies in what was called the Division of the West. Under Johnston, the Army of the Tennessee was formed under General Braxton Bragg, the vanquished at Perryville. After that defeat, Bragg fell back to Murfreesboro, Tennessee, to reorganize. Although Bragg had just suffered a major defeat and was heartily disliked by his subordinates (during the Mexican War, subordinates had even tried to kill him on two separate occasions), he was a personal friend of Confederate President Jefferson Davis, which is what allowed him to retain his command.

On the Union side, Major General William S. Rosecrans, "Old Rosy," the victor at Corinth, Mississippi, was given command of the Army of the Cumberland, with orders to occupy eastern Tennessee. Rosecrans was a skillful strategist and personally brave (though extremely excitable), but he had a frustrating tendency to spend a great deal of time gathering supplies and getting organized before he moved. Now, he characteristically delayed in Nashville, annoying Lincoln, who first exhorted him to move against Bragg and eventually threatened to replace him if he did not.

Meanwhile, Bragg knew that his Confederate cavalry was vastly superior to its Union counterparts, and he made good use of that, first by sending two of his cavalry commanders to harass Union supply lines, where they caused considerable damage. Two other cavalry units slowed Rosecrans's progress south, so that it took four days for him to move a little more than 20 miles over fairly good roads, and prevented the Union cavalry from scouting the area. When Rosecrans finally approached Murfreesboro on December 29, he had little information on the Confederates, while Bragg was well informed about his opponent's force. Once Rosecrans set up camp, one Confederate cavalry unit began attacking the Union rear, and by the next day, they had taken over 1000 prisoners and destroyed or captured vast quantities of Union supplies, wagons, and matériel.

Bragg had arrayed his Confederates in lightly entrenched defensive positions on the west side of the roughly north–south-running Stones River. Most of his army was massed on the west side of the river. But one division, commanded by Major General (and former Vice President of the United States) John C. Breckinridge, formed the right flank of the Confederate line, and protected Murfreesboro just east of Stones River on a group of hills that were the highest in the area.

On December 30, in heavy rain, Rosecrans's and Bragg's armies faced each other along a four-mile front. Ironically, Bragg and Rosecrans each planned to attack the right flank of the other's forces the next day and cut off his enemy from his line of communications. Since the two plans were basically identical, the advantage would go to the one who struck first and hardest.

That night the two armies were within earshot of each other, and the soldiers knew that there would be a brutal battle the next morning. It was then that one of the unique incidents of the war took place. Each army's band began to play, first trying to drown out the other and then alternating songs. The Confederate band played "Dixie," followed by the Union band's rendition of "Hail Columbia," followed by the Confederate's "Bonnie Blue Flag." At the end of the evening, both bands played "Home Sweet Home," which the troops on both sides sang together.

Bragg Holds the Upper Hand

At dawn on December 31, while some Union units were cooking breakfast, Bragg's army exploded out of the cedars into the Union right flank. While one division was forced back and some Union soldiers fled, another was able to form a battle line. For the moment, this Union line held, but Bragg also sent cavalry units far around the Union right flank to attack their rear. They overwhelmed a small Union cavalry unit and forced the Federals to withdraw their ammunition train, which would prevent future restocking when Union supplies ran low.

The Union left flank was blissfully unaware of these developments, and at seven a.m. General Horatio P. Van Cleve's division crossed Stones River, as planned, to attack Breckinridge on the Confederate right.

When Rosecrans was informed of

the severity of the situation, he rapidly changed from offense to defense and efficiently reorganized. He halted the attack on the Confederate right, recalled the troops that had crossed the river, and moved them toward the Union right, leaving a brigade to guard the fords. Rosecrans then rode off to his right wing, arriving to find that much of it had collapsed and panicked Union troops were pouring back through the woods.

By now, two of the three Union divisions on the far right of the Union line had collapsed, and the full force of the attack was concentrated on Union general "Little Phil" Sheridan's division. Sheridan was ready. During the night, his outposts had reported enemy activity, and he had mustered his forces at four a.m. to prepare for an attack. As the Confederate attack fell on them, Sheridan's men held. When the rest of the Union right flank had collapsed and Sheridan was in danger of being outflanked, he launched a vigorous counterattack that stopped the Confederates cold and allowed him to make a skillful, orderly withdrawal. He rotated his force so it was now perpendicular to his original line, and then joined with General James Negley's division on his left. The Union line now formed a rough V, with Negley and Sheridan at the angle in the center. General George Thomas, one of the best Union generals, commanded the overall Union center and fought the battle bravely and skillfully. In a lull, a fresh Union division joined to the right of Sheridan's position, establishing a new Union line, perpendicular to the original one on the Union right. Rosecrans rapidly extended this line with two more brigades to prevent it from being flanked.

On the battlefield, the limestone rocks provided shelter from fire, but they also caused problems for both sides. Many soldiers were wounded by limestone fragments and shells ricocheting off the boulders. The limestone made it difficult to move wagons and cannons, as their wheels caught in the cracks. Since many Union horses were killed during the battle and the Confederates advanced quickly, the Union troops were forced to abandon the cannons they could not move out quickly enough by hand. The rough terrain also limited the number of cannons the Confederates could bring forward as they advanced.

Temporarily, the battle stabilized.

William S. Rosecrans

After graduating fifth in his class at West Point in 1842, William Rosecrans served in the engineer corps, then as a professor at the Point, after which he retired from the army to become a successful architect, civil engineer, and inventor. At the outbreak of the Civil War, he returned to military service, and while he had several impressive victories early in the war—in Virginia, under McClellan, and in Tennessee under Grant—Rosecrans didn't receive the recognition he felt he deserved for his role in these battles.

Rosecrans was given command of the Union Army of the Cumberland in October 1862 and was mostly pitted against Braxton Bragg, whom he defeated at Stones River. He pushed Bragg back deep into Tennessee at the cost of only 50 casualties and took Chattanooga. But he made a costly mistake at Chickamauga, where he lost two thirds of his men, which resulted in his being replaced in December 1863 by George Thomas, the Union hero of Chickamauga. Rosecrans then held a minor command in Missouri until December 1864 when he was removed again. He resigned from the army in 1867.

The combination of open fields and groves of trees gave the Union forces plenty of areas to defend, but the Confederates' need to move rapidly channeled them into open areas. The Confederate units had become badly intermingled, and the men were tiring. By ten a.m., Bragg was aware that his attack was slackening, and he ordered Breckinridge to send two of his five brigades across the river to the Confederate left to reinforce the weary soldiers.

Critical Errors

Now, for the first time in the battle, things began to go wrong for the Confederates. Bragg and the popular Breckinridge disliked each other, and Breckinridge had little regard for Bragg as a commander. Confederate cavalry had reported to Breckinridge at seven a.m. that a Union division—Van Cleve's—was crossing the river and was preparing to assail his position. Breckinridge thought he was about to come under a strong attack, so he told Bragg he could only send one brigade. Unfortunately for the Confederates, their cavalry had not seen the Union forces pull back across the river and redeploy in response to the Confederate attack on the opposite side of the battle line. A frustrated Bragg ordered Breckinridge to advance and attack any Union forces east of Stones River. When Breckinridge moved forward, he made the embarrassing discovery that there were no Union troops on his side of the river. But before he could move his troops to carry out Bragg's orders, Bragg received a false report that a strong Union force was approaching from his right, so he told Breckinridge to keep his forces in place. Sloppy cavalry reconnaissance and Rosecrans's planned-but-never-realized attack on the Confederate right, mixed with a measure of personal animosity, caused the Confederates to make these two critical mistakes that may have cost them a victory.

On the main battlefield, dead and wounded cows, horses, sheep, and dogs from nearby farms lay around the field, which gave this area the name of the Slaughter Pens. On the Union side, Sheridan's men had staved off three heavy attacks. Two of his three brigade commanders had been killed (the remaining brigade commander would be killed later in the day), and now dead and wounded littered both sides of the battlefield. His men were exhausted and their ammunition was almost gone, with no way to resupply since the Confederate cavalry units had driven away the ammunition trains. Sheridan resigned himself to the

Braxton Bragg

Braxton Bragg was a strong disciplinarian and an able trainer of troops, turning the Confederate Army of the Tennessee into a well-coordinated group of soldiers. However, he didn't get along with either his subordinates or his superiors, which undermined his ability to lead a large army and inspire confidence. However, his friend Confederate President Jefferson Davis repeatedly retained Bragg in command despite Bragg's failures and the criticism of fellow commanders.

In charge of the Army of the Tennessee beginning in 1862, Bragg pushed his forces into Kentucky, but after a series of defeats he had to retreat through most of the Tennessee ground he had gained. As a commander, he made questionable tactical decisions, like continuing frontal assaults even after they had proven futile at Perryville, Kentucky, and Shiloh, Tennessee. He suffered a humiliating defeat by William Rosecrans at Stones River after taking an initial lead, followed by another loss at Chattanooga; but then he crushed Rosecrans at Chickamauga, redeeming himself in the Confederacy's only major victory in the West.

Nevertheless, Davis was finally forced to replace Bragg in November 1863 after another significant defeat, at Missionary Ridge, Tennessee. Davis kept him on, nominally, as an advisor, but Bragg had little authority in this role.

inevitable, notified the divisions on either side he was going to have to pull back, then retreated toward the Nashville Pike, hoping to gather some ammunition from one of the other corps' supplies.

As Sheridan's men pulled back, the Confederates poured into the gap. However, the Union divisions on either side of Sheridan also coolly pulled back and fought their way to high ground just south of the Nashville Pike. On the left, one brigade, commanded by Colonel William B. Hazen, held its strong position on a wooded ridge astride the Nashville and Chattanooga railroad line. This four-acre elevated oak grove, which reports of the battle call the Round Forest, was later renamed Hell's Half Acre by the troops because of the vicious fighting that took place there. There was an open field in front of the Round Forest, and Union artillery now came into play. The Union cannons, set slightly high on the embankments and firing double loads of canister antipersonnel rounds, ripped into the Confederates, taking a huge toll. The rough terrain and their rapid advance left the Confederates without their field artillery pieces, and they had no answer to the Union cannons.

Using Hazen's brigade as an anchor, Union forces pushed back wave after wave of attacks. Hazen's brigade was the only Union force to hold its position for the entire battle. The noise from the battle was so great that some soldiers reportedly pulled old bolls of cotton from the withered stalks and stuffed it into their ears.

Meanwhile, the Confederate cavalry, having forced one ammunition train to flee, now attacked Thomas's ammunition wagons. Fortunately for the Union, they were able to cobble together enough cavalry to save the train and force the Confederates away. For the rest of the day, the Confederate and the newly arrived Union cavalry sparred, but there was no more interference with the Union supply positions.

By noon, Van Cleve's men had arrived from Stones River, just in time to reinforce the Union positions. Rosecrans organized what turned out to be the final Union defensive line, roughly along the embankment of the Nashville Pike and the Nashville and Chattanooga railroad tracks, forming a V. The new Union position was very compact, and it was easy to move units back and forth quickly to counter an attack.

Bragg did not continue to attack the Union right, but instead decided that his best hope for a decisive victory lay in overwhelming the Union forces at Round Forest. He ordered the only fresh troops available for the attack—Breckinridge's four brigades—to cross the river and join the attack, but Breckinridge moved unenthusiastically and slowly. It was four p.m. when Breckinridge's first two brigades arrived on the scene, and they were committed to the battle piecemeal in a series of unimaginative frontal attacks. As soon as Breckinridge's next two brigades were available, they were also committed piecemeal into the fight, along with all the remaining available Confederate troops. Not surprisingly, the Confederates were repulsed with heavy losses, and the fighting tapered off as darkness fell.

That night was clear and cold, and Rosecrans met with his commanders to decide on the next day's actions. Some of the commanders felt the army was defeated and should retreat and retrench in front of Nashville before it was entirely cut off. Rosecrans, with strong support by Thomas and some others, disagreed and decided to stay and fight. The Union forces spent the night regrouping and preparing for the next round of fighting.

On the Confederate side, Bragg was certain that he had won a victory, and cabled the news back to Richmond, saying, "God has granted us a Happy New Year."

On New Year's Day, President Lincoln announced his formal Emancipation Proclamation in Washington.

Union Artillery Prevents Defeat

New Year's Day on the battlefield was relatively quiet and the weather was, for a change, clear. Before dawn, Rosecrans ordered Van Cleve's division (now commanded by Colonel Samuel Beatty because Van Cleve had been wounded), supported by another brigade, to cross the river and occupy a gradually sloping hill that overlooked two fords across Stones River. Later that day, Union forces pulled back from Round Forest. Confederates took possession of this position, and Breckinridge took two of his brigades back across the river to his prebattle positions. There were some Confederate probes

against the Union side, but most of the rest of the day was taken up with treating the wounded and burying the dead.

The Confederate cavalry continued to harass the Union rear along Rosecrans's line of communications to Nashville. They attacked a wagon train near LaVergne, routed the guard, and destroyed about 30 wagons. At this point, the Confederates made another mistake. Bragg took the cavalry reports of heavy activity along the roads as a sign that Rosecrans was preparing to retreat. He sat back, rested his troops, and waited for the Union forces to withdraw completely.

To Bragg's dismay, the next morning, January 2, Rosecrans was still in place and well dug in. Bragg also learned that Van Cleve's/Beatty's division had crossed the river and occupied high ground not far from Breckinridge's position. Bragg was afraid this high ground would be used to fire on Confederate lines, and he ordered Breckinridge to take the slope. This attack against the well-supported Union forces was ill advised.

At three thirty on that cold, rainy afternoon, the Confederate artillery began a preparatory barrage, and at four p.m. Breckinridge's division

"moved to the charge in perfect order." As the Confederate attack moved from east to west toward the river, it initially succeeded. Rosecrans later wrote, "Breckinridge advanced steadily, to within 100 yards of the front of Van Cleve, when a short and fierce contest ensued. Van Cleve's division giving way, retired in considerable confusion across the river at McFadden's Ford, followed closely by the enemy." As the Union troops were pushed back in disorder, their rapid withdrawal drew the Confederates to follow them.

But as the Confederates raced forward, they came into an open field in full view of the Union forces. On the other side of the river, less than a mile away, Major John Mendenhall had eight batteries of artillery, altogether more than 55 guns. As Breckinridge's soldiers came into range, the Union gunners opened fire, slaughtering the advancing Confederates. The Union infantry charged forward, cheering loudly, and Breckinridge was driven back to his starting point. Of the 4500 men he made the assault with, 1700 were killed, wounded, or missing. A member of General Bragg's staff described the episode as "a terrible affair, although short."

Samuel Beatty's brigade staggers Patrick Cleburne's attacking Confederates with a sharp volley on the first day of battle.

The next day, January 3, the Confederate cavalry was finally driven off, and a large supply train, escorted by a reinforced brigade, reached Rosecrans. Late in the day, Union forces attacked the center of the Confederate line and pushed it back. By that time, it was raining again and Bragg, having suffered heavy casualties and fearing that the rising Stones River would isolate his weakened forces, decided to retreat. Some of his generals argued against it, but that night the Confederates withdrew through the rain to Murfreesboro, and then continued to Tullahoma, Tennessee, 36 miles to the south.

The Aftermath

Bragg had fought fairly well, if not imaginatively. However, once again he had antagonized his subordinates, especially Breckinridge, whose command had been destroyed because of Bragg's foolish orders. Unfortunately for the Confederacy, Bragg's friendship with Davis trumped all his subordinates' complaints, and he remained in command.

Rosecrans emerged from the battle with his reputation enhanced. He had demonstrated cool under fire, even when a cannon ball decapitated his chief of staff, Lieutenant

Colonel Julius Garesché, who was riding next to him (Garesché's replacement as Rosecrans's chief of staff was Brigadier General James A. Garfield, later the 20th President of the United States). A Union history noted, "With blood from a slight wound on his cheek, in a light blue army overcoat, through the mud and rain of the battlefield, [Rosecrans] rode along the line inspiring his troops with the confidence he felt at the final result."

Stones River had been one of the bloodiest battles of the war. The numbers are imprecise, but Union forces suffered over 12,500 casualties and the Confederates over 10,000.

After the battle, Rosecrans occupied Murfreesboro; but, as usual, he settled in and made no effort to pursue Bragg, to Washington's chagrin. Still, Lincoln was gracious and effusive in his praise. Stones River was not much of a Union victory, but timing was everything. After the defeats at Fredericksburg and the Union's first attempt to capture Vicksburg in December 1862, Lincoln and the Union had not had a victory in months, and this cast a serious pall on the formal announcement of the Emancipation Proclamation. Stones River was no

Antietam, which had allowed Lincoln to make the Preliminary Emancipation Proclamation, but it was enough to bolster the troops.

Stones River National Battlefield

Almost immediately after the battle of Stones River, the soldiers of Colonel William B. Hazen's brigade built a memorial to their brigade near their defensive position at Round Forest, or Hell's Half Acre. It still exists today, probably the oldest intact Civil War monument standing in its original location. Aside from the Hazen Monument, little was done to the battlefield until 1896, when the Stones River Battlefield Park Association was formed to try to build a park to commemorate the battle and those who died there. In 1927 the area became the Stones River National Military Park, consisting of 324 acres next to the Stones River near Murfreesboro, Tennessee. In 1960, it became the Stones River National Battlefield.

Today the Stones River National Battlefield encompasses 584 acres, but much of the nearly 4000-acre battlefield is privately owned. In 1990, the Federal government listed Stones River National Battlefield as one of 25 Civil War battlefields most endangered by development.

Portions of the battlefield are accessible by walking or driving, and the Stones River National Cemetery, established in 1865, is sited there with more than 6000 Union graves. Inside the Visitors Center are numerous exhibits, including captured Confederate regimental flags, Union cannons captured by the Confederates, and a painting showing the Confederate side of the attack on Hell's Half Acre. The center also contains a time capsule containing a number of Confederate artifacts found in Hazen's monument in 1985 when it was opened for structural repairs; these include round and rifled cannon rounds, small arms rifled musket barrels, and a cedar staff. There are a number of theories about the significance of the items, from Masonic symbols to the speculation that some Confederates carried such staffs into battle because they had no weapons. Interestingly, the artifacts were placed in a location where it was clear they were not intended to be discovered.

The driving tour of the battlefield begins at the Visitors Center and has several stops with historic markers, including the Slaughter Pen, the Artillery Monument next to McFadden's Ford, the Round Forest, and the nearby Hazen Monument. The graves of more than 50 members of Hazen's brigade who died in the battle surround the large stone cube.

Some sites outside the main battlefield may be visited as well, including the headquarters of generals Bragg and Rosecrans, and Fortress Rosecrans—a large, earthen fortress and supply dump built in Murfreesboro shortly after the battle as a base for the Union campaigns against Chattanooga and Atlanta.

Allow two to four hours for a visit to the battlefield and Fortress Rosecrans, more to tour the battle sites outside the park boundary.

Visitor Information

615-893-9501;
www.nps.gov/stri/
Hours: Daily, 8 a.m. until 5 p.m.; closed December 25.
Admission: Free.
Accessibility: The Visitors Center information facilities are accessible to visitors who use wheelchairs or have sight or hearing impairments. Restrooms are accessible. A captioned version of the slide program and an audiotape tour of the battlefield are available upon request. Information about paved trails is available at the information desk. About 60 percent of the historic features can be viewed from a motor vehicle.
Special Events: From mid-June through mid-August, rangers offer regularly scheduled walks and talks. During the summer, there are evening tours called "Hallowed Ground: A Lantern Tour of Stones River National Cemetery." An annual artillery encampment featuring live cannon firing by several guns is held in July. Call for dates and times.
Getting There: The Stones River National Battlefield is 30 miles southeast of Nashville, Tennessee. Take I-24 to exit 78B, then follow state highway 96 east to the intersection of U.S. routes 41/70. Turn left and take routes 41/70 north to Thompson Lane, then turn left on Thompson Lane. Exit to Old Nashville Highway and follow signs to the Visitors Center.

This exhibit captures events that occurred at the Battle of Galveston, January 1, 1863, including a 32-pounder aimed at a large mural of Galveston's waterfront during the fighting.

Museum of Southern History

The Museum of Southern History is located on the beautifully landscaped grounds of Southern National Bank in Sugar Land, Texas, on the outskirts of Houston. The two-story brick building is modeled after Thomas Jefferson's Virginia country haven, Poplar Forest, begun in 1806. Also open to the public is an original sharecropper's home that was moved to the grounds. The museum's permanent exhibit chronicles the antebellum history of the South, the onset of the Civil War, and its effects upon generations of Southern society.

One of the centerpieces of the Civil War collection features Colonel Benjamin Terry's Texas Rangers, the 8th Texas Cavalry—the only Texas cavalry corps that served during the war. This exhibit narrates the history of the regiment and includes weapons and equipment used by its soldiers, such as a saber, a double-barrel shotgun, and a specially modified cavalryman's canteen. Colonel Terry's death during the regiment's first battle, at Woodsonville, Kentucky, is memorialized in a Bruce Marshall painting on display in the museum. There are also separate exhibits devoted to other members of Terry's Rangers, including Benjamin Weeks, whose collection includes his pistols, papers, and accounts of his postwar reunion activities.

Artifacts from the Battle of Galveston are displayed in another gallery. These include a large mural of Galveston's waterfront during the fighting, and a bell from the U.S.S. *Harriet Lane*. When the Confederates boarded the *Lane*, one of the victors, Albert Lea, found his son, a Union officer, dying on the deck.

The museum houses two weapons collections. One is of U.S. military pistols, including several models of the flintlock single-shot U.S. Martial Pistol, obsolete before the war but still used by some Confederate militia units. The second collection features an extensive array of major field artillery rounds from the early 1800s until the 1860s, along with other equipment used by artillerymen, including friction primers.

Several personal exhibits highlight a host of eclectic items from the period. The exhibit of Captain Wells Johnson, a Texas officer who served with the 36th Alabama Infantry, displays his regimental flag and the coffee can in which he hid it for years to prevent it from being taken by Union soldiers. Also on exhibit is a collection of wooden canes that Captain Frank Chilton, Company H, 4th Texas Infantry, recovered from several battlefields. The artifacts from the wife of Texas general Albert Sidney Johnston, killed at Shiloh, focus on the experiences of a soldier's wife and include personal possessions, as well as memorabilia from Civil War veterans conventions Mrs. Johnston attended.

Visitor Information

281-269-7171;
www.museumofsouthernhistory.org
Hours: Tuesday to Friday, 10 a.m. until 4 p.m.; Saturday and Sunday 1 p.m. until 4 p.m.
Admission: Minimal charge for adults and children over five.
Accessibility: The upper floor is accessible by elevator.
Getting There: The museum is located in Sugar Land, Texas.

From Houston: Go south on U.S. 59 (Southwest Freeway) and take the Sugar Land exit. Stay on the feeder and pass Dairy Ashford/Sugar Creek Boulevard. Turn right at the Southern National Bank, inspired by Monticello. Follow the driveway to the museum behind the bank.

From the Richmond–Rosenberg area: Go north on U.S. 59. Take the Sugar Creek/Dairy Ashford exit, turn left under the freeway, and left again at the feeder. Go 0.2 miles and turn right at the Southern National Bank. Follow the driveway to the museum behind the bank.

EDGED WEAPONS

Civil War actions rarely resulted in prolonged hand-to-hand combat, and edged weapons—bayonets, knives, and swords—accounted for very few wounds, perhaps 2 percent. One set of specific statistics showed that of the approximately 250,000 wounded treated in Union hospitals, only 922 were the victims of sabers or bayonets.

Bayonets

The bayonet, a blade attached to the muzzle of a musket, was a standard piece of equipment for both the Union and Confederate infantries. Before the Civil War, the bayonet was considered a key part of any infantry assault, but the long range of the rifled musket marked the end of the planned bayonet charge as an effective tactic.

There were two common types of bayonets—the socket bayonet and the sword bayonet. The socket bayonet was a triangular blade between a foot and a foot and a half long, intended to be used like a lance. It was light, with a tubular sleeve that fit over the muzzle and a slot to engage in the stud on the rifle. It was offset to one side so it did not interfere with the push of the ramrod when the musket was being loaded.

Sword or saber bayonets were similar to a knife, with a handle and a sharp edge. The hilt, offset like the socket bayonet so as not to interfere with the ramrod, slid onto a bar or stud on the barrel and usually had an encircling ring that fit over the muzzle. These were much heavier than the socket bayonet and made aiming musket fire more difficult, so they were not popular in combat. However, the sword bayonet was much more versatile than the socket bayonet, so it had a charm all its own. It was useful for digging in when under fire, for cooking and cutting food, and from time to time for fights in camp.

Swords and Sabers

Swords were rarely used as combat weapons in the Civil War, but they were very popular as symbols of rank and status. In 1861, the Union Ordnance Corps featured separate-issue swords or sabers for noncommissioned officers, musicians, foot artillery, light artillery, staff and staff corps, officers' light cavalry, foot officers, general staff, and the cavalry saber. The Confederacy had the same types of swords, and it is often difficult to tell them apart.

General officers and many others carried ornate and decorative sabers, never meant to be used in battle—gifts from friends or family or marks of esteem for distinguished service. Tiffany supplied swords to the Union army, and their presentation swords were very popular. They created gemstone-encrusted presentation swords for, among others, Admiral David Farragut and generals Ulysses S. Grant and William T. Sherman.

Both navies used cutlasses for their boarding parties. The 1841 Navy Cutlass was basically a short foot-artillery sword with a D-shaped guard around the handle. These were carried by the U.S. Navy during

U.S. Army field and staff officer's sword carried by Confederate general Thomas J. "Stonewall" Jackson

the Mexican War and used by the North (and variants by the South) during the Civil War. They were replaced by the U.S. Model 1861 Navy Cutlass (also known as the 1860 Cutlass), with a traditional full brass bowl guard, wire-bound leather grip, and curved blade. It was an efficient fighting tool and was used by the navy long after the war.

While swords were ceremonial and not really meant to be used in hand-to-hand fighting, swords were widely used by both sides in battle, especially for the seemingly innocuous task of brandishing. Officers usually fought with drawn swords so they could show leadership and give visual directions to their men in the deafening roar of the fight. During a line attack, for example, officers were spaced along the line and used their swords to wave directions to their men, to keep their portion of the line in order and moving at the proper speed.

Cavalry sabers were different. For the cavalry trooper, sabers were a legitimate weapon and formidable in the hands of someone skilled in their use. But using a large saber while

Union infantrymen proudly pose with their weapons fixed with socket bayonets. Bowie knives, right, were carried by both sides but were used more for utilitarian purposes than for fighting.

controlling a horse in battle took time to learn, and stories abound of Union cavalrymen cutting off the ears of their own horses early in the war. The most common saber early in the war, the Heavy Cavalry (Dragoon) Sabre, Model 1840, had a 36-inch blade and was known as being difficult to handle. It was replaced by the U.S. Cavalry Sabre, Model 1860. The blade was reduced in width, shortened to 34 inches, and the entire weapon was lightened. Almost all Confederate cavalry sabers were a copy of one or the other.

Knives

Soldiers on both sides carried knives. Union troops carried homemade ones, while the Confederates carried ones manufactured by the Confederate Ordnance Department, which called them side knives. Confederate knives were meant for fighting and generally had substantial knuckle guards, which Union knives lacked. Both sides called their knives Bowie knives, and there appears to be no difference between a Bowie knife and any other soldier's knife during this period. Confederate knives were large and serious weapons—one specimen has a blade 16 1/2 inches long, 2 1/2 inches wide, and 1/2 inch thick.

Pikes

Incongruously, the lance or pike also appeared in the war. At least one volunteer Union cavalry unit carried them until mid-1863, but they were clearly an anachronism in the Union army.

In the Confederacy, a weapons shortage led its leaders to give serious consideration to arming troops with pikes, which they considered an effective weapon. Cheap and easy to make, they were well liked by politicians and the media.

While pikes were rhetorically popular, the Confederate infantry was appalled at the idea of facing rifled muskets with them. When they were issued to the 31st Georgia, it almost sparked a revolt. One of the most foolish ideas was the "bridle pike," with a curved sickle on the end to catch a Union cavalryman's bridle. When told of this, Confederate general Albert Sidney Johnston sarcastically asked, "What would the troopers be doing with their pistols while these spearmen were catching their reins?"

Nevertheless, many pikes were made, though virtually all wound up stored in armories.

Battle and Surrender at Appomattox Court House

On April 6, 1865, the Confederacy was all but defeated. General Robert E. Lee and part of the Army of Northern Virginia slipped past the Union forces surrounding Petersburg and Richmond and headed west, with Union infantry close behind and Union cavalry on the flanks. The retreating Confederate troops, understandably demoralized, were involved in three sharp fights that day near Sailor's Creek. At the end of the battles 6000 Confederates had surrendered, leading Lee to cry, "My God! Has the Army been dissolved?"

The next day, April 7, Grant sent a letter to Lee pointing out the "hopelessness of further resistance on the part of the Army of Northern Virginia in this struggle . . . asking of you the surrender of the Army of Northern Virginia."

However, Lee was not ready to give up. In his reply to Grant's letter, he said, "I do not think the emergency has arisen to call for the surrender of this army." That evening,

Lee and his shattered force arrived in Appomattox County, Virginia, hoping to reach supply trains at Appomattox Station. He had sent General R. Lindsay Walker and a force of troops ahead to secure the supplies, but he learned that Union general Phil Sheridan and his cavalry had driven them off. Lee's supplies were now in Union hands.

Lee's men set up camp one mile north of a small hamlet, Appomattox Court House. There Lee met with his corps commanders, generals John B. Gordon and James Longstreet, and his nephew, cavalry commander General Fitzhugh "Fitz" Lee, to discuss their situation. Hoping that the Union force at the Station was only unsupported cavalry, Lee decided to attack. At nine a.m. on Palm Sunday, April 9, Lee ordered Gordon's decimated corps of a few thousand men (their normal size was at least 24,000) to attack, break through the Federal cavalry, and recapture the supplies. Fitzhugh Lee's cavalry led the advance, and

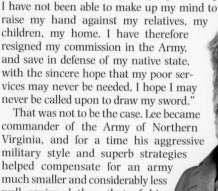

Robert E. Lee

Robert E. Lee, son of Revolutionary War hero "Light Horse Harry" Lee, was known for his military acumen and leadership skills, as well as his honor and moral character. After graduating second in his class at West Point, he held a variety of military posts and distinguished himself during the Mexican War under General Winfield Scott, who called Lee "the greatest military genius in America."

Although Lee disapproved of secession, his abiding loyalty to Virginia led him to the difficult choice of resigning from the U.S. Army on April 20, 1861. As he wrote to his sister, "With all my devotion to the Union and the feeling of loyalty and duty of an American citizen, I have not been able to make up my mind to raise my hand against my relatives, my children, my home. I have therefore resigned my commission in the Army, and save in defense of my native state, with the sincere hope that my poor services may never be needed, I hope I may never be called upon to draw my sword."

That was not to be the case. Lee became commander of the Army of Northern Virginia, and for a time his aggressive military style and superb strategies helped compensate for an army much smaller and considerably less well equipped than that of his opponent—until Ulysses S. Grant took command of the Union army. Against Grant's dogged fighting style, Lee could no longer make up for the deficit in men and supplies. He was forced to surrender on April 9, 1865.

the apprehensive Confederate soldiers moved forward.

The first forces Gordon's men encountered were a few Union cannons and a brigade of cavalry. The Confederates swept them away, but were then slowed by two fresh Union cavalry brigades. As they approached Appomattox Station, they found Grant had not only positioned more cavalry there but had also rushed in a large number of infantry. Gordon's force was met by elements of Union general Edward Ord's Army of the James, and after a brief firefight, Gordon's outnumbered and outgunned troops broke and fell back. At the same time, two Union corps had cut off Longstreet's rear guard. Grant had Lee surrounded on three sides. The only way Lee could move was northwest, but there were no supplies there.

Lee ordered truce flags sent out at about eleven that morning, then sent a messenger to find Grant. Meanwhile Grant, exhausted and suffering from a severe tension headache, approached the crossroads of Appomattox Court House, where Lee's messenger found him. Grant read the message, which said in part, "I now ask an interview, in accordance with the offer (of surrender)."

Grant's headache disappeared. He immediately dismounted, and wrote, "I . . . will push forward to the front for the purpose of meeting you," then sent it back to Lee.

After reading Grant's letter, Lee, his aide-de-camp, Lieutenant Colonel Charles Marshall, and Private Joshua O. Johns rode toward Appomattox Court House.

Marshall and Johns moved ahead to find a meeting place for the generals. In the village Marshall saw a local resident named Wilmer McLean near the courthouse. He asked McLean if there was a suitable place

for the two generals to meet. McLean first took them to an empty house with no furniture and then, when Marshall said that would not be acceptable for such a historic meeting, McLean offered his own home. Marshall looked at the fine house and, running short of time, accepted and sent word back to Lee.

That the meeting was held in the McLean home was one of the great ironies of the war. In 1861, McLean, a merchant and sugar importer, lived with his family along the creek of Bull Run in Virginia. There were two major battles fought virtually in McLean's front yard, as well as a constant parade of armies through the area. At the First Battle of Bull Run (Manassas), General P.G.T. Beauregard used McLean's home as his headquarters, and a Union cannonball went through the McLeans' outside kitchen. To get away from the war, McLean moved his family to Appomattox Court House, a quiet village about 90 miles southwest of Richmond. McLean must have been struck by the irony of having America's greatest war start in his front yard and end in his front room almost four years later.

Lee arrived at the McLean House first, about one o'clock, and he and two officers entered the large parlor. About half an hour later, General Grant entered alone, greeting Lee in the center of the room. Grant's staff waited outside, and after a few minutes, were called into the room.

Grant sat in the center of the room, and Lee sat near the front window. The contrast between the two has been extensively commented upon. The tall, erect Lee, with his fine silver beard and hair, had dressed that morning prepared to meet Grant and surrender. He wore full-dress grays buttoned at the throat, a gray hat, almost new clean boots, a fine sword, and long gloves.

Grant, darker, shorter, slightly stooped, had no idea what the day would bring when it began, so he had dressed in his standard uniform—unbuttoned blue blouse with a vest underneath, boots without spurs, and no sword. It has been famously noted that his uniform was that of a private soldier, except for shoulder boards showing his rank.

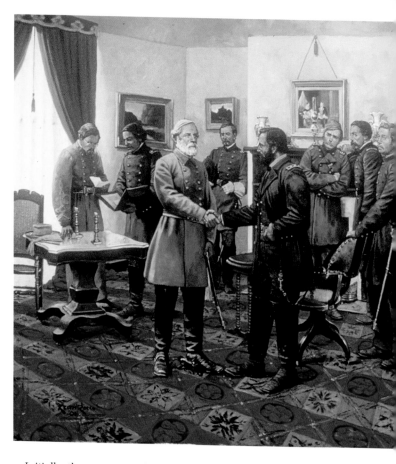

Initially the two generals talked about the Mexican War, and Grant told Lee they had met in Mexico. In what must have been an awkward moment, Lee said he had been told that but was not able to remember Grant's face.

The two talked about the Mexican War for almost half an hour, Grant probably too embarrassed to get to the point. Lee finally asked about the terms of the surrender and Grant said they would be as he had written Lee before. All officers and enlisted men would be paroled, but all Confederate military equipment must be surrendered. The conversation drifted again, then Lee asked Grant to put his terms in writing. Grant was provided with a small table where he rapidly wrote them out, using copying paper to make three copies. He noticed Lee's sword, then added a sentence that allowed the officers to keep their side arms, horses, and personal belongings. When Grant finished, he passed the document to Lee, who put on his glasses and read it over. General Horace Porter, one of Grant's staff members, was taking detailed notes of the meeting when Lee asked to write in a word that Grant had mistakenly omitted in the terms of surrender. Grant agreed but Lee had no pencil, so Porter lent his pencil to

Lee, realizing that it was about to become part of history. Fortunately for Porter, Lee returned it.

Lee pointed out that in the Confederate army, the enlisted cavalrymen and artillerymen owned their horses (Union soldiers' horses belonged to the government), and asked that they—in addition to the officers—be allowed to keep them to farm once they returned home. Grant agreed, but did not put it in the document. Lee wrote a letter formally accepting the surrender. Lee mentioned that his men had been without rations for several days, so Grant told his staff to have 25,000 rations distributed to the Confederates. A Native American on Grant's staff, Ely Parker, copied the final document of surrender.

At a little before three p.m., Lee shook hands with Grant, bowed to the other officers, and left the room. He mounted his iron-gray horse, Traveller, and General Grant stepped down from the porch. Grant saluted him by raising his hat, and all the Union officers did the same. Lee raised his hat in return, and then rode off to break the news to his army. The Union soldiers were understandably elated, but Grant stifled any excessive celebrations to avoid the appearance of gloating.

The formal surrender involved a

The first meeting of Lee and Grant in the McLean parlor. Shortly after the signing, Federal officers removed most of the furnishings as souvenirs, and since no sketches or photographs were taken of the actual event, contemporary artists were hampered in the accuracy of their depictions. This recent painting by Keith Rocco correctly portrays the marble-topped table used by Lee and the wooden spindle-legged one used by Grant to write out the terms of surrender. Officers in attendance included Colonel Charles Marshall (Lee's aide, far left) and General Phil Sheridan (leaning forward at right).

derly fold their flags, battle-worn and torn, blood-stained, heart holding colors, and lay them down." Reflecting on the deaths, the battles, and the future, he later wrote, "It was by miracles we have lived to see this day, any of us standing here . . . memories that bound us together as no other bond . . . was not such manhood to . . . be welcomed back into a Union so tested and assured."

The surrender of the infantry of Lee's Army of Northern Virginia took place on April 12, 1865, four years to the day after Confederate batteries fired on Fort Sumter.

ceremony known as the "stacking of arms," which took place three days later. It was presided over by Union general Joshua Lawrence Chamberlain, one of the heroes of Gettysburg, because generals Grant, George W. Meade, and Sheridan had all left Appomattox. Lee stayed, but understandably did not watch the ceremony.

Chamberlain noted it was a "depressing chill gray morning." As the Confederates moved forward to lay down their arms, Chamberlain—knowing he would be criticized for the gesture later—led his Union soldiers in a salute. He described the emotional ceremony later. "They fix bayonets, stack arms; then hesitatingly, remove cartridge-boxes and lay them down . . . [next] they ten-

Appomattox Court House National Historical Park

The present National Park area was authorized as a Battlefield Site on June 18, 1930, and then transferred from the War Department to the National Park Service on August 10, 1933. It was designated a National Historical Monument on August 13, 1935, and a National Historical Park on April 15, 1954.

The park encompasses approximately 1800 acres in rural central Virginia, three miles north of Appomattox. On the site are 27 original 19th-century buildings restored to their 1865 appearance. Markers designate Grant's and Lee's head-

One of the parole passes issued to a Confederate soldier at Appomattox on April 10 and 11, 1865, "to go to his home, and there remain undisturbed." Many Confederate veterans carried their passes as a badge of honor for serving with Lee to the war's end.

quarters, the site of the last shots fired by the Confederate artillery and infantry, and the road where the arms-stacking ceremony took place, as well as a small Confederate cemetery.

The Visitors Center is in the restored Appomattox Courthouse. The original courthouse was built in 1846, one year after Appomattox County was established, but it burned down in 1892 and was rebuilt in the town of Appomattox, three miles away. The present courthouse and square were reconstructed in 1963–64. It should be noted that the meeting between Lee and Grant did not take place in the original courthouse. The reason for the confusion is that the town's name was Appomattox Court House; Court House (two words) means the town, but Courthouse (one word) is the building. The two generals met in the parlor of the nearby McLean House.

The Visitors Center includes interpretive displays, museum exhibits, a theater, and a bookstore. A large "light map" systematically traces the movements of Grant and Lee to their final meeting, and there are many original artifacts from the surrender. Some of the more interesting are the pencil Lee used to write on the surrender document, and the only "outside observer" at the meeting—a rag doll left by McLean's young daughter Lula, in the parlor. Union lieutenant colonel Thomas W. C. Moore took the doll, and now the Silent Witness is on display in the Visitors Center.

A 70-seat theater shows two different 15-minute slide programs on an hourly schedule. One—a chronological slide program of the events from April 1 through April 12, 1865, that led to the meeting and surrender—is shown every hour on the half hour. The second program, shown every hour on the hour, consists of first-person accounts of soldiers who were present at the surrender.

The McLean House (Surrender House) was originally built as a tavern in 1848 and was used on April 9, 1865, for the surrender meeting between Lee and Grant. The house was also used the next day for the Surrender Commissioners meeting, and over the next few days as a Union headquarters.

In the fall of 1867, the McLeans left Appomattox Court House and defaulted on loans, so the Surrender House was sold at public auction on November 29, 1869. On January 1, 1891, the property was sold to speculators. The home was dismantled and packed for shipping to Chicago as an exhibit at the 1893 World's Columbian Exposition, but the project fell apart. Fortunately, the speculators made very detailed drawings of the house, so there was solid documentation of the building's location and appearance. Many of its dismantled bricks and other bits and pieces remained on-site. In 1940, after considerable debate, Congress created Appomattox Court House National Historical Monument. It

The McLean House also served as Union headquarters in the days following the Confederate surrender.

that worked 24 hours a day for three days printing over 28,000 parole passes for the Confederates who laid down their arms. Today it contains some of these parole papers.

In the village are also a law office, general store, stable, county jail, and four private homes from 1865. A full visit to the village will take at least two hours.

Visitor Information

434-352-8987, ext. 26;
www.nps.gov/apco

Hours: Daily, 8:30 a.m. until 5 p.m.; closed Thanksgiving, December 25, New Year's Day, and George Washington's and Martin Luther King's birthdays.

Admission: Moderate weekly charge per adult over 16 and per vehicle from Memorial Day until Labor Day; discounted fees during the off-season.

Accessibility: All parking areas, the Courthouse/Visitors Center, bookstore, restrooms, drinking fountains, and living-history programs are wheelchair accessible. A Braille map and folder, captioned slide program, and large-print brochures are available upon request. Wheelchairs are available for use in the historic village and a stair climber is available at the McLean House.

Special Events: From Memorial Day to Labor Day, and occasionally on weekends in the spring and fall, the park offers a full schedule of daily programs, including living-history programs, Ranger talks, and reenactors portraying historical figures from the 1860s. During the off-season, only audiovisual programs are available.

Getting There: The closest airport is Lynchburg, Virginia, 25 miles west.

From Richmond: Take U.S. 360 west to Jetersville, then state route 307 to U.S. 460. Go west on Route 460 to Appomattox. In Appomattox, take state route 24 east and follow the signs to Appomattox Court House National Historical Park, about three miles. The park is on the right.

From Roanoke: Take U.S. 460 east to state route 24, about 20 miles east of Lynchburg. Take Route 24 east and follow the signs to Appomattox Court House National Historical Park, about three miles. The park is on the right.

included the plan to reconstruct the area, but World War II intervened, and it was not until late November 1947 that bids for the reconstruction of the McLean House were opened. On April 9, 1949, 84 years after the historic meeting between Lee and Grant in its parlor, the National Park Service opened the McLean House. The McLean House is not a reconstruction but a restoration (defined in part as the replacement of missing elements).

Only a few of the furnishings in the house are original. General Ord paid 40 dollars for the marble-topped table where Lee sat. After offering it to Mrs. Grant (who graciously refused), he gave it to his own wife. Today the table is in the Chicago Historical Society's Civil War Room.

The small wooden table where Grant wrote the terms of the surrender went to General Sheridan, who paid 20 dollars for it. He gave it to his favorite staff officer, General George Armstrong Custer, whose wife Elizabeth carefully kept it for the rest of her life. One veteran called it "the Ark of the Covenant to all survivors of the Civil War." Today it resides in the Smithsonian's National Museum of American History, Behring Center, in Washington, D.C.

The rest of the area around the house—the McLean Ice House, the Outside Kitchen, and the McLean Slave Quarters—was reconstructed in 1965.

The Clover Hill Tavern, adjacent to the Courthouse, had a printing press

Arlington National Cemetery and the Robert E. Lee Memorial (Arlington House)

Though Arlington Cemetery may be better known for the modern-day Kennedy grave site and the Tomb of the Unknowns, its Civil War origins are in evidence throughout the grounds, as well as at Arlington House, the former home of Robert E. Lee that is now known as the Robert E. Lee Memorial.

Arlington National Cemetery was established in 1864 to handle Civil War fatalities, the growing numbers of which were overwhelming nearby cemeteries. By war's end, some 16,000 people had been buried here, among them both Union and Confederate soldiers and hundreds of former slaves.

Today there are more than 260,000 graves—veterans from every war our nation has fought (including the Revolutionary War, veterans of which were reinterred after 1900), those who have served in the military or been awarded military honors, as well as military spouses and dependent children.

History of Arlington National Cemetery and Arlington House

Perhaps there is no more poignant embodiment of the war's entwining ironies than these 600-plus acres. What began as a domestic shrine to the nation's most honored Founding Father and was passed in marriage to one of its leading military officers became a cemetery through the actions of a Georgia-born Union general whose hatred for the Confederacy was uncompromising.

The original owner of what is now the cemetery grounds and Arlington House, George Washington Parke Custis, spent his childhood at Mount Vernon, where he lived with his grandmother, Martha Washington, and his step-grandfather, George Washington. (Custis's father, John Parke Custis, was one of Martha Washington's children by her first husband. When he died of camp fever during the Revolutionary War, his children went to live with their grandmother.)

Upon the death of Mrs. Washington in 1802, George Washington Parke Custis inherited this land and erected Arlington House as a shrine to his step-grandfather. The house was accented with memorabilia of General and Mrs. Washington, and Custis reportedly would entertain guests by pitching the tents used by Washington at Yorktown and telling stories about his famous relation while playing the violin. Custis brought with him 60 slaves from Mount Vernon, using them to work his plantation.

Of Custis's four children, only one survived to adulthood, his daughter Mary Anna Randolph Custis. She married a distant cousin named Robert E. Lee, whose father, "Light Horse Harry" Lee, was a hero of the Revolutionary War and a member of one of the founding families of Virginia.

When Custis died in 1857, Mary inherited the house and the surrounding land, as well as her father's slaves. Robert E. Lee never legally owned the land, but he did supervise the plantation and the slaves who worked it.

In March of 1861, Lee was appointed commander of the 1st U.S. Cavalry by the newly inaugurated President Lincoln. After Virginia seceded in April, Lee sent a brief letter to the Secretary of War, resigning his commission and stating, "Though opposed to secession and deprecating war, I could take no part in an invasion of Southern States."

On April 22, Lee left Arlington for Richmond, where he accepted command of Virginia's military forces. He never returned to Arlington House. On April 27, he wrote to his wife, "War is inevitable and there is no telling when it will burst around you," and urged her to secure the silver and portraits brought from Mount Vernon and move to safety.

Three weeks later Mrs. Lee and the children left Arlington, and soon afterward Federal troops occupied the house and grounds. (With its elevated position, Arlington was an excellent defense point for the city of Washington.) The first soldiers to arrive did quite a bit of damage, desecrating what they couldn't remove. With the arrival of Brigadier General Irvin McDowell, who would use the house as his headquarters, an effort was made to save what he could of the family's possessions, especially those related to George Washington; but by the time order was established, much had been lost. For months after, it was said that peddlers were selling Washington-related artifacts on the city streets.

The following year, the U.S. government passed an act that required owners of properties in areas of insurrection to pay taxes in person.

Occupied in 1861 by Federal troops, the former estate of Robert E. Lee was confiscated by the U.S. government for delinquent taxes in 1864.

The house and estate at Arlington were valued at $26,810, and a tax of $92.07 was levied. Mrs. Lee tried to pay the tax through her cousin, but as he wasn't the legal owner, payment was refused and the land and all the property thereon were confiscated for nonpayment of taxes.

Creating the Cemetery

By 1864 cemeteries in and around the city of Washington were just about full. General Montgomery Meigs, Quartermaster of the U.S. Army, was given the task of finding outlying land suitable for a military cemetery. Almost immediately, the story goes, and without bothering to look elsewhere, he suggested the former home of Robert E. Lee.

Meigs, a native Georgian, was known to have an unflinching hatred for those of his Southern brethren who had sided with the Confederacy. What better way to punish the Confederacy's icon than to surround Lee's home with graves?

The first official burial took place on May 13, 1864, when William Christman, a private in Company G of the 67th Pennsylvania Infantry, was buried in what is now Section 27. Meigs was not happy with the placement. He'd ordered that burials be made in the immediate vicinity of

the house, but the officers residing there didn't fancy living that close to their fallen comrades.

Meigs not only saw to it that from then on graves were dug near the house, but he immediately began working on implementation of the Tomb of the Unknown Civil War Dead, which would eventually be erected in Mrs. Lee's rose garden.

After the War

At war's end, much of the former Lee estate was a graveyard, but in its southern section was a tightly knit community of African Americans called Freedman's Village.

Following the Act of Emancipation in September 1862, the city of Washington, D.C., had witnessed the arrival of thousands of former slaves. Washington—already bursting at the seams—had never been known for its abolitionist sympathies and was not prepared to absorb this new population, so the Federal government settled them on the southern end of Arlington Cemetery in what is now Sections 8, 47, and 25.

For the next 30 years, this was

home to more than 1100 residents who between them supported a school for both adults and children, a training facility for trades such as blacksmithing and carpentry, a home for the aged and disabled, a hospital, several churches, and a few farms. Eventually, however, the land was needed for more graves, and Freedman's Village was dismantled.

In the meantime, George Washington Custis Lee, Robert E. Lee's son, laid claim to the estate, which had been willed to him by his mother. In October 1882, the Supreme Court sided with Lee and granted him legal title to the land. Lee settled for a payment of $150,000.

In 1925 the U.S. Congress designated Arlington House as the Custis-Lee Mansion. In 1929 the house opened to the public, and in 1933 it was put under the jurisdiction of the National Park Service. In 1955 it was officially designated as the Robert E. Lee Memorial.

Arlington National Cemetery is under the jurisdiction of the U.S. Army's Military District of Washington, which oversees an average of 20 interments and inurnments (for those who have been cremated) a day. Officials estimate the current cemetery will reach full capacity sometime around 2020.

Civil War Points of Interest

Arlington Cemetery is a beautifully maintained shrine to those who have given of themselves for their country. At the Visitors Center, located off Memorial Drive, visitors are reminded that these grounds are not for recreation nor picnics.

A brochure with a map designating particular sites is available free at the center, where there are restrooms and an information desk, along with changing exhibits about the cemetery.

Section 1, along Meigs Drive, has a large concentration of Civil War grave sites. Among those buried here are the cemetery's creator, General Montgomery Meigs, and his son, John Rodgers Meigs. The son's grave includes a small monument with a bronze sculpture of a soldier lying dead on the ground, his gun just out of reach—a representation of the scene when Meigs's body was found. Young Meigs served with General Philip Sheridan in the Shenandoah Valley and was killed in what seemed like mysterious circumstances at the time. In retaliation for the death, Sheridan ordered the nearby town of Dayton, Virginia, burned to the ground, and, though some parts of the town were spared, many buildings were destroyed.

Alexander T. Augusta, among the first African American doctors to enlist in the Union army, is buried in this section, as is Abner Doubleday, erroneously credited with inventing baseball and (probably erroneously as well) with having fired the first Union shot at Fort Sumter.

Section 1 also includes the grave sites of Juliet Opie Hopkins, who was called the Florence Nightingale of the South for her heroic work at Chimborazo Hospital in Richmond, and naval hero John Rodgers, famous for his capture of the Confederate ironclad C.S.S. *Atlanta* in 1863.

In the center of the traffic circle near Section 1 stands the Philip Kearny Monument. Though little known today, General Kearny was renowned in his time as a heroic fighter. Born into a wealthy family (his father was one of the founders of the New York Stock Exchange), Kearny studied tactics at the French Cavalry School and won the Legion of Merit serving in Napoleon III's Imperial Guard. Returning home to America, he fought in the Mexican

The monument to Union lieutenant John Rodgers Meigs portrays his body as it was found at the time of his death.

War, where he lost an arm, and then in the Civil War, where he was killed at the Second Battle of Bull Run (Second Manassas). Robert E. Lee ordered Kearny's body, sword, and horse returned under a flag of truce.

Inventor and marksman Hiram Berdan is buried in Section 2, off Lee Drive, as is John Lincoln Clem. At the age of nine, Clem became a drummer boy for the 22nd Michigan Regiment and earned the nickname the Drummer Boy of Chickamauga through his bravery in that battle.

Also buried in Section 2 is David Dixon Porter, commander of the largest American fleet assembled up to that time in the 1864 attack on Fort Fisher. After the war, Porter became superintendent of the U.S. Naval Academy.

One of the Union's most famous generals, Philip Henry Sheridan, is buried in Section 2, as is the Confederate commander of the cavalry of the Army of Mississippi, Joseph "Fighting Joe" Wheeler. After the war, Wheeler was elected to Congress from the state of Alabama but was called into action again for the Spanish-American War. He is credited with urging his men on in the Battle of San Juan Hill with the incantation, "We've got the damned Yankees on the run!"

Section 2 is the resting place of a less famous soldier, but one who played an important role in American history. James Tanner lost both his legs at the Second Battle of Bull Run (Second Manassas), after which he became a clerk at the War Department in Washington. On the night of April 14, 1865, Tanner returned to his rooming house to find the street full of people waiting to hear the fate of President Lincoln, who lay fatally wounded in the Peterson house next door. When the call went out for someone proficient in shorthand to record the evening's events, Tanner volunteered. His record remains the most comprehensive of what occurred in the President's last hours.

Supreme Court Associate Justice Oliver Wendell Holmes, Jr., who was severely wounded at Antietam, is buried in Section 5, near the Kennedy grave site, and Robert Todd Lincoln, the only child of President and Mrs. Lincoln to reach maturity, is buried in Section 31, off Custis Walk. Custis and his wife are buried in Section 13, off Meigs Drive, on the crest of a hill in an area surrounded by an iron gate.

Veterans of the U.S. Colored Troops and residents of Freedman's Village are buried in Section 27, off Ord & Weitzel Drive (two names for one drive). Some of the U.S. Colored Troops are also buried in Section 23, off of McPherson Drive. Sadly, many of the gravestones of those from the village are marked only "Citizen" or "Civilian." Headstones for the U.S. Colored Troops are inscribed with the letters U.S.C.T.

Monuments and Memorials

In 1866 a burial vault was erected above the graves of the unknown Union dead whom Meigs had buried in Mrs. Lee's rose garden two years earlier. The Tomb of the Unknown Civil War Dead memorializes those buried here with this inscription:

BENEATH THIS STONE REPOSE THE BONES OF TWO THOUSAND ONE HUNDRED AND ELEVEN UNKNOWN SOLDIERS GATHERED AFTER THE WAR FROM THE FIELDS OF BULL RUN, AND THE ROUTE TO THE RAPPAHANNOCK. THEIR REMAINS COULD NOT BE IDENTIFIED. BUT THEIR NAMES AND DEATHS ARE RECORDED IN THE ARCHIVES OF THEIR COUNTRY: AND ITS GRATEFUL CITIZENS HONOR THEM AS OF THEIR NOBLE ARMY OF MARTYRS MAY THEY REST IN PEACE

In 1900 the U.S. Congress authorized that a section of Arlington Cemetery be designated for Confederate soldiers. A total of 482 soldiers from sites within the cemetery and from other nearby cemeteries were reinterred in Section 16. Unlike other gravestones in the cemetery, these are pointed. The popular explanation is that this was done to prevent Yankees from sitting on them.

In 1914 the Confederate Monument was built in the center of these graves, at Jackson Circle. The sculptor, Moses Ezekiel, himself a veteran of the Confederate army, is buried at the base of the monument, which depicts a classical female representation of the South extending a laurel wreath to the Confederate dead.

Seven years later, the Memorial Amphitheater, in Section 23, was dedicated to honor those who had died in American wars up to that time. Among the items placed in its cornerstone (laid in 1915) are a Bible; copies of the Declaration of Independence, the U.S. Constitution, and Pierre L'Enfant's design for the city of Washington; a U.S. flag; a Congressional Directory; and a photograph of President Woodrow Wilson, who attended the dedication

The Morning Room was the only place for entertaining until the center section of Arlington House was completed about 1818. In 1853 it became Mrs. Lee's Morning Room. As arthritis restricted her mobility, she answered her mail and managed the affairs of her household here. Today visitors see several original pieces in the room, including the sacks for General Washington's tents and a large painting of Washington at the Battle of Monmouth, New Jersey, painted by Mr. Custis to hang in the United States Capitol.

ceremony.

The names of the Civil War's most famous battles are among those inscribed around the frieze above the colonnade, and above the altar in the chapel are the words of Abraham Lincoln at Gettysburg: "We here highly resolve that these dead shall not have died in vain."

Arlington House

Sometime in late 1861, hearing about the damage done to their home, Robert E. Lee wrote his wife, "They cannot take away the remembrance of the spot, and the memories of those that to us rendered it sacred. That will remain with us as long as life will last, and that we can preserve."

In 1873, a few months before her death, Mrs. Lee returned to Arlington House. Since the end of the war, she and the general had been living in Lexington, Virginia, where Lee was president of Washington College, now known as Washington and Lee University. Her husband had died three years earlier and Mrs. Lee was in failing health. She was so weak that she couldn't alight from the carriage, but she could see that the mansion was in severe disrepair. "My dear home was so changed," she wrote a friend, "it seemed but a dream of the past."

How gratified Mrs. Lee would be to see Arlington House today, as it has been painstakingly restored by the National Park Service to its 1862 appearance.

A free brochure is available as visitors enter the house, and a park ranger is on hand to answer questions. Many of the furnishings are, necessarily, reproductions, but that doesn't detract from a sense of the pleasant home this must have been for the Lee family.

The Lees were married in the Family Parlor on the first floor. The portrait of Mary Lee over the parlor fireplace is an original, painted a few months before her marriage in 1831. The traveling desk, the green-silk-upholstered furniture, and the Carrara marble mantels (imported from Italy around 1825) were all brought here by the Lees.

Also on the first floor are the Center Hall, with murals high on the west end that were painted by George Washington Parke Custis about 1818; the Family Dining Room (the portrait, a copy, over the fireplace is of Custis); and the White Parlor, with crimson-upholstered furniture brought by the Lees from their time at West Point, where General Lee was superintendent for three years.

Next to the White Parlor is the Morning Room, which displays another of Custis's paintings, this one of George Washington at the Battle of Monmouth. From the

Morning Room, visitors can see the Store Room on one side and Lee's Office on the other, and, from Lee's Office, the Conservatory where Mrs. Lee kept her plants in winter.

In the north wing of the first floor are an Outer Hall Pantry, a Bath and Water Closet installed by the Lees in the 1850s and considered very modern at the time, and Mr. and Mrs. Custis's Chamber, whose wooden mantelpiece is the oldest in the house.

From the inner hall of the north wing, visitors can step down to the Winter Kitchen. This was the first part of the house built, and the Custis family lived here for several years, at which time there were 14 fireplaces and one stove for heating the structure and cooking. The Wine Cellar off the Winter Kitchen stored wine and brandy made from fruit grown at Arlington.

Off the Upper Hall on the second floor are the Lees' Chamber, where Robert E. Lee composed his letter of resignation; the Lee Boys' Chamber; and the Lee Girls' Chamber. On the mantel in the girls' chamber is a small sculpture of The Three Graces, which was a gift from their grandfather. A framed sketch sarcastically entitled *Roughing It At Arlington* was done by one of the Union soldiers who occupied the house.

Exiting to the back of the house brings visitors face-to-face with the ugly reality of plantation life, for here are the quarters of the slaves who worked the plantation and served the Lees in their home.

The Selina Gray Building (Gray was one of Mrs. Lee's personal slaves) contains an excellent exhibition about the daily lives of the slaves at Arlington, including ways in which they were allowed to earn their own money and how they spent their leisure time, like going swimming and ice skating. It's also noted that the Lees rarely sold a slave, which meant that families generally remained together.

Still, the horror of slavery is present in the details of how slaves were bought and sold as property. The well-earned honor afforded Robert E. Lee is tempered by the knowledge that not only did he use slaves to work his wife's plantation and provide the comforts of his home, but that given the opportunity upon the death of his wife's father to either free those slaves or keep them for five additional years, he chose to keep them.

At the end of the five years, in 1862, Lee wrote letters of manumission for each of the 55 remaining slaves, and sent these to Union administrators from the battlefield. One of those slaves, James Parks, remained at Arlington until his death at the age of 93 in 1929. The Secretary of War made an exception to cemetery policy and allowed Parks to be buried at Arlington, whose land he had worked as a slave early in his life and later as a free man. Parks is buried in Section 15, off of Farragut Drive.

Across from the Selina Gray Building is a small museum with an exhibition about Robert E. Lee's life and career.

Visitor Information

Robert E. Lee Memorial (Arlington House), 703-235-1530; www.nps.gov/arho
Arlington National Cemetery, 703-607-8000; www.arlingtoncemetery.org

Hours: Robert E. Lee Memorial (Arlington House), 9:30 a.m. until 4:30 p.m.; closed December 25 and New Year's Day. Arlington National Cemetery, open daily, 8 a.m. until 5 p.m., October 1 to March 31; 8 a.m. until 7 p.m., April 1 to September 30.

Special Events: Arlington House hosts seasonal interpretive talks and special activities on Robert E. Lee's birthday, January 19, and on the Lees' wedding anniversary, June 30.

Admission: Free for both.

Accessibility: Arlington House is accessible on the first floor, and the buildings behind the house are accessible. Arlington National Cemetery provides temporary passes to drive into the cemetery for those with accessibility needs.

Getting There: Arlington National Cemetery and Arlington House can be reached via Memorial Bridge coming out of Washington, D.C., or from the George Washington Memorial Parkway coming from Virginia. There is a small parking area near the Visitors Center. Visitors may also use the Metro (blue line), which has an Arlington National Cemetery stop on Memorial Drive. The Visitors Center is a five-minute walk from the Metro stop. Public buses do not go to Arlington National Cemetery. Tourmobile Sightseeing, a private touring bus company, includes stops at the Visitors Center, the Kennedy grave site, and the Tomb of the Unknowns.

The Battle of Brandy Station

The Battle of Brandy Station, on June 9, 1863, was the largest cavalry battle fought in North America, involving about 17,000 horsemen. The battle did not influence the war's outcome, but it was a harbinger of a shift in the winds of the conflict. Before the battle, the Confederate cavalry—made up of riders who had been in the saddle since they were small, knew the country, and rode their own horses—generally dominated the Union cavalry, filled with Northerners who knew little of horses and were riding on government-supplied mounts. While the Union cavalry was usually better armed with repeating rifles, Confederate skill was the determining factor in cavalry battles up to this point.

After victories at Fredericksburg and Chancellorsville, Robert E. Lee's Army of Northern Virginia moved in late May 1863 into Culpeper County, Virginia, about 75 miles southwest of Washington, D.C., and 80 miles north of Richmond. Lee was determined to strike north and to carry the war into Pennsylvania, both for strategic reasons and to provide his men with the food and clothing the chaotic Confederate supply system was unable to provide. He began to secretly move and mass his forces, and by June 5, two Confederate infantry corps were camped in and around Culpeper, while Lee's lone remaining corps pinned the Union army at Fredericksburg. At Brandy Station, six miles northwest of Culpeper, Confederate general J.E.B. Stuart was camped with his 9500 cavalry troopers along the Rappahannock River. His mission was to protect Lee against a surprise attack and to screen the Confederate army when it began to move to the Blue Ridge Mountains on its way to Pennsylvania.

Stuart requested that Lee hold a full field review of his troops to boost morale and to impress the local young women, whom Stuart had already hosted at two balls. Lee agreed, and on June 5 at Inlet Station, two miles southwest of Brandy Station, Stuart's mounted troopers passed the reviewing stand, first walking, then in full charge with sabers drawn, while cannons roared in the background. Lee could not attend the review on June 5, so Stuart repeated the whole performance on June 8.

While Stuart was parading, the Army of the Potomac commander, Major General Joseph Hooker, had reports of the Confederate cavalry's presence around Culpeper. He thought they were preparing for a raid on his supply lines, so Hooker ordered the Union cavalry commander, General Alfred Pleasonton, to take his horsemen to the area and break up Stuart's raid before it started.

Pleasonton's plan was to divide his force of 8000 cavalrymen into three divisions and attack from two directions. General John Buford's division would cross the Rappahannock at Beverly Ford two miles below Brandy Station, while generals David Gregg's and Alfred Duffié's divisions were to cross at Kelly's Ford about six miles away. Buford would attack the Confederate positions north of Brandy Station while Gregg and Duffié would attack from the Confederate rear and right flank. Unfortunately, during the Union staging the night of June 8, Duffié's force became lost, which meant Gregg's force had to wait. The opportunity for a coordinated attack was lost.

The Union's First Surprise

A dense fog hung over the Rappahannock River early on the morning of June 9. About four thirty a.m., Buford's column slipped across the river at Beverly Ford and swept past the Confederate pickets. At the sound of the first shots, Confederate brigadier general William "Grumble" Jones's brigade leapt on their mounts in various stages of dress to meet the attack. They engaged Buford's leading brigade, killed its commander, and temporarily slowed the advance. When Stuart heard gunfire from the river at his Fleetwood Heights headquarters, he moved to the scene to direct the battle.

Buford's Union horsemen moved past Jones's brigade, but then Confederate artillery on knolls at Gee House and St. James Church on either side of the Beverly Ford Road opened fire as the Union cavalry charged up the narrow road. Confederate reinforcements arrived and a battle began around the knolls. The 6th Pennsylvania Cavalry suffered the greatest casualties of the engagement when it unsuccessfully charged across a field straight into the Confederate artillery at St. James Church. Buford began to concentrate on the Confederate left, around the Cunningham farm. He

Close-hand fighting *with sabers was the order of the day at Brandy Station. In later years, sabers were abandoned in favor of more efficient weapons as they had little chance of success against veteran soldiers armed with modern weapons fighting from concealed positions. Colonel John Mosby is credited with the remark that the only real use for a sword was to hold a piece of meat over a fire for cooking.*

found a Confederate brigade blocking his advance there, behind a stone wall on a piece of high ground called Yew Ridge, and despite heavy losses Buford's men took the heights.

Around ten a.m., the Confederates finally held, then launched a counterattack against the Union front and both flanks. But now Stuart heard reports of possible enemy activity in his rear at Kelly's Ford and was told Union cavalrymen were approaching his headquarters on the prominent ridge of Fleetwood Heights. Whoever controlled this hill would have a great, perhaps decisive, advantage in the battle. Facing disaster, Stuart quickly sent two regiments to try to hold the position.

Gregg's and Duffié's Union divisions had crossed the Rappahannock at Kelly's Ford and then split up. A Confederate brigade blocked Gregg's route, so he slipped away on an unguarded but circuitous route. His lead brigade arrived below Stuart's headquarters at Fleetwood Heights at about eleven a.m.

Fighting at Fleetwood Heights

Stuart had only a token force remaining at his headquarters, along with a single 6-pounder howitzer, left by chance because it had no effective ammunition. When he saw the Union cavalry approaching, Stuart's aide had the gun moved to the crest of the hill and loaded it with whatever powder and shot the crew could find. As the Union troops moved toward Fleetwood Heights the cannon roared, firing the equivalent of blanks. It was enough. The leader of the Union advance force paused, concerned there might be a line of guns set just over the top of the hill (a favorite Confederate tactic). When the main Union force arrived, they charged up the western slope of the hill and near the top were met by the Confederate lead elements sent from St. James Church.

As the two groups clashed, a second Union unit swung around east and attacked up the eastern slope of Fleetwood Hill, but they were met by another force of Confederate horsemen from St. James. Soon the summit of the hill became the site of spectacular cavalry charges, clashing sabers, and dismounted troops firing as the horsemen thundered past.

Five miles south of Brandy Station, another battle was raging. Colonel Alfred Duffié had split from Gregg's wing to cover his left flank, then met and defeated two Confederate regiments. He drove his men toward Brandy Station on a route that would have brought him to the Confederate rear, a move that might have won the battle for the Union. However, Gregg sent him an order to come to Fleetwood Heights. Duffié had to turn around, backtrack several miles, and ultimately arrived too late for the battle.

The tide of the battle surged back and forth. Buford's men had pushed the Confederates back to the northern end of the Heights, and the battle was in balance when Pleasonton saw dust clouds in the distance that signaled approaching Confederate infantry. Pleasonton called for a general Union withdrawal. Because of a series of "just in time" arrivals, Stuart was able to hold the field and call it a victory, despite being surprised by his adversary twice in the same day. The Union forces suffered over 860 casualties, the Confederates over 510.

More important, Pleasonton reported back to Hooker that in addition to the cavalry, there were Confederate

James Ewell Brown Stuart

The "eyes of the army," as Robert E. Lee called him, J.E.B. Stuart cut a dashing figure on horseback, wearing his trademark plumed hat, gray cloak lined in red, and a red flower or ribbon in his lapel. He advanced rapidly in the Confederate army, moving from captain to brigadier general in only four short months in 1861, and took charge of the newly organized Virginia Cavalry Brigade. He eventually rose to the rank of major general and commanded an entire corps of cavalry.

Stuart was one of the finest cavalrymen of all time, and certainly the best in the Confederacy. He was indispensable in scouting troop strength and locations for Lee. Before Gettysburg, when he was out of touch for several days and didn't provide intelligence, Lee was at a great disadvantage, eventually losing the battle. In both June and October 1862, Stuart rode completely around McClellan's army while scouting, once on the Virginia Peninsula and once after Antietam, boosting Southern morale. Those rides also netted almost 450 prisoners, 1200 horses, and much-needed supplies for the Confederacy.

At the Second Battle of Bull Run (Second Manassas), Stuart's cloak and hat were captured, but Stuart later retaliated by stealing Union general John Pope's full dress uniform from his headquarters, along with valuable intelligence reports. Stuart died at age 31 on May 12, 1864, as a result of a wound he received while fighting Union major general Philip Sheridan's cavalry near Richmond, Virginia.

infantry units in the area. Hooker began to move his forces farther west—a route that would put the Army of the Potomac in a position to meet Lee later at Gettysburg—but conflicts with Lincoln and with Union general-in-chief Henry Halleck led to Hooker's replacement just before the battle.

While the Union cavalry had fought well before, at Brandy Station they matched the Confederate cavalry in a large battle for the first time during the war. The battle marked the end of the huge psychological advantage the Confederate cavalry had enjoyed. For the rest of the war, including the next month at Gettysburg, the Union cavalry held its own and eventually dominated the Rebel horsemen.

Brandy Station Park

From the late 1980s through the mid 1990s, the Brandy Station battlefield was the scene of a second "battle"—preservationists against developers. At one point, part of the battlefield was to be sold for light industrial development, and later for a Formula One auto racetrack. But when the developer was faced with local protests and financial problems, the Brandy Station Foundation, the Civil War Preservation Trust, and other preservationists around the country persuaded him to sell 944 acres of Brandy Station battlefield for $6.8 million. The Civil War Preservation Trust and its parent organizations, the Association for the Preservation of Civil War Sites and the Civil War Trust, contributed $2.6 million, and the rest came from the Commonwealth of Virginia and the Federal Civil War Battlefield Preservation Program (a program administered by the American Battlefield Protection Program, part of the National Park Service). The park was formally opened on June 6, 2003, three days before the 104th anniversary of the battle.

The "poster child" of the Brandy Station Park is the Graffiti House, purchased on August 27, 2002, by the foundation. The two-story frame dwelling was built in Brandy Station in 1858 as a tenant house, abandoned for much of the war, and then used as a hospital. In the early 1990s, a renovation of the three upstairs rooms in the house discovered hundreds of Civil War–era charcoal and pencil messages, signatures, and sketches under layers of paint and wallpaper. The graffiti includes dozens of individuals' names and regimental identifications, messages such as, "Yankees caught hell," and "Battle of Beverly's Ford April 16, 1863," and a three-foot drawing of a woman. It is the best and most extensive example of Civil War period graffiti discovered in recent years, and historians and archaeologists hope to uncover even more on the walls. The foundation plans to turn the ground floor of the Graffiti House into a full-service visitors center, while the upstairs will remain a museum.

The Brandy Station battlefield area still resembles the landscape during the Civil War, with little change in the houses, roads, and even fence lines. The park features historical signs, markers, and explanations to give visitors a sense of the battle and surrounding skirmishes. The Brandy Station driving tour includes the Grand Review Site, where Stuart held his reviews just before the battle; the site of Gregg's Attack; Fleetwood Hill, the location of Stuart's headquarters and the site of fierce fighting; the spot near Beverly Ford where the first engagements of the battle took place; and the St. James Church Site, scene of some of the heaviest fighting. Campsites and trenches are still visible along the driving tour and on the hiking trails, which include interpretive signs. Walking tour maps are available at the Graffiti House.

Visitor Information
703-403-1910;
www.nps.gov/frsp/brandy.htm or
www.brandystation.org/
Admission: Free.
Special Events: The park sponsors a number of special events, including a battle reenactment in early June; call for information.
Getting There: Brandy Station, Virginia, is about two hours southwest of Washington, D.C.

From Washington: Take I-66 to U.S. highway 29/15. Turn south on local route 663, then right on 762.

From I-95: Exit at state route 3 to Stevensburg, about 17 miles west of Chancellorsville. Turn right on local route 663 and go 3.8 miles to Brandy Station, where the main road will become Route 700. Follow Route 700 for 0.2 mile, and turn left on Route 669 for 0.1 mile. Turn left on Route 762 and travel two miles. Turn right on Route 342 and pull into the visitors parking area of the Virginia State Police area office.

CAVALRY

The Continental Dragoons, the ancestors of the U.S. Cavalry, were formed initially during the Revolutionary War. These units attracted an elite group of men and performed well, but they were disbanded after the war for budgetary reasons until March 1833. Then the first regiment of U.S. Dragoons was created to protect settlers in the West. In March 1855, at the request of Jefferson Davis, the recently appointed Secretary of War, Congress authorized two more cavalry regiments to combat Comanche raids in Texas. They became the 1st and 2nd Cavalry, the first regular American military organizations to bear the title of Cavalry.

The officers of the U.S. 1st and 2nd Cavalry were mostly Southerners. The officers in the units included John Bell Hood, George H. Thomas, Albert Sidney Johnston, Edmund Kirby Smith, and Robert E. Lee. Lee had his first independent command in the 2nd Cavalry, named "Jeff Davis's Own" after its formation, and the unit contributed more general officers to the Civil War than any other. Half of the full generals in the Confederate army had served with the 2nd Cavalry.

Ironically, a year after Davis formed the cavalry units, he asked Congress to appropriate $90,000 to develop a breech-loading carbine for the cavalry, designed to be easy to handle and quick to load in pressure situations. The request was approved. These carbines became the most important weapon used by the Union cavalry during the Civil War, and gave them a major advantage over their Confederate counterparts.

Cavalry and the Civil War

When the Civil War broke out in 1861, there were five regiments of U.S. horsemen with a total of 176 officers, 104 of whom left the U.S. army for the Confederate army, giving the Confederates a huge advantage at the outset of the war.

Initially, the Union thought that cavalry was a waste of money and turned away units that individual states offered. It was expected to take two years to produce a good cavalryman (interestingly, that proved to be about right), and most Union leaders thought the war would be over long before that time. For this reason, only seven troops of regular cavalry were available for First Bull Run (Manassas).

Cavalry units are expensive to equip and maintain, take longer to train than other forces, and in battle can be relatively vulnerable and difficult to replace. However, when employed properly and aggressively in combat, they could do things that no other arm could. At First Bull Run (Manassas), the Confederates had a full contingent of horsemen, notably Lieutenant Colonel J.E.B.

Stuart's 1st Virginia Cavalry, and they and other Confederate riders contributed greatly to the victory.

The First Bull Run (Manassas) disaster brought about a change of heart in Washington. By the end of the first year of the war, the Union army had formed 82 new regiments of cavalry.

Despite the increase in numbers, there were still major problems. Because so many cavalrymen had left to join the Confederate army, the new Union cavalry units had both new troops and a large number of inexperienced officers. Many of the recruits had never even ridden a horse before, and many of the men who were training and leading them knew little more than the rookies did.

While the Union cavalrymen were poorly trained and led, they were supplied with excellent equipment and weapons. At first this meant little because Union units were rushed into combat where they became easy prey for the more experienced Confederate horsemen. The Confederates were able to capture much of this quality equipment during skirmishes. However, as the war went on, there was a steady decline in the efficiency of the Confederate cavalry because the Confederacy was unable to match the high quality and quantity of Union arms and equipment. Making a reliable breechloader was beyond the technological

capability of Southern small-arms manufacturers. As the war progressed and the Union cavalry become stronger, fewer and fewer pieces of Union equipment were captured.

The Confederate cavalry had an early edge because it was better organized than its Union counterpart was. The Confederates had independent units that either cooperated with other units or worked on their own, while the Union cavalry units were attached to regiments and given a variety of extraneous duties by commanders who did not understand (or like) cavalry.

The Confederate superiority lasted for the first two years of the war. Confederate cavalrymen such as John S. Mosby and Nathan Bedford Forrest raided Union trains and outposts, captured and/or burned supply wagons, and generally raised havoc behind Union lines. The most famous exploit was Confederate cavalryman J.E.B. "Jeb" Stuart's ride around the Army of the Potomac in the spring of 1862, when he led 1200 troopers on a circling reconnaissance mission. Stuart's men covered more than 100 miles around General George B. McClellan's Union forces threatening Richmond, pinpointing Union positions, destroying outposts, and terrorizing Union cavalry units. His reports helped Lee launch the "Seven Days Battles" that pushed McClellan away from Richmond.

The situation was much the same in the West. Confederate cavalry under leaders like Forrest, John Hunt Morgan, and Joseph Wheeler regularly thrust deep into the Union rear to destroy high-value targets such as supply depots, bridges, or railroads. The Union generals in the West begged for more cavalry, saying "it was difficult to oppose the frequent raids of the enemy on communications and supply trains."

Gradually, the Union learned. Leadership and organization improved and in early 1863, the Army of the Potomac commander Major General Joseph Hooker created a unified cavalry corps. After some growing pains, the Union cavalry corps's numerical superiority in men and horses, combined with superior weapons, turned it into a force to be reckoned with.

The first solid indication of

A cavalry charge as sketched by Edwin Forbes.

change came on March 17, 1863, at Kelly's Ford, Virginia, in the first pure cavalry fight of any size east of the Mississippi. Union cavalry general William Averell wanted to impress Hooker by roughing up the Confederate cavalry in the region commanded by his old friend and West Point classmate, Confederate cavalry general Fitzhugh Lee. Lee had sent Averell several taunting messages, and Averell accepted the challenge. In the sharp cavalry battle that followed, the Confederates suffered 146 casualties, almost twice as many as Averell's men.

A few months later, the Gettysburg campaign began, marked by a series of almost daily cavalry skirmishes. The first great cavalry combat of the war took place at Brandy Station, Virginia, on June 9, 1863, full of charges and countercharges in a battle that lasted the whole day (*see* Brandy Station, page 224). The battle is generally acknowledged as the point where Union cavalrymen showed they could match the Confederate horsemen.

Less than a month later, on July 1 at Gettysburg, Union general John Buford and two brigades of his 1st Cavalry Division engaged a division of Confederate infantry. Fighting dismounted with Sharps breech-loading rifles, the Union cavalry stopped the Confederate advance for more than two hours, allowing the Union army to take Cemetery Ridge and the Round Tops, which would prove to be the key to the battle (*see* Gettysburg, page 161).

Not only was the Union cavalry improving, but the Confederate cavalry was steadily declining in numbers and efficiency. At the beginning of the Civil War there were about six million horses in the United States, only about 1.7 million of them in the South. As the war progressed, more and more horses were brought into military service, where they quickly wore out. Confederate cavalrymen owned their horses and were paid for their use or if they were killed in action; but if the horse "wore out" on long raids, the cavalryman usually had to buy a new horse himself. This was beyond the means of many as the war wore on. Toward the end of the war, many Confederate cavalrymen had no horses and their hard-won skills were useless. Union cavalrymen, on the other hand, rode on government-issued horses. By 1863, the Union wanted horses delivered

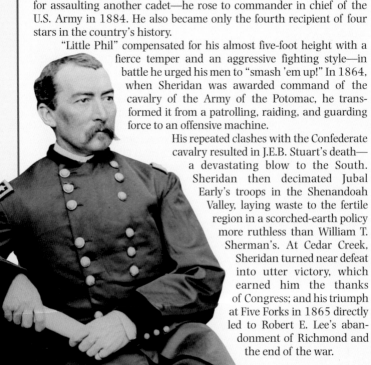

Philip Sheridan

Philip Sheridan was the Union's finest cavalry commander. From an unpromising beginning at West Point—he enrolled a year early by lying about his age, and graduated a year late due to disciplinary action for assaulting another cadet—he rose to commander in chief of the U.S. Army in 1884. He also became only the fourth recipient of four stars in the country's history.

"Little Phil" compensated for his almost five-foot height with a fierce temper and an aggressive fighting style—in battle he urged his men to "smash 'em up!" In 1864, when Sheridan was awarded command of the cavalry of the Army of the Potomac, he transformed it from a patrolling, raiding, and guarding force to an offensive machine.

His repeated clashes with the Confederate cavalry resulted in J.E.B. Stuart's death— a devastating blow to the South. Sheridan then decimated Jubal Early's troops in the Shenandoah Valley, laying waste to the fertile region in a scorched-earth policy more ruthless than William T. Sherman's. At Cedar Creek, Sheridan turned near defeat into utter victory, which earned him the thanks of Congress; and his triumph at Five Forks in 1865 directly led to Robert E. Lee's abandonment of Richmond and the end of the war.

Armed *with sabers and repeating rifles, the 8th Pennsylvania Cavalry collide with Confederate infantry on a country lane at the Battle of Chancellorsville. "We cut our way through, trampling down all who could not escape us," their commander later recalled.*

at the rate of 500 a day, and cavalry units had first call on the best.

For the last two years of the war, the Army of the Potomac's cavalry contributed much to the disruption of Lee's army, both in the Shenandoah and around Richmond and Petersburg. Sheridan was especially effective in the Shenandoah, but his most important contribution may have come during his Richmond raid, where his forces killed the illustrious Confederate cavalry leader, J.E.B. Stuart.

Cavalry Missions

For centuries, cavalry was used for shock attacks and to pursue a defeated enemy from the battlefield. Even through the Mexican War, the short range and inaccuracy of the smoothbore allowed cavalry with edged weapons to be a key attacking arm. Attempts to continue such tactics during the Civil War proved disastrous, and rifled muskets soon drove horsemen off the battlefield. During the war, the cavalry found new tactical roles and expanded old ones. Cavalry kept commanders informed of the enemy's movements and screened their own army's movements. However, their most glamorous role was as a mobile striking force disrupting enemy communication and supply lines, and it was these operations that immortalized Mosby, Forrest, and others.

But the cavalry's most useful con-tribution was probably fighting as dismounted infantry, a role first performed by the Confederates. Moving quickly on horseback to a critical location, dismounted cavalry could seize and hold ground until infantry arrived, fill gaps in lines of battle, and cover a retreat. At Chickamauga, two brigades of Union dismounted cavalry were able to hold back Confederate infantry after a Confederate breakthrough until the Union troops could re-form.

Generally, cavalry were maneuvered in columns of fours, which were flexible and easier to deploy. A troop of 96 men in columns of fours would be almost a hundred yards long, and a column of 10,000 cavalrymen could stretch for miles.

On the march, cavalry could cover some 35 miles in an eight-hour day under good conditions, though some units covered as much as 80 miles in a little more than a day. In late June 1864, Union brigadier generals James H. Wilson and August V. Kautz took their cavalry divisions from Petersburg to disrupt Confederate rail supply lines. The 5000 cavalry troops rode 300 miles in 10 days, often saddle-bound for 20 hours a day, while tearing up 60 miles of track, burning trains and railroad stations, and proving their value in combat operations.

The Battle of Fredericksburg

President Lincoln fired the politically popular George McClellan as commander of the Army of the Potomac after the election of November 1862, and on November 7 he chose the tall, handsome, affable Ambrose Burnside to replace him. Best known today as the namesake of the "sideburns" style of beard, Burnside had executed a successful amphibious operation along the North Carolina coast, where he captured Fort Macon. He supported John Pope adequately during the Battle of Second Bull Run (Second Manassas) and again at Antietam. Best of all, he seemed to have no political ambitions.

The problem was that Burnside knew himself well, and he realized he was not up to commanding the Army of the Potomac. He accepted the command reluctantly, and unfortunately was to show he was a good judge of his own abilities.

Immediately after his appointment, Burnside reorganized his army into three "grand divisions" of two corps each under major generals Edwin Sumner, William B. Franklin, and Joseph "Fighting Joe" Hooker, and a reserve corps under Major General Franz Sigel. He presented a plan to Lincoln and General Henry Halleck, commander of all the Union armies, to attack Richmond through Fredericksburg, Virginia. Burnside proposed to move to Warrenton, Virginia, to gather supplies and hold the Confederates in that area, then move rapidly southwest to Falmouth, across the Rappahannock River from Fredericksburg. He would then cross the river and take the town, threatening Richmond. Lee was sure to rush to defend the capital, and Burnside would fight him there. Lincoln was not enthusiastic—he would have preferred that Burnside attack Lee's army instead of Richmond—but approved the plan on November 14, saying, "It will succeed if you move very rapidly, otherwise not."

Burnside tried to move quickly. On November 15, the Army of the Potomac moved out; and on November 17 his leading element, under Sumner, entered Falmouth. The railroad line from Falmouth to the

Ambrose Everett Burnside

After graduating from West Point in 1847, Ambrose Burnside retired in 1853 to manufacture a breech-loading rifle he had designed. Unfortunately, he was not able to secure a government contract, and therefore his creditors took title to his patents. Ironically, more than 50,000 Burnside carbines were sold to the U.S. Army during the Civil War. His name was also used for his style of facial hair, which became known as burnsides or sideburns.

At the outbreak of the war, Burnside rejoined the army and had some victories at Roanoke Island, New Bern, and Fort Macon. In November 1862, after Antietam, Burnside finally accepted command of the Army of the Potomac—having twice refused President Abraham Lincoln's request—even though Burnside knew he lacked the necessary experience. He reorganized the army into three grand divisions, but was not particularly successful. His final humiliation was the debacle known as Burnside's Mud March, after which he asked that several of his subordinate officers be replaced. Instead, Lincoln replaced him with Joseph Hooker.

Burnside was reassigned to the Department of Ohio, where he had some success, most notably in defending Knoxville, for which he received the thanks of Congress. Sent back east, he took part in the Battle of Petersburg and was partly blamed for mishandling the follow-up to the Crater explosion. He was relieved of his command and never reassigned.

After the war, Burnside was elected governor of Rhode Island and to the U.S. Senate.

Confederate pickets stand tauntingly at the edge of the railroad bridge across the Rappahannock that they destroyed to prevent the Union capture of Fredericksburg.

secure Union supply port of Aquia Landing was in serviceable condition, and supplies were beginning to arrive. What had not arrived were the pontoons to build the six bridges Burnside needed to cross the river from Falmouth to Fredericksburg.

However, Sumner saw an opportunity to avoid the bridging operation. There were only a few Confederates near Fredericksburg, so he asked Burnside for permission to quickly ford the Rappahannock and occupy the hills, especially Marye's Heights, behind the town. Had Sumner moved, he could have brushed aside the small Confederate force; but Burnside hesitated, apparently because he saw dark rain clouds to the west and north. He was afraid rain and rising water might make the fords impassable behind Sumner and leave him isolated, so Burnside told him to wait for the rest of the force and the pontoons.

Lee thought Burnside might move to Fredericksburg, but the speed of the movement surprised him. When Sumner arrived at Falmouth, Lee realized the Union troops had won the race, and he was sure Burnside would cross quickly and the Confederates would have to fight farther south. He was relieved (and probably surprised) when the crossing was delayed.

Lee quickly sent General James Longstreet's 35,000-man corps to Fredericksburg, and by November 21 they were in position. The opportunity for the Union to make an unopposed crossing had disappeared, but Longstreet's line was seven miles long and quite thin. Lee held Stonewall Jackson's corps back

from Fredericksburg, concerned that Burnside might turn his army away from the town for an amphibious assault to the south. It was several days before Lee was convinced that Fredericksburg was the real target.

Lincoln and Halleck went to Falmouth on November 25 to discuss the operation with Burnside, the same day the first pontoons arrived (a week late). They thought the plan was risky, but Lincoln was under great political pressure to win a victory and passed that on to his generals.

While Burnside waited for the rest of the pontoons to arrive, on November 30, Lee decided that the main threat was to Fredericksburg. He sent Jackson there with four divisions, and now Burnside faced Lee's entire army. With Jackson in place, Lee hoped Burnside would attack Fredericksburg, because it was an excellent place to defend. Behind the town were open fields, and then high ground—Marye's Heights and Marye's Hill just behind the town and Prospect Heights just to the south. At the foot of Marye's Heights and Marye's Hill was a sunken road over 1000 feet long lined by four-foot-high stone walls. It formed a natural trench for Confederate riflemen, and the 600 yards of open ground in front of the wall defined the "kill zone."

By the first week in December, Burnside finally had all his pontoons, and he faced Lee with over 121,000 men, as well as a formidable artillery force including several of the large 4.5-inch Ordnance rifles set up just behind Falmouth on Stafford Heights. Burnside's plan

Federal troops row pontoons across the Rappahannock River toward Fredericksburg as engineers attempt to construct a pontoon bridge under heavy Confederate fire.

was to cross on six pontoon bridges, three directly into Fredericksburg and three more downstream about a mile to the south. By all accounts, when his staff heard the plan and looked across the river at the heights they would have to climb in the face of a large, dug-in Confederate army, several told him it was murder.

The night of December 10–11, Union engineers waded into the freezing waters to assemble the bridges. On the Union left, south of the town, the grand divisions of generals Franklin and Hooker (who would be between Franklin and Sumner) completed the bridges and made the crossing with little opposition, but Sumner's crossing into Fredericksburg turned into a battle. Confederate infantry firing from houses along the river picked off the engineers as they tried to lay their bridges into the town, and the construction came to a halt. To suppress the Confederate snipers, 150 Union cannons mounted on Stafford Heights fired 8000 rounds into the town, but the artillery fire actually helped the defenders, knocking down buildings and giving them more places to hide. When the Union artillery fire failed to dislodge the snipers, three regiments of Union volunteers had to paddle across the river in boats and seek out the Confederates in close-quarter house-to-house combat. By the time the operation was complete, it was almost dark, so there would be no attack that day.

The Union leaders used the next day, December 12, to plan, while Union troops looted the community.

The plan Burnside developed was straightforward. Franklin's left grand division would make the main attack in the south, supported by Hooker's grand division, and seize the heights of Prospect Hill. It would then turn right (north) and roll up the Confederate lines. Meanwhile, Sumner was to send one division against Marye's Heights behind Fredericksburg in a secondary attack. Burnside thought (hoped?) the two-pronged attack would force Lee's troops off the high ground.

Longstreet was well dug in on Marye's Heights, and his artillery included two 30-pounder Parrott rifles, previously considered too large for field use. Looking over the open ground between Marye's Heights and Fredericksburg, Longstreet asked his chief of artillery, E. P. Alexander, if he needed more guns. Alexander snorted and said, "General, we cover the ground now so well we will comb it as with a fine-tooth comb. A chicken could not live on that field when we open on it." This was to prove all too true.

When Burnside's written orders to attack arrived on December 13, they were not as clear as his plan the previous day. Franklin, whose force was to make the main attack, was the key to any chance the Union had of victory, because the terrain in front of Franklin's grand division was not as steep and had much more cover than the hills behind Fredericksburg. However, many Union generals seemed more concerned with not losing than with winning, and Franklin was afraid that he might lose his whole force. He chose to interpret Burnside's orders cautiously (and did not use his direct telegraph line to Burnside's headquarters to clarify his instructions). Rather than send his full force of 40,000 to the attack, Franklin only sent one division, about 4500 troops, supported by a division on the left and another on the right.

Nevertheless, despite being held up by two pieces of well-handled Confederate artillery, the attack started well. As the Union troops pushed forward, they found a gap between two Confederate brigades. They broke through to the second Confederate line and routed another Confederate brigade, bringing chaos to their defenses. However, Franklin did not send forward reserves to take advantage of what could have been a major breakthrough. Jackson rallied his troops and furiously counterattacked, pushing the Union forces down the hill. Two more Union divisions moved up and, supported by the Union artillery, stopped Jackson's attack in its tracks.

Burnside's confidence, never high, vanished early when he saw the Confederates hold Franklin's attack. He gave up on his plan to make his main attack from the left and decided to push from the right. As the fog lifted about noon, he ordered Sumner's grand division to attack Marye's Heights. There was a tragic irony in this—it had been Sumner who had wanted to cross the river before the Confederates arrived. Now Burnside, who had stopped him, was sending him and his men to attack these same heights when the Confederates were well dug in. The attacks would result in

one of the worst—perhaps the worst—massacres of the Civil War.

To reach Marye's Heights, Sumner's men had to advance across open ground, but in the middle of the ground was a steepbanked drainage ditch about 30 feet wide and six feet deep. Burnside had been warned about the ditch, but refused to believe it and threatened to court-martial a general who insisted it existed. Only two bridges crossed this obstacle, so the advancing Union troops had to march across the bridges, under fire, in columns, before they could spread out. This gave the Confederates on Marye's Heights and in the sunken road a clear target. As the Union attack began, the Confederates poured in reinforcements to the sunken road, and at times Confederate troops stood up to six deep waiting for their chance to fire. Union sharpshooters and artillery took a toll of the Confederates and killed two generals, but to no avail.

Division after division, Sumner's men moved forward, only to meet Confederate cannons firing explosive shells, then grapeshot and cluster shot (though one of the 30-pounder Parrotts exploded, almost injuring Lee). As they approached the sunken road, Confederates in the trench fired muskets at them using "buck and ball," a combination of a ball and three buckshots that was deadly at close range. By one thirty p.m., all of the attacks had been beaten back with heavy losses. After Sumner's grand division was decimated—he lost over 40 percent of his men—Burnside called upon Hooker to attack along the same

Confederate infantrymen, *at times up to six deep, alternately fire and reload from behind the stone wall in the Sunken Road at Marye's Heights.*

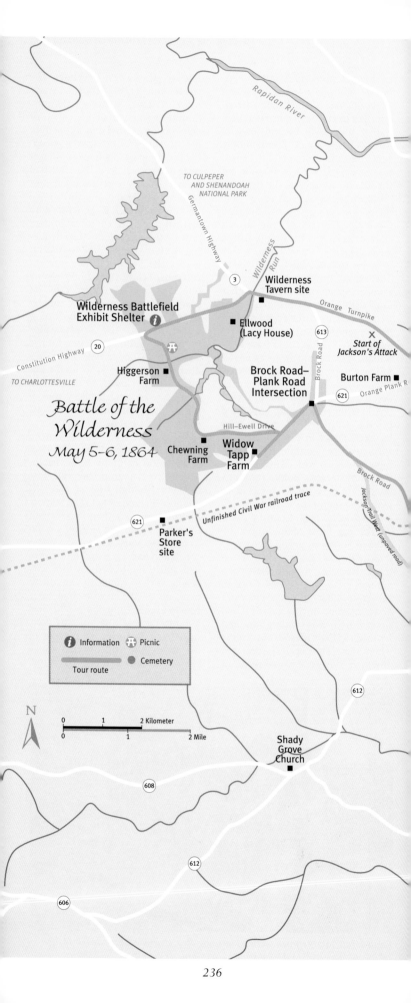

Rapidan River

TO CULPEPER
AND SHENANDOAH
NATIONAL PARK

Germantown Highway

Wilderness Run

③

Wilderness
Tavern site

Orange Turnpike

Wilderness Battlefield
Exhibit Shelter ⓘ

Ellwood
(Lacy House)

613

✕
Start of
Jackson's Attack

Brock Road

Constitution Highway

⑳

TO CHARLOTTESVILLE

Higgerson
Farm

Brock Road–
Plank Road
Intersection

Burton Farm

621

Orange Plank R

*Battle of the
Wilderness*
May 5–6, 1864

Hill–Ewell Drive

Chewning
Farm

Widow
Tapp
Farm

Brock Road

Jackson Trail West (unpaved road)

621

Parker's
Store
site

Unfinished Civil War railroad trace

ⓘ Information   🎪 Picnic

━━━ ● Cemetery
Tour route

N

0   1   2 Kilometer
0   1   2 Mile

612

Shady
Grove
Church

608

612

606

236

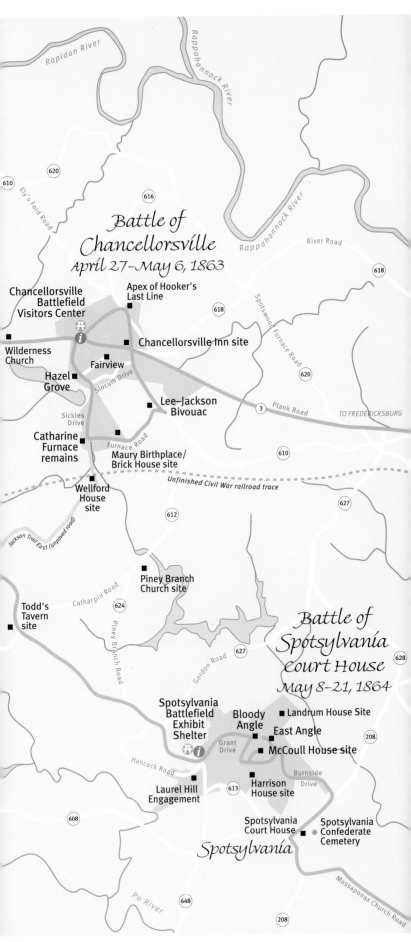

Rapidan River

Rappahannock River

610

620

616

Ely's Ford Road

River Road

Rappahannock River

618

Battle of
Chancellorsville
April 27–May 6, 1863

Chancellorsville
Battlefield
Visitors Center

Apex of Hooker's
Last Line

618

Spotswood Furnace Road

Wilderness
Church

Chancellorsville Inn site

620

Fairview

Hazel
Grove

Slocum Drive

Lee–Jackson
Bivouac

3   Plank Road   TO FREDERICKSBURG

Sickles
Drive

Catharine
Furnace
remains

Furnace Road

Maury Birthplace/
Brick House site

610

Unfinished Civil War railroad trace

627

Wellford
House
site

612

Jackson Trail East (unpaved road)

Piney Branch
Church site

Catharpin Road

624

Todd's
Tavern
site

Piney Branch Road

Gordon Road

627

Battle of
Spotsylvania
Court House
May 8–21, 1864

628

Spotsylvania
Battlefield
Exhibit
Shelter

Bloody
Angle

Landrum House Site

East Angle

208

Grant Drive

McCoull House site

Hancock Road

Burnside
Drive

Laurel Hill
Engagement

613

Harrison
House site

608

Spotsylvania
Court House

Spotsylvania
Confederate
Cemetery

Spotsylvania

Po River

648

208

Massaponax Church Road

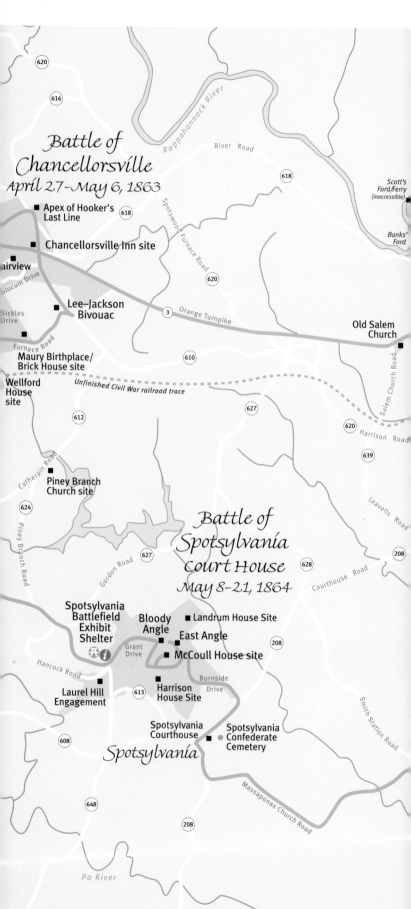

620
616

Battle of Chancellorsville
April 27–May 6, 1863

■ Apex of Hooker's
Last Line   618

618

Rappahannock River

River Road

■ Chancellorsville Inn site

Scott's
Ford/Ferry
(inaccessible)

airview

Banks'
Ford

Slocum Drive

Spotswood Furnace Road

■ Lee–Jackson
Bivouac

Sickles
Drive

620

■

Furnace Road

3   Orange Turnpike

Old Salem
Church

■ Maury Birthplace/
Brick House site

610

■

Salem Church Road

Wellford
House
site

Unfinished Civil War railroad trace

627

620 Harrison   Road

612

639

■ Piney Branch
Church site

Catharpin Road

624

Leavells Road

Piney Branch Road

208

Battle of Spotsylvania Court House
May 8–21, 1864

Gordon Road

627

628

Courthouse Road

Spotsylvania
Battlefield
Exhibit
Shelter

■ Bloody
Angle   ■ Landrum House Site

■ East Angle

208

Grant
Drive

■ McCoull House site

Hancock Road

Burnside
Drive

■

Laurel Hill
Engagement

613

■ Harrison
House Site

608

Spotsylvania
Courthouse   • Spotsylvania
Confederate
Cemetery

Smith Station Road

Spotsylvania

648

Massaponax Church Road

208

Po River

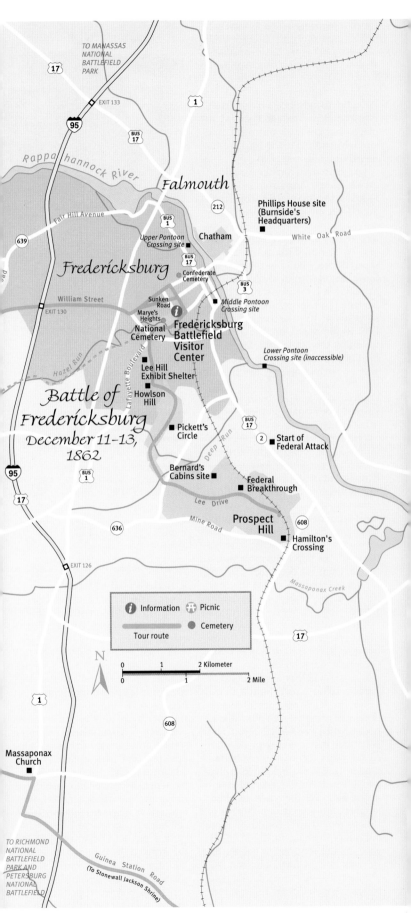

TO MANASSAS
NATIONAL
BATTLEFIELD
PARK

17

EXIT 133

95

BUS
17

Rappahannock River

Fair Hill Avenue

Falmouth

212

Phillips House site
(Burnside's
Headquarters)

White Oak Road

639

BUS
1

Upper Pontoon
Crossing site

Chatham

Fredericksburg

Confederate
Cemetery

BUS
17

William Street

EXIT 130

Sunken
Road

Marye's
Heights

National
Cemetery

BUS
3

Middle Pontoon
Crossing site

i

Fredericksburg
Battlefield
Visitor
Center

Lower Pontoon
Crossing site (inaccessible)

Hazel Run

Lee Hill
Exhibit Shelter

Howlson
Hill

Lafayette Boulevard

*Battle of
Fredericksburg*
*December 11–13,
1862*

Pickett's
Circle

Deep Run

BUS
17

2

Start of
Federal Attack

95

BUS
1

Bernard's
Cabins site

Federal
Breakthrough

17

Lee Drive

Mine Road

636

*Prospect
Hill*

608

Hamilton's
Crossing

Massaponax Creek

EXIT 126

i Information	🎪 Picnic
────	● Cemetery
Tour route	

N

0   1   2 Kilometer
0   1   2 Mile

17

1

608

Massaponax
Church

TO RICHMOND
NATIONAL
BATTLEFIELD
PARK AND
PETERSBURG
NATIONAL
BATTLEFIELD

Guinea Station Road
(To Stonewall Jackson Shrine)

***Union infantrymen** surge forward in another attempt to storm Marye's Hill. More than half of the Union casualties at Fredericksburg resulted from these charges.*

route as Sumner's men and for Franklin to advance on his front. Franklin demurred and stayed in place. Hooker was outraged and strongly objected to the waste of his men, but finally complied.

Lee, realizing Franklin would not attack, moved forces from in front of Franklin to Marye's Hill. The Union attack began again at three thirty p.m., and three more divisions went into the meat grinder without any results. Toward dark, a Union division attacked the Confederates' left flank instead of a direct frontal assault, but it too was thrown back. No Union soldier reached—or even came close to—the sunken road. Lee, as he stood on the heights watching the battle that day, made his famous remark, "It is well that war is so terrible, or we should get too fond of it." About 6000 Confederates and 20 cannons had stopped seven Union divisions—over 40,000 men—cold.

The next morning, after reflecting on his defeat, a distraught Burnside wanted to personally lead another assault but was dissuaded by his grand-division commanders. Both sides remained on the field during the 14th, strengthening their positions, and in the afternoon a truce was arranged to permit the burial of the dead. Lee hoped Burnside would attack again on December 15, but Burnside withdrew across the river the night before in a driving rainstorm.

The Confederates suffered over 5000 casualties, while the Union lost over 10,000, more than 6000 at the foot of Marye's Hill.

Burnside made one more effort at Fredericksburg. On January 20, 1863, he tried another pontoon-bridge crossing of the Rappahannock to turn Lee's left flank. It had potential, but it ended in disaster. Heavy rains turned the roads into muddy morasses and huge traffic jams ensued. The Confederate troops in the hills over the roads watched, laughed, and jeered as hundreds of Union troops tried to dig their wagons out of the mud. Burnside finally gave up and returned to Falmouth. He was at least fortunate that the weather had not turned cold and frozen his vehicles in their water-filled ruts for Lee to pick up at his leisure.

At the cost of over 10,000 Union soldiers, Burnside proved that his own doubts about whether he was qualified to lead the Army of the Potomac were correct. Burnside's subordinates, led by Hooker, were ready to mutiny (interestingly, Sumner, who had the most serious grievance, seemed to support Burnside). On January 25, President Lincoln relieved Burnside, Sumner, and Franklin, and awarded command of the Army of the Potomac to Hooker.

The Battle of Chancellorsville

When General "Fighting Joe" Hooker relieved Burnside in January 1863 after the disastrous Fredericksburg campaign, the Army of the Potomac was in pitiful shape, its morale in tatters and desertion rates soaring. Hooker was known as "a better conniver and carouser than commander" and an ambitious intriguer (Lincoln noted this in his appointment letter), but he seemed to be personally brave and proved to be a surprisingly efficient organizer and administrator. He improved training, tightened discipline, and made sure the army received better food, uniforms, and weapons—notably rifled cannons. Hooker junked Burnside's "grand divisions" and reorganized the Army of the Potomac into seven infantry corps and one cavalry corps, then introduced distinctive corps and division insignia, to the troops' delight. Operationally, he set

up an efficient military intelligence organization and consolidated the cavalry, which was to prove a huge boon to this much-maligned Union army—but not immediately.

Hooker learned Lee's forces were massed in a thinly stretched defensive line along the fortified south bank of the Rappahannock River, and that Lee had sent Longstreet south with two divisions to guard the Virginia–Carolina coast. Hooker had a decided numerical superiority, so he decided—under considerable pressure from Lincoln—to attack.

He began by sending virtually all the Union cavalry up the Rappahannock on a raid to destroy the Confederate communications. This was to cause Hooker innumerable problems during the battle. They were ineffective (primarily due to rainy weather) and the move left Hooker without a scouting force. Many of the myriad difficulties the Union forces would later encounter were caused by lack of intelligence—the kind cavalry would have provided.

On April 27, Hooker began his main move, employing both strategic and tactical deception. He took his primary force, three corps, and marched 40 miles up the Rappahannock to turn Lee's left flank. Two days later, he sent Major General John Sedgwick with two corps to Falmouth, just across the river from Fredericksburg, to threaten the town and distract Lee. He also sent Major General Darius N. Couch, his second in command (whom Hooker despised), with two divisions to cross at Banks' Ford, between the two converging wings of Hooker and Sedgwick. The Union moves confused Lee, and before he could react, Hooker's forces moved between Lee and General J.E.B. Stuart's cavalry, which had been raiding behind Union lines. On April 29, Lee, still confused about where Hooker would strike, moved the three divisions on his right flank closer to Fredericksburg. At the same time, he sent another division to occupy a position near the crossroads at Chancellorsville, 10 miles to the west of Fredericksburg. At Chancellorsville, this division encountered Hooker's advance force, realized they were outnumbered, and fell back.

Chancellorsville was in an area known as the Wilderness, full of thick pine and oak groves and heavy undergrowth, and cut by numerous small streams. The dominating terrain was a small plateau called Hazel Grove. The underbrush severely limited visibility and made movement off the few roads difficult or impossible, especially for artillery and cavalry. There was little room to spread out and maneuver, so a numerical advantage was almost meaningless, since it was virtually impossible to coordinate unit movements. By any measure, it was a terrible place to fight.

By three p.m. on April 29, Hooker's three corps were approaching Lee's rear near Chancellorsville, with Couch's two divisions close behind.

Had Hooker continued to advance, he would have moved through the Wilderness into open ground, where his numerical superiority would have put him at a great advantage. It would have also moved him closer to Sedgwick's corps, now across from Fredericksburg, trapping Lee in between. Overall, things were going according to plan, though Hooker's forces had met some resistance from Confederate skirmishers, and he had to advance blindly because he had no cavalry with him. Then, inexplicably, Hooker stopped his three corps at Chancellorsville and began to dig in. For whatever reason, "Fighting Joe" began to lose his nerve.

Meanwhile, Lee and Stonewall Jackson were trying to decide which wing of the Union army to attack, Sedgwick at Fredericksburg or Hooker at Chancellorsville. Lee realized Hooker was leading the main thrust and, since Sedgwick's forces were well supported by artillery on Stafford Heights, he left Jubal Early's small division at Marye's Heights behind Fredericksburg to pin down Sedgwick while he turned his attention to Chancellorsville. Hooker's observation balloons had detected Lee's movements and the weakness of Early's forces on Marye's Heights, and finally, late on the morning of May 1, he began to advance from Chancellorsville to meet Lee.

Jackson's forces engaged Hooker to try to slow down the advance, and Lee and his men soon joined in. Initially they stopped Hooker's progress, but the Union force had the numbers and the initiative and began to push them back. Then, suddenly and unaccountably, Hooker ordered his troops back into their positions of the night before around Chancellorsville. This was done over the indignant protests of his corps commanders, and one commander said, "My commanding general was a whipped man." Once back in Chancellorsville, Hooker occupied the high ground at Hazel Grove and dug in behind his log breastworks.

When the Union forces withdrew, the Confederates followed carefully, fearing a trap. Lee assessed the situation and realized that despite Hooker's retreat, the Confederates were in a precarious position. Hooker's position was too strong for a frontal attack, and if Sedgwick were to attack aggressively at Fredericksburg, Early could not hold him.

Lee decided to attack. His cavalry commanders reported that Hooker's right flank was weak and suggested an attack there, and a local Confederate sympathizer offered to lead them through the tangled woods to the Union flank. It was an incredible gamble. Lee was already outnumbered more than two to one. If he attacked, he would have to divide his army into three parts, then put them in positions where they could not support each other. If Hooker attacked Lee, or if he detected Jackson and attacked him, the Confederates would be defeated. The same would apply if Sedgwick struck at Early on Marye's Heights.

Lee sent Jackson and about 26,000 men, screened by Stuart's cavalry, to march 14 miles by narrow roads across the front of Hooker's army and circle around to attack the Union right flank. Lee and his remaining 17,000 men would keep Hooker engaged from the front.

Meanwhile, Hooker's corps commanders—many of whom disliked him personally—were concerned about his lack of aggressiveness and perhaps suspected he had been drinking. Sedgwick received no orders to attack Fredericksburg, so he stayed in place across the river.

Jackson began his flanking move-

"Fighting Joe" Hooker

Joseph Hooker was a capable division and corps commander, proving his talents in the Peninsula campaign, Second Bull Run (Manassas), and Antietam; but his brief stint commanding an entire army—the Army of the Potomac from January to June 1863—was a dismal failure.

Hooker was arrogant and didn't get along with his fellow officers, though he was well liked by his troops. He was also a heavy drinker and a carouser.

Upon replacing Ambrose Burnside in command of the Army of the Potomac, Hooker said, "May God have mercy on General Lee, for I will have none." President Abraham Lincoln's orders appointing Hooker included a combination of advice, warnings, and support, ending with the statement, "Beware of rashness, but with energy and sleepless vigilance go forward and give us victories." That was not to be. After an initially bold offensive move, Hooker inexplicably lost his nerve and was defeated by Lee's forces at

Jackson's attack on the Union right flank was ordered by Lee in spite of the fact that the Confederates were outnumbered. This tactic would also split their forces into three parts, where none could support the other.

Confederates passing steadily across the Union front, and finally got permission to make a "reconnaissance in force." Sickles's men harassed but could not halt Jackson's march, but their report back to Hooker was completely misconstrued. Hooker decided that Jackson was retreating after Sickles's light probe, and gave orders to prepare to pursue. As part of this maneuver, he ordered Sedgwick to attack across the river to Fredericksburg and take Marye's Heights, an attack that would have unexpected consequences.

By two thirty p.m., Jackson had moved around the Union right flank, but the terrain was so rough it was five thirty before he was organized enough to attack. Meanwhile, Hooker had not visited Howard's corps to see if they were prepared for an attack. Had he done so, he would have found Howard had disregarded the warnings and had only 700 men on the right.

Lee probed the Union center to pin down as many troops as possible, and two hours before dark, Jackson attacked. The right flank of Howard's corps was quickly scattered (many of the soldiers were German American and acquired the nickname "the Flying Dutchmen" after the rout), but Colonel Adolphus Buschbeck's brigade was well dug in and held Jackson for a time. Meanwhile, Union forces set up 24 cannons—six 3-inch Ordnance rifles, six 10-pounder Parrotts, six light 12-pounders, and six Napoleons—on Hazel Grove to await Jackson's troops. As the jubilant Confederates burst out of the tree line in a dense formation, the Union artillery greeted them with canister, along with solid bolts from the Ordnance rifles that skipped along the ground so they hit the tightly packed lines at waist height. The quick slaughter stopped the attack,

ment at about six a.m. on May 2. By nine a.m., Hooker knew Jackson was on the move. He suspected an attempt to turn his right flank, and he warned General Oliver Howard, on his right, about the movement. One of Hooker's other corps commanders, General Daniel Sickles, wanted to attack the parade of

Chancellorsville. Lincoln replaced Hooker with George Meade a month later.

Hooker later served in a lesser capacity with the Army of the Cumberland, leading his troops to victory at Lookout Mountain in Tennessee, and he fought well in the Atlanta campaign. However, when Oliver O. Howard, instead of Hooker, was promoted to head the Army of the Tennessee, Hooker was affronted and resigned. He spent the rest of the war in a quiet command in Michigan, Ohio, Indiana, and Illinois.

and the Confederates fell back to the tree line and dug in.

As darkness fell, a stroke of fate caused lasting repercussions for the Confederates. Jackson went forward in search of a route that would enable him to cut off Hooker from the river. Returning, he and several of his officers were shot by Confederate soldiers, perhaps unnerved from an earlier chance clash with Union cavalry. Jackson's left arm was amputated and he seemed to be recovering, but he contracted pneumonia and died a few days later. Many have said that Confederate hopes for a victory in the war died with him. Shortly after, A. P. Hill, Jackson's second in command, was wounded, and Confederate operations against the Union right came to a confused halt.

The next morning, May 3, Hooker had the advantage. He still had a two-to-one numerical superiority, the Confederate leadership was in some disarray, and the dominating Union position on Hazel Grove split the Confederate army in front of him. The Confederates could not support each other, and a Union attack from Hazel Grove could strike the flank of either half of Lee's army. Confederate general J.E.B. Stuart, who had taken over Jackson's command, realized the importance of Hazel Grove and prepared to launch a desperate all-out attack on the Union forces there at dawn.

It was unnecessary. Early in the morning, Hooker unaccountably ordered his army to pull back to a prepared line north of Chancellorsville. This withdrawal had catastrophic results. Lee and Stuart quickly rejoined, to the wild applause of their troops. Now they held the dominating terrain in the area. Lee moved to occupy Chancellorsville, while Stuart rapidly set up 31 cannons—later increased to 50—on Hazel Grove. The cannons pounded the Union lines while Stuart sent the rejuvenated Confederate infantry in charge after charge against the earthworks of the new Union perimeter. After several hours of vicious fighting, Confederate attacks slowly gained ground as the Union troops began to run out of ammunition.

Thomas "Stonewall" Jackson

There is a heavy mystique surrounding Thomas Jonathan "Stonewall" Jackson, the physically imposing general who rose from poverty and barely any schooling to become a respected graduate of West Point and one of the most revered generals of the Confederacy. His nickname, coined for his steadfastness at First Bull Run (Manassas), stuck with him until his death.

Jackson was eccentric and a hypochondriac, who sat ramrod straight so as not to compress any of his internal organs. A devout Calvinist, he believed that the Christian faith and the cause of the Confederacy were intertwined. As a commander, he expected blind obedience from his subordinates and viewed secrecy as a paramount military tactic; he even kept those carrying out his orders uninformed of his overall strategy or goal.

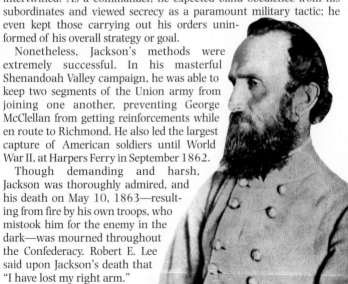

Nonetheless, Jackson's methods were extremely successful. In his masterful Shenandoah Valley campaign, he was able to keep two segments of the Union army from joining one another, preventing George McClellan from getting reinforcements while en route to Richmond. He also led the largest capture of American soldiers until World War II, at Harpers Ferry in September 1862.

Though demanding and harsh, Jackson was thoroughly admired, and his death on May 10, 1863—resulting from fire by his own troops, who mistook him for the enemy in the dark—was mourned throughout the Confederacy. Robert E. Lee said upon Jackson's death that "I have lost my right arm."

Hooker did little to try to control the battle from his headquarters, the Chancellor House. He was standing outside, leaning against one of the front-porch pillars, when a Confederate shell from Hazel Grove struck the pillar and knocked him unconscious. When Hooker regained consciousness, he was in great pain and partially paralyzed. He took a drink of brandy and then, when asked, refused to turn over command to Couch, his deputy. The chief Union medical officer refused to declare him "medically disabled," so he remained in charge.

Lee, sensing an opportunity to destroy Hooker's force, goaded his tired troops forward, when he received a stunning message—Union forces had taken Marye's Heights outside Fredericksburg. Lee had to stop his attack on Hooker and rush reinforcements to meet this new threat.

Union general Sedgwick had received Hooker's order to attack Fredericksburg and occupied the town early in the morning. At daybreak, while Lee and Stuart were rejoining, Sedgwick's troops attacked Early's strongly fortified but thinly held Confederate position at Marye's Heights behind the town. The first three Union assaults were repulsed, but the fourth effort succeeded. Sedgwick pushed the Confederates south, leaving a small division to hold Marye's Heights. As Sedgwick advanced, the Confederate reinforcements sent by Lee moved to Salem Church, about four miles west of Fredericksburg, and took position there. When Sedgwick arrived at four p.m., he did not realize that he was outnumbered, and attacked. His attacks were turned back, but he stayed in the area during the night, prepared to resume the fight the next morning.

Lee now decided to concentrate on destroying Sedgwick. The morning of May 4, he left Stuart with 25,000 men to contain Hooker's 75,000 (a telling comment on his assessment of Hooker's generalship) while he moved with 21,000 men to attack Sedgwick's 19,000.

Early that same morning, Sedgwick received a message that Hooker intended to await Lee's attack in his new position, and that Sedgwick had permission to retreat if necessary. Sedgwick had his forces dig into a semicircular defensive position with their backs to the river, then set up a pontoon bridge across

the Rappahannock so they would not have to fight their way back to Fredericksburg to cross if they had to withdraw. His force was well positioned across a main road, and this disrupted Confederate communications and coordination. Lee was not able to attack until about five thirty in the afternoon, and then only in piecemeal fashion. (Hooker, though he could hear cannon fire in the distance and knew that Lee had moved his forces, did not move.) Meanwhile, Early returned with reinforcements to Marye's Heights and forced the outnumbered Union division to fall back into Fredericksburg. They and Sedgwick recrossed to the north bank of the Rappahannock early in the morning of May 5. When Sedgwick escaped, Lee turned back to face Hooker, and the Confederates concentrated every available man for an assault on May 6.

Lee was to be frustrated again. The night of May 5–6, Hooker called his corps commanders together, and after some wrangling, Hooker ordered a withdrawal across the Rappahannock. It was a difficult operation, because rain had swollen the river and the pontoon bridges were becoming too short as the river widened. Nevertheless, Hooker crossed with the artillery during the night, and his infantry began to cross at five a.m., just before Lee was to attack. Couch had been left in command and seems to have been preparing to fight, but Hooker, seemingly anxious to deny Couch any chance at glory, sent his deputy a strongly worded order to withdraw. When Lee moved the next morning, he was astonished to find the Union forces had escaped.

However, though they controlled the battlefield, the Confederates probably suffered the most. While their losses were less—approximately 13,000 to the Union's 17,000—they could not afford even this exchange ratio. Additionally, they lost the irreplaceable Jackson. Almost unnoticed were the incremental improvements in the Union army in intelligence, artillery, and now cavalry, once the exclusive domain of the Confederates. What the Union needed was a general who could exploit these advantages.

The Wilderness

Early in March 1864, Lieutenant General Ulysses S. Grant took command as General in Chief of all the Union armies, replacing General

Henry Halleck, who was promoted to the newly created position of Chief of Staff, where he could indulge his considerable talents in administration.

Lincoln brought Grant in to fight, and he got to it quickly. His overall plan—with Lincoln's enthusiastic support—was to keep constant pressure on the Confederates at all points. The two main pressure points were to be in Georgia, where General William T. Sherman was to attack Confederate general Joseph E. Johnston's army, and Virginia, where the target was Robert E. Lee's Army of Northern Virginia. Grant let General George Meade, the victor at Gettysburg, retain command of the Army of the Potomac, but Grant decided to accompany the army on its attack.

It was a poor command structure. In effect, it meant two generals commanded the Army of the Potomac, and their respective responsibilities were never clearly defined. While Grant and Meade were able to work with each other, there was great tension between their staffs, with considerable backbiting, jealousy, and one-upsmanship. The result was often confusion and occasionally worse. However, in the end the final decisions were Grant's, as overall commander of the Union armies.

Grant realized that Lee's entrenched position along the Rapidan River was too strong to be taken by a frontal attack. An attack on Lee's left (western) flank would allow Union troops to move across favorable terrain, but it would expose the Union lines of communication to a sudden northward Confederate thrust. An attack on Lee's right (eastern) flank would screen the Union supply lines and place the Army of the Potomac close to another Union army, Benjamin F. Butler's Army of the James, for mutual support. However, to attack Lee's right flank, the Union army would have to move through the same Wilderness that had hampered Hooker the year before. Nevertheless, beginning the night of May 3, Grant moved to the fords across the Rapidan, crossed with almost 120,000 men, and moved into the Wilderness. The force was divided into two columns that planned to move down three of the parallel northeast–southwest-running roads through the Wilderness— the Orange Turnpike, the Orange Plank Road, and Catharpin Road. The roads were only about four miles apart, but the terrain in between was so overgrown that there would be little opportunity for one force to support the other except by marching down one of the few intersecting roads. The most prominent of these was the Brock/Germantown Road.

Grant hoped to slip through the Wilderness before Lee could gather a large enough force to engage, so he left behind part of his artillery and took only essential supplies. Still, his supply wagon train was about 65 miles long. The supply train soon lagged behind, and the main force had to stop in the Wilderness early in the afternoon of May 4 to let them catch up. The northern column, led by General Gouverneur Warren's corps, stopped on the Orange Turnpike, while the southern column, led by Winfield Hancock's corps, stopped about seven miles away, on Brock Road, on their way to the Catharpin Road. John Sedgwick's and Ambrose Burnside's corps followed them.

Lee had been seeking an opportunity to launch another major attack against the Army of the Potomac, and was pleased to see Grant move into the Wilderness. He had hoped that the Union forces would be foolish enough to come into the area where their superior numbers and artillery would be nullified by the terrain. The bad news was that Lee's Army of Northern Virginia was scattered. Lee had two corps available (against Grant's four)—Richard "Old Baldy" Ewell's and A. P. Hill's— but General Longstreet's corps was at Gordonsville, 42 miles away.

Lee hoped to hold the Union forces in the Wilderness long enough for Longstreet to arrive. On May 4, he sent Ewell's corps to face Warren and sent Hill's to intercept Hancock.

The first clash was the next morning, May 5, and as at Gettysburg, it was an accident. Ewell's Confederates were advancing eastward along the Orange Turnpike about seven a.m. when they met the forward elements of Warren's corps, and skirmishing began. Grant was anxious to get out of the Wilderness and thought Warren had met a small delaying force, so he ordered Warren to launch a full attack to determine their actual strength. The Union forces attacked briskly and pushed the Confederates back, but then Ewell sent in his reserves, counterattacked, and recovered the ground he had lost. Both sides began to dig in, and the fight stalemated.

The Wilderness *consisted mainly of underbrush and brackish water, and fighting in the area became an ordeal. The two sides were often invisible to each other and were able to move only by the use of a compass or the sounds of gunfire. During the battle, much of the underbrush caught fire and many of the wounded suffocated or burned to death.*

Meanwhile, on the parallel Orange Plank Road, Confederate general Hill's men encountered a detachment of Union brigadier general James H. Wilson's cavalry. Wilson's men, though outnumbered, were armed with repeating rifles and the terrain was perfect for a small, well-armed force to defend. The Union force made a slow, fighting retreat toward the Orange Plank Road–Brock Road intersection, forcing the Confederates to struggle for every inch.

Grant ordered reinforcements to support Wilson's men in holding the crossroads, and he also ordered Hancock to march his corps quickly north to the Orange Plank Road–Brock Road junction to meet them and prevent them from being separated from the rest of the army.

About two p.m., Hancock's corps began coming into line, and the Union commanders decided to take advantage of Longstreet's absence. Late that afternoon the Union forces attacked Hill's position. The battle raged back and forth and more Union forces were fed in, but they appeared to make little progress in the difficult terrain.

In fact, they had made significant progress. Hill's Confederates were hanging on by their fingernails, almost out of ammunition, and their right flank was ready to collapse. Hill, normally an able and hard-fighting commander, was sick with a combination of liver problems and venereal disease and was unable to properly organize his defenses.

Lee expected Longstreet to arrive by the next morning, May 6. He planned to use Longstreet's corps to help the beleaguered Hill and then turn the Union left flank. Hill, anticipating Longstreet's arrival, did not redeploy his troops to new positions.

The Union forces were also planning an attack the next morning, but on all fronts. Grant ordered Sedgwick and Warren to attack along the Orange Turnpike, and at the same time, Hancock would push Hill down Orange Plank Road.

There was no sign of Longstreet when the Union attack began at five a.m. To the north, Ewell held on; but in the south, 23,000 Union troops struck the front and flank of Hill's unprepared forces and quickly overwhelmed them. Except for the Confederate artillery, Lee's entire right flank crumbled, and he sat on his horse helplessly as his broken troops came pouring by him.

Just then Longstreet's Texas Brigade came down the road. His troops had run the last five miles, and Lee was so excited by their just-in-time arrival, he turned to lead them personally in the counterattack. His subordinates had difficulty restraining him, and only the shouts of the soldiers, "Lee to the rear," made him give up. Longstreet went directly into action and pushed forward to a line about a mile west of Brock Road, but the counterattack stalled. For the rest of the morning, the armies attacked and counterattacked, without result—except for huge casualties.

The fighting in the Wilderness

frustrated the soldiers and their commanders. Attacks went forward noisily and blindly, while defenders simply lay in wait to fire at close range. Numbers were frequently an encumbrance on the narrow trails, and during any movement it was virtually impossible to keep formations together in the limited visibility. It was dirty, dangerous close-in combat.

By eleven a.m. the battle slowed, but it was only a lull. Grant had ordered Sedgwick and Warren to stop their attacks on the Orange Turnpike, dig in, and send troops to reinforce Hancock on Brock Road. Inexplicably, the Union cavalry was not scouting their flanks; and as usual, Lee would make them pay for such an oversight. A Confederate reconnaissance patrol had discovered that the south flank of Hancock's lines was unprotected and that there was a 12-foot-wide bed of an unfinished railroad running parallel to the Orange Plank Road. This would make it easy for troops to advance quickly through territory that was otherwise impassable. Longstreet had kept several brigades in reserve and now, with Lee's approval, he prepared a Chancellorsville-style flank attack to roll up the Union line.

The flank attack slammed into Hancock's south flank and, as at Chancellorsville, the Union forces began to collapse. Only the steadiness of several regiments from Vermont kept Longstreet from taking the Orange Plank–Brock Road intersection.

Then there was yet another repeat of Chancellorsville. Longstreet was pushing the Confederate drive forward when he was shot in the neck and right shoulder by his own men. (He recovered, but only returned to duty about five months later with a paralyzed right arm.) The attack was delayed for several hours until Lee took over, and it was late afternoon before it resumed. Meanwhile, Hancock had rallied his Union troops behind the fortifications he had built the day before, and the Confederate attack was defeated.

Lee must have wondered what evil spirit lived in the Wilderness that had cost him two of his best commanders to friendly fire, but the Union generals were more concerned about their own evil spirit, Lee. Grant was so frustrated at their comments as the fighting slacked off that evening that he said, "I am heartily tired of hearing about what Bobbie Lee is going to do. Some of you always seem to think he is suddenly going to turn a double somersault and land in our rear and on both of our flanks at the same time. Go back to your commands, and try to think about what we are going to do instead of wondering what Lee is going to do." They did.

Spotsylvania

On May 7, the day after the Battle of the Wilderness wound down, the two armies were three quarters of a mile from each other behind their fortifications. Union losses had been between 15,000 and 18,000, and Confederate between 7750 and 11,400. Union general Hooker, in a similar situation, had accepted defeat and fallen back toward the north, leaving the field to Lee. Now the Army of the Potomac packed up, and at eight thirty that night moved out. Many of the troops believed that they had been beaten again, and were heading back north with their tails between the legs. Then, on the road, they turned south; they realized that Grant was not retreating but was going to advance and fight again, and for many their spirits rebounded.

Grant tried to outflank Lee by sending Gouverneur Warren's and John Sedgwick's corps around Lee's right to New Spotsylvania Court House, hoping to beat Lee there and cut him off. A detachment of General James Wilson's Union cavalry, which had fought so well in the Wilderness, was sent ahead to scout the town. They found a small force of Confederates there, overwhelmed them, and settled into the town. At eight thirty the next morning, May 8, Warren's infantry came out of the Wilderness into the open ground near Alsop, about three miles west of Spotsylvania. It seemed Grant had won the race.

Then, suddenly, Warren's corps came under attack by a large Confederate force—Longstreet's corps, now commanded by Major General Richard Anderson, which was there almost by accident. The night before, Lee had ordered Anderson to take over Longstreet's corps, withdraw from his position on the Orange Plank Road, and then gather his men in a rear area where they could rest for a few hours. After resting, early in the morning they were to march to Spotsylvania, where Lee expected Grant to move, not knowing that by that time Grant's troops would have been on the road for seven hours. Anderson began his withdrawal at eleven p.m. but could not find a place to rest his entire command, so he simply pushed on, planning to rest at Spotsylvania. He and his exhausted men arrived just in time to meet and stop Warren's equally tired Union troops. Now Confederate troops, led by cavalry, began to pour into Spotsylvania. It was clear that Wilson's small Union force could not hold the village, so he withdrew. That afternoon, more Union forces arrived as Sedgwick's corps joined Warren. Grant wanted them to attack, but it was late in the afternoon before the two were able to coordinate their forces, and the attack failed.

As the Union force moved toward Spotsylvania, General Phil Sheridan, commander of the Union cavalry, quarreled with Meade, still the commander of the Army of the Potomac, about the cavalry's role in the upcoming battle. Sheridan wanted to ride to Richmond to search out and destroy the Confederate cavalry under J.E.B. Stuart. Meade refused; but Grant, knowing Sheridan had twice as many horsemen and that they were armed with repeating rifles, sided with Sheridan. He allowed Sheridan to take most of the Union cavalry south, leaving the Army of the Potomac, like Lee at Gettysburg, deep in enemy territory with only a small cavalry force.

By the afternoon of May 9, both armies were pouring forces into Spotsylvania. Lee dug in, emplacing artillery all along his breastworks and installing trees with sharpened branches—called an abatis—in front of the trenches. The exact line of the Confederates' emplacements was hidden by trees and undergrowth, and they sent forward skirmishers and sharpshooters to keep Union scouts from reconnoitering the defenses. Sedgwick, one of the Union corps commanders, went forward, and when he saw his men ducking behind cover, he said, "What are you dodging for? They cannot hit an elephant that far." A few seconds later he was hit below the left eye by a Confederate ball and died instantly.

Because they dug many of their defenses at night, the Confederates made a mistake on their trench line. When they were complete, the fortifications created a salient, or bulge, a half mile wide at the base and a mile long, shaped like a horseshoe or mule shoe. It was given the name the Mule Shoe, and while entrenchments there were strong—an abatis and four-foot-high walls, backed up by a partially completed second line—the position was vulnerable because it could be attacked from three sides by troops and artillery.

By nightfall on May 9, most of Grant's corps were deployed. Almost as an afterthought, Grant sent Winfield Hancock and his corps to cross the Po River to see if they could turn Lee's left flank. Hancock made a difficult river crossing, and by the next morning his corps had turned Lee's left flank. Had Grant sent more forces to support him, Lee would have been flanked and forced to abandon his strong position.

However, the Union commanders were focused on planning a frontal assault, and missed the chance. Around three thirty p.m., Warren said that he thought he could break through with an immediate frontal attack in his sector. At this point, few of the senior officers on either side understood the value of well-manned field fortifications and did not realize that one man well dug in was the equal of three men in the open. Warren was given permission to try, and was bloodily repulsed. It was a hint of things to come.

During reconnaissance near the Mule Shoe, Union forces saw a belt of woods 200 yards in front of the Confederate works that could conceal Union troops during an attack. An energetic young commander, Colonel Emory Upton, organized a special task force of 12 regiments to try to take the salient. It was to be a mass attack, with troops in four lines of three regiments each. They were not to stop to fire—they would simply charge with bayonets as fast as they could and break through quickly. When the first

General John Sedgwick *was mortally wounded by a sniper while trying to reassure his men that they were in no danger from sharpshooters.*

line was through the Confederate line, it would fan out and widen the penetration; the second line was to do the same to the second Confederate line, while the last two formed the reserve. Another Union division would follow them to exploit the breakthrough.

At about six p.m. on May 10, the attack began. Upton's men went through and over both lines of entrenchments, beating back heavy opposition and capturing about 1000 prisoners. But the division that was supposed to follow was poorly led and was scattered by Confederate artillery fire, so Upton and his men were left isolated. They hung on until dark, and then withdrew.

There was little fighting on May 11, but Grant sent an infantry brigade on a reconnaissance mission that had unforeseen consequences. Lee saw the movement and, still not understanding Grant's aggressive mentality, thought that Grant was planning a night retreat to Fredericksburg after his failed assaults. Lee was still convinced that the only chance for a Confederate victory lay in successful offensive operations. If Grant retreated, Lee wanted to be ready to attack him, so he told his commanders to prepare to move that night on short notice. When he visited the Mule Shoe, he realized it would be difficult to remove the entrenched cannons at night, so he told the commanders to move most of the cannons back before dark and prepare them to move.

Grant was indeed carrying out a major movement, but it was not the one Lee anticipated—in fact, just the opposite. He was planning a repetition of Upton's attack on the early morning of May 12, but on a massive scale. Two full corps would make the attack, with other troops ready to exploit any successes.

A steady rain partially masked the noise of the Union approach that night. A heavy fog set in, and it was four thirty-five a.m. before it was light enough to begin the attack. The Union forces had been gathered in large, tight formations to keep better control in the dark and fog, and to get the greatest possible number of men into the Confederate works with the first charge. The Union commanders did not know that Lee had ordered most of the cannons withdrawn from the Mule Shoe, and they expected slow going and heavy casualties until the Confederate batteries could be overrun.

In the Mule Shoe, the Confederate outposts heard the Union troops gathering and passed the word back. The artillery returned hurriedly, and troops moved back to the fortifications. About an hour later, the guns were being wheeled back into position when, out of the predawn darkness and fog, a huge wave of Union troops surged over the fortifications. The Union troops swept away the Confederates and captured the returning cannons before they could be set up. They moved on to the next line of fortifications, but the unexpected speed of the movement and the Union troops' dense formations wedged them together and slowed them down. The attack captured nearly a division of Lee's army (as well as the cannons) and came near to cutting the Confederate army in half, but the logjam of troops retarded the Union advance enough for the Confederates to begin to plug the gaps.

The Confederates organized a counterattack that Lee wanted to lead personally, but—as in the Wilderness—his men restrained him. The Confederate counterattack forced the Union troops out of much of the Mule Shoe, but they clung to the log breastworks on the outer edge. Throughout the day and into the night, for nearly 20 hours, the fighting raged savagely, especially along a few hundred yards of trenches known as the Bloody Angle on the west face of the salient. It was probably the most ferociously sustained combat of the Civil War.

The infantry knew what the stakes were. One Union soldier wrote later, "Whoever could hold 'The Angle' would be the victors; for with 'The Angle,' either party could possess themselves of the whole line of works. . . . A breastwork of logs separated us from the Rebels. Our men would reach over this partition and discharge their muskets in the face of the Rebels, and in return would receive the fire of the Rebels at the same close range. Finally, the men began to use their muskets as clubs and then rails were used. Neither side backed down, even as a steady rain fell."

Another soldier remembered, "So continuous and heavy was our fire that the head logs of the breastworks were cut and torn until they resembled hickory brooms. Several large oak-trees, which grew just in the rear of the works, were completely gnawed off by our converging fire." The trenches filled with water and

The Bloody Angle *was the scene of some of the bloodiest fighting of the campaign.*

blood, and as reinforcements came in to continue the fight, they trampled the dead and badly wounded into the muddy quagmire.

While the two armies fought stubbornly, Lee's engineers scrambled to build a new fortification line across the base of the Mule Shoe. The rain and the battle delayed the work, and it was not until after midnight that Lee was able to gradually withdraw his tired soldiers to new fortified trenches. The Union had the Mule Shoe, but it was of no use, and they were too tired for a follow-up attack.

The next day, May 13, Grant decided to attack Lee's right flank south from Spotsylvania Court House, hoping to turn it before Lee could reinforce the area. Warren's corps was ordered to move south after dark and attack at four a.m. Warren's men did their best, but heavy rains, fog, and swollen creeks slowed the movement. Instead of being ready to attack the morning of May 14, it took the whole day to get into position and organize his men, and Grant finally called off the attack. Grant's move caught Lee off guard, and it was fortunate the weather had saved him from a serious surprise. He immediately began to shift troops and extend his trenchworks southward.

Meanwhile, Sheridan's Union cavalry had achieved considerable success. He had ransacked Confederate supply lines, and then clashed with the preeminent Confederate cavalry commander, J.E.B. Stuart, at Yellow Tavern, outside of Richmond, on May 11. Stuart, wearing his trademark plumed hat, was shot and killed by a Union marksman, and the Union cavalry won their first clear victory against a large Confederate cavalry force.

From May 14 to 17, the two armies dug in and fought a series of skirmishes that produced no gains but a steady flow of casualties. On May 18, Grant tried another attack on the Confederate left flank, but Confederate scouts and patrols detected the movement and the Union forces were shot to pieces by Confederate artillery. By about ten a.m., even Grant was willing to halt the operation. On May 19, a Confederate attempt to turn the Union right flank at Harris Farm was beaten back with many casualties. On May 20, Grant ordered Hancock to march southward along the line of the Fredericksburg and Potomac Railroad, five miles to the east. On May 21, Grant disengaged his entire force and continued his advance on Richmond, with Lee in lockstep.

Union losses during the fighting around Spotsylvania Court House are variously reported but appear to have been between 17,000 and 18,000. Confederate casualties are unknown, but since their forces fought behind fortifications during most of these engagements, their losses must have been considerably less—perhaps between 9000 and 10,000.

Fredericksburg and Spotsylvania National Military Park

The park preserves portions of four major battlefields—Fredericksburg, Chancellorsville, the Wilderness, and Spotsylvania—in the city of Fredericksburg, Virginia, and the nearby counties. More than 15,000 men were killed and 85,000 wounded in this area during the Civil War, making it the "bloodiest landscape in North America." All of the battlefields are within a 17-mile radius of Fredericksburg, and park roads link a series of 16 tour stops that provide a complete self-guided tour of all four battlefields. The park maintains two battlefield visitors centers: the **Fredericksburg Battlefield Visitor Center** and the **Chancellorsville Battlefield Visitor Center.**

The **Fredericksburg Battlefield Visitor Center** contains two floors of museum exhibits and a 12-minute slide program explaining the battle. The center also offers brochures for walking and driving tours.

Behind the Visitor Center is a path that leads along the Sunken Road. Along the path are signs, monuments, pictures, and an audiovisual program that describes the battle. A painting in the Visitor Center depicts the topography of the area in 1862.

The Lee Drive/Fredericksburg Battlefield Drive begins one half mile south of the Fredericksburg Battlefield Visitor Center, at the entrance to Lee Drive, the starting point for a five-mile tour following the line of Confederate trenches and artillery emplacements. Markers, maps, paintings, and exhibits line the drive. A paved trail goes to the top of Lee Hill, where General Robert E. Lee watched the battle.

The **Chancellorsville Battlefield Visitor Center** offers a 12-minute slide presentation explaining the battles of Chancellorsville, the Wilderness, and Spotsylvania, as well as exhibits and dioramas. Behind the Visitor Center is a monument on the site where Stonewall Jackson was accidentally wounded by his own men on May 2, 1863, and a walking trail to nearby trench works.

The Chancellorsville Battlefield Drive begins next to the Visitor Center parking lot. There are stops along the five-mile drive at the important landmarks on the battlefield, including the Chancellorsville house site, Hazel Grove, and the spot where Confederate generals Lee and Jackson met to plan Jackson's march around Union general Joseph Hooker's right flank. A short walking trail leads to the Hazel Grove and Fairview artillery positions.

The park also includes the Wilderness Battlefield Exhibit Shelter and the Spotsylvania Battlefield Exhibit Shelter, but there are no visitors centers at those battlefields. Tours are self-guided, and the shelters at the entrance to each battlefield offer explanations and maps of the battles. There are usually historians there on summer weekends. Driving tours begin near the shelters.

In addition to the battlefield visitors centers and exhibit shelters, the park contains five other historical sites open to the public.

The **Stonewall Jackson Shrine** is the building where Confederate General Thomas Jonathan "Stonewall" Jackson died after he was wounded at Chancellorsville. There are interpretive signs and a large painting depicting the arrival of the wounded Jackson, and an audio program explaining the picture. The building is furnished with period pieces and includes the original deathbed, blanket, and clock.

The 18th-century **Chatham Manor** was a Union headquarters, communications center, and hospital during the battle. Outside there is an excellent view of Fredericksburg and of Union pontoon-bridge sites on the Rappahannock.

Ellwood Manor was owned by the same family that owned Chatham Manor. Jackson's amputated arm is in the family cemetery.

Old Salem Church was involved in pivotal fighting during the Chancellorsville campaign and served as a hospital when the fighting ended. The building is open only on weekends during the summer, but there is a self-guided walking tour around the grounds.

Fredericksburg National Cemetery on Marye's Heights is across the Sunken Road from the Fredericksburg Battlefield Visitor Center and was once an artillery position for Confederates. Today the cemetery contains the graves of more than 15,000 United States soldiers. Several monuments are scattered about the cemetery, and at the crest of the hill is a painting depicting the Battle of Fredericksburg from that view, as well as a short audio program.

Numerous walking trails provide access to additional areas, and folders and maps of these trails are available in the visitors centers and at the exhibit shelters. These walks include Sunken Road, National Cemetery, Marye's Heights, Chancellorsville History Trail, Hazel Grove, Salem Church, McLaws Walking Trail, Wounding of Jackson Trail, Gordon Flank Attack, Widow Tapp Field, Spotsylvania History Trail, and the Bloody Angle. Regularly scheduled historian-guided tours are available during the summer season and on some weekends during the spring and fall.

There are several bookstores in the park. The main one is located at the Fredericksburg Battlefield Visitor Center complex, with others in the Chancellorsville Battlefield Visitor Center, Chatham Manor, and Stonewall Jackson Shrine.

Visitors who want to tour the Wilderness or Spotsylvania Battlefields should begin at either of the visitors centers, where they can pay the entrance fee and receive maps and information about the battlefields. Allow two full days to visit the entire park.

Visitor Information

Fredericksburg Battlefield Visitor Center 540-373-6122; Chancellorsville Visitor Center 540-786-2880; Chatham Manor 540-654-5121; Jackson Shrine 804-633-6076; http://www.nps.gov/frsp/index.htm
Hours: The grounds are open from sunrise to sunset. **Fredericksburg Battlefield Visitor Center** and **Chancellorsville Battlefield Visitor Center:** Weekdays, 9 a.m. until 5 p.m.; weekends, 9 a.m. until 6 p.m.; closed December 25 and New Year's Day. **Wilderness Exhibit Shelter:** Summer weekends, 10:30 a.m. until 5:30 p.m. **Spotsylvania Battlefield Exhibit Shelter:** Summer weekends, 10 a.m. until 6 p.m. **Stonewall Jackson Shrine:** Friday through Tuesday, 9 a.m. until 5 p.m.; closed Wednesday and Thursday. **Chatham Manor:** Daily, 9 a.m. until 5 p.m. **Ellwood Manor:** Weekends, 11 a.m. until 5 p.m. from Memorial Day to Labor Day, and 11 a.m. until 5 p.m. for the anniversary of the Battle of the Wilderness, May 3–4. **Old Salem Church:** Open summer weekends. Call ahead for information about the hours of the sites.
Admission: Moderate charge per adult 17 and older; National Parks Pass, Golden Eagle, Golden Age, and Golden Access are honored.
Accessibility: All park buildings,

except for the basement level of the Fredericksburg Battlefield Visitor Center and the upper floor of the Stonewall Jackson Shrine, are accessible to wheelchairs. All buildings have wheelchair access to restrooms. For inaccessible exhibits, the park has a photo album of the exhibits with explanatory text. Handicapped parking is located at all visitor facilities. Text versions of the audiovisual programs are available for the hearing impaired.
Special Events: In summer, the Fredericksburg and Spotsylvania National Military Park offers a series of free evening "History at Sunset" programs that consider the realities of a community and a nation at war. Most are held on Friday evenings. Some recent programs included Chaos in the Night: The Wounding of "Stonewall" Jackson; City of Hospitals: The Aftermath of Battle; History Unveiled: Archaeology at the Sunken Road and Marye's Heights. Call for information.
Getting There: Fredericksburg, Virginia, is located approximately 50 miles south of Washington, D.C., and 50 miles north of Richmond, Virginia. The town is about three miles east of I-95. Various shuttle services that can transport individuals to Fredericksburg operate to and from area airports—Washington-Reagan National, Dulles International, Baltimore-Washington International, and Richmond International. Amtrak provides train service to downtown Fredericksburg.

To the Fredericksburg Battlefield Visitor Center from Washington, D.C.: Take I-95 south to state Route 3 east. Drive east approximately two miles to the traffic light at the intersection of Route 3 (Blue and Gray Parkway) with business Route U.S. 1 (Lafayette Boulevard). Turn left and go approximately 1/2 mile to the Fredericksburg Battlefield Visitor Center, on the left.

To the Fredericksburg Battlefield Visitor Center from Richmond, Virginia: Take I-95 north to the Fredericksburg exit. Drive about one mile on U.S. 1 (Jefferson Davis Highway) to the traffic light where U.S. 1 splits. Bear right on business Route 1, Lafayette Boulevard, and drive about four miles to the visitors center, on the left.

To the Chancellorsville Visitor Center: From I-95, take state route 3 west at exit 130, and proceed approximately seven miles. The visitors center is on the right.

PHOTOGRAPHY

The new technology of photography came into its own during the Civil War. Whereas earlier wars had been captured through artists' pen-and-ink sketches, this war saw the evolution of photography as the most realistic and evocative means of visually recording the war for the citizenry of both sides.

This war wasn't the first to be captured in photographs (the Crimean War in 1855 was covered by photographer Roger Fenton for the *London Times*), but the extent to which battlefields, ravaged cities, and the common soldier were photographed was unprecedented. In fact, photographs of the common soldier made up the majority of the more than one million photographs taken during the war.

Dozens of "portraitists" traveled from camp to camp, immortalizing the war in the faces of its soldiers. The average photographer was thronged with visitors from morning to night, soldiers of all ranks eager to record themselves in uniform for the folks back home.

As described in the book *The Blue and the Gray* by Martin Graham, Richard Sauers, and George Skoch, the process of taking a photograph was time consuming and elaborate: "When ready to photograph, the artist coated a glass plate with collo-

Mathew Brady spent most of his time supervising his corps of photographers.

dion made of a solution of nitrocellulose in equal parts of sulphuric ether and 95-proof alcohol. The surface of the plate was then sensitized by adding bromide and iodine of potassium or ammonia. After letting this mixture evaporate to the right consistency, the plate was immersed from three to five minutes in a bath holder solution of silver nitrate. . . . The photographer then uncapped the lens to permit an exposure of from five to thirty seconds, depending on available light. Following the capping, the photographer then had only a few minutes to develop the plate in a solution of sulfate of iron and acetic acid. Then he washed the plate with a cyanide of potassium solution to remove any surplus silver. Finally he washed it yet again, dried it, and varnished it."

Imagine doing this from the back of a wagon and you have some idea of the difficulties of being a Civil War photographer.

Illustrated weeklies, such as *Harper's Weekly* and *New York Illustrated News*, chose to use the old-fashioned sketch artist, but following a New York exhibition by Mathew Brady of "The Dead of Antietam" in September 1862, photographic images were suddenly in demand.

Mathew Brady remains the most famous of the Civil War photographers and it is his images that are often called to mind—a soldier sprawled in a ditch like a broken doll, mangled horses across a muddy field, silent cannons on a hilltop. Brady himself was nearly blind and depended on his assistants, Alexander Gardner and Timothy O'Sullivan, to take shots—often posed to greatest effect. Once, Gardner dragged the corpse of a Confederate soldier some 40 yards to a sniper's nest in order to create a dramatic statement.

Other Union photographers included Captain Andrew J. Russell, the army's official photographer, and George N. Barnard, who traveled with William T. Sherman to Atlanta and photographed the city after its capture.

After the war, the public lost interest in photography. Mathew Brady went bankrupt and was forced to sell thousands of his glass plate negatives to gardeners, who used them as glass panes in their greenhouses.

"Decidedly one of the institutions of our army is the travelling portrait gallery. A camp is hardly pitched before one of the omnipresent artists in collodion and amber bead varnish drives up in his two-horse wagon, pitches his canvas gallery, and unpacks his chemicals. Our army here (Fredericksburg) is now so large that quite a company of these gentlemen have gathered about us. The amount of business they find is remarkable. Their tents are thronged from morning to night. . . . In one day since they came here they took . . . 160 odd pictures at $1 each."
—*From* Scientific American, *October 18, 1862*

A photographer's wagon, top, served as the traveling darkroom. The box camera, above, held an 8-by-10-inch glass negative. Sharpening was accomplished by moving the plate forward or back in the inner box. Finer focusing was achieved by turning the knob on the lens.

Alexander Gardner's famous photograph A Sharpshooter's Last Sleep *was actually staged by hauling a dead Confederate infantryman up to the Devil's Den at Gettysburg.*

Fort Ward

When the Civil War broke out in April 1861, the Union capital of Washington, D.C., was surrounded by Confederate sympathizers and was virtually undefended. When Virginia seceded, Union troops quickly moved to protect the capital. They crossed the Potomac and occupied Alexandria, the home of Robert E. Lee at Arlington Heights, and other areas in northern Virginia. There the Union troops began building earth forts to use as supply bases for Union operations deeper into Virginia.

In July 1861 the Confederate's victory at First Bull Run (First Manassas) caused panic in Washington. The battlefield was just 30 miles from the capital, and soon afterward Union general George McClellan began a huge expansion of Washington's defenses, soon known as the Defenses of Washington or Mr. Lincoln's Forts. Fort Ward, situated on the highest point in Alexandria, was completed in September 1861 and was the fifth largest of the over 160 forts and batteries eventually built around the

capital. The fort was named for Commander James H. Ward, the first Union naval officer killed in the Civil War.

Fort Ward was a standard mid-19th-century earth fort, first built with a perimeter of 540 yards and emplacements for 24 guns. After another Union defeat, at the Battle of Second Bull Run (Second Manassas) in August 1862, Fort Ward was strengthened; and when the war

The Northwest Bastion, together with its counterpart the Southwest Bastion, were the major defensive elements of Fort Ward. Armed with two 24-pounder howitzers, three 4.5" ordnance rifles, and a 6-pounder James rifle, the Northwest Bastion guarded the approach to Alexandria along the Leesburg Turnpike.

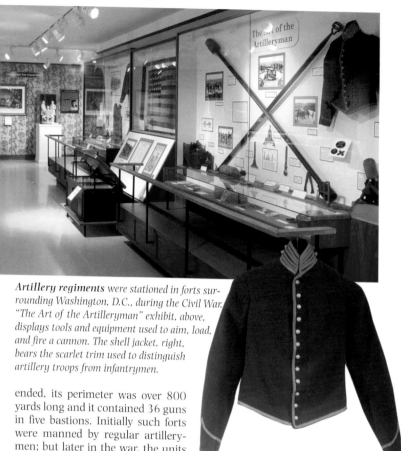

Artillery regiments were stationed in forts surrounding Washington, D.C., during the Civil War. "The Art of the Artilleryman" exhibit, above, displays tools and equipment used to aim, load, and fire a cannon. The shell jacket, right, bears the scarlet trim used to distinguish artillery troops from infantrymen.

ended, its perimeter was over 800 yards long and it contained 36 guns in five bastions. Initially such forts were manned by regular artillerymen; but later in the war, the units were pulled out and sent to the front (where many of them suffered heavy casualties). Freed slaves and soldiers recovering from wounds or disease replaced these regular crews. Fort Ward was abandoned and torn down in late 1865, leaving Alexandria with nothing but a deep depression in the ground.

In 1961 the City of Alexandria began restoration work on Fort Ward as a Civil War Centennial Project. Working from photographs of Fort Ward and other area forts (including some taken by famous Civil War photographer Mathew Brady), the city reconstructed part of the fort and a museum inside a 45-acre park. Today Fort Ward is the best preserved and restored of the capital's protective system of Civil War Union forts and batteries, and the only remaining fort in the system with a permanent museum and interpretive program.

Fort Ward Museum and Historic Site

The two-story museum was completed in 1964 and is patterned after a wooden Union headquarters building. Its wooden trim below the rooflines is called gingerbread, a fanciful but popular architectural style in the 1800s. The museum features exhibits on a variety of Civil War topics and is home to the Dorothy C. S. Starr Library.

An orientation video, *Fort Ward and the Defenses of Washington, D.C.: Silent Guardians of the Capital City,* provides an overview of the history of Fort Ward and its place in Washington's wartime defenses. The museum collection contains a large number of Civil War artifacts and photographs, including objects related to Alexandria's Civil War past, as well as descriptions of life in Union-occupied Alexandria, where most of the citizens were Confederate sympathizers. The exhibits also describe the city's role in the Union army supply system and the lives of Civil War soldiers and civilians. Among the artifacts and photographs displayed are letters, uniforms, weapons and military equipment, surgeons' tools, musical instruments, sketchbooks, diaries, and a set of jackstraws carved by a Confederate prisoner of war.

The museum also contains a three-dimensional small-scale model of Fort Ward, as well as a large map that outlines the extensive ring of forts that made up the capital's defenses. The museum shop offers books and other items, as well as exhibit brochures and a self-guided tour map of the fort.

The Dorothy C. S. Starr Library inside the museum is open to the public for on-site research when the museum is open, until a half hour before closing. Written requests are answered on a case-by-case basis. The small staff tries to respond to written queries but cannot conduct extensive research.

The self-guided Fort Ward walking tour follows an interpretive trail through the reconstructed ceremonial entrance gate (on its original site), a reconstructed wooden Officers Hut where high-ranking soldiers lived, and underground bomb shelters, called bombproofs, each designed to hold 500 men. The fort's completely restored Northwest Bastion has reproductions of Civil War cannons and an interesting powder magazine and ammunition-filling room. The adjacent North Bastion contains a connecting rifle trench, intended to allow troops to move under cover to other forts and batteries during a battle. The earthwork walls show the characteristics of major earthen fortifications that were part of the Defenses of Washington. The walking tour takes approximately 45 minutes.

Visitor Information
703-838-4848;
oha.ci.alexandria.va.us/fortward/
Museum Hours: Tuesday to Saturday, 9 a.m. until 5 p.m.; Sunday, noon until 5 p.m.; closed Thanksgiving, December 25, and New Year's Day.
Historic Site Hours: Daily, 9 a.m. until sunset.
Admission: Free.
Accessibility: The museum exhibit areas are wheelchair accessible. The Fort Ward video is close-captioned for the hearing impaired. Large-print, Braille, French, German, and Spanish brochures are available. An individual with a disability who wishes to request a reasonable accommodation may contact the museum at 703-838-4848.
Special Events: The park includes an amphitheater where musical concerts are held every Thursday night from June to August. Because of its proximity to the nation's capital, the park grounds attract a number of Civil War reenactments and living-history programs. The museum offers a wide range of educational programs throughout the year, including a lecture and video series and tours. Call for details.
Getting There: Fort Ward Museum is located in Alexandria, Virginia,

Drummers *were expected to master all of the 148 regulation calls and tunes by the first day of enlistment. The most important use of drums was on the battlefield, where they were used to communicate orders from the commanding officers and to signal troop movement.*

across the Potomac River approximately six miles south of Washington, D.C.

Public Transportation: Take the Yellow or Blue Line Metro to King Street Station in Alexandria, or take Amtrak or Virginia Railway Express to the Alexandria Union Station. The DASH bus stop is in the King Street Station across from the Alexandria Union Station. The AT5 DASH bus to Landmark stops at Fort Ward. Call 703-370-DASH for bus schedules and information.

From Old Town Alexandria: Follow King Street west to T. C. Williams High School, and turn right on Kenwood Avenue. Turn left on West Braddock Road, and proceed about a mile. The museum entrance is on the right.

From I-395: Take the Seminary Road East exit. At the fourth traffic light (Alexandria Hospital) turn left onto North Howard Street. Follow North Howard to its intersection with West Braddock Road and turn right. The museum entrance is on the left.

From Washington, D.C., and National Airport: Follow road signs to I-395 south, and follow those directions, above.

From I-95/I-495 (Capital Beltway): Follow road signs to I-395 south, and follow those directions, above.

From Dulles Airport: Take Dulles Access Road east to I-495 south (Capital Beltway). Follow road signs to I-395 south, and follow those directions, above.

There is ample free parking for cars and buses, and handicapped parking is available in the museum lot.

The First Battle of Bull Run (Manassas)

When the Civil War began in April 1861, many Americans expected the conflict to be brief, with a single battle deciding the outcome. The logical place for this Armageddon seemed to be between the two capitals—the Confederate one at Richmond, Virginia, and the Union capital in Washington, D.C.—100 miles apart.

Both sides rushed to create an army, and volunteers flooded the recruiting offices. "On to Richmond" was the rallying cry of the Union newspapers, and President Abraham Lincoln was willing to risk a rapid offensive strike into Virginia, even though the commander of the Union army, the 75-year-old General Winfield "Old Fuss and Feathers" Scott, opposed it. He preferred a slow strangulation of the South by a blockade, known as the Anaconda Plan (*see* sidebar, page 117), with the intention of ending the war with a minimum of bitterness and casualties. However, Scott was too old to be the commander that Lincoln wanted, so command of the Union army devolved to the newly promoted Brigadier General Irvin McDowell. McDowell was reluctant to go on the offensive quickly, even though he had assembled 35,000 men—the largest army ever seen in North America. Like Scott, he had little faith in his untrained army, mainly made up of 90-day volunteers. However, Lincoln argued famously, "You are green it is true, but they are green also." McDowell was ordered to move south before the end of July, so he did not have time to train his troops.

For his first attack, McDowell selected Manassas Junction, 29 miles to the southwest of Washington. It was the link for two railroads, the Manassas Gap and the Orange & Alexandria. These two railroads were crucial because they linked Washington, central Virginia, and the Shenandoah Valley. The Orange & Alexandria line could be used both to transport and to supply a Union army marching south. The Manassas Gap railroad line was important because it linked the area around Washington with the Confederate stronghold in the Shenandoah Valley.

McDowell knew the Confederate forces in northern Virginia were divided, with Brigadier General Joseph E. Johnston's 11,000 Confederates somewhere in the Shenandoah Valley and another larger force around Richmond. This was part of a deliberate Confederate plan to use the railroads to move troops rapidly, separating their forces to meet Union probes and then quickly joining them as needed

In early July, McDowell began the Union attack by sending Major

Irvin McDowell

Irvin McDowell was the first commander of the Union army around the capital at the outbreak of the Civil War, due to both his excellent reputation up to that point and his friendship with Secretary of the Treasury Salmon Chase. While McDowell's battle plan for First Bull Run (Manassas) was well regarded, political pressure forced him into action before his inexperienced troops were prepared for this first major battle of the war. The Union performance was dismal, and McDowell was replaced by George McClellan only four days later.

Bull Run was to be McDowell's nemesis. As a corps commander in the Army of the Potomac, he was blamed for the Union defeat at the Second Battle of Bull Run and relieved of his command. A court of inquiry eventually cleared his name, but he never again led a battle, and he served in administrative roles until his retirement in 1882.

General Robert Patterson and 18,000 troops into the Shenandoah Valley. Patterson's mission was to keep Johnston away from the rail line to Manassas while McDowell attacked the other forces. If Patterson was successful, McDowell would have 35,000 troops massed against about 21,000 Confederates.

Confederate brigadier general P.G.T. Beauregard, the victor at Fort Sumter, was the commander of the Confederate troops between Washington and Richmond. His forces were spread out around Manassas, Centreville, and Fairfax Court House; and like the Union soldiers, the Confederate troops were enthusiastic but raw recruits. Beauregard was not expected to mount an offensive, only to defeat any Union attack. The Manassas Gap rail line would link Beauregard with Johnston so the two could concentrate their forces where the threat was greatest.

Beauregard expected McDowell to try to capture the rail center at Manassas Junction, so he set up his defense line three miles east of the rail center, behind a stream named

Bull Run. He needed to bring in Johnston's troops from the lower Shenandoah Valley in order to avoid certain defeat. But first he had to get the Confederate government to allow Johnston to abandon the Shenandoah and bring his troops to Manassas before McDowell struck. Then, once they received permission to move, Johnston's Confederates would have to elude Patterson's men in order to board the trains to get to Manassas. It was not clear which would be more difficult.

Beauregard's seven infantry brigades were all led by either West Point graduates or veterans of previous wars, or both. (It was the superiority of these Southern combat leaders that made their early victories possible.) He began to strengthen his line on a six-mile front along the south bank of Bull Run, concentrating most of his forces on his right center astride the Centreville–Manassas Road since he did not have enough men to cover the entire Bull Run stream and its numerous fords.

Union general McDowell organized his 60 separate regiments and

---

P.G.T. Beauregard

Pierre Gustave Toutant Beauregard was an able military commander for the Confederacy, but his ego and poor relations with Confederate President Jefferson Davis prevented him from advancing beyond second-in-command and from getting plum assignments.

Known as Little Napoleon for his French-Creole background and haughty demeanor, Beauregard achieved early fame in the Confederacy for his successful bombardment of Fort Sumter in April 1861, and for his role in the First Battle of Bull Run (Manassas). Though he performed well, Davis sent him to the western theater under Albert Sidney Johnston, where he took command at Shiloh after Johnston was wounded and led the withdrawal to Corinth.

After a sick leave, Beauregard returned to Charleston, where he successfully held off Union attacks on the coast, incorporating ironclads, torpedoes, and a submarine into his defense. In the spring of 1864, he supported Robert E. Lee in Virginia, commanding a victory at Drewry's Bluff and holding Petersburg against Ulysses S. Grant until Lee's arrival. At the end of the war, Beauregard was again reassigned under Joseph Johnston in the Carolinas until the surrender.

Unlike most former Confederate officers, after the war Beauregard spoke out in support of civil and voting rights for recently freed slaves.

batteries into larger brigades and divisions to ease command and control, but none of his five division commanders had ever seen, much less commanded, the numbers they would have to control at Bull Run.

On July 16, Confederate spies brought Beauregard the news that McDowell had begun to move into the Virginia countryside. Beauregard relayed this information to Richmond, hoping this would be the catalyst necessary for them to approve Johnston's move to join him, which they did a few days later.

Because of the heat and the lack of road-march discipline, McDowell's advance was slow. On July 18 he sent General Daniel Tyler's lead division to seize Centreville and probe carefully beyond it. Tyler took Centreville but became involved in a sharp skirmish just beyond the town, where his men were badly chewed up.

Once in Centreville, McDowell stayed there for two days to organize. He decided to attack at Sudley Ford on the Confederate left, a few miles upstream from Stone Bridge, where Warrenton Turnpike crossed Bull Run. The attack would begin before dawn on July 21, with Tyler feigning an attack at Stone Bridge to make Beauregard think this was the main Union thrust. Meanwhile, two other divisions would march northwest to Sudley Ford, cross Bull Run, then march south along the Manassas–Sudley Road to turn Beauregard's left.

The plan, while a reasonable one, assumed that Patterson would keep Johnston from leaving the Shenandoah Valley and reinforcing Beauregard. Unfortunately for McDowell, instead of concentrating on Johnston, Patterson began to worry about his rear and pulled back from the railroad line. Before dawn on July 18, Johnston used General J.E.B. Stuart's cavalry to screen him from Patterson's men and was able to load his forces onto trains on the Manassas Gap Railroad. His first brigade, led by Brigadier General Thomas J. Jackson, reached Manassas Junction on July 19, and Johnston and parts of two other brigades arrived at Manassas on July 20. However, the railroad had limited capacity and—amazingly—the Southern railroad staff refused to work overtime, so the units were moved slowly and piecemeal to the front.

Because Johnston was senior to Beauregard, he assumed overall command of the Confederate forces when he arrived, and the two planned a spoiling attack on the Union left. They concentrated most of their strength on the right of their eight-mile line. On their far left, where the Union attack was to come, Colonel Nathan G. Evans's brigade was alone, overlooking the Stone Bridge. Beauregard had no reserves in the rear.

McDowell Attacks

On July 21, still unaware that Johnston's troops had escaped the valley and were arriving in Manassas, McDowell ordered his army forward. The plan quickly went awry. Tyler's division moved slowly and delayed the two flanking divisions, who were trying to share part of the road to move quickly to Sudley Ford on the Confederate left. Additionally, the other road the flanking divisions had to use was very narrow, which further slowed their movement. The 13,000-man Union attack force did not begin crossing Bull Run until nine thirty a.m., over two hours behind schedule.

Tyler also began his feint too early, long before the flanking force had reached its crossing point, and his diversion was so unenthusiastically executed that Evans suspected a ruse and prepared to move. He notified Beauregard and Johnston, but they vacillated between proceeding with their attack and defending, and most of their early orders were confused and contradictory.

At eight a.m., Evans's suspicions were confirmed when he received a warning from a Confederate signal station: "Look out for your left, you are turned." Evans had only a small brigade to meet the larger Union force, but he did not hesitate. He left 200 men to watch Tyler, and then led 900 men north toward Sudley Ford. He arrived on Matthews Hill, a short distance from the ford, just in time to meet the first 6000 Union troops that had crossed Bull Run. He held his position alone at first, but by midmorning he was joined by reinforcements recently arrived from the Shenandoah. The Confederate force on Matthews Hill had grown to 2800, and their goal was simple— hold on and buy time until Beauregard and Johnston could shift forces north to reinforce the Confederate flank.

The force on Matthews Hill bought about two hours, but by eleven thirty a.m. McDowell's larger

force pushed them off the hill and into full retreat south across the Warrenton Turnpike and to a cleared plateau called Henry Hill, six miles north of Manassas Junction. McDowell was beside himself, screaming "Forward. Victory! Victory! The day is ours." Then, at the base of Henry Hill, he halted for an hour to regroup his disorganized troops. Beauregard and Johnston took full advantage of the lull by rushing reinforcements to Henry Hill.

Jackson's brigade reached Henry Hill around noon, and he ordered his five regiments of infantry to take cover on the reverse slope, just over the crest of the plateau and out of sight of the Union troops. When the broken Confederate forces crossed the crest they saw Jackson's brigade forming into battle line, and General Barnard E. Bee uttered the immortal words (or some variation thereof), "There stands Jackson like a stone wall. Rally round the Virginians!" A legend was born, and the Confederate troops moved into the line. By the time McDowell realized he had a fight on his hands for Henry Hill, Jackson had 13 guns in position and Beauregard and Johnston had gathered approximately 7000 men along the rear edge of the plateau.

Still, McDowell retained a significant numerical advantage. He now ordered two artillery batteries to move to Henry Hill and blast Jackson's line at close range. A massive duel commenced between their 11 guns and Jackson's artillery. The Union troops were using Parrott rifles, superior in range and accuracy to the Confederates' smoothbores, and Union guns blasted Confederates out of the Henry House (in the process killing widow Judith Henry). However, many of the advantages of the rifled Union weapons were lost at the close range where the battle was taking place. McDowell tried to move up infantry to support his artillery batteries, but the Confederate artillery cut them down.

Disaster for the Union
Captain Charles Griffin, in charge of one Union artillery battery, realized he would have to move his guns to break the Confederate defenses. He took two cannons and established a new position perpendicular to the Confederate line. From there, Griffin could fire from the flank down the length of the entire Confederate line, and could turn the tide of the battle for the Union. About three p.m., just as he was setting up his guns, Griffin saw a formation of troops moving toward his new position. Although a number of the men wore blue uniforms, Griffin decided that they were

Confederate cavalry under Colonel J.E.B. Stuart attack the colorful 11th New York Fire Zouaves and the 69th New York, a solidly Irish regiment. While the print accurately portrays the fervor of the battle, the Zouaves were actually clothed in blue pantaloons, some with red flannel shirts.

Jackson ordered two of his regiments to charge the other Union battery, where they captured the Union guns. Though the guns were to change hands four more times during the fighting, this initial capture was the turning point of the battle.

McDowell finally managed to get Union infantry up to the top of Henry Hill, and a desperate struggle ensued around the abandoned guns. As the battle on the plateau raged, McDowell ordered one brigade to Chinn Ridge on the western flank of Henry Hill. If the Union could seize the ridge, they could strike the exposed flank of the Confederate line. But the last Confederate brigades from the Shenandoah Valley reached the battlefield just then and quickly moved to Chinn Ridge, forcing the Union troops away. Around four p.m., Beauregard ordered his entire line forward. The Union right began to crumble, and a spirited charge pushed the last Union forces off Henry Hill.

At four thirty p.m., the Federal retreat began across Stone Bridge and Sudley Ford, but a Confederate artillery shell blew over a wagon on the Cub Run Bridge, another withdrawal route. The bridge was blocked, and this was the straw that broke the Union forces. Order disappeared and panic gripped the

Confederates and ordered his men to load their guns with canister. Then McDowell's chief of artillery, William B. Barry, stepped in and said, "Don't fire there. Those are your support." Griffin argued, and then reluctantly gave in.

In fact, the unidentified force was a battalion of Virginia Confederate troops. They moved close to Griffin's position, raised their muskets, and mowed down the Union gunners with a murderous volley. Seeing this,

Federal retreat turned into panic after an escape route became blocked. An eyewitness said riderless horses and wrecked wagons, "flying at their utmost speed and whacking against other vehicles, produced a noise like a hurricane at sea."

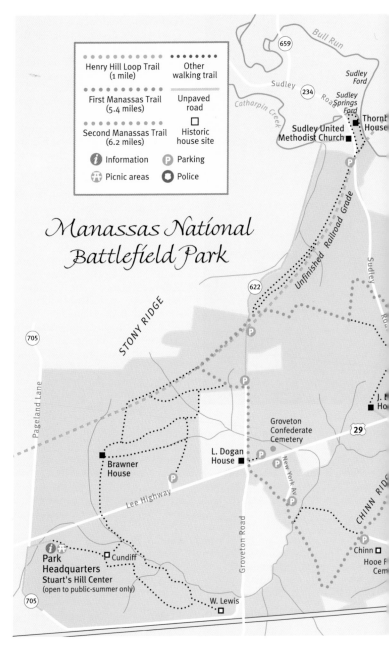

Manassas National Battlefield Park

Legend:
- Henry Hill Loop Trail (1 mile)
- First Manassas Trail (5.4 miles)
- Second Manassas Trail (6.2 miles)
- Other walking trail
- Unpaved road
- Historic house site
- Information
- Parking
- Picnic areas
- Police

exhausted troops and the civilians who had come out to watch the battle. What had been a nearly even contest became a rout of the Union forces. A Union commander said later, "Panic seized all the troops within sight. The men seemed to be seized simultaneously by the conviction that it was no use to do anything more and they might as well start home." However, the Confederate army was equally disorganized and in no condition to pursue, despite the urgings of Jackson and others.

Union general McDowell suffered almost 3000 casualties and abandoned a great deal of equipment in the panicky retreat. The Confeder-ates had less than 2000 casualties, but both sides lost a disproportionate number of officers trying to lead their inexperienced troops from the front. The losses were small in comparison with later battles, but nonetheless shocked those who had expected a bloodless war. Southerners had anticipated that one victory such as Bull Run would persuade the North to abandon the war; but President Lincoln quickly made it clear that he would continue the fight, and he organized new armies for a long conflict. McDowell was blamed for the defeat, and Lincoln appointed Major General George B. McClellan to replace him.

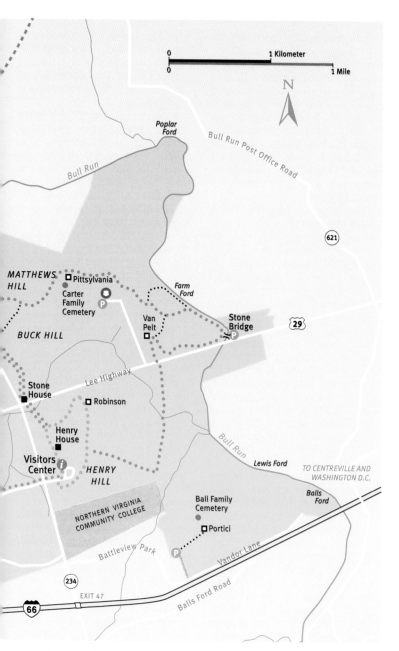

The Second Battle of Bull Run (Manassas)

After defeating Union major general George B. McClellan's Army of the Potomac in the Seven Days Battles in June–July 1862, Confederate general Robert E. Lee turned north to face a second Union threat. President Abraham Lincoln had created a new army, the Army of Virginia, and chose Major General John Pope to lead its 50,000 men. Pope was supposed to wait for McClellan's army to arrive, and then the combined armies would attack Lee. Meanwhile, Lee knew that if McClellan joined Pope in northern Virginia, the Confederates would be outnumbered more than two to one. He had to defeat Pope before McClellan's army could join him.

On August 9, Lee ordered Major General Thomas J. "Stonewall" Jackson's corps of 24,000 men to move north toward Pope and the Army of Virginia. A few days later, Lee marched northwest with Major General James Longstreet's corps of 31,000 men to join Jackson against Pope.

Lee planned to cross the Rapidan River on Pope's left while his cavalry struck behind Union lines to burn bridges over the Rappahannock River and isolate Pope from reinforcements, allowing Lee to defeat him before McClellan arrived. However, as the Confederate army began to move, a Union cavalry detachment defeated part of J.E.B Stuart's cavalry and discovered Lee's communication regarding battle plans. (They almost captured Stuart and did get his plumed hat and cloak.) Now warned, Pope fell back behind the Rappahannock on August 18. There, reinforced by the vanguard of McClellan's army, he established a strong defense front from Kelly's Ford to Rappahannock Station to prevent Lee's troops from crossing the river.

Time was running out, and McClellan was on the move. Lee realized he could not break through Pope's main defensive line, but he was still determined to attack. On August 25, while Longstreet skirmished with Pope's men along the Rappahannock, Lee sent Jackson's corps and Stuart's cavalry to move behind Pope's right flank and cut Pope's supply line, hoping to force Pope away from his defenses on the Rappahannock and back toward Washington. Late on August 26, Jackson's advance force captured Bristoe Station, and then moved north along the railroad to Manassas Junction, the location of Pope's huge supply depot. They had marched 54 miles in 36 hours.

Easily scattering the few defenders, Jackson's men took possession of the Junction after dark and brushed off an attack by a Union brigade. Although surprised to hear that Jackson was at Manassas Junction, Pope quickly realized that he had Lee's army separated in two parts and could defeat them one at a time. He boasted he would "bag the whole crowd." On August 27, Pope left his defensive line on the Rappahannock and marched toward Manassas (as Lee had hoped he would), planning to attack Jackson before Longstreet's corps arrived.

Through the night of August 27 and into the morning of the 28th, Jackson's men settled into positions hidden in the woods and in ridges behind an old, unfinished railroad bed north of the Warrenton Turnpike at the base of Stony Ridge, near Sudley Springs and the Brawner Farm. Jackson wanted to avoid detection until Longstreet's men arrived. As Union troops converged on Manassas Junction, they found that Jackson had slipped away.

Late that afternoon, one of Jackson's outposts reported a Union division-sized column moving along the road in front of his position.

Jackson knew Lee and Longstreet were close and that they would join him the next day, so he decided to attack this force and pull in the rest of Pope's forces. Then when Lee and Longstreet arrived, they would find Pope distracted.

A few minutes later, Confederate artillery shells began exploding around the Union column. The Union troops quickly formed into battle lines and moved across the fields and woods toward the Confederates. Considering the Confederates had the advantage of surprise and were dug in, it was a surprisingly bloody battle that went on until dark, two hours later. A third of those engaged became casualties before the Union troops withdrew.

After the engagement, Pope issued orders for his divisions to converge on the area and attack, assuming he had Jackson cornered. The next morning, August 29, Union artillery fire began the day. Jackson had deployed his three divisions along the cuts and fills of the unfinished railroad. His left rested near the village of Sudley Springs on Bull Run, while his right was at the Brawner Farm. He put his artillery at the base of Stony Ridge, a formation that rose behind his lines. Pope, despite his boasts that he would "bag" Jackson, only launched a series of small attacks against the Confederates behind the railroad cut. But each time they broke through Jackson's line, Pope hesitated, then did not send in his reserves, and the attacks were eventually repulsed.

Longstreet and Lee arrived on Jackson's right before noon. Lee sent Longstreet and his men to extend Jackson's line and wrap it around Pope's left flank. Three times Lee asked Longstreet to attack that afternoon; but each time, Longstreet demurred, instead sending out probes to determine the enemy strength. Had he attacked, the Confederates might have won a massive victory.

The next morning, Pope believed that the Confederates were retreating, even though he knew Longstreet was on the field. After a morning of light skirmishing and cannon fire, Pope decided to launch a massive attack on Jackson. He gathered 10,000 men and attacked Jackson's line at three p.m. at a point along the rail line later named the Deep Cut.

As the Union troops moved forward, Longstreet's artillery—set up

Edwin Forbes of Frank Leslie's Illustrated Newspaper *sketched the rout of Federal troops by General John B. Hood's Texas Brigade on August 30th. In order to reproduce these battlefield drawings, artists would translate them into wood engravings.*

on the end of Pope's line—raked the Union attack while Jackson's men, protected by the unfinished railroad, cut them down with artillery and small arms fire. "What a slaughter! What a slaughter of men that was!" remembered one Georgian. "They were so thick it was just impossible to miss them." After 30 minutes of heavy fighting, the Union troops broke and fell back.

As Pope's attack failed, Lee saw his opportunity. At four p.m. he ordered Longstreet forward in a massive counterattack against the Union left, and Confederates swept the Federals east to the high ground at Chinn Ridge, already famous from the First Battle of Bull Run (Manassas) 13 months before. Five Union brigades held on at Chinn Ridge, and each side threw in regiments and brigades as fast as they arrived. The fighting raged on the ridge, but the Union troops managed to hold until about six p.m., long enough for Pope to form another line on Henry Hill. Longstreet sent his troops against this new line, but darkness ended the fighting. That night, Pope had the option of bringing in reinforcements to strengthen his strong position and perhaps turn the defeat into a victory, or at least a stalemate. Instead, with his confidence shattered, he ordered a retreat and led his men back toward Washington. Less than a week later Pope was sent to Minnesota to fight Indians. The Union lost well over 14,000

men, the Confederates about 8500.

After this battle and the Seven Days, Lee and the Confederacy were at the height of their power. Now Lee decided to invade Union territory for a final victory.

Manassas National Battlefield Park

Shortly after the First Battle of Bull Run (Manassas), Confederate soldiers from Colonel Francis S. Bartow's brigade placed a marble column on Henry Hill on the spot where he was killed, making Manassas one of the first Civil War battlefields to receive a memorial marker. Four years later, in June of 1865, Union troops constructed a 20-foot-high, sandstone obelisk on Henry Hill, with a similar 16-foot monument at the Deep Cut railroad embankment where Stonewall Jackson turned back Union attacks during Second Bull Run (Second Manassas). Both were decorated with cannon shells from the battle, and both were inscribed IN MEMORY OF THE PATRIOTS WHO FELL. In the years that followed, more monuments and markers were erected.

In 1922, the Sons of Confederate Veterans acquired the 128-acre Henry farm and established a Confederate memorial park there. A number of new monuments were installed, including some dedicated to Southern heroes by the local chapter of the United Daughters of the Confederacy. This same chapter held annual well-attended commemorations for each battle.

In May 1940, the historic farm and 1475 acres of the "Bull Run Recreational Demonstration Area" were given to the National Park Service and officially proclaimed the Manassas National Battlefield Park. An important part of the agreement called for the erection of a huge bronze equestrian statue of Stonewall Jackson on Henry Hill, where he won his nickname. The state of Virginia commissioned Joseph Pollia to create the statue, and today it overlooks the battlefield.

The park slowly expanded after World War II to include sites from the Second Battle of Bull Run (Second Manassas) and grew to its present 5100 acres. It now includes the Stone Bridge over Bull Run, Sudley Springs Ford, Matthews Hill, the Stone House at the intersection of the Warrenton Turnpike and Sudley Road, Battery Heights, the Brawner Farm, Stuart's Hill, and Chinn Ridge. The unfinished railroad embankment, including the Deep Cut, is also preserved.

The Henry Hill Visitor Center includes the park museum, bookstore, and restrooms. The museum gallery contains artifacts and exhibits pertaining to the First Battle of Bull Run (Manassas). A six-minute audiovisual map presentation describes troop movements during this battle. Ranger-guided 30-minute tours interpreting the battle take place throughout the day, starting at ten fifteen a.m. The tours begin at the visitors center.

There are also several self-guided walking tours. From the visitors center, a mile-long loop with audio messages and interpretive signs tells the story of the first Battle of Bull Run. There are also two separate five-mile-long trails that cover the battlefields from both the first and second battles. A 16-mile driving tour covers 11 sites that figure prominently in Second Bull Run (Manassas), including the Deep Cut, Matthews Hill, and Stone Bridge. Maps are available at the Visitors Center.

The center shows the 45-minute film *Manassas: End of Innocence* daily, every hour on the hour starting at nine a.m., with the last show beginning at four p.m. It covers both the first and second battles. There is a minimal charge for admission, separate from the park entrance fee.

The Stuart's Hill Center is oriented more toward the Second Battle of Bull Run (Manassas). It is located at the intersection of state route 29, Lee Highway, and Pageland Lane, and includes the Stuart's Hill Museum and restrooms.

Visitor Information

703-361-1339:
www.nps.gov/mana

Hours: The park is open daily during daylight hours. The Henry Hill Visitor Center is open year round from 8:30 a.m. until 5 p.m., with extended hours in summer; closed Thanksgiving and December 25. The Stuart's Hill Center is open during the summer on weekends from 8:30 a.m. until 4 p.m.; closed the rest of the year; call for exact dates.

Admission: Minimal charge per adult with an additional charge for the movie; National Parks Pass, Golden Eagle, Golden Age, and Golden Access are honored

Accessibility: The Henry Hill Visitor Center and Stuart's Hill Center are fully accessible; all audiovisual programs and films are captioned.

Special Programs: From time to time park volunteers conduct approximately five mile, five hour walking tours of the battlefields. Each tour focuses on one of the two battles. There are also regular Civil War reenactments, especially around the anniversaries of the battles, as well as on Memorial Day. Call for information.

Getting There: The park is approximately 25 miles south of Washington Dulles International Airport.

From Washington, D.C.: Travel west on I-66 to exit 47B, Virginia Route 234 north. Go through the first traffic light, and the Henry Hill Visitor Center is located at the top of the hill on the right.

From south of Washington: Take I-95 to exit 152, state route 234. Turn left at the traffic light onto Route 234 north. The Henry Hill Visitor Center is located approximately 20 miles on the right, north of the city of Manassas.

From west of Washington: Travel east on I-66 to exit 47A, state Route 234 north. Turn left on Route 234. Go through the first traffic light, and the Henry Hill Visitor Center is located at the top of the hill on the right.

Of Note: Local residents consider the last "Battle of Manassas" to have been fought in 1993 when the Walt Disney Company proposed building a history theme park 3.5 miles from the battlefield. The proposal became highly controversial, and Disney

The Mariners' Museum

This museum has a number of Civil War–related artifacts, the most famous of which are those recovered from the Union ironclad U.S.S. *Monitor*, which foundered off the coast of Cape Hatteras, North Carolina, in December 1862. Since the remains of the ship were discovered in the 1970s, this museum, working with the National Oceanic and Atmospheric Administration (NOAA), has salvaged and begun or completed preservation of several large pieces from the ship, including its 30-ton steam engine, its massive gun turret (with cannons attached), and its anchor, as well as many other smaller pieces. Visitors can view preserved pieces in the Monitor Conservation Area, and see the preservation process in the glass-enclosed conservation lab.

In 2007 the museum will be opening its Monitor Center, a new wing devoted entirely to the ironclad and its history. The exhibits will explain the design and technological innovations of the ironclad ships that changed naval warfare. It will also explain how this ship was discovered underwater and then recovered. It will be possible to visit a re-creation of Civil War–era Hampton Roads with the *Monitor* at dockside, and to view cutaway portions of her living accommodations and engine rooms. Also on display will be some of the crews' journals and letters and various artifacts of their lives. In addition, the exhibit will explore the experiences of African Americans who served on board.

In the meantime, besides the *Monitor* artifacts, a permanent exhibit, *Defending the Seas*, includes a

Sinking of the U.S.S. Monitor *in 1862.*

section on the maritime history of the Civil War called "A New Era of Battles, Missions, and Technologies."

Visitor Information

757-596-2222; www.mariner.org
Hours: Open daily, 10 a.m. until 5 p.m.; closed Thanksgiving and December 25.
Admission: Moderate charge for adults and children six and over.
Accessibility: Handicapped accessible.
Getting There: The museum is located at 100 Museum Drive, at the intersection of Warwick and J. Clyde Morris boulevards in Newport News, Virginia. Take I-64 to exit 258A and continue 2.5 miles to the museum entrance.

Dents in the Monitor's *turret are evidence of the nine shots that struck the revolving turret during the encounter with the C.S.S.* Virginia (Merrimack).

Museum of the Confederacy

The Museum of the Confederacy has the world's largest and most comprehensive collection of artifacts, manuscripts, photographs, and other material from the Confederate States of America, and it's the leading center for their preservation, display, and study. The museum also serves as an international center of study on the role of the Confederacy in the American Civil War, as well as organizing and sponsoring lectures and a variety of other special events and programs.

There are over 15,000 artifacts in the museum's collection, which is best known for its uniforms, flags, and the personal effects of soldiers, as well as those of many famous Confederate generals. Among these are the Bible that General "Stonewall" Jackson carried with him during the war, the bloodstained uniform of the soldier who carried Jackson from the battlefield when he was mortally wounded, and the personal effects of J.E.B. Stuart, the great Confederate cavalryman killed outside Richmond. There are also 215 uniforms, including prewar militia uniforms, handmade ones, and regulation uniforms issued late in the war from the

Robert E. Lee's uniform coat worn at the surrender at Appomattox stood in marked contrast to Grant's apparel that fateful day—a private's uniform with general's shoulder bars to signify his rank.

Confederates' Richmond depot.

One of the most prized items in the uniform collection is General Robert E. Lee's uniform coat worn at the surrender in Appomattox, and the most famous sword in the weapons collection is the one worn by Lee for that same meeting. The uniforms of Richard S. Ewell, William Dorsey Pender, John Bell Hood, Patrick Cleburne, and Ambrose P. Hill have also been donated to the collection.

The collection contains 300 edged weapons and 250 firearms, both European-made weapons brought in by blockade runners and those made in the South, such as Leech & Rigdon and Griswold & Gunnison revolvers, the Robinson "Sharps" carbine, and rifled muskets from the Richmond and Fayetteville armories. The visitor can see unique weapons, including a breech-loading carbine manufactured by George W. Morse's Atlanta firm and a Richmond-made sharpshooter's rifle for special service against Union ironclads sailing on the James River.

A poignant exhibit shows the sword that General Lewis Armistead used to hoist his hat aloft as he led his brigade in Pickett's Charge at Gettysburg, where he was mortally wounded. The firearms collection also includes the personal sidearms of Lee, Stuart, P.G.T. Beauregard, and John Hunt Morgan.

Over 550 Confederate flags are on display in the museum, including government-issue colors and non-regulation oil-painted silk flags. There are also 25 sculptures, including busts of Jefferson Davis and Stonewall Jackson by Frederick Volck. Over 1000 postwar "memorial period" artifacts include badges and ribbons from veterans' reunions, and souvenirs from the dedications of monuments to the memory of comrades who lost their lives in the war.

Permanent exhibitions include "The Confederate Years," a chronological history of the Confederacy and the Civil War; "Victory in Defeat: Jefferson Davis and the Lost Cause," a brief history of the museum and the Davis family; "The Hope of Eight Million: The Confederate Soldier," with artifacts, letters, and personal diaries that tell the enlisted men's story; and the iconic *The Last Meeting of Lee and Jackson* painting by E.B.D. Julio.

The museum's rich and diverse

Major General
William Dorsey Pender led the Light Division at Gettysburg. While trying to ready his troops, Pender was wounded in the thigh by a shell fragment. His leg was eventually amputated but Pender died within a few hours after the operation. Lee was to later remark that had Pender been able to stay on his horse another half an hour at Gettysburg, he would have won the day.

photographic collection consists of more than 6000 original images and more than 7000 negatives and color transparencies, as well as thousands of research prints. There are more than 310 "cased image" photographs of Confederate soldiers and Southern civilians, both white and black. Most are those of women and children—many of them unknown—that were found among the effects of dead soldiers. The collection features portraits of Confederate civilian leaders such as President Davis and rare prewar portraits of generals Hill and Cleburne. More than a third of the cased images are of Confederate soldiers, the largest known group of identified, uniformed Confederate soldiers images in existence.

The museum also has a collection of 2500 of the very popular cartes de visite, approximately 2 1/2-by-4-inch cards that were a craze at the time and are the ancestors of today's trading cards. Confederate First Lady Varina Howell Davis donated several albums of Civil War–era cartes de visite to the museum.

The museum's collection of photographs of the postwar Confederate memorial period includes individual and group portraits of Confederate veterans and the United Daughters of the Confederacy at postwar veterans' reunions and monument unveilings.

The museum is also home to the Eleanor S. Brockenbrough Library, with thousands of prints, hundreds of maps, and over 10,000 books and bound periodicals. Holdings include the Provisional Confederate Constitution, a draft of Lee's resignation letter from the U.S. Army, one of the world's largest collections of Jefferson Davis papers, and an extensive collection of Confederate currency and bonds.

(See page 273 for Visitor Information)

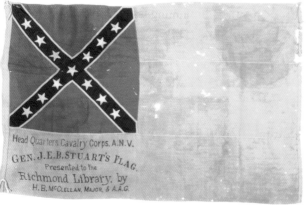

J.E.B. Stuart's headquarters flag is one of 550 flags on display in the museum. It was inscribed after the war by his assistant adjutant general, Major H.B. McClellan. Headquarters flags were generally flown over campsites but not carried into battle.

271

White House of the Confederacy

The White House of the Confederacy was originally known as the Brockenbrough House, after John Brockenbrough, who commissioned it. When completed in about 1818, it was a two-story home with a flat slate roof, on a hill at the corner of 12th and Clay Streets overlooking Shockoe Valley. In 1857 it was bought by a wealthy local businessman, Lewis Crenshaw, who added the third floor.

In May 1861, the city of Richmond purchased Crenshaw's house and its contents and leased it to the Confederate government to serve as Confederate President Jefferson Davis's executive mansion. The Davises moved in, in August of 1861, and it functioned much like the Washington White House, as a center of social, political, and military planning activities.

The first floor was reserved for formal state affairs. The President's offices were on the second floor, along with his secretary's, as well as the family's private quarters. His secretary, military aides, the housekeeper, and family guests had rooms on the third floor. The basement contained the family dining room and associated facilities. There were several outbuildings, including slave quarters, a two-story brick kitchen, a stable and carriage house, and a gardener's cottage. Tragically, one of Davis's sons, five-year-old Joseph

Evan, fell to his death from the east portico of the house in April 1864.

Davis and his family evacuated the city on April 2, 1865, leaving the White House intact. On April 4, 1865, President Abraham Lincoln came to Richmond to see the Confederate capital and the Confederate White House, where he was shown into Davis's office. Lincoln sat in Davis's chair and "crossing his legs, he looked far off with a serious, dreamy expression." One wonders what he was thinking just a few days before the end of the horrible conflict. A few minutes later the housekeeper showed him around the rest of the house.

The house later became a Union military command center, and souvenir hunters took many items. The large furniture was sold at public auction in the fall of 1870, and the building became a public school until 1889, when it was scheduled for demolition. It was saved by a group of Richmond women, members of the Confederate Memorial Literary Society, and was reopened as the Confederate Museum on February 22, 1896—the national repository of Confederate memorabilia. Varina Davis, the President's wife, returned several times to consult as the home became the Confederate Museum.

It served as the Confederate Museum until the mid-1970s, and

The White House of the Confederacy *served as the official residence of President Jefferson Davis, his wife, Varina, and their children. The house was also the social, political, and military center of the Confederacy.*

The parlor of the White House of the Confederacy as it might have been decorated for the Christmas season. The first floor was reserved for formal state affairs, with the exception of a small private library. The mansion has been restored to the splendor of its mid-19th century phase, with over half of the original furnishings from its wartime role as the Confederate White House.

then for 10 years it was carefully restored to its appearance as Jefferson Davis's executive mansion. Many of its original furnishings were returned, and today 11 period rooms are open to the public and feature over 1000 objects, more than half of which are original furnishings, and the majority have a Davis family provenance. They are supplemented by a variety of period objects, including paintings, sculpture, and furniture. There is a fine garden with a fountain in the rear of the mansion.

Visitor Information

804-649-1861; www.moc.org/ www.moc.org/exwhite.htm

Hours: Monday to Saturday, 10 a.m. until 5 p.m. and Sunday noon until 5 p.m.; closed Thanksgiving, December 25, and New Year's Day. The White House can be visited only for the regularly scheduled guided tours. The 40-minute tour starts in the basement and includes the first and second floors. Tours are available Monday, Wednesday, and Friday, every 45 minutes beginning at 10:30 a.m.; Tuesday and Thursday, every 45 minutes beginning at 11 a.m.; Saturday, every half hour beginning at 10:30 a.m.; and Sunday, every 45 minutes beginning at 12:30 p.m. The last tour

every day is at 4 p.m. Additional tours are added as needed.

Admission: There is a relatively high charge for adults for either the museum or the White House; discounted combined passes are available; discounts are also available for seniors and students.

Accessibility: The museum building is handicapped accessible and takes at least an hour to tour. The White House is not handicapped accessible.

Getting There: The Museum of the Confederacy and the White House of the Confederacy are located in Richmond, Virginia, at 12th and Clay streets in the historic Court End neighborhood, about two blocks from the historic State Capitol and Capitol Square.

From I-95: Take exit 74C to U.S. 250 west (Broad Street). At 11th Street turn right and go two blocks to Clay Street. Turn right on Clay. The museum and White House are on the corner of 12th and Clay streets. Parking is available in the Medical College of Virginia Hospital visitor patient parking deck at the end of Clay Street. Visitors' parking tickets will be validated at the front desk of the museum.

Of Note: The complex houses the Haversack Store, which offers a wide variety of Confederacy gift items as well as an extensive bookstore.

The Battle of New Market

In May 1864, Union general Ulysses S. Grant crossed the Rapidan River and began a campaign to destroy Confederate general Robert E. Lee's Army of Northern Virginia. Grant sent Major General Franz Sigel to neutralize Confederate forces in the Shenandoah Valley, the "breadbasket" of the Confederacy. Grant disliked Sigel, a politically powerful German American who had an unsuccessful military career in Europe before coming to the United States in 1852. But while Sigel was a mediocre combat leader (at best), he had been successful in attracting many German American recruits into the Union army. Most of his staff and some of his units were German American, and they would often speak German among themselves.

On May 2, Sigel and almost 10,000 men began to advance from Martinsburg, Virginia, on their way to destroy the railroad yards and canal complex at Lynchburg and generally to distract Lee as much as possible. Lee had his hands full with Grant, so he turned the Valley's defense over to Major General John C. Breckinridge, telling him simply, "Drive the enemy back." Breckinridge, a former U.S. Vice President, mustered all the troops he could in southwest Virginia, and was eventually able to cobble together a force of two brigades of infantry, militiamen and 14 cannons, as well as about 260 members of the Corps of Cadets from Virginia Military Institute (VMI) at Staunton, Virginia, to meet the Union advance. Breckinridge's strength was a superior 1500-man cavalry force commanded by Brigadier General John D. Imboden.

Imboden immediately set to work on Sigel's army as they meandered slowly through the Valley. Sigel stopped frequently to drill his men, while Confederate cavalry harassed his rear. On May 5, the Confederates destroyed the Baltimore & Ohio Railroad's repair shop and machine shops, a railroad bridge, nine locomotives, 80 freight cars, and several miles of telegraph lines. A few days later they took three full freight trains, and they even captured Sigel's personal supply train. On May 9, Imboden's horsemen ambushed Sigel's patrols, causing 150 casualties and further slowing his movement. On May 11, Confederate cavalry surprised and captured about 450 Union cavalry near Port Royal.

Breckinridge prepared to move while Imboden tried to hold Sigel's army north of the village of New Market. Skirmishing between the two sides began in earnest, but by nightfall on May 14 the lead Union column had established a line on the north side of New Market and on the high ground to its west. However, the rest of the Union forces were well back, and Sigel was about 18 miles north of the village that night.

Imboden had been forced to fall back, and on May 15 Breckinridge and about 5000 men arrived in the area of New Market around daybreak. He set up his artillery just to the southwest, on Shirley's Hill, and set the rest of his force on the high ground farther south.

It had been raining for four days, and it continued that morning. Breckinridge repeatedly attempted to prod a Union attack, but Sigel had still not joined the Union forces, and the Union commanders were not inclined to launch an attack without his approval.

Finally, a frustrated Breckinridge decided to attack the Union positions. At eleven a.m. he sent his two infantry brigades forward with a regiment of dismounted cavalry between them, maneuvering them to give the impression of a large force. As they moved forward, they appeared to be three strong battle lines, when in reality there was only one line staggered. The VMI cadets were held in the rear as a reserve. Breckinridge also sent Imboden's cavalry with a battery of four guns to harass the Union flanks, with additional orders to burn the bridge over the North Fork of the Shenandoah River, hoping to trap Sigel's force.

The Confederate attack was in full swing when Sigel arrived around noon. He quickly realized that in the rainy weather his forces in the rear would not arrive at the Union defensive line in time to hold back the attack, so he began pulling the Union line back to a new position two miles north of New Market, on a ridge known as Bushong's Hill, about 300 yards north of the Bushong Farm. It was a solid position, with the Shenandoah on one side and Smith's Creek on the other. Sigel set up 18 cannons on the forward-sloping crest of a ridge and waited.

The Union rear guard resisted briefly and then pulled back, and a little before one p.m. the Confederates moved into New Market, to the cheers of the inhabitants. As the

Civil War enthusiasts in traditional uniform reenact the parts of Confederate infantry-men during the Battle of New Market at the New Market Battlefield Museum.

thunderstorms became increasingly violent, the Confederates pressed forward toward the final Union position. The fields the Confederates marched across were a muddy quagmire. Many soldiers had their shoes pulled off by the suction of the mud, giving the area the name The Field of Lost Shoes.

As the Confederates approached, the Union artillery fire took a greater and greater toll. By the time Breckinridge's units approached the line of the Bushong Farm, they began to waver. Breckinridge had hoped to keep the VMI cadets in reserve, but at this critical moment he reluctantly ordered, "Put the boys in." The cadets moved forward in tight parade-ground formation rather than the looser line used by veteran troops, but despite unnecessarily heavy casualties they moved to within 300 yards of the Union lines, took their positions and exchanged fire with their enemies.

Sigel moved to counterattack as the thunderstorms increased in intensity. He sent a cavalry charge against the Confederate lines, but Confederate artillery caught the horsemen in a crossfire that sent them reeling back with heavy losses. Sigel then ordered an infantry attack, but it was halfhearted and easily repulsed.

Meanwhile, the Union artillery batteries were taking heavy fire from Confederate skirmishers and artillery. Sigel then made a critical mistake. He ordered his artillery to withdraw and regroup out of range of the snipers, and this loss of firepower doomed the Union infantry line.

When Breckinridge saw the Union cannon fire drop off, he called for a charge all along his line, and the Confederates smashed through the Union lines. Sigel ordered a retreat and, according to a member of his staff, began to give his orders in German, adding to the confusion.

Artifacts from the Battle of New Market include a wooden canteen, a Confederate flag, a Spanish saber, and a leather trunk. All were carried into battle on the VMI cadet corps baggage wagon.

In the rush, several Union cannons became stuck in the mud and abandoned, to the great delight of the VMI cadets who captured one, as well as taking a number of Union prisoners. Breckinridge removed the cadets from the advance about three thirty, telling them, "Well done Virginians, well done men!"

Sigel's force was on the verge of a complete rout when a Union battery, commanded by Captain Henry A. Du Pont, intervened. Du Pont had been held back in reserve and seemingly forgotten; but when he saw how the battle was going, he moved his cannons forward on his own initiative. As the Union forces retreated, Du Pont fired on the advancing Confederates, and then coolly pulled his cannons back two by two, one pair firing while the other moved. The covering fire allowed Sigel's retreating army time to cross the North Fork of the Shenandoah, where Imboden had been unable to destroy the bridge because of high water in the creeks. Sigel eventually got all of his forces across the river, and Du Pont destroyed the Mount Jackson Bridge to prevent pursuit.

In Sigel's rush from the battlefield, he abandoned a number of seriously wounded Union soldiers. A few days later Sigel was relieved of his command, and one of his officers said, "We can afford to lose such a battle as New Market to get rid of such a mistake as General Sigel."

The Union forces suffered almost 850 casualties. Confederate losses were about 550, including about 55 of the VMI cadets and officers, 10 of whom were killed or died of their wounds.

Sigel was replaced by General David Hunter, who later moved into Lexington and burned down VMI.

New Market Battlefield Historical Park and Military Museum

New Market Battlefield Historical Park was established by Virginia Military Institute in 1967, on land owned by the institute. The park covers about 280 acres and contains about 10 percent of the New Market battlefield, including several areas of the most severe fighting. The Hall of Valor was opened in 1970.

The New Market battlefield has 15 granite and marble monuments, including ones that mark the positions of the first Union line of defense and the Confederate second line of advance. Two of the monuments were erected by veterans of the New Market Battle—the Missouri (Woodson) Monument near the Bushong House and the 54th Regiment Pennsylvania Infantry Monument, located directly east of Bushong's Hill but separated from the main park by I-81. These are currently the only battlefield markers on any of the Shenandoah Valley battlefield sites.

There is a self-guided 1.5-mile walking tour of the battlefield, and 45-to-60-minute guided tours are given during the summer at 10 a.m., 1:30 p.m., and 3 p.m. Visitors can also see the Bushong Farm House, with nine structures interpreting Civil War–era Shenandoah Valley farm life.

The park's Hall of Valor Museum includes various artifacts, an interactive orientation to the park, a hands-on program called "Equipping the Soldier," and an Emmy Award–winning documentary film on the battle, *The Field of Lost Shoes*, as well as a film about the Shenandoah campaigns. General Breckinridge's sword is among the exhibits.

The nearby New Market Battlefield Military Museum is privately owned. It is situated in a reproduction of Robert E. Lee's Arlington House at Arlington National Cemetery. It houses a large collection of antique military memorabilia from the 1750s and is focused on the Civil War and the Battle of New Market. The exhibits include 2500 artifacts in 125 displays, including Stonewall Jackson's family Bible. There is also a 30-minute film on the battle.

Visitor Information

New Market Battlefield Historical Park and Hall of Valor Museum, 540-740-3101; www.vmi.edu/museum/nm/index.html
The New Market Battlefield Military Museum, 540-740-8065; www.newmarketmilitarymuseum.com
Hours: New Market Battlefield Historical Park and Hall of Valor Museum, daily, 9 a.m. until 5 p.m.; closed Thanksgiving, December 25, and New Year's Day. New Market Battlefield Military Museum, call for hours.
Admission: New Market Battlefield Historical Park and Hall of Valor Museum, moderate charge for adults 16 and up; discounts for children six to 15. New Market Battlefield Military Museum, moderate charge for adults 15 and up; discounts for children six to 14.
Accessibility: There are wheelchair-accessible parking spaces at Battlefield Park Visitor Contact Station and the New Market Battlefield Station. For guests with hearing impairments there are written scripts. For guests with visual impairments, there are documents in large print on a nonglossy surface. Restrooms and pathways are accessible.
Special Events: There is an annual reenactment of the Battle of New Market in May on the weekend closest to the anniversary. Call for dates and times. A special day camp for children ages 7 to 12 is offered weekly in July and August, which introduces them to the life of a Civil War soldier. Space is limited; call 540-740-8124 to reserve a spot.
Getting There: Take I-81 to exit 264 onto Route 211 west. Make an immediate right onto Route 305 (George Collin Parkway). The Battlefield Park Visitor Contact Station is immediately on the left. New Market Battlefield Military Museum is 1/4 mile farther up the road on the left, next to the Days Inn.

Old Court House Civil War Museum

This museum in Winchester, Virginia, is housed in the Frederick County Court House. The exhibits focus on three themes.

The life of the common soldier, especially of those who were prisoners of war, is told through photographs and with medical and personal items. The collection also highlights artifacts relating to technology in the war. The evolution in uniforms portrays changes from a volunteer army to a national military.

Winchester changed hands more than 70 times during the war, and prisoners from both sides were housed in this building. Framed graffiti, rescued when the museum was being developed, testifies to their thoughts on their situation and the war in general. (Left in place on the south wall is a strongly worded curse aimed at Jefferson Davis, President of the Confederacy.) There are also armaments and other relics of the war, and visitors are invited to ring the courthouse bell.

Visitor Information

540-542-1145; www.civilwarmuseum.org
Hours: Friday to Sunday, 10 a.m. until 5 p.m.; Sunday, 1 p.m. until 5 p.m.; closed major holidays.
Admission: Minimal charge for adults and children five and over.
Getting There: Winchester, Virginia, is 60 miles west of Washington, D.C., on state route 7, or via I-66 to I-81 northbound to exit 313. It is 40 miles south of Hagerstown, Maryland, off I-81 at exit 315. The museum is at 20 North Loudon Street in the central City Hall district, which is bounded by U.S. 11 (northbound Cameron Street on the east and southbound Braddock Street on the west), and by Piccadilly Street on the north and Boscawen Street on the south. Parking is available in a parking garage at the corner of Cameron and Boscawen streets or in a metered lot one block north. (There is no charge for meters on the weekend.)

Pamplin Historical Park and the National Museum of the Civil War Soldier

The 422-acre Pamplin Historical Park and the National Museum of the Civil War Soldier are located in Petersburg, Virginia, on the site of the last engagement of the Battle of Petersburg, the breakthrough of April 2, 1865. The park includes the Battlefield Center and Military Encampment, the Breakthrough Trail that leads through part of the Petersburg battlefield with original fortifications, and the Tudor Hall Plantation.

The 25,000-square-foot National Museum of the Civil War Soldier focuses on the experience of the common soldier of the Civil War. In the museum's main gallery, "Duty Called Me Here," the visitor uses a CD player to select a soldier "comrade" from a group of real Civil War infantrymen, both Union and Confederate. Children have the option of choosing a 13-year-old drummer boy as their comrade. The comrade then leads the visitor through the galleries, often using his own words taken from diaries and letters. At the end of the tour, each visitor learns the ultimate fate of his or her soldier comrade. Vibrant sound and Civil War artist Keith Rocco's murals provide backdrops for the camp and battle scenes. In the gallery entitled "Trial by Fire," the visitor experiences a taste of Civil War combat, complete with the sensation of whistling bullets. Numerous interactive computer kiosks bring to life a variety of soldiers' activities as well.

The Battlefield Center displays over 3000 artifacts, including a Confederate battle flag captured during the breakthrough. A fiber-optics map and interactive computer displays describe eight of the most important battles around Petersburg, while a theater offers a surround-sound presentation of the April 2 battle.

For children, there is a hands-on area where they can try on Civil War uniforms and equipment, and there is also a tour designed especially for them. Outside the center is a full-scale replica of part of the formidable Confederate defensive breastworks. There is also a year-round Military Encampment, where some costumed interpreters offer artillery or rifle-firing demonstrations, and others explain the soldiers' daily routine and the experiences of the common soldier. The camp is modified throughout the year to reflect the change in seasons, just as the soldiers experienced them.

Just outside the Battlefield Center, the self-guided Breakthrough Trail takes the visitor through the battle

Park interpreters dressed as Confederate artillerymen demonstrate how to load and fire a field piece. One crewman sponges the bore to remove any burning residue from the previous round while another receives the next to place in the muzzle. Right, a display of artillery shells includes top row, a Hotchkiss shell and cross-section; second row, a tall canister round, Read shell, and cross-section of a Hotchkiss Bolt; third row, cross-sections of spherical shells and case shot showing their deadly fillings.

Earthwork fortifications *include an abatis (pronounced AH-ba-tee)—a barrier of felled trees with sharpened ends pointing toward the enemy to impede their advance.*

that occurred in this area. The protracted campaign for Petersburg involved the construction of elaborate earthen fortifications, and about two miles of the original Confederate earthworks and field fortifications are preserved at the park, some eight feet tall. Optional loops on the trail cover almost two miles and include interpretive wayside plaques and markers, some with audio presentations, which interpret the route the Union attack took on the final day. The trail also leads to a grouping of recreated Confederate winter huts from the desperate winter of 1864–65. There are also guided tours of the trail daily.

The Boisseau family built the Tudor Hall Plantation in about 1812, but during the siege, Confederate general Samuel McGowan (whose men built many of the original fortifications) requisitioned the home for his brigade headquarters. Today Tudor Hall has been restored to its Civil War appearance. Half of the house has been furnished as the Boisseaus' home, while the rest was restored as a brigade headquarters.

The basement of Tudor Hall interprets the building's history as part of the antebellum South. Interactive videos allow visitors to "role play" positions on the plantation, or in the Confederate brigade. Visitors can see a reconstructed kitchen duplex with two downstairs rooms (a kitchen and laundry) and upstairs rooms used as quarters for the house slaves and their families, as well as listen to an audio description of slave life and how the building functioned in the overall operation of the plantation. Guided tours of Tudor Hall are offered daily.

The site also has a café and Civil War store with a large selection of books and gifts.

Visitor Information

804-861-2408 or 877-PAMPLIN (toll-free); www.pamplinpark.org/
Hours: Mid June through Labor Day,

A display of firearms includes, top to bottom and left to right, a Gallagher carbine, a Confederate Sharps carbine, a Remington New Model Army revolver, a Smith and Wesson Army revolver, a French-made LeMat revolver, and a Griswold and Gunnison revolver. The Lemat packed greater firepower than any other Civil War handgun, firing nine successive shots followed by a single round of buckshot. The Griswold and Gunnison Revolver was produced by slaves working in a converted cotton-gin factory in Georgia.

Dressed as a Federal infantryman, right, an interpreter demonstrates how to load and fire a musket

daily, 9 a.m. until 6 p.m. and until 5 p.m. the rest of the year; closed Thanksgiving, December 25, and New Year's Day.

Admission: There is a high fee for adults, a moderate fee for children 6–11, and free admission for children 5 and under; group discounts are available with prior reservations.

Accessibility: The park is fully accessible, except for the first and second floors of Tudor Hall (the basement and its exhibits are accessible); complete picture albums are available for the first and second floors.

Special Events: There is a Civil War weekend in mid-April and an annual Civil War Symposium in mid-October. Call for information about multiple other special programs.

Getting There: Pamplin Historical Park is 35 minutes from downtown Richmond.

From Richmond and the north: Take I-95 south to I-85 south to exit 63-A (U.S. 1 south). The park entrance is one mile on the left.

From the south: Take I-95 north to I-85 north to exit 63-A (U.S. 1 south). The park entrance is one mile on the left.

From the west: Take U.S. 460 east to U.S. 1 north; entrance is a half mile on the right.

From the east: Take U.S. 460 west (it becomes I-85 in Petersburg) to exit 63-A (U.S. 1 south). The park entrance is one mile on the left.

The Petersburg Campaign

After his devastating defeat at Cold Harbor in June 1864, Grant decided that instead of attacking Richmond and its formidable defenses directly, he would capture the Confederate capital's crucial supply center, Petersburg. Petersburg was 25 miles away on the southern bank of the Appomattox River, where five railroads and nine wagon roads met. Every railroad to Richmond but one came through Petersburg. If the Union could capture the town, Lee's supply line would be down to a single rail line from the southwest, and Richmond would have to be abandoned. Ironically, while Grant and Lee were engaged at Cold Harbor, a Union probe by units from General Benjamin Butler's Army of the James had tried but failed to capture Petersburg.

As Grant began to disengage from Lee's army at Cold Harbor, he first feinted toward Richmond to confuse Lee. Then, during the night of June 12–13, he began moving his forces toward Petersburg. Lee knew Grant was moving; but for several crucial days, he believed that Grant was still attacking Richmond and was simply adjusting his lines.

On June 14, Union engineers began to build a technological marvel—a huge 2100-foot pontoon bridge—that would allow large army units to cross the James River despite its strong tidal currents and four-foot tides. When the Union corps began to pour across the James toward Petersburg at midnight, Lee was still defending Richmond, unaware of Grant's intentions. The capture of Petersburg seemed inevitable.

In Petersburg, Confederate general P.G.T. Beauregard had his men arrayed behind the formidable Dimmock Line, 55 artillery batteries in redans (positions that allow fire to the front and to the side) behind abatis (trees with sharpened branches) in a 10-mile arc of earthworks. But Beauregard had only 2500 men, not even enough to man all the cannons and far too few to hold back a serious Union attack.

Union major general William F. "Baldy" Smith's troops were the first to arrive in front of Petersburg from Cold Harbor. On June 15 his force attacked with General Edward W. Hincks's division of U.S. Colored Troops (USCTs). Hincks's 1300 USCTs pushed aside a small force of militia and opened a mile-wide gap in the Confederate line. Smith could have easily moved into Petersburg, but lost his nerve when he heard a rumor that Lee was sending reinforcements. This has been characterized as "one of the war's biggest failures of generalship." Beauregard, amazed at his luck, immediately ordered that Confederate troops down the peninsula at Bermuda Hundred move to Petersburg. He wrote after the war, "Petersburg at that hour was clearly at the mercy of the Federal commander, who had all but captured it."

On June 16, three more of Grant's corps arrived, but in a late afternoon attack they only captured a few redans and suffered heavy losses. On June 17, an early morning Union surprise attack captured a number of sleeping Confederates, but the overall Union attacks failed again. That day Lee finally understood what was happening and rushed elements of the Army of Northern Virginia to reinforce Petersburg's defenses. That night, Beauregard craftily withdrew from his forward lines and fell back to another line of fortifications just outside the city limits.

The next morning Union forces tried a massive three-corps attack, but by the time the Union commanders realized the enemy had pulled back, they were off balance and had to reorganize for a new attack. By then Confederate general A. P. Hill's corps and other units arrived with more than 18,800 men, and stopped several disorganized Union attacks that afternoon. In one of them, the 1st Maine Heavy Artillery, fighting as infantry, suffered the greatest percentage of losses of any regiment in any action in the war, 635 killed and wounded out of 900 engaged. Grant's well-thought-out and carefully executed strategy came to naught. The chance for a quick victory was gone, the victim of timid Union generals and Beauregard's steadfastness and ingenuity.

The Siege of Petersburg

Grant settled in for a siege and set up his headquarters at City Point, 10 miles east of Petersburg, where the James and Appomattox rivers meet. The town quickly became a small city, full of supplies, soldiers, and sailors; and a railroad was set up to take men and supplies to the battlefield.

Meanwhile, the political situation was deteriorating for Lincoln. With

Confederate fortifications stretched 10 miles around Petersburg. Traverses set at right angles were established in the trench lines so that troops would not be vulnerable to enfilading fire as Federal troops stormed the defenses.

Sherman stuck in Georgia and Grant stalled outside Petersburg, the war seemed stalemated, and it seemed certain that Lincoln would not be reelected in November 1864. Grant badly wanted a victory to save his President.

There seemed to be an opportunity for one in late June. A group of coal miners from the 48th Pennsylvania Infantry, Burnside's Corps, proposed digging a long tunnel under a Confederate strongpoint, filling it with black powder, and blowing up that part of the Confederate line. Union troops could then swarm in through the breach and overwhelm the stunned Confederates. The idea was not a new one—it had been used for at least two centuries in European siege warfare—but it seemed to be worth a try. The coal miners began to dig a 510-foot tunnel from the Union lines to beneath the Confederate stronghold at Elliott's Salient. Once it was completed, they would plant 8000 pounds of black powder in the tunnel, as well as in tunnels dug out to the sides, forming an explosive-filled T under the Confederate positions.

The operation was scheduled for the early morning of July 30, and Union guns were set up to open fire on the Confederate positions as soon as the tunnel blew up, to keep

Confederate reinforcements away from the assault. On July 26, Grant began an elaborate series of movements to occupy Lee's attention.

A division of USCTs under Union brigadier general Edward Ferrero had been chosen to lead the assault. The troops were fresh and willing, but there were conflicting reports about whether they were trained for the attack. Training was important, because the key to success was for the attackers to go around—not through—the crater made from the blast, to avoid being trapped in the pit.

As the operation approached, Grant became nervous, afraid that if it did not go well he would be accused of sacrificing the USCTs. Less than 12 hours before the attack, he told Burnside to substitute a division of white soldiers for Ferrero's

The entrance to the tunnel that was dug under the Confederate lines.

men. Brigadier General James H. Ledlie's division was chosen, but there was no time to train them. Additionally, Union engineers failed to move their own fortifications out from in front of their lines to allow Ledlie's men to move forward quickly for the attack.

When the mine exploded at 4:45 a.m. on July 30, 1864, it sent guns, dirt, and Confederates flying into the air and blew a crater 170 feet long, 60 feet wide, and 30 feet deep. Five hundred yards of the Confederate fortifications were now empty as Ledlie's men went forward. Ledlie himself took a pass on the assault, staying in his bunker drinking rum. His poorly trained and leaderless troops struggled to get past their own fortifications, and once they got to the crater they moved down into it. There they were trapped because they had not brought ladders. Two more divisions followed, and soon the crater was filled with thousands of panicky trapped Union soldiers.

Meanwhile, the Confederates were recovering. Lee pulled brigades from all sides to counterattack, and three hours later the Confederate defenses were solid again. Confederate mortars began to lob shells into the crater, and sharpshooters picked off first the Union officers, then the troops. Ferrero's division was the fourth to arrive; but when the black soldiers fanned out around the crater, they were easy targets for the prepared Confederates. Ferrero did not join the attack, but instead joined Ledlie drinking in his bunker. The Confederates gradually took the crater back, capturing many of the white soldiers while killing many of the USCTs. A little after noon, the last Union soldier surrendered. The Union lost almost 6000 men, the Confederates less than 1500. Grant reported back to Washington, "It was the saddest affair I have witnessed in the war." It was a political disaster as well; Burnside was made the scapegoat and relieved of his command.

Weldon Railroad at Globe Tavern

As the siege of Petersburg progressed, Grant noted that Lee would respond to any move against Richmond by aggressively pulling troops out of the Petersburg trenches. He begin to use this against the Confederates, and sent General Gouvernor Warren's reinforced corps on a hit-and-run raid to cut the Weldon Railroad at Globe

Tavern, a yellow brick building six miles south of Petersburg. The Union troops arrived early in the morning of August 18, brushed aside Confederates outposts, and by nine a.m. were energetically tearing up the tracks in the muggy, wet weather. The Confederates responded, and that afternoon there was heavy fighting. That night, Union forces dug in north of Globe Tavern, cut off from the Union trench lines and thus vulnerable.

Lee sent reinforcements. The next afternoon, August 19, Confederate general Hill launched a well-coordinated, two-pronged counterattack that found a break in the Union lines, ripped through, and took almost 2700 prisoners. A Union counterattack stopped the breakthrough, and Warren withdrew a short distance to a stronger position on high ground to the south.

Now Grant sent in reinforcements because he saw an opportunity for Union troops to fight a defensive battle from behind prepared positions. On August 20, while the Confederates reorganized, the Union forces extended their trenches to connect their fortified position to the main Federal lines. What had started as a raid had become a permanent extension of the Union siege lines, and now Warren's men were no longer isolated. When the Confederates tried a frontal attack the morning of August 21, they were cut to pieces by the Union artillery and the dug-in Union infantry. With the Union troops now straddling the railway, Lee was forced to off-load supplies from rail cars farther south and haul them by wagon to Petersburg—inconvenient, but not incapacitating. But Grant continued to attack the rail line, eventually rendering it useless to the Confederates.

Through the fall, Grant launched a number of probes, called "offenses," seemingly intended to give the impression of activity and to aid Lincoln politically in the November elections. However, by September, Sherman's capture of Atlanta and the securing of Mobile Bay relieved the pressure on Lincoln, and he was reelected easily in November. Winter weather brought a halt to combat activities, except for minor skirmishing and artillery duels. The citizens of Richmond and Lee's army were on short rations, while the railroad from the huge Union supply base at City Point kept the Union soldiers supplied.

Virginia

By early February 1865, Lee had only 60,000 soldiers to oppose Grant's force of 110,000. With improving weather, Grant extended his lines to his left, stretching the Confederates thinner and thinner. In March 1865, Phil Sheridan had defeated the last Confederate forces in the Shenandoah Valley and Sherman swept through the Carolinas, clearly on his way to join Grant at Petersburg. It was apparent to Lee that sooner or later Grant's larger forces would either turn the Confederate right flank or stretch Lee's men so thin that Grant could break through wherever he chose. Given Confederate President Jefferson Davis's commitment to continuing the war, Lee realized that something had to be done.

Fort Stedman

Lee's last grand offensive was a surprise attack to loosen the Union stranglehold on Petersburg. The goals were modest—a breakthrough that would penetrate Grant's front and force the Federals to tighten and deepen their lines, opening an escape route to the west for Lee. The Army of Northern Virginia could then break out of Petersburg and link up with the Confederate army in North Carolina. Fort Stedman, a Union redoubt only 150 yards from the Confederate trenches, seemed to be the ideal target. There were few abatis in front, and there were more small forts and a supply depot on the Union railroad less than a mile behind it. Three Confederate "special forces" units of 100 men each were sent to capture these areas to help the breakthrough.

Confederate corps commander John B. Gordon began his attack at four a.m. on March 25, 1865. Gordon's first wave overwhelmed Union pickets and cleared out the fixed defenses, and then they were followed by more troops. The Confederates captured Fort Stedman and the three artillery batteries just to the north and south of it, as well as taking 1000 prisoners, including a Union general. There were few Union commanders in the area, and a division commander, General John Hartranft, took control of the

The "Dictator" was a 13-inch Model 1861 seacoast mortar that was mounted on a specially reinforced railroad car and could lob a 200-pound explosive shell about two miles. It was usually positioned in a curved section of the Petersburg & City Point Railroad and was employed for about three months during the siege.

The Union artillery bombardment on April 1, 1865, as described by an eyewitness: *"From hundreds of cannon, field guns and mortars came a stream of living fire . . . the shells screamed through the air in a semi-circle of flame."*

defense. Union artillery joined in the battle, and Hartranft's infantry stopped the attack. The battle now turned. Gordon's special operations units returned without locating the rail line or the other forts, and the Confederates were gradually forced back into defensive positions. Hartranft was reinforced and launched a vigorous counterattack, and by eight a.m. the Confederates had withdrawn to their old positions. A large number of Confederates, about 1900, surrendered, probably realizing their cause was doomed.

Five Forks

The end of the Confederacy was now just a matter of time. A few days later, on March 29, Grant sent Sheridan and his corps to capture Five Forks, an intersection 17 miles southwest of Petersburg, and cut the South Side Railroad, the last rail line into Petersburg. If Grant could take the railroad, Lee would have to evacuate Richmond and Petersburg.

The 19,000 Confederates manning the defenses were commanded by General George Pickett, of Gettysburg "fame." Lee, though he had a low regard for Pickett, had sent him reinforcements with the admonishment, "Hold Five Forks at

all hazards." In a driving rainstorm, Sheridan attacked on May 31, but Pickett's men held and pushed Sheridan back. Pickett then dug in along a two-mile-long fortified line.

The next day, Sheridan feinted at Pickett's front with dismounted cavalry, planning to have Union infantry under Warren strike the Confederate flank. Warren's men were delayed, much to Sheridan's annoyance, and the attack did not begin until four p.m. This was fortunate for the Confederates, because just before the attack, Pickett left his post and went to a "shad bake," where he and his commanders ate shad and drank whiskey, oblivious to the danger and Lee's instructions.

When Warren finally began his attack, he found that Sheridan had given him an incorrect report on the Confederate positions and a bad map, so Warren's first attack found nothing on one of its flanks. Warren regrouped, wheeled, and then overwhelmed the Confederate left, where his men almost captured Pickett. Union cavalry, led by General George Armstrong Custer, tried to cut off the Confederates' retreat. Only a desperate stand by Confederate cavalry under General Fitz Lee held them off, and Pickett and the remnants

Grant's City Point headquarters cabin was presented to the citizens of Philadelphia in recognition of their loyal support. The cabin stood as a major tourist attraction in Fairmount Park for many years but eventually fell into neglect. In 1981, the National Park Service returned the cabin to its original City Point site.

of his command escaped.

Petersburg still had strong fortifications, but not enough men to man them. On April 2, Grant ordered an all-out assault, and Lee's right flank crumbled. Two forts, Whitworth and Gregg, hung on grimly for several hours, though the Confederates inside were outnumbered almost 10 to one. This gave Jefferson Davis and the other members of the Confederate government time to evacuate Richmond. Now Lee's only hope was to dash west and gather supplies. That night the remainder of Lee's troops filed out of Petersburg, hoping to reach supplies at Appomattox Court House.

Petersburg National Battlefield

Between June 9, 1864, and April 2, 1865, the Union and Confederate armies fought the longest continuous engagement of the Civil War, with six major battles, almost 100 other clashes, and 70,000 casualties. In the best American tradition, the Petersburg battlefield tourist industry began almost immediately after the war. In August 1864, tourists were visiting the Crater, while a former Confederate opened a concession stand near Fort Stedman. Later, a local hotel sold what is believed to be the first Civil War battlefield guidebook, which included a 20-mile horseback tour of the battle sites. The owner of the Crater site, William H. Griffith (whose house was destroyed during the siege), left it intact and created

the Crater Museum, which was visited by many of the famous, near famous, and ordinary from the two armies.

Petersburg became a popular place for veterans' gatherings, and on February 11, 1925, President Calvin Coolidge signed a bill establishing a small 185-acre park, and the area began to grow, supported by local citizens. It became a National Military Park on July 3, 1926, and a National Battlefield on August 24, 1962. Today the Petersburg National Battlefield's 2700 acres encompass many of the sites associated with this fighting and are divided into three units: the Eastern Front Unit, where much of the hardest fighting occurred; the City Point Unit, where Grant's headquarters and supply depot were located; and the Five Forks Unit, where Lee's last supply line was finally cut.

The Eastern Front Unit Visitors Center features an electronic map, audiovisual presentation, museum exhibits, dioramas, a bookstore, and rangers who offer guidance for visiting the battlefields. A taped tour of the park is available, as is material for the Lee's Retreat Tour segment of Virginia Civil War Trails. From the Visitors Center there is a four-mile self-guided battlefield tour, Park Tour Road, that takes the visitor past areas immortalized during the siege. The tour has eight interpretive stops and four trails from the road into battlefield sites. The impressive Crater is one of the stops, where the results of the Union attempt to blow a huge hole in the Confederate lines are still visible. Another site is Fort Stedman, the site of Lee's last, unsuccessful attempt to break the siege just before the war ended. Close to Fort Stedman is the memorial to the 1st Maine Heavy Artillery, the regiment that suffered 70 percent casualties in the battle there in June 1864. There is a fine collection of 85 cannons in the park, including an 8-inch iron siege howitzer, many 24-pounder Coehorn mortars, three 3.80-inch bronze James rifles, a 2.75-inch Whitworth breech-loading rifle, and a 4.2-inch army Parrott rifle.

Outside the main park, the 16-mile Siege Line Tour covers many of the events that took place during the siege, as well as battlefields and fortifications. It includes the Poplar Grove National Cemetery, with its 6178 Union graves—4110 unidentified. (Most Confederates are buried in the Blandford Cemetery in Petersburg.) Also on the Siege Line Tour is Fort Gregg, where the Confederates held off Union troops on April 2, 1865, and allowed Davis to escape from Richmond.

The City Point Unit focuses on Ulysses S. Grant's headquarters and supply base in Hopewell. The Visitors Center offers tourist information, an introductory video, and a diorama that describes the huge Union supply depot and communications hub there, as well as the hospital. Nearby is Appomattox Manor, a plantation house with furnished rooms and outbuildings. Visitors may watch a 15-minute video as well as visit the parlor, library, Grant's cabin, and the outbuildings. There is also an Open Air Museum Walking Tour with 25 points of interest about the people and events of City Point during the Civil War. A walking tour brochure is available at the Visitors Center.

The Five Forks Visitors Center features a 17-minute relief-map presentation shown every half hour.

Visitor Information

Petersburg National Battlefield, 804-732-3531; www.nps.gov/pete; Grant's Headquarters at City Point, 804-458-9504; Five Forks Battlefield, 804-265-8244

Hours: All the units' visitors centers are open daily, 9 a.m. until 5 p.m.; grounds are open from 8 a.m. until dusk; closed Thanksgiving, December 25, and New Year's Day. Poplar Grove National Cemetery, open year round, staffed on weekends June to August, from 9 a.m. until 5 p.m.

Admission: Petersburg National Battlefield, minimal charge per person or per carload; National Parks Pass, Golden Eagle, Golden Age, and Golden Access are honored. Grant's Headquarters at City Point, free; Five Forks Battlefield, free.

Accessibility: The visitors centers at Petersburg National Battlefield and Grant's Headquarters at City Point are wheelchair accessible.

Special Programs: During the summer there are numerous special programs and ranger-led tours. Recent tours from the Eastern Front center have included the "Guided Siege Line Tour," a three-hour ranger-led auto tour of the siege lines of Petersburg, "Siege Life," and "The Battle of the Crater." Five Forks tours have included "The Battle of Weldon Railroad/Reams Station" and "The Alamo of the Confederacy." There are also a variety of presentations with costumed interpreters throughout the park during the summer months. Call for sites and times. At Five Forks, from mid-June through mid-August, costumed living-history reenactors gallop into the area with cannons and limbers drawn by a six-horse team. They also demonstrate mortar and cannon firings and the soldiers' life. Call for information.

Getting There: Eastern Front Visitors Center: Take I-95 or I-85 to the Wythe Street (state route 36 east) exit. This leads to a one-way road. Follow it 2.5 miles to the park entrance on the right. Or from I-295 take exit 9B onto state route 36 west to the park entrance on the right, just past Fort Lee.

Grant's Headquarters at City Point: Take I-95 or I-295 to state route 10 east toward Hopewell. Cross over the Appomattox River and turn left at the second traffic light past the bridge onto Appomattox Street. Follow it until it meets Cedar Lane, and then turn left. The parking lot is on the left.

Five Forks Battlefield: Take I-95 to exit 51 onto I-85 south, then take exit 61 onto U.S. 460 west. Continue for seven miles and turn left onto local Route 627 (Court House Road). Go three miles to the Ranger Station, on the left. Or from I-85 north: Take exit 53 and turn left onto local Route 703. Take a left onto Route 1, and then a right onto Route 627 (Court House Road). Travel 5.1 miles to the Ranger Station on the right.

The Battles for Richmond—The Seven Days Battles

In March 1862, Union attacks on Richmond were planned both over-land and by sea. On land, Union major general George B. McClellan's 100,000-man Army of the Potomac began a move to capture the Confederate capital at Richmond. A month later, McClellan was seven miles east of the Confederate White House, intending to mount his heavy siege artillery and bombard Richmond until it surrendered. But his advance was slowed by rains that made roads impassable.

Meanwhile, since Union gunboats could navigate the James River all the way to the capital, Richmond was vulnerable by water as well. The key to the city's river defenses was a small fort seven miles south of Richmond on Drewry's Bluff, which rose 90 feet above the water on a sharp bend in the river. In mid-March 1862 the Confederates had built Fort Darling, with earthworks, barracks, and artillery emplacements of three large seacoast guns—one 10-inch Columbiad and two 8-inch Columbiads.

On May 9, 1862, Norfolk fell to Union forces, and the ironclad C.S.S. *Virginia (Merrimack)* left and made a run for Richmond. However, her draft was too deep, so she was burned to prevent her from falling into Union hands. Her crew and guns were sent to Drewry's Bluff.

To block the passage of any enemy ships, the Confederate fort commander took over several civilian vessels, loaded them with stones, and sank them in front of the fort to act as a barricade. Additionally, a battalion of Confederate sharp-shooters was deployed along both riverbanks to pick off anyone above decks on Union ships.

The Battle for Drewry's Bluff

In early May 1862, U.S. Navy commander John Rodgers planned to take five ships up the James to Richmond and shell the city as General George B. McClellan's Army of the Potomac advanced. On the morning of May 15, Rodgers's squadron, consisting of the ironclad U.S.S. *Monitor*, the gunboats *Port Royal*, *Aroostook*, and *Naugatuck*, and the U.S.S. *Galena*, steamed around the

Parrott guns, Coehorn mortars, and solid shot await loading onto transport ships at Yorktown to accompany General George B. McClellan on his Peninsula Campaign in May 1862. Eventually, Union forces would field a total of 353 guns.

With the U.S.S. Galena in the lead, the U.S.S. Monitor, followed by the gunboats Port Royal, Aroostook, and Naugatuck, attempt to knock out the fortifications on Drewry's Bluff. The Galena, left, was forced to withdraw after a shell penetrated the gundeck and ignited some loose powder.

bend in the river below Drewry's Bluff. The *Galena* was in the lead—a new steam-powered ironclad gunboat with a light iron shell around her superstructure. Unlike the *Monitor,* she had no armor around her hull.

The five Union ships anchored in the river below the fort, and at seven fifteen a.m. the *Galena* opened fire. Fort Darling's guns immediately returned fire from their Columbiads, primarily aimed at the three smaller gunboats. The Union ships were in a very narrow channel of the narrow river, almost in a cul de sac, where they could neither maneuver to assist each other nor get beyond the point-blank range of the enemy's batteries without withdrawing. After about an hour, the small gunboats fell back. Because of her poorly designed single turret, the *Monitor* was unable to elevate her guns high enough to reach the Confederate guns atop the bluff, so she moved away. The *Galena* was now alone, and Confederate shells were plunging onto her thin decks at a steep angle. On the bluff, the defenders also had problems. The 10-inch

Columbiad's recoil broke its carriage, and a casemate protecting one of the guns outside the fort collapsed, knocking out that gun.

After four hours of exchanging fire, at about eleven a.m., a fire broke out aboard the *Galena* when a shell penetrated the gun deck and ignited loose black powder. When the smoke reduced visibility, Rodgers, low on ammunition, broke off the attack.

As the flotilla disappeared around a bend in the river, a cheer arose from the Confederates. They had lost only seven men killed and eight wounded. The *Galena* was less fortunate. A witness noted that she "looked like a slaughterhouse" after the battle. Rodgers reported that his ship had taken at least 28 direct hits from the Rebel artillery, and many of the cannonballs remained lodged in the ship's wooden decks and bulkheads. He wrote, "She [the *Galena*] was being roughly used as shot & shell went crashing through her sides. . . . Her sides look as though she had an attack of smallpox." About 13 men were killed and about the same number wounded, though the other ships in the force suffered almost no losses.

McClellan Faces Lee

As McClellan's Army of the Potomac prepared to attack Richmond, a fierce but unsuccessful Confederate counterattack at Fair Oaks on May 31 and June 1 convinced McClellan that he needed reinforcements, even though the Union forces treated the Confederates roughly and seriously wounded their overall commander, General Joseph E. Johnston, one of the heroes of First Bull Run (Manassas).

In June, Confederate President Jefferson Davis replaced Johnston with General Robert E. Lee, one of his military advisors. The press and public had modest expectations for Lee, who had finished number two in his class at West Point and had been highly regarded in the prewar U.S. Army, but had done little in the Confederate army.

When Lee took command of the Confederate armies in the field, he knew that if he waited until McClellan received fresh divisions and deployed his huge guns, Richmond would fall. He planned to disrupt McClellan's plans through a series of fast-moving battles. First, though, Lee needed to improve his own defenses. He had his troops build eight miles of earthworks running north from White Oak Swamp to the Chickahominy River, then along the south bank of that marshy, swollen stream.

Fortunately for the Confederacy, it rained continuously the first ten days of June, and McClellan could not move up his heavy artillery train. The Confederates brought up heavy artillery of their own—a 32-pounder artillery piece mounted on a railroad car, that could move no matter what the weather. It was the first "railroad gun" in history.

The Union front covered a distance of approximately 10 miles and was as close as five miles to Richmond on its far right flank. Its entrenchments were too strong for a direct assault, so Lee decided that he would need to turn one of the Union flanks. McClellan had split his corps, putting them on both sides of the Chickahominy River, linked by

---

George B. McClellan

George Brinton McClellan was deft at organizing and training an army—which he did for the Army of the Potomac after the Union's loss at First Bull Run (Manassas)—but his cautious nature prevented him from using that army's skills to win the war, and he squandered several opportunities.

McClellan graduated second in his West Point class in 1846. A gifted engineer, he adapted European cavalry saddles into the "McClellan Saddle," which was used regularly by the U.S. Army until the early 1940s.

McClellan was only 34 years old when he was made commander in chief of the Union armies in November 1861. He inspired confidence in his men, who fondly called him Little Mac, but his interpersonal skills were poor, and he alienated his civilian superiors. McClellan succeeded in advancing to within sight of the Confederate capital of Richmond but refused to press onward, overestimating the numbers and strength of the defenders—a mistake he would make repeatedly.

In September 1862, at Antietam, his troops vastly outnumbered Robert E. Lee's. Lee had his back to the Potomac in an unfavorable defensive position, but McClellan was again overcautious and failed to vanquish Lee and his men.

Finally, Lincoln had had enough. "My dear McClellan," he wrote, "If you don't want to use the Army I should like to borrow it for awhile." In November 1862, Lincoln replaced McClellan with Ambrose Burnside.

Two years later, McClellan unsuccessfully ran as the Democratic presidential nominee against Lincoln.

none-too-sturdy bridges, creating an opportunity for Lee. The Union left, on the south side of the river, was heavily defended by a series of strong fortifications and heavy guns, but the Union right wing, north of the Chickahominy, appeared to be less well defended.

Lee began to bring in reinforcements until he had a force of about 85,000. On June 12, he sent his cavalry commander, Brigadier General James Ewell Brown "Jeb" Stuart, to reconnoiter to determine whether an assault on the Federal right was practical. Stuart headed north with 1200 cavalry and a section of artillery, giving the impression that he was going to join Stonewall Jackson in the Shenandoah Valley. The next day he turned east—spreading confusion as he and his men rode completely around the Union army, locating the Union's lines of communication. After covering 100 miles in three days, Stuart returned and reported to Lee that the Union right flank lay unprotected. Lee prepared to attack.

Lee's plan was to leave 30,000 troops south of the Chickahominy to hold McClellan's 75,000 on that side of the river, then use his remaining 55,000 Confederates troops to crush the Union units on the north bank. If Lee was successful in defeating and destroying a large portion of this force, he could then capture McClellan's supply base and storage area at White House Landing on the Pamunkey River and force him away from Richmond.

Ironically, Stuart's ride had two unintended consequences that were to throw off Lee's plan. First, McClellan, realizing his supply port at White House Landing was in danger, ordered his supplies moved to Harrison's Landing on the James River. Next, McClellan moved one corps south of the Chickahominy, leaving only Brigadier General Fitz-John Porter's corps, with 30,000 troops, north of the river. Porter was to guard White House Landing until the supplies were transferred. Lee's attack now faced smaller numbers, but his basic intention would be negated by McClellan's decision to move his supply center.

On June 24, Lee ordered Jackson and his 18,500 veterans in the Shenandoah Valley to leave there and march with his Army of the Valley to join the Confederate forces outside of Richmond. Lee planned the Confederate attack for June 26 to be sure Jackson would be in position. Early that day, generals D. H. Hill's, James Longstreet's, and A. P. Hill's divisions would cross to the north bank of the Chickahominy to pin Porter's troops behind Beaver Dam Creek near Mechanicsville. Jackson's men would then turn the Union right flank and swing around to the Union rear and cut Porter's supply line, then surround and defeat Porter's corps.

Lee's plan entailed great risk. McClellan had 60,000 soldiers south of the Chickahominy, more than enough to overpower the remaining Confederates and move easily into Richmond. Lee was gambling that McClellan was too conservative to move. On June 25, the day before the attack, McClellan sent a significant force to secure a road leading to Porter's isolated wing. The attack did not secure the position, but this aggressive move highlighted Lee's gamble. Would McClellan launch a Union attack south of the Chickahominy before the Southern offensive commenced?

In fact, McClellan was contemplating such an attack on June 26, but he still believed that Lee outnumbered him two to one, so McClellan delayed again, waiting for reinforcements. Had he attacked as planned, he might have taken Richmond. Instead, he was to begin a period of retreating and fighting that would become known as the Seven Days Battles.

First of the Seven Days Battles

On the morning of June 26, Lee waited for Jackson's corps to arrive. The arrival would be the signal for Longstreet and both Hills to cross the river and begin the attack. But Jackson was several hours behind schedule. He had started late, then Union cavalry blocked the road after a Confederate deserter told them Jackson was on the move. That afternoon, when Jackson finally reached the place he thought he was supposed to meet Lee, no one was there. Since he had heard nothing from Lee all day, Jackson and his men settled down and made camp.

As the day slipped away and Jackson failed to appear, it seemed that surprise was going to be lost. Finally A. P. Hill, impatient over the delay, disobeyed orders and began the attack on his own, reinforced by one of D. H. Hill's brigades. They forced Porter's skirmish line into the Beaver Dam Creek defenses, and at three p.m. launched a frontal assault with 11,000 troops on Porter's line. The attack was across a wide, marshy creek, and Porter's well-entrenched soldiers, protected by 32 guns in six batteries, chewed up the onrushing Confederates. The impulsive attack cost 1400 Confederate casualties.

Tactically, the Battle of Beaver Dam (Mechanicsville) was a Confederate disaster, but it threw McClellan off stride. Lee had boldly taken the offensive, and when McClellan heard that Jackson's Shenandoah Valley divisions had arrived, he believed his army was further outnumbered and now outflanked. The Confederate buildup on his right flank threatened the Richmond & York River Railroad north of the Chickahominy River. There was no other railroad to his new supply base on the James River, and concerned about supplies, he abandoned his plan to take Richmond by siege. That night, the Army of the Potomac began to retreat from Richmond after having prepared for months for a full-scale attack, now stillborn. McClellan directed all the remaining supplies at White House Landing to be immediately moved to his new base at Harrison's Landing or destroyed. He also told Porter to pull back to a position just beyond Gaines' Mill, behind a marshy waterway called Boatswain's Swamp, and dig in again.

The Battle of Gaines' Mill

The morning of June 27 was hot and sultry as Union general FitzJohn Porter's corps settled into their prepared positions in Gaines' Mill, close to the Union bridges over the Chickahominy. Lee planned to attack again, using the same basic plan he had used the previous day. Jackson, who had finally joined Lee, would turn Porter's right flank and threaten the supply line to White House Landing, and when Porter moved to guard his flank, Longstreet and A. P. Hill would attack from the front. Lee didn't know the Union supplies were being moved, and Porter had no reason to protect a supply line that no longer existed, so he did not move the way Lee expected him to move.

Porter's defensive line had been well chosen. It stretched for two miles, with the left anchored on the Chickahominy River and the right protecting the main road, so he could not easily be flanked. The first line was at the foot of a partially wooded plateau just beyond Boatswain's Swamp, while the second was set up on the plateau's crest. Artillery covered the open fields in front of the plateau. Porter had one infantry division plus two regiments of cavalry in reserve, and behind him were three bridges across the Chickahominy if a retreat was necessary.

Just after two thirty p.m., A. P. Hill's Confederates attacked from the woods, moving across several hundred yards of cultivated fields. Union artillery opened fire, tearing great gaps in the Confederate line as it moved across the open areas. When the Confederates closed, one of the units that met them was the 5th New York Zouave regiment, dressed in crimson red pants and short blue coats. After a spirited struggle, the Confederates fell back. After four hours of what many felt had been the heaviest fighting of the war, both sides paused, and an ominous silence settled over the battlefield.

For the second day in a row, Jackson was late. His experienced guide (who had guided Stuart on his ride around the Union army earlier) misunderstood Jackson's destination and led him down the wrong road. Jackson had to backtrack, and it was five p.m. before his three divisions arrived. Lee greeted him with what was, for the extravagantly polite Lee, anger and sarcasm. "General. I am very glad to see you," said Lee. "I had hoped to be with you before."

Now, Lee finally had over 50,000 men on the battlefield, and at about seven p.m. he ordered an all-out assault with the most troops the Confederacy had ever concentrated on a single battlefront. The main effort focused against the Union center, over much of the same ground where A. P. Hill's six brigades had been ravished. This time Brigadier General John Bell Hood's brigade spearheaded the attack. As Hood's men advanced over and through the bodies of their dead and wounded compatriots, some of the wounded tried to grab them, perhaps for help, perhaps because they thought the attack was suicide. However, the Confederates had made a tactical change. Instead of stopping to fire when they were in range of the Union line, they would move as fast as they could straight ahead with bayonets, hoping to break through with speed and shock.

The rush succeeded. Hood's brigade made the first penetration, and his breach forced a general

Union retreat along the entire front. In the resulting confusion, the Confederates captured 14 guns as Porter's men slipped away. Gaines' Mill cost Lee 8800 and Porter 6800 men, but it was the first major victory of Lee's career.

After Gaines' Mill, McClellan told his corps commanders to withdraw to the safety of the navy's guns at Harrison's Landing, his new supply outpost. The retreat was so skillfully masked that it was not until late on the night of June 28 that Lee learned that the Union supply base had been relocated and that the Army of the Potomac was well on its way toward a new position on the James River. Lee began to pursue.

McClellan had to cross the White Oak Swamp, but once across it, all roads led to a junction called Glendale. It was certain to be a bottleneck, because from Glendale there was only a single road that led south to the Union base on the river. Lee sent generals A. P. Hill and Longstreet to begin a wide sweep to the southeast of the Glendale intersection while other Confederate units attacked the Union flank and rear to buy time for Longstreet and Hill to reach Glendale, which would be no sooner than June 30.

The movement through the White Oak Swamp was difficult for McClellan's supply train of 5000 wagons and 2500 head of cattle. The Confederates were able to catch the Union rear guard near Savage's Station, another Union supply base, where stockpiles of equipment, ordnance, and commissary stores were to be destroyed. As darkness fell, Union general Edwin "Bull" Sumner's forces held off rushed and disorganized Confederate assaults while the rest of the Union forces escaped southward. That night, under cover of an intense thunderstorm, Sumner withdrew, abandoning supplies and more than 2500 wounded Union soldiers in a field hospital.

Once they had crossed the White Oak Swamp Creek, the Union army burned the bridge and deployed on the heights south of the creek to hold off the Confederate pursuit. Nevertheless, by June 30, Lee had enough forces to cut off McClellan's force at Glendale. He planned a massive combined attack with Benjamin Huger's, Longstreet's, and A. P. Hill's divisions now converging on the retreating Union army around the road intersection.

But the plan fell apart early. Huger found his road blocked by trees cut down by the retreating Union army, and instead of moving them, Huger opted to build an alternate road through the dense forest. While the battle took place, his 9000 much-needed Confederate troops were building this road instead of fighting.

Confederate major general T. H. Holmes tried to turn the Union left flank at Turkey Bridge, but a bombardment by land-based Union artillery and gunboats in the James River stopped his advance.

Jackson's 25,000-man corps had the longest distance to cover and, after many delays, reached the north bank of White Oak Swamp Creek at noon. He found the bridge destroyed, and exhausted by a lack of sleep, Jackson told his staff to rest until the next day.

As a result, only Longstreet's and A. P. Hill's troops were involved in the five p.m. attack. They briefly penetrated the Union defense, routing a Union division and capturing its commander, but the Confederate forces were too small to hold. Union counterattacks sealed the breach and saved their line of retreat, and a frustrated Lee witnessed the loss of another 3300 of his men, as well as his best chance to cut off McClellan's retreat.

The Battle of Malvern Hill

On June 1, 1862, Confederate general Robert E. Lee had been an unknown quantity to both Confederacy and Union. Now, one month later on July 1, he was recognized as the general who saved Richmond and seemed to be on his way to destroying McClellan and the Army of the Potomac before they could reach the protection of the U.S. Navy on the James River. On July 1, McClellan made his last stand on well-fortified Malvern Hill, seven miles from the new Union base at Harrison's Landing. It was a beautiful day—hot, but with a cool breeze—and Lee saw victory within his grasp.

Malvern Hill is a large, crescent-shaped plateau, about a mile and a half long and three quarters of a mile wide, 150 feet high at its loftiest point. Swamps, ravines, and creeks protect the sides—terrain that made a flanking attack, for all practical purposes, impossible. In front, the ground gradually slopes down from the crest, open and rolling for about 1000 yards, ending in marshy woods. It was a fine kill zone. The Union position on the hill was held, once again, by General Porter; but this time he had 80,000 Union troops and 250 cannons, protected by earthworks.

In a serious lapse of judgment, Lee decided to attack this formidable Union position, even though, as an engineer, he certainly appreciated the strength of the defenses. Confederate general Longstreet reconnoitered the area and found a plateau on the Confederate right where he thought he could move 60 guns and, with Jackson's cannons on the left, catch the Union troops in a crossfire that would give Lee's infantry a chance of success.

Lee authorized the artillery movement and bombardment and ordered D. H. Hill's, John Bankhead Magruder's, and Huger's divisions to follow the barrage with an attack on the Federal line. Two of Jackson's divisions were kept in reserve, and Longstreet's and A. P. Hill's divisions were to be held back from the action because of their losses the day before at Glendale.

D. H. Hill (whose men would lead the attack) had looked at the defenses on Malvern Hill and told Lee, "If General McClellan is there in force, we had better let him alone." Longstreet (not scheduled to attack) sarcastically replied, "Don't get scared, now that we have got him whipped." Lee agreed with Longstreet, though he realized his men had to cross a long stretch of open ground under artillery fire before they even began to scale the heights.

It was noon when the bulk of Lee's army began forming a mile-long front at the base of the hill. They were without Magruder's six brigades, who had taken a wrong turn and were marching down a road that led away from the rest of the Confederate army. This mistake was to have tragic consequences for Lee's attack.

At about one thirty p.m., Lee sent a message to his commanders: "Batteries have been established to rake the enemies' line. If broken, as is probable, [Brigadier General Lewis A.] Armistead, who can witness the effect of the fire, has been ordered to charge with a yell. Do the same."

It soon became apparent that it was not "probable" that the Confederate artillery would "rake the enemies' lines." Longstreet could not move his artillery across the swampy, heavily wooded terrain to their firing positions, and only 20 guns out of the planned 140 in total were deployed. As soon as the Confederates mounted a battery and fired, dozens of pieces of Union artillery would fire back and destroy it, and the expected Confederate artillery bombardment

---

Taps

Taps, the military bugle call now used at lights-out, funerals, memorial services, and the lowering of flags, is a revision of an earlier bugle call, Tattoo. During the Virginia Peninsula Campaign in July 1862, General Daniel Butterfield, with the help of his bugler, Oliver W. Norton, ordered that a 24-note modification of the last five measures of the Tattoo be played instead. It became popular throughout the Army of the Potomac and was even adopted by some Confederate units.

The melody was first used at a funeral during that same campaign. Captain John C. Tidball ordered that Taps be played rather than the traditional firing of three volleys—out of concern that the explosions would alert the enemy. Taps became an official bugle call after the war, and its use became mandatory at military funerals by 1891.

After the Battle *of Malvern Hill the Union army continued McClellan's retreat to Harrison's Landing. Along the way the rear guard, seen here arriving at camp, dispatched a party to destroy Turkey Bridge and block the road beyond with felled trees.*

never materialized. When Lee saw what had happened to his artillery, he realized the frontal attack would not succeed, and at about two thirty he began to change it to a flank attack. Unfortunately, he failed to keep his commanders informed, and they continued operating on the assumption they were to attack when Armistead did.

Then fate intervened. Armistead's men came under steady fire from a small force of Union skirmishers. In an effort to protect themselves, they moved forward a few hundred yards and slowly forced the Union troops to retreat out of their firing pits. Just then General Magruder arrived on the battlefield from his wanderings. Seeing Armistead's troops moving forward, Magruder sent word to Lee that the Confederate attack was under way. Not realizing that Armistead's men were not launching a full-scale assault and seeing some Union troops falling back, Lee sent Magruder and Huger orders to "press forward our whole line and follow up Armistead's successes."

At four forty-five p.m., Huger and Armistead's men began to advance, and the confusion spread. D. H. Hill heard Huger's men attack and thought it was the signal referred to in Lee's orders, so he sent his five brigades forward shortly before six p.m. As the Confederate troops moved up the open slopes, Union

solid shot and cannon balls skipped through their ranks, leaving straight lines of dead and wounded. When the wide Confederate battle line reached the base of Malvern Hill, the Union artillery switched from solid shot to canister, and the Union infantry began to fire their rifled muskets. Despite rapidly mounting casualties, the Confederates kept coming, and artillery and infantry continued to cut them down. The Union infantry was firing so rapidly that their gun barrels overheated and the men had to wrap their leather rifle slings around the barrels to keep from burning their fingers. In some places the Confederates were forced to pile up their dead and use them as a shield against the storm of fire. None reached the Union lines. Finally the pressure was too much, and at about seven p.m. the Confederates began to fall back. D. H. Hill, whose division had been cut to pieces in a few hours, wrote afterward, "We attacked in the most desultory, harum-scarum way. . . . It was not war, it was murder."

When night fell, more than 5500 Southerners covered the battlefield. A Union soldier on Malvern Hill looked down and said, "A third were dead or dying, but enough of them were alive and moving to give the field a singular crawling effect." The next day the battlefield was a morass of blood, mud, and corpses.

Despite the victory, and against the wishes of some of his generals, McClellan evacuated Malvern Hill that night, and the next day the Union army continued its retreat to Harrison's Landing, where McClellan was protected by the guns of the U.S. Navy. He claimed victory, but the Union soldiers knew better, and one said, "We retreated like a parcel of sheep."

Realizing that there was nothing else he could do, a frustrated Lee directed his army to return to its former positions around Richmond on July 8, ending McClellan's "Peninsula Campaign." The Seven Days Battles had cost the Union almost 16,000 killed, wounded, or captured. Lee's losses totaled about 21,000, but he stopped the most serious threat to Richmond yet mounted. The battles also established his reputation as a field commander. But his plans had been continually frustrated by inaccurate maps, poor staff work, miscommunications, and difficult road conditions, all of which led to late, poorly coordinated, and piecemeal attacks. Jackson's performance was especially disappointing. When told after the final battle that McClellan would escape, a frustrated Lee said, "Yes, he is getting away because I can't get my orders obeyed."

While the Army of Northern Virginia was never quite able to defeat the Army of the Potomac, in retrospect it seems remarkable that Lee came so close, given the disparity in numbers. One wonders if Lee really understood the situation when he later wrote, "Under ordinary circumstances, the Federal army should have been destroyed."

With McClellan holding at Harrison's Landing, Lee directed Jackson to seize the initiative and move the war north of the Potomac River, where the Union was forming the Army of Virginia under Major General John Pope.

Drewry's Bluff in the Campaign

Following the repulse of the Union flotilla in May 1862, Drewry's Bluff saw no action for two years. Captain Sydney Smith Lee (Robert E. Lee's brother) took command of the site, and it grew into a permanent fort protecting Richmond. It also was the training ground for the Confederate Naval Academy and the Confederate Marine Corps and soon became almost a village, with log houses built for families and the refugees from Norfolk and Portsmouth, a hotel, a post office, a chapel, and a Masonic Lodge.

On May 5, 1864, Union major general Benjamin F. Butler and his Army of the James landed at Bermuda Hundred, a neck of land 15 miles south of Richmond. Marching overland, they advanced within three miles of Drewry's Bluff by May 9. On May 12, Butler moved north against the Confederate line at Drewry's Bluff, but his move was not supported by Union gunboats and

*A **Confederate artilleryman** relaxes at the entrance to his underground earthwork fortification at Drewry's Bluff while one of three Columbiads awaits the onslaught of Federal troops.*

his attack failed. Confederate infantry under General P.G.T. Beauregard counterattacked on May 16 and drove Butler back to his Bermuda Hundred line. Drewry's Bluff remained part of Richmond's defenses until the fall of Petersburg in April 1865. The garrison at Drewry's Bluff evacuated the position on April 2–3, 1865, and the soldiers, sailors, and marines from the fort joined the Confederate army's move westward, ultimately surrendering at Appomattox Court House.

The Battle of Cold Harbor

Beginning in May 1864, Ulysses S. Grant's Army of the Potomac battled Robert E. Lee's Army of Northern Virginia for six weeks across central Virginia, inexorably moving toward Richmond. In a series of battles, Lee delayed, but failed to stop, Grant's southward progress.

On May 31, 1864, Grant ordered Major General Philip Sheridan to move south with two small divisions of Union cavalry and capture the crossroads at Old Cold Harbor (named for a local establishment that served only cold food). Using the roads radiating out from there, Grant could threaten the Confederate army as well as Richmond, just 10 miles to the southwest beyond the Chickahominy River. He could also cover his new supply depot at White House on the Pamunkey River.

When they approached Old Cold Harbor, the Union force ran into Major General Fitzhugh Lee's Confederate cavalry. Sheridan was able to drive the Southern horsemen, plus a small infantry foot brigade, off the important crossroads. On May 31, Sheridan received reports of a large Confederate force approaching and began to withdraw, but he was ordered to hold the intersection at all costs. On June 1, Confederates tried to retake the area, but Sheridan's dismounted cavalry, armed with Spencer repeating carbines and light "horse artillery," generated enough firepower to hold them off. The Confederates withdrew onto a north–south ridge a half mile to the southwest, between Old and New Cold Harbor, and began to dig in.

Grant arrived, along with a steady stream of reinforcements that brought his strength to three corps, and he began an attack on New Cold Harbor at five p.m. Four divisions struck west from Old Cold Harbor and drove Confederate skirmishers

from a wood line, and then continued over the broad open slope up toward the Confederate entrenchments. The two center divisions broke through a 50-yard gap between Confederate units and routed two Confederate brigades. However, before the Union troops could exploit the breakthrough, a Confederate counterattack forced them back and ended the action.

Grant planned another attack the next day, but one corps got lost on its way to its assigned position, then was too exhausted to fight. Grant reluctantly agreed to wait until early the next morning, June 3.

The Union delays gave Lee time to strengthen his defenses. By nightfall of June 2, the Confederates had dug a deep, interlocking series of earthworks from a point called Turkey Hill northwest along the low ridge, with a slightly graded, open slope offering excellent fields of fire. With water on both sides and trenches with overlapping fields of fire in front, Lee's men were ready, though Lee himself was ill and confined to his tent.

The Union commanders did little reconnaissance of the Confederate fortifications, but the Union troops watched the Confederates digging the entire day and into the night, and they knew what it meant. They began writing their names on pieces of paper and pinning them to the back of their uniforms so they could be identified when they were killed. One soldier wrote in his diary on June 2, "June 3, Cold Harbor. I was killed." He was correct.

At about five a.m. on June 3, almost 50,000 Union troops began their attack. There was no plan—simply a frontal charge against Lee's dug-in Confederates by three Union corps. They attacked simultaneously, but their advance soon became uncoordinated. One Union division was caught up in a swamp, another in a ravine, and both were shot to pieces. In less than an hour, 7000 Union soldiers lay dead and dying between the lines. Grant would have lost more, but his corps commanders simply ignored another order to attack. The Confederate musket and artillery fire was so severe that Union troops could neither advance nor retreat to their own lines. Using whatever utensils they could find, including cups, they dug in and cowered in the shallow trenches.

Under cover of darkness, the Union soldiers joined and improved their trenches, and soon a long

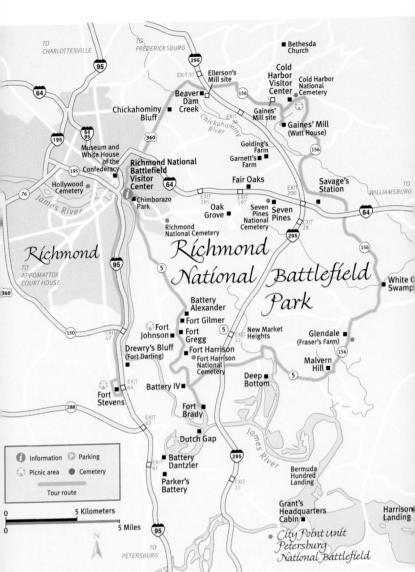

series of lines was set up some 50 yards from Lee's lines. Grant refused to raise a white flag of truce to take his wounded off the battlefield (as was his general policy), so the armies remained in place and sniped at each other for four days while hundreds—perhaps thousands—of wounded Union soldiers remained on the battlefield unattended in the sweltering heat. When Grant finally agreed to raise a truce flag on June 7, virtually all of the wounded had died. At Cold Harbor, the Union army lost 13,000 men against a loss of only 2600 for the Confederates, and Grant understandably received a huge amount of criticism for it. After the war he said, "I have always regretted that the last assault at Cold Harbor was ever made."

Cold Harbor was Lee's last major field victory. Grant withdrew the night of June 12 and abandoned further direct moves against Richmond, turning instead to Petersburg and the railroad links there. This move took away Lee's initiative and forced the Confederates into close defense of Richmond and Petersburg. Nevertheless, the losses at Cold Harbor had a chilling effect on Union commanders and their men, and there would be few frontal charges against prepared positions after this time. It was a decision that was long overdue.

The Battle of Chaffin's Farm

New Market Heights and Fort Harrison were part of a single large operation, known collectively as the Battle of Chaffin's Farm.

On the night of September 28, 1864, Major General Benjamin F. Butler made a forced march with 20,000 Union troops, including 3000 blacks designated U.S. Colored Troops (USCTs), out of Petersburg around General Robert E. Lee's left flank. They were to make a surprise attack against the Confederate defenses protecting Richmond, hoping for a breakthrough and the capture of the Confederate capital. The next day, September 29, Butler faced a small force of 2000 Confederate soldiers scattered from New Market Heights, southeast of Richmond, to Drewry's Bluff on the James River. Just before dawn, Butler launched a two-pronged attack.

General Butler ordered Brigadier General Charles Paine's 3rd Division of USCTs, all experienced veterans of Petersburg, to lead a Union attack on New Market Heights. He believed New Market Heights offered a perfect opportunity for the USCTs to prove the black troops could fight as well as whites. To maintain an element of surprise, Butler decided to attack without artillery support. Paine's troops were to charge with bayonets alone, counting on speed and shock to break through.

At about five thirty a.m. on the foggy morning, the attack began against the Confederate trenches, but it started badly. Colonel Samuel Duncan's brigade, comprising the 4th and 6th Regiments USCT, moved forward. There was a line of cut trees (an abatis) 150 yards in front of the Confederate earthworks, and when the lead elements of the Union troops took out their axes and began to chop at the trees, the Confederates opened fire. All of the axmen in the first wave went down, but the soldiers behind them took the axes and opened a path. Sergeant Christian Fleetwood and Private Charles Veal led a small band of survivors in one final push to reach the Confederate works, but their effort failed. Fleetwood and Veal returned safely, but over half of the almost 700 that charged were killed. A short time later, a second attack began, but the soldiers had to go through the openings already cut in the abatis, and the Confederates massed their fire on these points. The three black regiments lost most of their officers early in the attack and were pinned down by Confederate artillery fire for about 30 minutes. Finally the USCTs made a desperate charge against the earthworks, but during the middle of this charge the Confederate commander had to withdraw most of his men to defend Fort Harrison, the second prong of Butler's attack. The USCTs took New Market Heights, and the other prong of the Union offensive captured Fort Harrison and a small section of Richmond's outer defenses. Later that day, Confederates moved up and stopped the advance. The Heights and Fort Harrison were occupied and enlarged by the Union forces and forced a realignment of Richmond's southern defenses.

Butler lost over 3000 Union troops in the attack against New Market Heights and Fort Harrison. USCTs made up almost 50 percent of the casualties, even though they were less than one third of the Union soldiers on the field. The Medal of Honor was awarded to 14 African Americans, including Fleetwood and Veal, for their actions at New Market Heights.

Richmond National Battlefield Park

Memorials to the Confederate victories of the Seven Days Battles were relatively slow in coming. In 1925, a local Richmond citizens' group and the state of Virginia began placing roadside markers on some of the sites of the Seven Days Battles, and a corporation was formed later to purchase land to preserve the battlefields, including Beaver Dam Creek, Gaines' Mill, Malvern Hill, and Drewry's Bluff. On March 2, 1936, President Franklin D. Roosevelt signed a bill authorizing the Richmond National Battlefield Park. The corporation and state lands, as well as 570 acres of sites from the 1864 campaign, were transferred to the Park Service in 1944. In the 1950s, the city of Richmond lent the park six acres in the Chimborazo Park and the on-site building that is the Confederate medical museum.

Today the battlefield park includes 1750 acres with 11 different sites associated with those campaigns. The principal visitors center is in downtown Richmond at the Tredegar Iron Works, with another center at Chimborazo Park and a third at Cold Harbor. Those three are open year-round. Additional visitors centers are open seasonally.

An 80-mile, approximately four-hour, driving tour covers the sites of both the 1862 and 1864 fighting, and passes many sites outside the park. On the route are audio stations, wayside interpretive shelters, maps, and mounted photographs. There are marked walking trails for guided and unguided hikes throughout the park, including Gaines' Mill, Cold Harbor, Malvern Hill, Fort Harrison, and Drewry's Bluff. Some of the battlefields that are not part of the park are Seven Pines/Fair Oaks, Oak Grove, Savage Station, and White Oak Swamp. State historical markers and monuments explain

The Chimborazo Medical Museum is at the site of the Civil War hospital, which had between 75 and 80 wards. Each ward was a hut of whitewashed boards for up to 40 patients, for a total capacity of over 3000. Every division had its own laundry, kitchen, and bathhouse, and a central bakery and dairy serviced the entire facility, making Chimborazo one of the Confederacy's best-equipped hospitals.

the fighting at these battlefields.

It should be noted that much of the Union war effort was focused on Richmond, and the battlefields of 1862 and 1864 are interspersed. On the driving tour, it is sometimes difficult to keep from getting confused, especially since some of the sites are well separated and pass through developed areas. The Visitors Center and the maps it provides try to draw the scattered sites into a coherent picture.

The main visitors center is the Civil War Visitor Center at Tredegar Iron Works on the James River. Three floors of exhibits, artifacts, and audiovisual displays introduce visitors to the Richmond-area battlefields, military and civilian experiences, and the city's other Civil War history resources. An orientation film is shown throughout the day. Park rangers provide information and park maps for touring the battlefields, and a cassette tape for the Seven Days Battles is available for sale at the bookstore.

The Chimborazo Medical Museum is located at the site of the 1861 hospital building that treated over 76,000 patients during the Civil War. It includes medical exhibits and descriptions of hospital life, such as personal stories of the men and women who staffed the hospital. Exhibits include a 12-foot panoramic photograph of Richmond taken shortly after the Civil War, with the location of the city's hospitals marked, and exhibits that explode myths about Civil War medicine. A film, *Under the Yellow Flag*, describes the medical history of the site and hospital.

The Cold Harbor Battlefield Visitor Center contains exhibits and artifacts, as well as a five-minute electric-map program that describes the 1864 battle. From the Visitors Center, a mile-long walking trail moves through both the Union and Confederate lines and offers examples of Civil War field fortifications.

Two other centers are open limited hours. Maps and guides are available at the main Visitor Center. The Fort Harrison Visitor Center, highlighting the role of the USCTs in attacking the Confederate fortifications guarding Richmond. It contains a relief map of the fort and a self-guided 20-minute historical walking trail that begins at the Visitor Center.

The Glendale/Malvern Hill Battlefields Visitor Center has a five-minute electric battle map that describes the last two battles of the 1862 Seven Days campaign. Malvern Hill is the most completely preserved battlefield in Richmond National Battlefield Park, and a walking tour of the battlefields begins at the National Cemetery. The short walking trail shows the steep slopes that protected the Union left flank, with interpretive signs. There are also numerous cannons along the walk.

Chickahominy Bluff, Gaines' Mill, and Drewry's Bluff have short, self-guided trails that include interpretive signs and audio stations.

At Chickahominy Bluff, portions of the earthworks remain and there is a view of Mechanicsville and the Chickahominy River Valley. This was where General Robert E. Lee watched the beginning of the Seven Days Battles.

At Gaines' Mill, the restored Watt House on the battlefield is near the site of General Porter's headquarters, and a short walking trail takes the visitor to rifle pits where Texas and Georgia Confederate troops broke through for Lee's first victory.

South of Richmond on Drewry's Bluff there is a large, 8-inch, Columbiad, as well as the defender's view of the river. There is a self-guided walking tour through the fort and the site of the Confederate Naval Academy. The site contains a historical marker, dedicated in May 2000, commemorating the area where Corporal John Freeman Mackie became the first U.S. Marine to win the Congressional Medal of Honor.

Visitor Information

804-226-1981;
www.nps.gov/rich
Hours: The battlefields are open from sunrise until sunset; closed Thanksgiving, December 25, and New Year's Day. Civil War Visitor Center at Tredegar Iron Works, Chimborazo Medical Museum, and Cold Harbor Battlefield Visitor Center, daily, 9 a.m. until 5 p.m.; closed Thanksgiving, December 25, and New Year's Day. Glendale/Malvern Hill Battlefields Visitor Center, Wednesday to Sunday, 9 a.m. until 5 p.m.; closed Thanksgiving, December 25, and New Year's Day.

Fort Harrison Visitor Center, summer only; call for details.
Admission: Free.
Accessibility: Each of the park units is wheelchair accessible. Wheelchairs are available on site at the Fort Harrison Visitor Center.
Special Events: Cold Harbor Battlefield Visitor Center, June 3–4 anniversary of the Battle of Cold Harbor; call for details. Fort Harrison Visitor Center, annual Memorial Day program at Fort Harrison National Cemetery and from September 30 to October 1 the fort celebrates the anniversary of the Battle of Fort Harrison with living-history programs; call for information.
Getting There: Civil War Visitor Center at Tredegar Iron Works:

From I-95: From the north take exit 74C west, or from I-95 south use exit 75, and then follow signs to the Civil War Visitor Center located at 490 Tredegar Street.

From I-64 east: Go to I-95 south, and then follow directions above.

From I-64 west: Take the 5th Street Downtown exit for the Richmond Civil War Visitor Center at Tredegar Iron Works. Take 5th Street to the end, turn right onto Tredegar Street, and then right again.

Chimborazo Medical Museum is located at 3125 East Broad Street in Richmond.

Cold Harbor Battlefield Visitor Center is located five miles southeast of Mechanicsville on state route 156.

Glendale/Malvern Hill Battlefields Visitor Center, take U.S. Route 60 east from Richmond. Two miles beyond the exit for I-64, take a right onto state route 156, and follow the park signs to Glendale.

Fort Harrison Visitor Center is located on Battlefield Park Road off state route 5, Richmond.
Of Note: Richmond hosts an annual Civil War Day, usually in late April/early May. The purpose is to increase awareness about Richmond's role in the Civil War and the war's role in American history. The event includes living-history interpreters explaining and illustrating the roles of civilians and minority populations in the city, as well as those of the soldiers who fought around Richmond. There are also regular battlefield encampments during the summer. Call for details and dates.

Stonewall Jackson's Headquarters Museum

When General Joseph E. Johnston took command of the Southern army after the Battle of First Bull Run (Manassas) in 1861, he sent General "Stonewall" Jackson to Winchester, Virginia, to plan an offensive out of the Shenandoah Valley. From Winchester, Jackson could watch the 27,000 Union troops in western Virginia (today West Virginia) and maintain contact with Johnston's army at Manassas.

Jackson knew the Union forces were scattered and had poor communications, and he requested reinforcements to launch an offensive against the Federal force in Romney, Virginia, manned by about 5000 men. Three brigades were transferred to Jackson, and on New Year's Day, 1862, Jackson marched 10,000 soldiers north from Winchester toward Berkeley Springs (now in West Virginia) and Hancock, Maryland, to eliminate the Federal garrisons there and prevent them from interfering with the main thrust at Romney. Jackson also hoped to cut the Baltimore & Ohio Railroad telegraph to make communications between the scattered Union forces even more difficult.

Unfortunately for the Confederates, the weather—pleasant at the beginning of the movement—turned nasty. A snow-and-ice storm wreaked havoc on the roads and slowed the march, and when the Confederates arrived at Berkeley Springs, they found that the forewarned Union troops had abandoned the position. There was a brief skirmish on January 4, 1862, and Jackson came out of it profoundly disturbed by the lack of aggressiveness shown by one his subordinates, Brigadier General W. W. "Old Blizzards" Loring.

On January 5, Jackson's force reached the Potomac River opposite the Union-occupied town of Hancock, but the Union commander refused to surrender. Jackson conducted a desultory artillery attack for two days on the town while he looked for a place to cross the river in the miserable weather. When he was unable to find one, on January 7 he withdrew and marched on Romney.

Delayed by the road conditions, Jackson did not reach Romney until January 14, and once again he found that the Union forces had withdrawn. (During the war, Romney changed hands between Union and Confederate troops at least 56 times; Winchester changed hands more than 70 times.) His men were exhausted, so Jackson decided to leave Loring and his troops to occupy Romney while he took the remainder of his army back to winter quarters in Winchester.

This decision may have been personal. Loring's men had not only performed badly in combat, but they were also undisciplined, poor marchers, and had a high desertion rate. Loring, who had lost an arm in the Mexican War, was outspoken and did not conceal his dislike for Jackson.

When Jackson ordered him to remain in Romney, Loring rebelled. Shortly after Jackson departed, Loring sent him a letter signed by 11 of his officers protesting their assignment. Loring expected Jackson to ignore the letter, so he sent one of his aides to the Confederate capital in

Richmond with a second copy. The aide arrived in Richmond complaining about Jackson's high-handed ways, and received an audience with Confederate President Jefferson Davis. Foolishly, Davis sided with Loring and told Secretary of War Judah P. Benjamin to fix the situation. A few days later, Jackson received a telegram from Benjamin telling him to recall Loring and his men because they were in danger of being cut off by Union forces.

Jackson was stunned, but followed orders and recalled Loring to Winchester. He then wrote a letter of resignation to Johnston, his immediate superior, with a copy to Secretary of War Benjamin. Jackson also sent a personal letter to his close friend and sponsor, Virginia governor John Letcher, complaining about Benjamin's attempt to control military operations from his desk in Richmond. He strongly made the point that allowing troops to defy orders by "going over their commander's head" to politicians would be the end of discipline in the Confederate army.

Letcher realized that the Confederacy could not afford to lose Jackson, and went to the Confederate leadership to repair the blunder. Benjamin agreed to postpone his acceptance of the resignation until Letcher had time to contact Jackson. Confederate Congressman Alexander R. Boteler—a close personal friend of Jackson's and a part-time member of his staff—helped by a flurry of letters from clergymen, eventually convinced the religious and mercurial Jackson to change his mind. The letter of resignation was withdrawn, Loring was transferred to a minor post in the West, and the crisis settled. Jackson later demanded Loring be court-martialed because of his actions in battle on January 3–4, but this faded away.

Jackson proved to have considerable political clout. After the incident, Benjamin was forced to leave his post as Secretary of War and was moved to Secretary of State. (Many thought this was a better fit for him both politically and personally.) Loring contributed little during the rest of the war, and then went to the Middle East. He was well thought of there and highly decorated, eventually being made a Féreek Pasha (major general), the highest grade in the Egyptian and Turkish military.

The major purpose of the Thomas Jonathan "Stonewall" Jackson Head-quarters Museum is to interpret Jackson's operations early in the Civil War and to honor Jackson as a "military genius and Robert E. Lee's most valuable officer." The museum is located in the house Jackson used for his headquarters in Winchester to plan and launch his campaigns in 1861–62. It was built in the Hudson River Gothic style in 1854 and sold to Lieutenant Colonel Lewis T. Moore, of the 4th Virginia Volunteers, in 1856. In the winter of 1861–62, Moore invited Jackson to use his house as headquarters.

Jackson's office is essentially the same as it was when he used it to plan the Romney Campaign and the operations in and defense of the Shenandoah Valley. Here he wrote his resignation letter, and here Boteler talked him into withdrawing the letter. The office includes Jackson's personal prayer table and initialed prayer book. The room reflects attention to detail. In a letter to his wife, Jackson wrote that the office walls were "papered with elegant gilt paper," and the museum operators found a remnant of the wallpaper and had it reproduced for today's office. Other personal items on display in the museum belonged to Jackson and to members of his staff, notably his topographer, Jedediah Hotchkiss, and cavalry generals Turner Ashby and Bradley Johnson.

Visitor Information
540-667-3242;
www.winchesterhistory.org/winchesterhistory/index.cfm?section=museumJH1
Hours: Daily, April 1 to October 31, Monday to Saturday, 10 a.m. until 4 p.m., Sunday, noon until 4 p.m.; November 1 to March 31, Friday and Saturday, 10 a.m. until 4 p.m., Sunday, noon until 4 p.m.
Admission: Moderate charge for adults; discounts available for seniors, students, and families.
Accessibility: The museum is handicapped accessible.
Getting There: Winchester is located in Frederick County, Virginia, 155 miles west of Washington, D.C. near the West Virginia state line, along I-81. From I-81, take exit 313, and then follow U.S. Route 50 west to Winchester, where U.S. 11 will join it. When Route 50 turns left, stay on U.S. 11 for seven blocks, then turn left on Wyck Street. Go two blocks on Wyck and turn left on Braddock. The museum will be on your right.

The Virginia Military Institute Museum

The Virginia Military Institute (VMI) Museum is in the lower level of Jackson Memorial Hall, which also houses the Cadet Chapel and a large oil painting of the charge of the VMI Cadets at the Battle of New Market in 1864. The 15,000 artifacts in the museum's collection recognize the exploits of VMI alumni, including George Patton and George Marshall.

Two exhibits devoted to the Civil War are "VMI's Involvement in the Civil War" and "'Stonewall' Jackson at VMI." Between 1842 and 1861, VMI graduated about 1900 students. During the Civil War, almost 1700 of these alumni served in the Confederate army, but only 16 served in the Union army. Not surprisingly, VMI is considered the "West Point of the South."

Thomas Jonathan Jackson, known almost universally by the sobriquet Stonewall after the Battle of First Bull Run (Manassas), was an instruc-

tor at VMI before the war, and is arguably its most cherished associate. His exhibit includes the minié ball–ripped coat he was wearing when he was shot by his own soldiers at Chancellorsville. It also includes a hide of Little Sorrel (the horse Jackson rode to battle) mounted on a plaster-of-Paris mold. The rest of Little Sorrel's remains were

VMI, above, as it appeared in the 1850s. Right, Thomas "Stonewall" Jackson with paintings and artifacts of his life and the raincoat he was wearing the night he was mistakenly shot by his own troops. Opposite page, VMI cadets bravely charge Union artillery to fill a gap in the Confederate line at the Battle of New Market.

buried with full honors at VMI in front of Jackson's statue on July 20, 1997, 111 years after the horse died.

While not exclusively focused on the Civil War, the Stewart Collection of firearms, with over 800 pieces, is considered one of the finest in the country. Part of the collection features the search for rapid-firing weapons in the 19th century, and displays a number of experimental solutions. The collection also includes some one-of-a-kind or only-known-surviving pieces.

Visitor Information

540-464-7334;
www.vmi.edu/museum/

Hours: Open daily, 9 a.m. until 5 p.m. The museum is closed for the same holidays as the school; call for information.

Admission: Free.

Accessibility: The museum is handicapped accessible.

Getting There: VMI is located at the southern tip of the Shenandoah Valley, in the town of Lexington, Virginia. It is a 2 1/2-hour drive from Richmond, 3 1/2 hours from Washington, D.C., and four hours from Charlotte, North Carolina.

From I-81: Take exit 191 to I-64, then take exit 55 off I-64. Follow U.S. Route 11 south. Where U.S. 11 splits over the Maury River Bridge, merge to the right (Business Route 11) to downtown Lexington, then turn right on Letcher Avenue. The museum is on the right.

Warren Rifles Confederate Museum and Belle Boyd Cottage

The Warren Rifles Confederate Museum and the Belle Boyd Cottage, residence of the Confederate agent Belle Boyd, are located nearly side-by-side in Front Royal, Virginia. The Warren Rifles Chapter of the Daughters of the Confederacy operates the museum, which aims to interpret historical and cultural aspects of the Confederacy, as well as to preserve both military and civilian items of the citizens of the Confederate states. Guided tours are offered.

The museum has an eclectic collection of arms, battle flags, uniforms, letters from Confederate soldiers, and other personal artifacts that belonged to generals "Stonewall" Jackson, Robert E. Lee, and Turner Ashby, among others.

It has a strong local emphasis, and two memorial units in the main room honor two prominent local families. The McKay Memorial is an arch dedicated to the 11 members of the McKay family who served in the Confederate army. At the other end of the room is a flag niche that memorializes the Buck family.

The Belle Boyd Cottage is an 1860s middle-class home where Belle Boyd's aunt and uncle lived. At one time, the teenage Belle Boyd was a Washington, D.C., debutante, but she later shot and killed a Union soldier who had offended her mother. (Boyd was acquitted.) She stayed in the cottage when she visited Front Royal to spy on Federal troops occupying the town, then went on to become a Confederate courier carrying information and medical supplies. She was made a captain and honorary aide-de-camp in the Confederate army, while being arrested six times and imprisoned twice. Released from prison because of poor health, she went to England carrying information for the Confederates, and then returned on a blockade runner that was captured by a Union warship. She promptly fell in love with the Union officer who had taken command of her ship. He married her and left the Union navy, but died shortly thereafter. After the war, Boyd wrote an account of her life as a spy, became an actress in England, and later toured the United States in an acting company.

Since the Civil War, the cottage has served a variety of roles, including tavern, military headquarters, and storeroom. Today it has been restored in the period decor as a museum

Confederate spy Belle Boyd, having charmed a Union officer into revealing military secrets, said of him, "I am indebted for some very remarkable effusions, some withered flowers, and a great deal of important information."

depicting Warren County during the Civil War. Guided tours feature the story of Boyd, her life as a Confederate spy, and interpretations of life in this small Virginia town during the Civil War. The Warren Heritage Society operates the facility.

Visitor Information

Museum: 540-636-6982, 540-635-2219, or 540-635-3463; Cottage: 540-636-1446; users.erols.com/va-udc/museum.html

Museum Hours: April 15 to November 1, weekdays, 9 a.m. until 4 p.m.; Sundays: noon until 4 p.m.; by appointment the rest of the year.

Boyd Cottage Hours: May to October, Monday, Tuesday, Thursday, and Friday, 12:30 p.m. until 3:30 p.m.; Saturday and Sunday by appointment.

Admission: Minimal charge for adults 13 and over; discounts for students.

Accessibility: The museums are handicapped accessible.

Getting There: The museum and cottage are on Chester Street (between North Royal Avenue and Main Street in Front Royal, Virginia, about 60 miles west of Washington, D.C. Front Royal is at the north end of the Skyline Drive, just off I-66 near the Shenandoah River and Sky Meadows State Park, along U.S. Routes 522/340.

Harpers Ferry National Historical Park

Arguably, the Civil War began in Harpers Ferry, Virginia (now West Virginia), on October 16, 1859, when a radical abolitionist named John Brown seized the United States Armory and Arsenal there. Since the U.S. government had purchased the 125-acre site in 1796, it had become a significant resource, both for the government's arms supplies and for the local economy. By 1810 the arsenal was producing about 10,000 muskets, rifles, and pistols annually, and by 1859 its workforce had grown to about 400 from the town of 3000. The armory was one of only two federal armories at the time of the Civil War, and the town's location on the Baltimore & Ohio Railroad and the Shenandoah and Potomac Rivers all made it a significant site during the war. Troops clashed there frequently, and over the course of the war, the site changed hands numerous times.

John Brown's Raid

John Brown had a long record of violence in the Kansas Territory, and between 1856 and 1859 he had focused all his attention on how to vanquish slavery using force. His plan here was to seize the Harpers Ferry armory and arsenal, arm the local slaves, and then move south and launch attacks on slaveholders.

Although Brown's scheme was funded by Northern abolitionists, some of his early supporters, notably Henry Highland Garnet and Frederick Douglass, tried to dissuade him from the plan as the date of the raid approached.

Brown would not be deterred. On the night of October 16, he took his grandly named "Provisional Army" of the United States into Harpers Ferry. The five black and 16 white men, including two of Brown's sons, cut the telegraph wires and quickly captured the armory and arsenal. They took over the fire engine house, held several local citizens hostage, and waited for the slaves to come pouring in to support their cause. None did.

When Brown and his men fired on an incoming train, the local militia gathered and began to snipe at the raiders. Meanwhile, President James Buchanan heard of the attack and sent troops from Maryland, Virginia, and the District of Columbia. More than a third of Brown's men had been killed by the time the main force of U.S. Marines arrived, led by brevet colonel Robert E. Lee and including Lieutenant J.E.B Stuart. On the morning of October 18, a dozen Marines stormed the fire engine house, taking the seriously wounded Brown captive. Ten of Brown's men were killed, including both of his sons, four were captured, and seven escaped. Two of those who escaped were later captured and put on trial.

The prisoners were taken to Charlestown, Virginia (now Charles Town, West Virginia). Brown was tried, convicted, and hanged on December 2, 1859, for conspiring with slaves to commit treason and murder. The other six prisoners were also convicted and hanged over the next few

John Brown led a group of abolitionist insurgents to Harpers Ferry, where they briefly seized the U.S. Arsenal. His actions generated sympathy for the abolitionist cause.

months. Before he died, Brown prophetically pronounced, "I, John Brown, am now quite certain that the crimes of this guilty land will never be purged away but with blood."

Brown's attack had a traumatic effect on virtually all segments of the American public. Brown was considered a hero by abolitionists, but he was the Southerners' worst nightmare. The abolitionists' deification of Brown led Southerners to believe that these raids would become more common. Brown's raid provided a backdrop to the debate that eventually resulted in the Civil War.

The Outbreak of War

Eighteen months after John Brown's raid, on April 17, 1861, when Virginia passed its ordinance of secession, the Harpers Ferry Armory and Arsenal became an immediate target for the Virginia militia. Several companies moved toward Harpers Ferry from nearby Charlestown hoping to take over the armory and its arsenal and claim its stockpile of weapons. In Harpers Ferry, U.S. army lieutenant Roger Jones realized he could not defend the facility with the small number of regulars and volunteers under his command. He and his men torched the buildings to keep them out of Confederate hands and then crossed the Potomac River to safety. The arsenal and about 15,000 weapons were destroyed, but most of the weapons-making equipment survived and was shipped to other armories in the Confederacy. Two months later, the Confederates abandoned the town, burning most of the rest of the armory buildings and blowing up the railroad bridge.

Fighting for Control

In the spring of 1862, Union colonel Dixon Miles led Federal troops to reoccupy Harpers Ferry. While the armory was a burned-out hulk and most of the townspeople had fled, the site was still of strategic importance. Miles's assignment was to protect the two railroad lines and the canal that ran through the town to the east, and prepare them for use as a supply base for Union operations. By September 1862, Miles commanded 14,000 men stationed at Harpers Ferry and nearby Martinsburg, Virginia.

Defending Harpers Ferry was a formidable task. The town lies in a lowland V where the Shenandoah River flows from the southwest to join the Potomac River flowing in from northwest, which then continues its flow to the east. It is surrounded by three cliffs—the steep Maryland Heights directly across the Potomac, Loudon Heights south across the Shenandoah, and the significant Bolivar Heights directly behind the town to the west.

John Brown's fort—the structure used as the armory's fire- and guardhouse—where John Brown and several of his followers barricaded themselves during the final hours of their ill-fated raid of October 16–18, 1859.

Maryland Heights was the most dominating location, so Miles built a few fortifications and mounted three large and four small cannons there. Another force was placed west on Bolivar Heights, but only a token force protected the third high point, Loudon Heights.

On August 30, 1862, Robert E. Lee's Army of Northern Virginia won another victory at Second Bull Run (Second Manassas). To keep the positive momentum from the victory and to reduce the burden of the war on the people of northern Virginia, Lee decided to invade the North. He hoped to gain local support and to favorably impress European countries, which were considering granting diplomatic recognition to the Confederacy.

On September 4, 1862, Lee moved into Maryland. He realized the Union troops at Harpers Ferry were a threat to his stretched supply lines, but he also believed the Union forces were demoralized following their recent defeat. On September 10, Lee took a gamble to neutralize Harpers Ferry. He split his army, sending Major General Thomas J. "Stonewall" Jackson with almost 23,000 men to capture Harpers Ferry. The task would have to be accomplished within three days so the Confederate forces could then rejoin Lee in

The remains of the B & O Railroad bridge at Harpers Ferry in September 1862. Considered an important military target, the span was destroyed by Confederate artillery but rebuilt by Federal engineers nine times during the war.

Maryland before the main Union army caught up with him.

Jackson divided his forces into three columns, sending General John Walker to take Loudon Heights and generals Richard Anderson and Lafayette McLaws to seize Maryland Heights, while Jackson's own force would attack the Union garrison in Martinsburg and then proceed to Harpers Ferry and capture Bolivar Heights. It was a complex operation; Jackson's columns would be traveling to Harpers Ferry by three different routes and approach from three different directions, yet all had to arrive at about the same time.

At Martinsburg, Virginia, when Union brigadier general Julius White heard of the Confederates' approach, he ordered his 2500 men to retreat to Harpers Ferry. There he met Colonel Dixon Miles, who showed him a message from General H. W. Halleck, the Union general-in-chief, telling Miles, "Harpers Ferry must be held to the latest moment."

White was not overly impressed with Miles's preparations. The most important position, Maryland

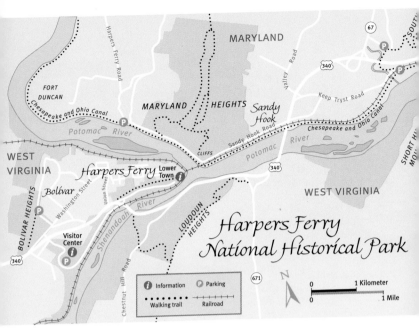

Heights, had about 1600 men on it, many of them inexperienced. Bolivar Heights was fortified with about 7000 men, and the remaining troops were at Loudon Heights and guarding the bridges across the rivers. White noted that the most critical points were not properly fortified, nor could they support each other in case of assault.

On September 13, generals McLaws and R. H. Anderson arrived at Maryland Heights. Seeing it as the key to victory because of its elevation, McLaws ordered two infantry brigades to attack along the northern extension of the plateau. The Confederates broke the Union resistance quickly, and by that afternoon they were setting up cannons overlooking the town. At about the same time, General Walker took possession of Loudon Heights with virtually no Union opposition. That same day Jackson's 14,000-man force arrived across from Bolivar Heights, after marching 51 miles in less than two days. Harpers Ferry was surrounded.

That night Jackson ordered General A. P. Hill to move to the south of Bolivar Heights and flank the Federal position on the Heights. Hill moved his forces toward the Shenandoah River and, hidden by ravines, maneuvered five artillery batteries into position half a mile from the Union forces' south flank.

The morning of the 14th, the Confederate artillery fire began to rain down on the surrounded Union troops. Colonel William H. Trimble of the 60th Ohio wrote that there was "not a place where you could lay the palm of your hand and say it

was safe." The barrage continued all day, and that night another Union soldier noted in his diary, "We will have to surrender or be cut to pieces."

One Union officer was not ready to surrender, however. Under cover of darkness, Colonel Benjamin Davis led his cavalry command of about 1500 men across the Potomac River on a pontoon bridge and, moving undetected toward Sharpsburg, wreaked havoc on surprised Confederates along the way. He reached the safety of the Union lines on the morning of September 15.

At the same time Davis was making his way to safety, the Union commanders at Harpers Ferry agreed to surrender. About 9 a.m. they raised the white flag from their positions on Bolivar Heights. However, news of the surrender was passed slowly. A few minutes later, a Confederate shell from across the river at Loudon Heights killed the Union commander, Colonel Miles.

Jackson took over 12,500 Union troops prisoner at Harpers Ferry, the largest number of Federals captured during the entire war, as well as 13,000 small arms and about 45 pieces of artillery. Once the battlefield was secured, Jackson and his forces raced north to help Lee at Sharpsburg, arriving just in time to prevent Lee's defeat. Virtually all the Union prisoners accepted parole and were left behind.

Post Battle

A month later, after the Battle of Antietam, the Federals reclaimed Harpers Ferry. This time, they learned their lesson; the three heights were quickly fortified to protect the town and the vital railroad lines and canal. Harpers Ferry also became one of many Union towns that offered shelter to "contrabands"—runaway slaves. The town's final contribution to the war effort was as General Philip Sheridan's supply base for his critical 1864 campaign against Confederate forces in the Shenandoah Valley.

With the destruction of the armory in 1861, most of the townspeople had moved away from the fighting, and Harpers Ferry was economically devastated. Following the Civil War, New England Freewill Baptist missionaries acquired several vacant armory buildings on Camp Hill. In 1867, they founded Storer College, an integrated school designed primarily to educate former slaves. It closed in 1955 and is used today by the National Park Service as a training facility.

The armory's engine house and guardhouse—"John Brown's Fort"—remained intact and had an itinerant career. It was moved to the Storer College campus, then was taken to the World's Exposition in Chicago in 1893, and then it went back to the town. In the late 1960s, it was moved back near its original location. The engine house fire bell was taken by the 1st Massachusetts Regiment and today is in Marlboro, Massachusetts.

Harpers Ferry National Historical Park

On June 30, 1944, Congress authorized the Harpers Ferry National Historical Park. During the next 10 years, the state of West Virginia purchased land on Loudon Heights, Bolivar Heights, and in the town itself and donated it to the National Park Service. Three years later, Maryland donated land on Maryland Heights, and in 1962 the area was officially designated the Harpers Ferry National Historical Park.

The Lower Town Historic District has been preserved and remains much as it was during the Civil War. Sites of interest include the engine house that was John Brown's fort, the John Brown Historical Exhibit, and the sites of the armory and arsenal. There are also numerous museums. Additionally, rangers conduct a daily hour-long walking tour of sites in the Lower Town.

Across the Potomac, the key point of the battle, Maryland Heights, is a rewarding (if strenuous) walk. The view from the top allows visitors to see the contours of the battle and makes it clear why this area was of such strategic importance. Visitors can also see the remains of many Civil War fortifications.

Park Rangers regularly conduct daily and weekend discussions and tours, notably a weekend tour called "Training Ground, Battle Ground and Staging Ground" on the Bolivar Heights battlefield.

In November 2001, Harpers Ferry National Historical Park and the town of Harpers Ferry hosted filming for the motion picture *Gods & Generals* about Stonewall Jackson.

Visitor Information
304-535-6298; www.nps.gov/hafe
Hours: Summer, daily, 8 a.m. until 6 p.m.; winter, daily, 8 a.m. until 5 p.m.; closed Thanksgiving, December 25, and New Year's Day.
Admission: Three-day and annual passes are available. Golden Age, Golden Access, and Golden Eagle passes are accepted. Commercial tour fees are available on request by calling 304-535-6299.
Accessibility: A shuttle system connects the park Visitors Center with the Lower Town District. Most exhibits and museums are accessible. Wheelchairs are available.
Special Events: The park has special programs on Earth Day and July 4. On the anniversary of Election Day 1860, living-history volunteers and reenactors parade in the lower town on Shenandoah Street.
Getting There: Harpers Ferry is approximately 65 miles northwest of Washington, D.C., 20 miles southwest of Frederick, Maryland, and six miles northeast of Charles Town, West Virginia.

From Baltimore, Maryland, take I-70, and from Washington, D.C., follow I-270 to I-70 at Frederick, Maryland. At Frederick, take U.S. 340 south to Harpers Ferry. The Visitor Center is located on Cavalier Heights about one mile west of the Shenandoah River Bridge, just off U.S. Route 340.

Amtrak's Capital Limited stops at Harpers Ferry daily with service from Washington, D.C., Pittsburgh, Cleveland, and Chicago. MARC Rail operates several commuter trains Monday through Friday between Harpers Ferry and Union Station (Washington, D.C.). For information on MARC and Amtrak schedules and fares, call 800-325-7245.

Selected Bibliography

BOOKS

Anders, Curt. *Hearts in Conflict: A One Volume History of the Civil War.* Secaucus, NJ: Carol Pub. Group, 1994.

Batty, Peter, and Peter Parish. *The Divided Union: The Story of the American Civil War, 1861–65.* London and New York: Viking/Rainbird, 1987.

Blight, David. *Race and Reunion: The Civil War in American Memory.* Cambridge, Mass.: Harvard University Press, 2001.

Boge, Georgie, and Margie Holder Boge. *Paving Over the Past: A History and Guide to Civil War Battlefield Preservation.* Washington, DC: Island Press, 1993.

Campaigns of the Civil War. 8 vols. New York: Thomas Yoseloff, 1963.

Canney, Donald L. *Lincoln's Navy: The Ships, Men, and Organization, 1861-65.* Annapolis, MD: Naval Institute Press, 1998.

Catton, Bruce. *This Hallowed Ground: The Story of the Union Side of the Civil War.* Garden City, NY: Doubleday, 1956.

——, *Army of the Potomac* (3 volumes) Garden City, NY: Doubleday, 1962.

——, *Grant Takes Command.* Boston: Little, Brown, 1969.

Colby, C. B. *Civil War Weapons: Small Arms and Artillery of the Blue and Gray.* New York: Coward-McCann, 1962.

Congdon, Don, ed. *Combat: The Civil War.* New York: Delacorte Press, 1967.

Cowley, Robert, ed. *With My Face to the Enemy: Perspectives on the Civil War.* New York: G. P. Putnam's Sons, 2001.

Cozzens, Peter. *Battles and Leaders of the Civil War.* 5 vols. Urbana: University of Illinois Press, 2002.

Craven, Avery. *A Historian and the Civil War.* Chicago and London: University of Chicago Press, 1964.

Dew, Charles B. *Apostles of Disunion: Southern Secession Commissioners and the Causes of the Civil War.* Charlottesville: University of Virginia Press, 2001.

Edwards, William B. *Civil War Guns: The Complete Story of Federal and Confederate Small Arms.* Harrisburg, PA: Stackpole Co., 1962.

Eicher, David J. *The Longest Night: A Military History of the Civil War.* New York: Simon & Schuster, 2001.

Foner, Eric, and Olivia Mahoney. *A House Divided: America in the Age of Lincoln.* New York: W. W. Norton & Company, 1990.

Foote, Shelby. *The Civil War: A Narrative.* New York: Random House, 1963.

Forman, Stephen. *A Guide to Civil War Washington.* Washington, DC: Elliott & Clarke Publishing, 1995.

Graham, Martin, Richard Sauers, George Skoch, and William Davis. *The Blue and the Gray: The Conflict Between North and South.* Lincolnwood, IL: Publications International, Ltd., 1997.

Hattaway, Herman. *Shades of Blue and Gray: An Introductory Military History of the Civil War.* Columbia: University of Missouri Press, 1997.

Heidler, David S., and Jeanne T. Heidler, eds. *Encyclopedia of the American Civil War: A Political, Social, and Military History.* Santa Barbara, CA: ABC-CLIO, 2000.

Horowitz, Tony. *Confederates in the Attic: Dispatches from the Unfinished Civil War.* New York: Vintage, 1999.

Kincaid, Paul. *The Timechart History of the Civil War.* Ann Arbor, Mich.: Lowe & B. Hould Publishers, 2001.

Leckie, Robert. *None Died in Vain: The Saga of the American Civil War.* New York: HarperCollins Publishers, 1990.

McPherson, James M. *Battle Cry of Freedom: The Civil War Era.* New York: Oxford University Press, 1988.

Miller, Francis Trevelyan. *The Photographic History of the Civil War.* 10 vols. New York: The Review of Reviews Co., 1911.

Musicant, Ivan. *Divided Waters: The Naval History of the Civil War.* New York: HarperCollins Publishers, 1995.

O'Reilly, Noel S., David C. Bosse, and Robert W. Karrow, Jr. *Civil War Maps: A Graphic Index to the Atlas to Accompany the Official Records of the Union and Confederate Armies.* Chicago: Newberry Library, 1987.

Ross, Charles D. *Trial by Fire: Science, Technology and the Civil War.*
Shippensburg, PA: White Mane Books, 2000.
Still, William N. *Iron Afloat: The Story of the Confederate Armorclads.*
Columbia: University of South Carolina Press, 1985.
Time-Life Books, *The Civil War: An Illustrated Guide.* 28 vols.
Alexandria, Virginia: Time-Life Books, 1987.
——, *Echoes of Glory.* 3 vols. Alexandria, Virginia: Time-Life Books, 1998.
Ward, Geoffrey, with Ric Burns and Ken Burns. *The Civil War.*
New York: Knopf, 1990.
Weigley, Russell Frank. *A Great Civil War: A Military and Political History,*
1861–1865. Bloomington: Indiana University Press, 2000.

PERIODICALS
The American Historical Review, American Historical Association,
Washington, DC.
America's Civil War, Primedia History Group, Leesburg, VA.
Blue and Grey Magazine, Columbus, OH.
Civil War Regiments, Savos Publishing, El Dorado Hills, CA.
Civil War Times, Primedia History Group, Leesburg, VA.
The Journal of Military History, George C. Marshall Library, Lexington, VA.
The Journal of Southern History, Rice University, Houston, TX.
North & South Magazine, Tollhouse, CA.

Acknowledgments

No other event in America's past approaches the significance of the Civil War
in history, memory, and myth. There are a large number of Americans who
are helping preserve the legacy of the Civil War, and I have been fortunate to
meet many during the course of writing this book. It would be impossible to
name all of the people who walked me across Civil War battlefields or took me
through their museums and memorials to explain the significance of the
events in their area. They also answered innumerable questions by phone and
e-mail after my visits, and many took the time to read parts of this manuscript
and make useful suggestions. There were many others who patiently shared
their expertise in various areas, and of course I was able to draw from numerous chroniclers of the war in all its aspects, from immediately after its conclusion to the present day. I hope that this book will lead readers to visit many of
the Civil War sites described within and that they will gain a greater appreciation of the events and personalities of the conflict.

I wish to personally thank the following individuals for their invaluable
contributions:

Diane Ney for contributing the following articles:
Timeline of the Civil War; Ford's Theatre and the Petersen House National
Historic Site; The Smithsonian Institution's National Museum of American
History, Behring Center; New York State Military Museum and Veterans
Research Center; United States Military Academy at West Point and the
West Point Museum; Civil War Library and Museum; Grand Army of the
Republic Civil War Library and Museum; National Civil War Museum;
Arlington House and the Arlington National Cemetery; The Mariners'
Museum; and the sidebar about Photography.

Meredith Wolf Schizer for contributing the Union and Confederate
biographies and the sidebar about *Taps.*

Jane Neighbors and Dave Hall for their superb copyediting skills and tough,
critical eyes.

Amy Wilson for her dogged pursuit of elusive site contacts and their even
more elusive photographs. Also for her aid in preparing text and map files
for the designer.

Picture Credits

Library of Congress, Prints & Photographs Division:
Page 5, 16, 19, 25, 26, 27, 30, 31, 34 bottom, 35, 36, 37 top, 38, 44, 46, 47, 55, 58, 63 top, 64 bottom, 67, 68, 69, 70, 71, 73, 80, 97, 102, 106, 107, 108, 109, 110, 111, 112, 115, 116, 117, 118 top, 122–123 top, 134, 138, 142–143, 146, 160 top, 163 bottom, 166, 169, 176, 176–177, 178, 181, 195 bottom, 203, 204, 211 top, 212, 219, 226, 230, 232, 243 bottom, 254, 244, 247, 249, 254, 255 top and bottom, 259, 260, 269, 282, 283, 284 bottom, 288, 289, 295, 296 top, 305 middle, 306, 309.

Page 14–15 chromolithograph published by L. Prang & Co., 1887, from a painting by Thure de Thulstrup; 15 bottom Courtesy West Point Museum, US Military Academy, photographed by Henry Groskinsky; 17 © Lowell Georgia/ CORBIS; 21 © David Muench/CORBIS; 22–23 235 From *Battles and Leaders of the Civil War*, published by the Century Company, NY; 28 © Kevin Fleming/CORBIS; 32 top © Bettmann/CORBIS; 32 bottom Smithsonian Institution; 34 top Ford's Theater National Historic Site; 37 Smithsonian Institution; 39, 40, 41 Smithsonian Institution; 43, Courtesy Andersonville National Historic Site/ National Park Service; 48–49, 50, 51, 52, 53 © Paul Franklin; 54 © Dave G. Houser/CORBIS; 61 © Dave G. Houser/CORBIS; 62–63 bottom Naval Historical Foundation; 64–65 top © CORBIS; 65 bottom © Lee Snider/CORBIS; 66 Atlanta Historical Society, Atlanta, GA; photographed by Michael W. Thomas; 72 chromolithograph published by L. Prang & Co., 1887, from a painting by Thure de Thulstrup; 75, 76 bottom Courtesy The National Civil War Naval Museum and Port Columbus Civil War Naval Center; 76 top Naval Historical Foundation; 78 Courtesy Pickett's Mill State Historic Site; 79 Courtesy Southern Museum of Civil War and Locomotive History; 81, 82 Courtesy Fort Scott National Historic Site/ National Park Service; 84, 84–85, 86 bottom Courtesy The Confederate Museum (Memorial Hall); 86 Rosemonde E. and Emile Kuntz Collection, Manuscripts Dept., Tulane University Library, New Orleans, LA; 88-89 Buck's Historical Society, photo by Al Freni. Courtesy PRC Archive, Boston, MA; 92-93 Painting by Thure de Thulstrup, courtesy Seventh Regiment Fund, Inc., photographed by Al Freni; 94 © Lee Snider/CORBIS; 96 © David Muench/CORBIS; 98 © CORBIS; 100 Courtesy Fort.Washington Park; 104 Courtesy National Museum of Civil War Medicine; 105 Museum of the Confederacy, Richmond, VA. Photographed by Larry Sherer; 113 © David Muench/CORBIS; 118 bottom Painting by Julian O. Davidson, American Heritage Picture Collection; 119 Courtesy Old Court House Museum, Vicksburg, MI; 122 bottom © David Butow/CORBIS SABA; 124, 125 Courtesy General Sweeny's Museum of Civil War History; 129 © CORBIS; 130 © Dave G. Houser/CORBIS; 132, 133 Courtesy New York State Military Museum and Veterans Research Center; 134–135 West Point Museum, U.S. Military Academy. Courtesy PRC Archive, Boston, MA; 136 © Bob Krist/CORBIS; 137, 141 top Naval Historical Foundation; 141 bottom Courtesy C.S.S. *Neuse* State Historic Site; 144-145 Courtesy Beverly R. Robinson Collection, U.S. Naval Academy Museum, Annapolis, MD;

Courtesy Museum of the Confederacy, Richmond, VA. Photograph by Katherine Wetzel; 150–151 top © CORBIS, 150–151 center, 151 bottom Courtesy Fort Macon State Park; 154, 155 Naval Historical Foundation; 157 © Philip Gould/CORBIS; 158 © CORBIS; 159 © Tria Giovan/CORBIS; 160 bottom Private Collection. 162–163 top Painting by Peter F. Rothermel, Collection of the State Museum of Pennsylvania, photographed by Henry Groskinsky; 170,170–171,172 © Jim Schafer Location Photography, Pittsburg, PA; 174 Courtesy United States Naval Academy Museum; 177 right Courtesy Fort Sumter National Monument and National Park Service; 180 Naval Historical Foundation; 182–183 top © CORBIS; 182–183 bottom Courtesy Fort Donelson National Battlefield/ National Park Service; 184 Private Collection/Harper's Weekly; 186 © Kevin Fleming/CORBIS; 187 Courtesy Chicago Historical Society; 188–189 Courtesy National Park Service. Artwork by Donna J. Neary; Gettysburg National Military Park; 190 Courtesy Beverly R. Robinson Collection, U.S. Naval Academy Museum, Annapolis, MD; 194-195 top © CORBIS; 196–197 Courtesy The Cincinnatti Historical Society; 198 National Archives; 201 © David Muench/CORBIS; 206–207 © CORBIS; 209 Courtesy Museum of Southern History; 210, 211 right Courtesy Museum of the Confederacy, Richmond, VA. Photographed by Larry Sherer; 213, 214-215 top, 215 bottom, 216–217 Courtesy Appomatox Court House National Historic Site/ National Park Service; 220 Courtesy Arlington National Cemetery; 222 © James P. Blair/CORBIS; 225 Wadsworth Atheneum, Hartford, CT. The Ella Gallup Sumner and Mary Catlin Sumner Collection. Photographed by Joseph Szaszfai; 228–229 © CORBIS; 231 Painting by A. Tholey, Fredericksbug National Military Park/National Park Service. Photographed by Larry Sherer; 233 © CORBIS; 234, 235 From *Battles and Leaders of the Civil War*, published by the Century Company, NY; 240–241 © CORBIS; 243 top © Bettmann/CORBIS; 251 top Painting by Thure de Thulstrup, courtesy Seventh Regiment Fund, Inc., photographed by Al Freni; 255 middle Courtesy George Eastman House, Rochester, NY; photographed by Vincent Rotella; 256, 257, 258 © Paul Franklin; 262 Chromolithograph by Kurz & Allen, Library of Congress. Courtesy PRC Archive, Boston, MA; 263 From *Battles and Leaders of the Civil War*, published by the Century Company, NY; 267 © CORBIS; 269 Naval Historical Foundation; 270, 271 Courtesy Museum of the Confederacy, Richmond, VA; 272 © Richard T. Nowitz/CORBIS; 273 Courtesy White House of the Confederacy, Richmond, VA; 275 © Richard A. Cooke/CORBIS; 276 Courtesy New Market Battlefield Historical Park and Hall of Valor Museum. Photographed by Michael Latil; 278, 279, 280 © Paul Franklin; 284–285 top © CORBIS; 286 © Dave Bartruff/CORBIS; 296 bottom Naval Historical Foundation; 300 © Buddy Mays/CORBIS; 302 © Richard T. Nowitz/CORBIS; 304 bottom Painting by Benjamin West Clinedinst, Jackson Memorial Hall, Virginia Military Institute, Lexington. Photographed by Michael Latil.; 305 bottom left and right Courtesy Virginia Military Institute Museum; 307 © CORBIS; 308 © Mark E. Gibson/CORBIS.

Index

Page numbers in **boldface** refer to illustrations and maps.